3 2044 059 946 707

D0926522

The Persuaders

The Persuaders

When Lobbyists Matter

Steve John

8941386

First published 2002 by
PALGRAVE MACMILLAN
Houndmills, Basingstoke, Hampshire RG21 6XS and
175 Fifth Avenue, New York, N.Y. 10010
Companies and representatives throughout the world

PALGRAVE MACMILLAN is the global academic imprint of the Palgrave
Macmillan division of St. Martin's Press, LLC and of Palgrave Macmillan Ltd.
Macmillan® is a registered trademark in the United States, United Kingdom
and other countries. Palgrave is a registered trademark in the European
Union and other countries.

ISBN 0–333–98588–5

This book is printed on paper suitable for recycling and
made from fully managed and sustained forest sources.

A catalogue record for this book is available
from the British Library.

Library of Congress Cataloging-in-Publication Data
John, Steve.
        The persuaders : when lobbyists matter / Steve John.
        p. cm.
        Includes bibliographical references and index.
        ISBN 0–333–98588–5 (cloth)
        1. Lobbying—Great Britain. 2. Pressure groups—Great Britain. I. Title.
JN329.P7 J64 2002
324'.4'0941—dc21   20010156370

10   9   8   7   6   5   4   3   2   1
11   10   09   08   07   06   05   04   03   02

Printed and bound in Great Britain by
Antony Rowe Limited, Chippenham and Eastbourne

Contents

Preface

In light of the mystery surrounding the role of spin doctors and back-room figures, this book assesses the effectiveness of professional lobbyists.

The data that exist on influence have thrown up contradictory answers on the impact of lobbyists. There are two versions of the impact of a lobbyist: lobbyists are either bit players who cannot upset a system that takes decisions based on merit, or they are effective operators and deliver success.

When do lobbyists matter? The book assesses the relationship between professional lobbying and policy outcomes, and the impact of external variables. Lobbyist's impact on policy-making varies according to context. Whilst the effectiveness of professional lobbyists is partly a function of internal variables such as skill, contacts and resources, external contextual factors are more often the key determinants of policy. Contextual variables include factors external to government (the world economy and judicial decisions), and factors internal to government (party ideology and the autonomy of government actors).

Its four case studies – representing a range of issues, from high to low profile, and varying in degrees of technicality and politicality – test various propositions against evidence from in-depth interviews, governmental and parliamentary papers, and the press.

When context is favourable, lobbyists have the greatest effect on non-contentious, technical and non-partisan issues. On low-profile issues, when low-profile tactics have failed, lobbyists can be effective if they use high-profile tactics to increase the salience of the issue *within* government. On issues initially and inherently high-profile, non-technical and political, there are more variables so the lobbyist's impact is proportionally less.

Though lobbyists on occasion affect policy, they are rarely at the centre of decision-making. Policy outcomes are decided by bigger factors than the activities of lobbyists. Their impact is at the margins of policy, and the perception they and the press hold about their major effects is illusory.

The book concludes that lobbyists' effect on policy is less significant than commonly believed. Whilst lobbyists themselves rarely influence policy significantly, they do sometimes matter and can help clients influence policy. They bring economies of scale and are often a worthwhile investment. They have experience, they educate clients, they know key players and processes and can overturn established procedure. More importantly, at key moments when the context is right, lobbyists really do matter.

STEVE JOHN

Acknowledgements

This book is the outcome of doctoral research. I am particularly grateful to Professor George Jones and Alan Beattie of the London School of Economics (LSE). They were supportive, diligent and generous PhD advisers. The LSE's Professor Patrick Dunleavy and Tony Travers both offered valuable assistance in the structure of case studies and the survey. Professor Grant Jordan, Professor Helen Margetts, Professor Beth Leech, Professor Keith Downing, Dr Martin Smith, John Barnes and June Burnham all provided useful comments at various stages.

The Economic and Social Research Council funded the research (grant number: R00429634186).

Many from the lobbying profession helped, including Steve Atack, Adam Atkinson, Andrew Currie, Charles Miller and Tim Clement-Jones.

My friends helped read the work as it developed. Andrew Blick, Shelley Deane, Angela Dunn, Steve East, Eva Gronbech, Scott Kelly, Martin Lodge, Francisco Paris, Ranjita Rajan, Fabian Richter, Mike Sedgley, Nick Sitter, Marit Sjøvaag and Jason Stacey all deserve a mention.

I owe a debt to many policy-makers, and those close to them, who were interviewed and whose identity is withheld. This book could not have been completed without the co-operation of these people.

Most of all, the love and support of my family made writing this book possible.

STEVE JOHN

List of Abbreviations

ADM	Annual Delegate Meeting
APL	Autonomous Policy Leader
APPC	Association of Professional Political Consultants
BR	British Rail
CBI	Confederation of British Industry
CHL	Chelsea-Hackney Line
CLRS	Central London Rail Study
CTRL	Channel Tunnel Rail Link
DIY	Do-it-yourself
DJC	Docklands Joint Committee
DLR	Docklands Light Railway
DoE	Department of the Environment
DTI	Department of Trade and Industry
DTp	Department of Transport
E&Y	Ernst & Young
EC	Executive Committee
ECJ	European Court of Justice
ECU	European Currency Unit
EDL	London Cabinet Sub-Committee
EDL (L)	Cabinet Sub-Committee – London
EDM	Early Day Motion
EDX	Cabinet Committee on Public Expenditure
EIB	European Investment Bank
ELRS	East London Rail Study
EP	European Parliament
ERM	Exchange Rate Mechanism
GBC	Grant Butler Coomber
GDP	Gross Domestic Product
GLC	Greater London Council
HMT	Her Majesty's Treasury
ICAEW	Institute of Chartered Accountants for England and Wales
IGA	Ian Greer Associates
IoD	Institute of Directors
J&S	Joint and Several
JLE	Jubilee Line Extension
KSSC	Keep Sunday Special Campaign

LBTH	London Borough of Tower Hamlets
LCD	Lord Chancellor's Department
LDDC	London Docklands Development Corporation
LDSP	London Docklands Strategic Plan
LEG	Legislation Committee of the Cabinet
LLP	Limited Liability Partnership
LRG	Liability Reform Group
LRT	London Regional Transport
LSE	London School of Economics
LT	London Transport
LUL	London Underground Limited
NDPB	Non-Departmental Public Body
OPEN	Outlets Providing Everyday Needs
O&Y	Olympia and York
PFI	Private Finance Initiative
PLP	Parliamentary Labour Party
PPS	Parliamentary Private Secretary
PPU	Public Policy Unit
QFL	Queen's Speech and Future Legislation Committee
RAM	Residents' Association of Mayfair
REST	Recreation, Emergencies, Social Gatherings, and Travel
RSAR	Retailers for Shops Act Reform
RSC	Rowland Sallingbury Casey
SHRC	Shopping Hours Reform Council
SOP	Standard Operating Procedure
SOS	Sort Out Sunday
TWA	Transport and Works Act
UCTA	Unfair Contract and Terms Act
UDC	Urban Development Corporation
USDAW	Union of Shop, Distributive and Allied Workers

1
Introduction

Are the lives of professional lobbyists pointless? Many journalists, politicians and political commentators would answer in the affirmative. Assessing the effect of lobbyists is controversial, and the current debate shows a wide variation in judgements about the efficacy of lobbyists. Do lobbyists advance special interests over the collective interest? Who is right: the critics who deplore the activity of lobbyists, assuming their effectiveness, or those who dismiss their effect? This book will explain when lobbyists matter and when they do not.

A classic study of 'the lobby' in 1950s and 1960s Britain identified those innumerable and ubiquitous groups that influenced public policy.[1] Finer's anonymous Empire has since emerged from the shadows and the participation of outside interests in policy-making is now institutionalised. Formal consultation procedures, departmental select committees, and legislative inquiries on draft Bills provide groups with formal mechanisms to contribute to policy-making.

Since the early 1980s the 'Empire' has commissioned an anonymous and discreet mercenary army of professional lobbyists. British political science has largely ignored this development in interest-group politics. What Salisbury said of Washington lobbyists in the mid-1980s foreshadowed the plight of British lobbyists today: the real world accords lobbyists importance but they are designated as insignificant by social scientists.[2] Yet outside interests are increasingly aided and abetted by professional lobbyists. Finer's words forty years ago fit professional lobbyists today: 'their day-to-day activities pervade every sphere of domestic policy, every day, every way, at every nook and cranny of government'.[3]

Pick any domestic policy on the government's agenda, and professional lobbyists are likely to be involved somewhere, somehow. Political science has overlooked this subtle evolution. There is a need to bring

1

together the current academic understanding of interest-group impact on policy and the new reality of professional lobbying. The widespread involvement of professional lobbyists is unmistakable, but their impact on policy-making is uncertain.

The question of who influences policy formulation is central to political science, and the effect of professional lobbyists has implications for the study of public policy. The increase in professional lobbying has raised fears about a policy-making system exposed to bias. It is time to re-evaluate these fears in light of the evidence presented in this book.

For scholars interested in lobbying, effectiveness is a captivating subject. There are limitations to the existing literature, in particular a paucity of data on effectiveness and some contradictory conclusions. The literature on effectiveness and influence 'is an interesting example of avoidance based on a recognition that previous studies have mostly generated more smoke than fire, more debate than progress, more confusion than avoidance'.[4] Grant concludes his study on British pressure groups by stating: 'if we are interested in finding out who wins and who loses in the political process, and why they win and lose, the question of effectiveness cannot be ignored by pressure-group analysts'.[5]

Questions which need answering include whether lobbyists are influential, and under what circumstances are they effective? Jordan sums up neatly, asking whether lobbyists are unfairly useful or fairly useless.

Clients pay high fees for lobbyists' services to influence policy, yet the return on investment is uncertain and difficult to substantiate.[6] Berry notes: 'the question remains, however, to what extent these techniques are effective in any meaningful way?'[7] Jordan has asked for 'detailed examples of the *impact* of these increasingly expensive activities'.[8] He continues:

> If there are lobbyists active on both sides of a question, there are bound to be plenty of cases where the lobbyists can claim to have been effective...whether the client wins because of the impact of the lobbying or whether the lobbying was merely incidental is something that requires detailed investigation. Such an assessment however requires more detailed case study evidence than is yet available.[9]

This book provides the case-studies and analysis.

Whilst the market for professional lobbying suggests that they are a worthwhile investment, Warhurst suggests the market is not always right and that lobbyists would not describe their own work as ineffective.[10] Whilst this statement is true, it also pays for lobbyists to show real results; repeat business and referrals are important in a market which has moved from being based on a regular monthly fee to one-off case work.

Similarly Berry wonders whether 'the tendency [of the media] to emphasise the "influence" of lobbyists, and to place them at the centre of the decision-making process, is borne out by more than hearsay and unsubstantiated newspaper speculation?'[11] Effective lobbying may be impossible to discover because 'a great lobbyist is like the perpetrator of the perfect crime. At the very best there is no indication the crime has even been committed. When they have done their job well, there are no fingerprints.'[12] Although the lobbying industry is increasingly discreet in the face of recent press coverage, now is an opportune moment to undertake research. Some lobbyists are aware of the reasons why they should be the subject of academic scrutiny; for example, the creation of the Association of Professional Political Consultants (APPC) has shone light on the lobbying industry.

Attention is being paid to effectiveness. The public relations journal *PR Week* launched its '10 per cent Campaign' to encourage practitioners to allocate 10 per cent of their budget to assessing the value and impact of their services.[13] Similarly, more attention is being paid to lobbying by practitioners and journalists, reflecting its higher profile and increasing importance.[14] Lobbyists entered popular culture, with even the *News of the World* reporting their activities.[15] Restricted scholarly interest in professional lobbying continues: a special edition of *Parliamentary Affairs* examined the regulation of lobbying.[16] Regulation is a questionable enterprise unless decision-makers can be sure lobbyists are influential. A study is needed to assess the views of the press, which ascribes influence to lobbyists, and of the civil service and ministers, who suggest the journalists' interpretation is inaccurate.

The debate between those suggesting lobbyists are effective and those arguing they are an information service staggers on. By explaining what factors facilitate effectiveness, this book will resolve questions about the influence of lobbyists in order to explain how the policy process operates and how different actors interact.

Since the attention given to professional lobbyists in UK academic circles is less extensive than in the USA, some of the material cited is of American origin. This work is referred to only when its analysis or insights are applicable to the UK.

The debate so far

The literature that exists on influence and effectiveness has failed to reach concrete conclusions, or rather has thrown up contradictory answers on the impact of lobbyists.[17] To understand when, how and why lobbyists are effective will allow for an improved understanding of public policy-making.

Many lobbyists seek to portray their work as simply a service to complement a client's strategy. But this definition fails to withstand practical application. Lobbyists often have a vested interest in denying their activity can be measured. The attempt to maintain a 'professional mystique' indicates that lobbyists wish to be measured by their inputs into the policy process and not outputs. However, promotional literature is laden with bravado about policy successes from effective lobbying.

This book will assesses whether lobbyists meet their clients' targets. It will seek to distinguish between the publicly-expressed and private objectives of the client. In order to do this, it will be important to distinguish between the lobbyist's skills (internal variables) and contextual factors (external variables). Context is key. Assessment of effectiveness requires attention to the policy outcome. A lobbyist will be judged effective if the policy outcome meets the client's objective, and if that outcome can be traced at least in part to the activity of the lobbyist.

Lobbyists, like academics and journalists, have two versions of their effect. Version one is for the media and the public: the lobbyist is depicted as an adviser who has little ability to upset a system that takes decisions based on merit. Version two is for clients: the lobbyist is portrayed as an effective operator and the key to success. The two faces of the lobbyist are reflected in the literature on the value of lobbying, which comprises two schools: first, that lobbyists have little effect and their influence is trivial; second, that lobbyists do affect public policy.

Lobbyists are fairly useless

The American 'communications school' of lobbying, proposed by Milbrath amongst others, argues that lobbyists do not have a significant effect on the decisions of officials or legislators.[18] Lobbyists have been portrayed as timid, approaching only those decision-makers that agree with them and acting as a service bureau.[19] Lobbyists are simply channels of information to improve decision-makers' knowledge.[20] Lobbyists are not influential; in fact, they are ill-informed and badly organised. Part of the reason lobbyists were deemed ineffective was because they did not lobby; or rather their lobbying was directed at those who were already convinced.[21] This school encouraged political science to move away from analysing the policy process and to concentrate on internal group dynamics.[22]

Recent research in the UK 'suggests that commercial lobbyists achieve low levels of effectiveness, defined as the ability to achieve pre-stated measurable goals by their own behaviours'.[23] It is not only academics who dismiss the impact of lobbying as superficial; government also denies lobbyists are effective.

John MacGregor, MP, a former Cabinet Minister and Leader of the House of Commons, in evidence to the Committee on Standards in Public Life, argued that the work of one lobbying company, Decision Makers, added nothing to the decisions being taken by government. Ministers, he argued, made their decisions based on representations received and the clear benefits.

MacGregor went on to say:

I think the role and so-called influence of lobby firms needs to be put into its proper perspective. In my experience and judgment it is greatly overstated. They do not have preferential access to and influence with government. Presumably if such claims are made, they are made to potential clients for marketing purposes and to win business. On the other hand, lobbying firms do have a legitimate role. For those companies, organisations and pressure groups who do not have their own resources they can provide a proper and useful information service ... They can provide technical knowledge on how government and Parliament work, and they have experience in knowing how best to present a case.[24]

If MacGregor's interpretation holds true, much of the hyperbole about lobbyists and their impact is empty boastfulness on the part of firms seeking business. Similarly, a parliamentary question about the effect of lobbyists produced the following unambiguous response: 'Lobbyists play no role in decisions made by my Department' (Welsh Office).[25]

Lobbyists are unfairly useful

Others have shown lobbyists to be effective. The press in Britain and in America has been captivated by the influence of lobbyists.[26] *The Guardian* and *The Independent* in the UK have long run stories about their access and supposed efficacy.[27] This journalistic obsession was illustrated in 1998 by a team from *The Observer* posing as representatives of an American energy company.[28] The story rested on the foundation that lobbyists were unduly effective. The lead journalist argued that Labour modernisers were 'now boasting that the contacts they made when the party was in opposition can now be used to gain access to and information from their erstwhile fellow-modernisers playing key roles in government'.[29] Although government dismissed the investigation as empty boasting by ambitious thirty-somethings, Palast disagreed: '*The Observer* has demonstrated the boasts were well-founded.'[30] He pointed to a No. 10 Policy Unit member who said one lobbyist was part of the inner circle and offered preferential access.[31]

Two Cabinet ministers, David Clark and Clare Short, expressed concern at lobbyists flitting around special advisers and ministers like moths around a flame. Short argued that ministers should not deal directly with lobbyists and advised colleagues: 'we should frown on it and completely distance ourselves from it'.[32] The Association of Professional Political Consultants' report, which pointed to human error rather than management system deficiencies, extinguished the matter.[33]

Journalistic commentators suggest professional lobbyists have too much influence over policy-making. However, a correlation does not prove a causal relationship, and the press has frequently taken a one-dimensional view of policy-making. In general the validity of journalistic assertions has been difficult to establish.

In support of the journalists some scholars advocate the 'interest-group dominance' thesis, suggesting lobbyists and groups play an important role in policy communities and can be dominant.[34] Schattschneider's study of tariff policy found that interest groups were effective.[35] Various scholars make normative judgements about the desirability of their activity and deem lobbyists effective only because they judge their activities undesirable.[36] Lobbyists are alleged to be detrimental to good government. They supposedly pull decision-makers away from the public interest.[37]

This book moves on from the sterile debate on whether or not lobbyists matter. The two camps talk past one another 'with academics dismissing the validity of popular claims in a few paragraphs and the popular press ignoring the research of scholars or quickly rejecting its methods and conclusions as irrelevant'.[38] Confusion is inflated by concealment. Twelve ministerial departments failed to answer parliamentary questions about the meetings ministers, officials, special advisers and parliamentary private secretaries had with lobbyists. Ministers replied baldly that meetings are all governed by the 'Ministerial Code', the 'Civil Service Code' and 'Guidance for Civil Servants: Contacts with Lobbyists'.[39]

The contradictory conclusions in the lobbying literature are partly explained by the perspectives of the researchers, their methodology and those to whom they speak. An incomplete explanation of the variation is that some academic studies concentrate on legislative voting and find little effect. In a parliamentary system, for example, it is almost certain that such studies look at the wrong stage in the process. Second, to look at an issue from the perspective of the lobbyist, researchers concluded lobbyists were often ignored, spent most of their time submitting information, and were ineffectual. From the standpoint of government, however, researchers who saw decision-makers under pressure from lobbyists and interest groups accorded them influence.

Neither finding is wrong. The difference between the two approaches appears irreconcilable only if debate is limited to the misleading question of whether lobbyists are important, and if that answer must be defended over time and under all circumstances. There is sufficient anecdotal evidence to suggest lobbyists make a difference on a case-by-case basis. This book moves forward by recognising that the existing literature allows us to state that lobbyists matter sometimes. What is worth examining is the circumstances under which lobbyists matter.

The contradictions are variations that need to be explained.[40] It is necessary to examine the *circumstances* under which lobbyists are effective. This research adopts a contextually-rich approach to the policy process to explain effectiveness.[41] It recognises that lobbyists' effectiveness depends on context. Policy outcomes depend on the combined influence of a number of factors.

The principal argument

The effect of a lobbyist will depend on both external and internal variables. With the context of a congenial external environment, success will depend on the lobbyist's possession of the internal characteristics necessary for effectiveness.

The central proposition of this book is based on three external variables: lobbyists tend to be effective on low-profile, non-political and technical issues. Lobbyists certainly 'operate more regularly, and more effectively, at the level of incremental day-to-day policy-making rather than at the more visible level of medium and high policy'.[42]

As the effect of lobbyists depends on the presence or absence of a range of variables, *ceteris paribus* lobbyists will be effective when other variables do not impinge on decision-makers.[43] On high-profile, political and general issues the concept of effectiveness becomes more diffuse as lobbyists have to wade through areas of subjective human factors.

On low-profile, non-political, technical issues lobbyists are effective because contacts, persuasion and reasoned argument matter more. Within a closed community external variables do not operate as powerfully as they do outside. Organised opposition and media interest are less likely on technical issues. Lobbying, which on high-profile matters would not exert influence, can tip the balance on low-profile, non-political, technical issues. These are the factors that influence effectiveness.

Lobbyists are not masters of their own destiny, so it is important to account for both internal and contextual factors that are fundamental determinants of effectiveness.

What counts as lobbying?

It is difficult, and not really necessary, to give a precise definition of the activity of professional lobbyists. The concept of lobbying has meanings so varied as to lead inevitably to misunderstanding.[44] Salisbury, writing about lobbyists in America, noted of the word 'lobbying', 'that much-abused word is so fraught with ordinary language meaning, most of it unsavoury, as to defy rehabilitation anyway, but it is also true that none of its historic uses comfortably fits with what many Washington representatives do'.[45]

The term 'lobbying' need not be hostile, but attempts at close definition can be self-defeating. Statutory definitions of lobbying are 'either hopelessly restrictive infringements on free speech or because they are so narrow ... only a few rare behaviors are affected'.[46] Salisbury argues the word does not reflect what 'lobbyists' do, such as the presentation of a technical case or a legal challenge; he prefers the term 'interest representation'.[47] In reality professional lobbyists can be described in a number of ways, such as public affairs consultant, government relations counsellor, communications adviser, regulatory specialist or parliamentary officer. 'What lobbying is even goes beyond the elephant problem of being something one instantly recognises but cannot define precisely, because what may be lobbying to one individual, or in a particular cultural setting, may be a routine exchange to another.'[48]

There are some boundaries: lobbying relates to government decision-making; it is motivated by a desire to influence government decisions; it implies the presence of a representative; and it involves communication.[49]

One definition of a lobbyist is any person who, for payment, attempts to influence, directly or indirectly, the passage of legislation or the taking of public policy decisions.[50] Some scholars have argued lobbying occurs only when an individual or group acts on behalf of someone else.[51] However, the definition of lobbying does not necessarily have to centre on the act of representing an interest to and before Parliament, government and officials.

Lobbying may include non-direct work such as providing strategic advice and monitoring, since both fall under the concept of representation. The fact is that most of the day-to-day work of lobbyists is monitoring and intelligence gathering. However, monitoring can be 'seen as a form of representation [because it] requires the third party's presence to be meaningful'.[52] Therefore the distinction between advocacy and advice should be disregarded because the attendance of the lobbyist is a requirement of both services.

Rush *et al.* defined lobbyists as:

- professional lobbyists or consultants whose business is to advise their clients on lobbying, and sometimes to lobby on their behalf;
- organisations outside Parliament and government who themselves seek to lobby, ranging from those who are fully professionalised or bureaucratised ... to entirely voluntary bodies, who have no paid staff and only limited resources;
- MPs and other individuals with direct access to parliament who also have a pecuniary interest in a particular policy area or who receive some sort of remuneration to represent the interests of an outside organisation;
- MPs and other individuals with direct access to Parliament who have non-pecuniary interests in a particular policy area and who represent the interests of, or make representations on behalf of, an outside organisation.[53]

Lobbying involves communicating the client's aims and preferences and advising clients how to influence public policy. The most comprehensive definition of a lobbying firm is provided by the Association of Professional Political Consultants:

Individual partnership or company (including divisions of companies) who either hold themselves out as offering consultancy services (meaning advice, representation, research, monitoring or administrative assistance provided for commercial gain by a professional political consultant relating to the institutions of UK central and local government and/or other public bodies) whether such activities are the principal business of that consultant or are ancillary or incidental to it, such work in each case being undertaken for their parties for commercial gain.[54]

It follows that a 'lobbyist' is a principal of a lobbying company, whilst the verb 'lobbying' encompasses the representative work undertaken by the lobbyist on behalf of a third party. The APPC paper continues:

These criteria therefore cover advisers, the majority of whose trading revenue is derived from advice or advocacy related to dealings with public authorities, or those undertaking one-off or ad hoc projects, and others, such as law and accounting firms, who may deal with Government on behalf of third parties but only on a basis incidental to their main business since in undertaking such work they are implicitly holding themselves out as possessing professional competence.[55]

Who counts as a professional lobbyist?

Lobbyists often have experience in political parties.[56] One firm, the Public Policy Unit (PPU), described itself as 'a group of former officials, Ministers, MPs, Peers and political advisers who now act as policy analysts and consultants on dealing with political and regulatory bodies at central and local government levels in the UK and EC'.[57] In Washington, DC, the majority of lobbyists are lawyers. This legal dominance does not apply to the UK, where British lobbyists tend to have political and/or administrative experience. They bring with them a detailed knowledge of the policy process and friends within the political system.

An advertisement in *The House Magazine*, from a leading professional lobbying firm seeking a managing director, sought a candidate with a 'Westminster, Whitehall, Brussels or similar background, together with existing consultancy experience. Experience in publishing, information services, journalism or economic consultancy would also be considered.'[58] Many have experience at the periphery of the political arena, such as civil servants, lobby correspondents, or departmental press officers.

Lobbyists are mainly an amalgam of ambitious white male middle-class political activists and a gaggle of aristocrats. They all have in common experience of and contacts in politics, the administration, the monarchy or elite business circles.

Several types of consultancies offer lobbying services. First, the specialised professional lobbying consultancies, which are members of the

APPC, tend to be the largest firms and the market leaders. Second, there exist smaller independent professional lobbying consultancies, eligible to become members of the APPC, but who choose not to for various reasons. Third, there are several large public relations companies with large public affairs departments and genuine experience (some US-owned): for example, Burson-Marsteller and Hill & Knowlton. Fourth, there is a vast number of smaller public relations companies which offer 'political services', treating government as another 'public' or 'stake-holder'.

Fifth, a host of 'one-man bands' exploit their contacts and experience of the political system. Sixth, the larger legal practices have public affairs departments (DLA and Clifford Chance). The boundary between the services provided by a lobbying company and those provided by a legal firm is hazy. Lobbyists have seen 'increasing competition from law firms in Brussels and the UK [and] from a number of merchant banks'.[59]

Seventh are registered parliamentary agents, with passes giving privileged access to the Palace of Westminster, who offer political consultancy services.[60] Since the replacement of the Private Bill with the Transport and Works Act (1992) and subsequent Orders and Regulations, they have moved into lobbying. The distinction between professional lobbyists and some parliamentary agents is no longer relevant. Both are concerned with case-building and advocacy.

Eighth, the 'Big Five' accountancy firms have established offices in Brussels to monitor and lobby the EU Commission and EU Parliament. Some firms provide a full range of legislative lobbying services, whilst others offer monitoring and strategic planning but avoid advocacy. The accountancy firms have developed sophisticated systems to track EU legislative processes. UK-based accountancy houses also offer legislative and policy services to their clients.

Finally, journalists have stepped in to exploit the lobbying market. The European Parliament has noted: 'some journalists express a specifically political agenda; and sometimes even...receive income from industrial or commercial interests for their advice and insights'.[61] Peter Luff, MP, argued in evidence to the Select Committee on Members' Interests that:

there are a number of paid relationships between outside interests and Lobby correspondents who are able to obtain more information on a confidential basis than even Members of Parliament, and if there were any attempt to curtail Members' ability to maintain relationships with outside interests...one could easily be left with a situation where others … had privileged access and would be more furtive than any of the possible abuses we are seeking to curtail here.[62]

Therefore professional lobbyists exist in a range of forms and might have previous experience as a local government officer or councillor, party official, civil servant, Commission official, non-departmental public body (NDPB) official, MP, special adviser, journalist, in-house specialist, regulatory expert, academic, lawyer, accountant or trade association official. They are an eclectic collection of individuals, each with a distinctive area of expertise and knowledge.

Who hires professional lobbyists?

Following Mancur Olson, the term 'interest group' became synonymous with membership organisations.[63] However, earlier interest groups embodied a range of organisations, including professional lobbyists, industries, foreign and local governments and corporations.[64] It was a mistake to restrict the definition of groups to membership organisations because it dragged political science away from examining those non-membership organisations so influential in policy development.[65]

It is also arguable that the cost of concentrating on internal structure was significant since it led to 'the marginalization of interest group studies as they lost their relation with the core issues of democratic governance'.[66] Olson and those who followed him concentrated on internal factors to the detriment of the contextual. More recently academics have broadened the concept of interest groups to include corporations, institutions and other organised interests.[67] This book refers to all non-governmental organisations as interest groups.

Put simply, lobbyists are employed by interest groups able to afford the fee. Clients are typically business organisations and companies. Even large companies with in-house staff employ external consultancies. Foreign governments use lobbyists as an alternative channel to traditional diplomacy. Executive bodies, executive agencies and local government use lobbyists to help them understand informal policy development in Whitehall. Government even hires lobbyists: the Department for International Development hired the Public Policy Unit.[68]

The services of lobbyists are 'sought when, and only when, the client firm requires those services, and their billing is usually based on an hourly charge', but it can also be based on a flat retained fee.[69] Clients frequently have several criteria when judging whether to embark upon lobbying: the relative importance of the issue to the interest; the probability of success; the complexity of the issue; whether the organisation is obliged to get involved; an assessment of other actors already involved; and the topicality of the issue.[70]

The potential market size is large. Every company is affected by public policy decisions. In its nascent years lobbying-industry clients were mainly large business and City financial institutions.[71] By the mid-1990s the lobbyists' client base had become more diverse. Although private companies are the largest client group, trade unions, local authorities, public bodies and campaign groups also hire lobbyists. The increased use of professional lobbyists by the private sector has forced parts of the public sector to follow because they often do not have good relations with central departments.

Figure 1.1 shows the breakdown of Association of Professional Political Consultants' members' clients. Companies accounted for 69 per cent of clients, and public bodies accounted for 9 per cent, whilst trade associations accounted for 13 per cent.

Some blue-chip UK companies do not employ professional lobbyists. One reason offered is that the government may perceive hiring lobbyists as a sign of weakness, although this reason is less valid today as lobbying has become ubiquitous. Second, Jordan opines that large, politically-aware companies have no need to purchase lobbying skills from professional lobbyists;[72] they can afford to employ in-house representatives to ensure their views are heard. However, it is often the case that in addition to in-house teams, lobbyists support large companies

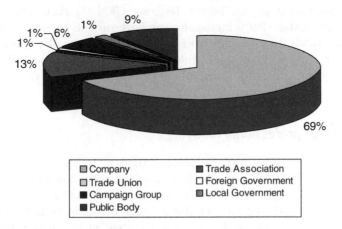

Figure 1.1 APPC client profile

because they can be closer to decisions and usually deliver high-quality intelligence.

Contrary to what Jordan says, a trend in Washington indicates that the complexity of the policy system has encouraged large companies to hire representatives: 'Ford, General Electric, IBM, GM, Exxon, and other giants may hire eight or ten separate outside representatives in addition to working through trade associations and their own substantial government relations staff.'[73] Likewise, in the UK British Gas hired several lobbying firms during the deregulation of the gas market for two reasons: the issue was complex, and their competitors were left with a restricted choice of adviser.

So lobbyists often support large companies with an in-house government affairs department. They may work for companies because an issue may be important, it may be particularly demanding for a short time, or the company may face a crisis. The issue may also be too complex to be handled in-house, or the company could have been forced to participate in policy-making and needs advice. The company may see a potential competitive advantage in hiring a lobbyist to bring about change. Some lobbyists are also acknowledged experts in specific policy areas and many larger firms are building specialist teams in subjects such as merger and acquisitions, financial services, defence, health, transport and local government.

Lobbying companies' clients also include trade unions such as the Transport and General Workers' Union and the Association of University Teachers; campaign groups such as the Multiple Sclerosis Society, Fast Tracks to Europe Alliance and National Anti-Vivisection Society; and companies such as BG, British Telecom, GKN Westland and Glaxo-Wellcome. Other clients include foreign governments such as the British Virgin Islands, the Azerbaijan Republic and the State of Bahrain. One lobbying firm, Bell Pottinger (which is not a member of the APPC), was hired by the Chilean Reconciliation Movement to run a campaign in defence of General Augusto Pinochet.[74]

Growth of professional lobbying

Interest in the circumstances under which lobbyists matter is partly a product of the increase in lobbying. Lobbyists are now hired by thousands of organisations. APPC members alone had 747 clients serviced by 268 staff. Because of the number of lobbyists now working in the UK, the value of the industry and their pivotal involvement in policy-making, an assessment of the circumstances under which they are effective is needed.

The development of professional lobbying is often described as an explosion; however, given the UK government's long tradition of dealing with consultants it may be more accurately viewed as the latest stage in a continuum. Although new public management increased government's demand for business input, the involvement of the private sector in Whitehall dates back far longer.

There are many reasons explaining the growth in lobbying in the UK over the past 20 years.

Government

1. Government has become dependent upon interest groups for information, advice and the implementation of policy. Statutory co-option of groups allowed for specific interests to be included in the political system. In some cases there was a continuous dialogue with permanent lobbies. The element of 'bureaucratic accommodation' to policy-making increased.[75] A 'consultation culture' developed following the Second World War.[76] War brought outside interests closer to government, and the interaction that began during the war became established by the post-war period.

2. Increased lobbying may be the consequence of government's increased scope in setting corporation tax and regulations.[77] As government has become more intrusive, organisations have been forced to become politically involved.[78] 'If government is a significant actor in a corporation's environment, then, *ceteris paribus*, that corporation will be politically active.'[79] Government matters because of its expenditure and increased. Interest groups cannot afford to be inactive.

3. The Conservative governments brought the professional lobbyist to the fore. Reforms distanced formerly public organisations from central government. These processes meant there were more potential clients and more organisations keen to retain contact with policy-makers. Privatisation and sub-contracting became commonplace. Professional lobbying is a consequence of those trends. Privatisation expunged the incestuous relationship that existed between the centre and nationalised industries. Consequently, although the system consults more, arguably it deals with outsiders less. Privatisation erected Chinese walls that distanced 'the system' from outsiders. Business thinks lobbyists help them scale these Chinese walls.

4. The changing structure of government has also encouraged a prolifer-
ation of lobbying. EU institutions have broadened their policy competence.[80] The Single European Act enhanced the power of the
Commission, which can now initiate policy in several areas. The power
of the European Parliament has also increased given the co-operation
procedure, and Parliament now influences the detail of Community
legislation. Similarly the Labour government's devolution programme
encouraged lobbying in Edinburgh and Cardiff.[81]

Business

1. The private sector increasingly relies on public subsidies and general
   economic decisions. The increase in lobbying may be the consequence of a shift from distributive to redistributive policy. More
   interest groups seek a share of increasingly limited resources.
2. The lack of innate empathy between government and organisations
   dealing with it has contributed to the rise of professional lobbying.[82]
   Those individuals able to link government and business have become
   indispensable. The decline of the 'Establishment', and of lobbying by
   social affiliation in the last 30 years, has allowed for the emergence of
   the professional lobbyist. In the run-up to the 1997 General Election
   business believed it did not know how to talk to the prospective
   Labour Government, leading many lobbying firms and large businesses to recruit Labour apparatchiks.
3. Business reacted slowly to the activity of environmentalists and consumer protection groups in the 1970s. Trade associations were established to represent their interests. Corporations also hired professional
   lobbyists to fight their corner.[83]

Parliament

1. The increased workload of ministers and MPs means the old style of
   personal contact lobbying is less effective. MPs also lack the opportunity, because they are both too busy and not expert enough, to act
   as an interface between interest groups and government. Therefore
   outside groups turn to lobbyists.
2. The complexity and length of parliamentary processes has encouraged lobbying. Similarly, the behavioural changes of Parliament have
   altered, giving rise to more independent voting and making the legislature a more relevant target; before 1970 lobbyists rarely troubled
   MPs.[84] The select committee system has also given groups a platform
   and encouraged lobbying.

3. There was also an increase in the willingness of MPs to engage in lobbying work. During the 1980s many MPs were directors of lobbying companies. In the mid-1980s 39 MPs were part-owners or employees of consultancies.[85] The new generation of MPs includes many who were professional lobbyists in their previous careers. Younger MPs are more used to lobbying and dealing with the business community.

Supply

1. Modern communications technology has allowed the identification of new coalitions around relatively narrow issues.[86] These new issues have altered the role of the political party. The Internet helps lobbyists and interest groups to activate grass-roots supporters and disseminate information quickly, easily and cheaply.
2. Professional lobbyists are political entrepreneurs similar to those noted by Kavanagh.[87] Though he concentrates on 'think-tanks', lobbyists also enter this category. Growth may be supply-led because these entrepreneurs exploited a market opportunity. There is a saloon door mentality in professional lobbying: a two-way process from lobbyist to politician and vice versa.
3. A 'me too' philosophy applies to lobbying. Organisations tend to hire a professional lobbyist if their competitors have done so.[88] Foreign firms might also be in part responsible for the growth. An American journalist argued that: 'American companies and their money are pushing the UK lobbying industry to provide the same sort of service they would expect in Washington.'[89] Corporations demand 'the same levels of access and political intelligence to which they have become accustomed at home'.[90]

The focus of professional lobbyists

To understand when lobbyists matter it is necessary to understand the circumstances in which they operate. There are two principal foci of professional lobbying: Parliament and the civil service.

Lobbyists have focused increasingly on Parliament. Norton writes: 'since 1979, the government has been perceived as more resistant to interest group influence, and so groups were turning increasingly to Parliament for a hearing'.[91] There is substantial debate on the appropriate focus of professional lobbying. Some practitioners argue that those who direct their activities at select committees and MPs in general are 'professionally bankrupt'. They argue that for a professional lobbyist to direct 'clients down the parliamentary road because he knows no better, is to turn what is often an administrative or technical matter into a political one'.[92] Miller claims it is a misdirection of effort caused by an exaggerated media interest in Parliament (because it is easy to report).[93] He argues that they are profile-raising techniques which are essentially ineffective.

It may be that a failure to persuade key actors in Whitehall will lead professional lobbyists to target Westminster. Professional lobbyists often operate across 'all fronts'. Though Parliament sometimes contributes to policy-making, it more often confers legitimacy on policy. However, Parliament can be an important route of access to ministers (for example, through the medium of the Parliamentary Private Secretary, or PPS).

Parliament

Arguably the concentration of interest groups in Parliament is out of proportion with the legislature's influence. This imbalance may be the consequence of an inaccurate perception held by outside interests of Parliament's influence, or a reliance on Parliament when other channels have failed.[94] Some practitioners argue that reactions to professional lobbying have over-emphasised the significance of Parliament in the decision-making process,[95] and the role of lobbyists is to disabuse clients of the misapprehension that Parliament is the key to influencing policy.

However, Parliament is important and is a part of the policy-cycle which needs cultivation. As a 'policy influencing' chamber, the House of Commons is a relevant target for lobbyists. To be effective in Parliament lobbyists require knowledge of personalities and procedure. Rush *et al.* support this argument. They refute the notion of the UK as a post-parliamentary democracy and argue that Parliament makes a difference and is relevant to influencing policy.[96]

The focus of professional lobbyists on Parliament can be both cosmetic and substantive.[97] It is cosmetic, because dining in the Palace of Westminster and meeting MPs is mostly ineffective but can impress clients. But Parliament is substantive because it influences some important decisions, such as moral issues. Although Miller reduces Parliament to the 'gift-wrapping of Government', he is forced to concede that Parliament is important when government majorities are low.[98] The events of the late 1970s and the Major governments in the 1990s justify a lobbyist's attention to Parliament.

Various types of MP are targeted by lobbyists. Policy advocates can be ideologues, generalists or specialists. Specialist policy advocates are the most professional, seeking to influence policy 'carefully ... persistently and effectively in narrow policy areas'.[99] Such specialists rely on outside contacts for advice and often work with lobbyists. MPs who are ministerial aspirants are concerned with power, whereas policy advocates seek influence. Ministerial aspirants would be prepared to work with professional lobbyists on policy issues if they could foresee political advantage. Members who are primarily concerned about their constituents will usually work with professional lobbyists when the lobbyist's cause brings benefits for their constituents. 'Parliament men', notes Searing, include 'spectators' (those who want to be at the centre of things), and 'club men', who are more active than spectators but who absorb themselves in the atmosphere and collegiality of the Commons.[100]

To some the Conservative reforms of the 1980s encouraged lobbyists to focus on Parliament. The reforms of the Thatcher governments divested central government of its operational involvement and embraced the private sector. Because of the speed of the reforms lobbyists targeted parliamentarians rather than civil servants.[101]

Standing and select committees

Lobbying of members of standing committees is extensive. Interest groups contact some or even all members of Standing Committees, and many ask MPs to table amendments. Only a few Bills each session are intensely political, and the bulk of business is routine. Briefing material from lobbyists allows MPs to participate in deliberations. Lobbying improves the knowledge of standing committee members, and reduces the ability of the government to rely on the party majority automatically to approve its policy. Lobbying at committee stage, argues Norton, renders legislation more acceptable. He suggests that interest groups hiring professional lobbyists are more effective, since they can monitor committee proceedings and are 'better placed to have some influence than those who cannot afford such assistance'.[102]

The select committee system is organised around departmental business and encourages a specialised focus on public policy issues. Lobbyists are adept at exploiting this platform and often use it as a route to departmental policy-making. They train clients as to how to promote their case in front of MPs anxious to portray themselves in televised select committee hearings as defenders of the public interest.

Charles Miller claims that whilst select committees have increased parliamentary scrutiny of ministerial and official actions, they have not been a complete success because their reports are rarely debated and are too late to affect policy.[103] However, since many witnesses are representatives from outside groups, the process of giving evidence provides the opportunity to influence the recommendations of the select committee and to gain the attention of ministers and civil servants who have to note and reply.[104] Agriculture, Education, Energy, Social Services and Trade and Industry committees obtain over half their evidence from outside groups.[105] Some select committees would not be able to operate were it not for interest-group involvement. Several scholars have shown that select committees provide interest groups with valuable information about how departments are thinking.[106] Consequently select committees have acted as a magnet for outside interests and lobbyists. Backbench party committees and all-party groups also play some part in setting the policy agenda.

However, it is select committees that are able to place issues on the House's agenda or to increase their standing in Whitehall. Committee reports usually filter down to debate and questions in the chamber of the Commons. Sir Clifford Boulton noted that 25 per cent of select committee reports were the subject of debate in the House, but only a small proportion had been the subject of a substantive motion or an adjournment motion.[107] There have been many requests for extra parliamentary time to be set aside for debate of select committee reports.

Select committees are used to attract the attention of players outside the legislature. Although Whitehall is the key arena for most policy, select committees force ministers and civil servants to listen or to respond to committee reports containing the group's evidence.

The civil service

For every policy decision government is forced to change as a consequence of high-profile pressure, there are likely to be 'several hundred where decisions are made or influenced purely through the undramatic submission of a well-researched, well-argued and representative case'.[108] The word 'pressure' does not adequately describe the professional lobbyist–civil servant relationship: '"pressure" implies that some kind of sanction will be applied if a demand is refused, and most groups, most of the time, simply make requests or put up a case; they reason and they argue'.[109]

The civil service has undergone massive change since 1979. A central theme to the reform of the civil service has been the devolution of managerial authority and responsibility. Managerial devolution implies discretionary judgement by officials, opening the way for different solutions to similar problems.[110] Junior officials have enhanced autonomy and are increasingly important targets for lobbyists.

The quiet approach is the most effective when dealing with civil servants, argue many commentators:

> The safest solution for the corporate lobbyist is to fix his [client], and then to watch his [client] fix the civil service. For once the deal is done, the honour of the civil service is engaged. If it fails to deliver its Ministers bound hand and foot, it hangs its head in shame. Whereas the lobby which [only] converts the politicians is inevitably confronted by the resistance of the civil service.[111]

Similarly, Miller argues that there are 'few civil servants at principal grade and above who do not spend some of every day giving advice to, engaging in consultations or professional negotiations with, or simply meeting representatives of their sponsoring area of responsibility'.[112]

Guidance on contact with lobbyists

Following newspaper allegations about the effect of lobbyists on policy, the Prime Minister instructed the Cabinet Secretary to investigate. Informal guidance was produced for civil servants about their contact with lobbyists. The report amplified the Civil Service Code and reminded officials of the high levels of integrity and honesty demanded of them.

Some years earlier the Committee on Standards in Public Life rejected the arguments for regulating lobbyists and placed the burden on the institutions of government to 'develop ways of controlling the reaction to approaches from professional lobbyists in such a way as to give due weight and attention to their case while always taking care to consider the public interest'.[113] The pivotal role of lobbyists in policy-making was accepted and the 1998 paper dismissed a ban on dealings with lobbyists.

The report identified degrees of severity. The most serious offences were for civil servants to leak confidential or market-sensitive information to a lobbyist, and to help a lobbyist attract business by giving privileged access to ministers or undue influence over policy.[114]

In essence the advice was for officials to exercise their common sense. Civil servants were instructed not to:

- do or say anything that could be seen as granting lobbyists preferential or premature access to information;
- accept gifts or hospitality that could lead to an obligation to the donor;
- give the impression that the idea of a lobbyist's client would be decisive;
- do anything to breach parliamentary privilege;

- use insider knowledge to impress lobbyists;
- use insider status to get lobbyists an undeserved benefit;
- offer or give the impression of offering preferential access to lobbyists.

Civil servants should:

- declare all personal or family business interests;
- take care when accepting hospitality from lobbyists;
- consider, when meeting one group, how their views could be balanced by other groups.

The Cabinet Secretary noted sardonically that if civil servants 'have a friend who is a lobbyist you do not have to sever your friendship and stop meeting them socially. If you are married to one you do not have to get divorced!'[115] He urged that common sense should prevail. Officials with concerns about their relations with lobbyists should be cautious, consult a manager and make a note on the file to show they had considered issues of propriety. Most important was the *'Private Eye* test'. Officials should do nothing about which they would feel embarrassed were it to become public knowledge.

The burden of fairness and transparency was placed on the public servant. Because many lobbyists have other roles (local councillors, journalists, consultants), civil servants could not 'expect the lobbyists to keep their different roles in watertight compartments'.[116] Since lobbyists can be shameless self-publicists who talk up their own influence, Sir Richard Wilson concluded: 'It is the job of all civil servants to make sure that they conduct their dealings with lobbyists in a manner which is proper and not open to misinterpretation.'[117]

Even critics of lobbying recognise that professional lobbying is now an entrenched part of policy-making.[118] It is considered less an unbecoming political activity imported from the USA and increasingly as a legitimate part of the policy process. Sir Richard Wilson's tone indicated his acceptance of professional lobbying and his reliance on the integrity of the civil service to prevent misbehaviour. A former Cabinet Secretary has also written about how professional lobbying plays a valuable role in policy-making and there is nothing intrinsically wrong in it.[119] In many respects the lobbying industry has emerged from its various crises as an accepted and integral part of the policy-making landscape.

Conclusions

The number and activity of professional lobbyists have grown rapidly since Finer's examination of interest groups of the 1950s. Lobbyists pervade many areas of government's domestic policy-making, and their activity has caused concern.

The two schools of thought on the effect of lobbyists (the communications school and the interest-group dominance thesis) have clouded the debate on effectiveness. Clarity can be brought to the subject by recognising that the two schools are variations that can be explained by attention to context and circumstances.

Four policy areas are examined later in this book. The following chapters explain when lobbyists matter by taking account of the contextual variables that impinge on decision-makers in each case, as well as the variables within the control of lobbyists and their clients. This approach enables researchers to assess which contexts are most amenable to effective lobbying. It allows the study to identify which internal factors (those within the lobbyists' control, such as skill and resources) are important, and when and why they are important.

2
What Effectiveness Means
for Lobbyists

Effectiveness is a fuzzy concept. Attention to the idea of effectiveness is important and worthy of investigation. This chapter provides a working definition of what effective lobbying is. It investigates the different perceptions of effectiveness and the difficulties of judging it. The chapter reviews the literature on practical attempts to measure and improve effectiveness, before presenting a method to assess it.

To help in this assessment, the chapter identifies two sets of variables that affect influence: external independent variables and internal independent variables. These two variable types are the building blocks of the propositions presented in Chapter 3.

Sensitivity to context is key to explaining when lobbyists matter. External variables are, by and large, beyond the control of the lobbyist and the client, operating at the macro and meso levels. The lobbyist and client generally only have control over internal variables. Therefore, other things (a favourable external context) being equal, a lobbyist tends to be effective if he or she possesses the internal independent variables in greater number (contacts, knowledge of rules, resources, client-lobbyist relationship, a dependency relationship, long-term relationships and credibility).

What is effectiveness?

There is no consensus on what effectiveness means for lobbying. Effectiveness could be based on having an effect on votes in the legislature,[1] gaining access to decision-makers,[2] customer satisfaction, or having an effect on policy outcome.[3] An effective lobbying campaign may simply be routine monitoring and agenda setting.[4]

Effectiveness depends on what the client wants. Since there is no one route to an effective campaign, effectiveness must mean different things to different people. Once a definition has been selected, effectiveness (say, at meeting the client's objectives) might be achieved not because of the activity of the lobbyist but because of contextual factors. Therefore, when examining policy outcomes, it is as important to assess the impact of the range of factors on policy as it is to examine the activity of the lobbyist. The lobbyist is just one of many independent variables that interact to produce the dependent variable: the policy outcome.

Government since 1979 has become more concerned with effectiveness, efficiency and economy. The advent of New Public Management, including the Rayner scrutinies, the Financial Management Initiative, contracting-out, the Private Finance Initiative (PFI) and Value-For-Money audits, has increased the profile of effectiveness. The term effectiveness, when applied to policy-making, is challenging to conceptualise.[5] There are several definitions of effectiveness relating to policy-making, but the most appropriate is:[6] 'Effectiveness is concerned with the relationship between the intended and the actual results of projects, programmes or other activities. How successfully do outputs of goods, services or other results achieve policy objectives, operational goals and other intended effects?'[7]

The common theme to the definitions is that effectiveness refers to the value given to the relationship between activity and its effects. This relationship causes conceptual problems.[8] There exists a loose consensus on what the effects of activity are. Outputs are the direct products of certain processes: for example, in a lobbying campaign briefs will be circulated, meetings held and information gathered. Outcomes are the measurable consequences of a strategy. These effects can be external to the activity itself; lobbying by one interest may spur an opposing group into activity. Impacts are the ultimate effects of a policy, representing the change in gross and net values.

The motive most often behind lobbying is to influence governmental decisions. But other factors influence the policy process, and one must distinguish between intended and unintended effects. It is essential to demonstrate a causal link between outcomes and the intended actions of a lobbyist. Functionality is the relationship between an activity's underlying purpose and its effects, and this is at the heart of the concept of effectiveness. Effectiveness can be restricted to intended effects; if an action does not meet its intended effects it is not 'effective', however valuable the actual outcome. Definitions limiting effectiveness to the extent to which effects are desired do not capture the essence of effectiveness. Effectiveness is a measure of the functionality of activities and effects and, only secondarily, the extent to which they are intended and desirable.[9]

There should be a distinction between substantive effectiveness and evaluative effectiveness. *Substantive effectiveness* is the contribution of activities and their effects to designated purposes. It is concerned with the direct relationship between an activity and its effects. Substantive effectiveness has two sub-divisions, managerial effectiveness and policy effectiveness. Managerial effectiveness is the extent to which management style can bring about functional outputs. It is concerned with direct outputs and is expressed as output effectiveness. For inputs to be transformed into outputs requires funds, labour, skill and expertise. Policy effectiveness relates to whether inputs produce outputs/outcomes that are consistent with the underlying aims. Policy effectiveness is concerned with outcome effectiveness.

Evaluative effectiveness is the capability of strategies to measure their own substantive effectiveness and improve it. The inability of lobbyists to evaluate their own activity lessens their learning potential and thus reduces their substantive effectiveness. Evaluative effectiveness depends on an ability to examine one's technical capability, such as the possession of databases and information systems, and an expertise in the quantitative and qualitative methodologies necessary to undertake evaluation. An ability to judge the organisational structures of a campaign, such as reporting links, lines of responsibility and decision-making functions, is necessary to improve substantive effectiveness.

Attempts to measure the effectiveness of lobbying activity are likely to be politically sensitive. Economists use cost-benefit analysis, and statisticians measure effectiveness by means of causal models and simulations, but these methodologies are of little use to the political scientist. Methodology strategies can improve measurement of effectiveness by asking three types of question: descriptive, explanatory and normative. Descriptive questions require information about specific conditions, while explanatory questions seek to establish causes and effects of activities, such as 'Did lobbying lead a civil servant to change his mind?' Normative questions ask whether goals were achieved; for example, while a civil servant may have altered his or her position, policy may not have changed. This book asks and provides answers to these three questions.

A particular effectiveness study may explore simultaneously different forms of effectiveness, leading to a number of differing questions that, in turn, demand differing measurement approaches. There are several models employed in judging effectiveness. First, a case study approach describes and analyses the relationships within and surrounding a complex event. Second, survey research analyses a structured collection of data from a sample of those affected by policy. Survey research is primarily descriptive, but it allows actors scope to offer subjective evaluations of effectiveness. Unstructured interviews, structured interviews and questionnaires are used to assess effectiveness by seeking the subjective opinions of the political actors involved.

The issue of effectiveness has been addressed by Milbrath and Berry using surveys, but they asked lobbyists what strategies they considered most effective; they did not analyse effectiveness in specific policy cases.[10] A subsequent, more comprehensive, survey asked what attributes helped lobbyists be effective, and showed that the lobbyist's contacts, client and years in government were associated with effectiveness.[11] It asked lobbyists if they believed they had been effective. The team of researchers then sought to confirm or refute self-assessment reports by interviewing government officials and politicians.

Finally, performance indicators are quantitative expressions of various characteristics or consequences of an activity. Indicators focus on levels of performance. Absolute indicators report volume or incidence, and indices report relative achievement. Their function is primarily descriptive and they are unlikely to provide explanations.

The problems of judging effectiveness

Since policy influence is awkward to operationalise, political science is unclear over how to assess the influence of lobbyists.[12] Methodological problems prevent an accurate judgement of effectiveness.[13] There exists no methodological or quantitative framework to judge the effectiveness of one lobbyist against another.[14] Berry says:

> Whilst Washington lobbyists express a high degree of certainty in evaluating lobbying success, political scientists are considerably more cautious, finding it very difficult to evaluate the effectiveness of interest groups' advocacy campaigns. In carrying out such analyses, political scientists face formidable obstacles in developing scientifically valid measures of influence.[15]

There are nine reasons why judging effectiveness is problematic.

1. The most obvious problem is that there are too many variables. There are usually other interests and other lobbyists involved on any one issue. Berry argues: 'If all the individual relationships among the numerous variables were drawn in with appropriate lines and arrows, one fears that all would be obscured in a hopelessly tangled maze.'[16]

There is no obvious way to isolate and measure adequately the causality of the activities and advice of lobbyists on policy outcomes: this task is made more difficult in larger campaigns which have more variables.[17] Berry says:

> any attempt at evaluation, however, is limited by the method-ological difficulties to be encountered in trying to operationalise the concept of influence. The problems of distinguishing the influence of interest groups upon policy makers, as distinct from other influences such as the press, general public opinion, and other political elites, remain rather substantial.[18]

2. Correlation does not prove causation.[19] A statistical relationship may exist between lobbying and policy because unobserved or omitted variables may determine the outcome.[20] Salisbury has argued: 'it is exceedingly difficult to identify when influence has occurred and when there is really only a parallelism of purpose and action between the lobbyist and government official'.[21] Berry comments: 'the crux of the issue, therefore, is actually "proving" that the interest group *caused* government officials to change their behaviour in some manner. How is one actually to know that it was an interest group that caused an observed change in behaviour on the part of a governmental policy maker?'[22] Similarly, Grant says: 'there is never a tangible end-product which can be attributed to the efforts of the lobbyist; if the campaign is successful, it may have nothing to do with the lobbyist's efforts'.[23]

3. Assumptions and assertions about the effect of lobbying are flawed because studies have been unable to establish convincing counterfac-tuals (i.e., what effect an organisation would have on policy if lob-byists' activities were not performed). The qualitative studies, which consist of anecdotes and interviews, and quantitative correlation stud-ies arguably fail to prove a link between lobbying activity and policy outcome.[24] However, establishing a counterfactual is impossible.

4. Self-reports on influence by lobbyists are, by their very nature, unre-liable, but have been used in US studies.[25] Lobbyists probably exag-gerate their impact. There is an element of 'Emperor's clothes' to the work of consultants.[26] They might view a successful outcome as tes-timony to their effectiveness even though that outcome may have been the consequence of contextual factors.[27]

5. '[R]eliable conclusions about the true influence of one political actor over another requires knowledge of the initial sincere preferences of both actors uncontaminated by considerations of anticipated reactions

which may influence what one actually tries to achieve.'[28] Actual influence may be less than potential influence because of a deficiency in consciousness.[29] Similarly, policy-makers may be unwilling to admit they have been swayed by lobbyists. Civil servants are unlikely to acknowledge the true impact of lobbyists, though it may be 'not so much a case of officials wanting to hide something as it is the selective perception that leads them to believe that their decisions were based on other factors'.[30] Officials are not likely to admit to having been influenced by 'pressure'.

6. Policy-making is often hidden and transient. Much lobbying is specific and short-lived; or 'like the dog that Sherlock Holmes realised had not barked in the night, effective representation may entail doing nothing'.[31] Most of what lobbyists do is not on public record. Client lists have only recently been made public by the voluntary APPC. It is also difficult to uncover the government's true intention. 'Sometimes government may toughen up a Green Paper or a White Paper so that it has something to give away to pressure groups at a later stage without compromising its core position.'[32] Lobbyists may appear to have been effective, but the concession may have been an inexpensive loss-leader for government. The government keeps intact its over-riding objectives.

7. The scale of the change and the importance of an issue to an interest group make judging effectiveness problematic. Grant asks: 'how does one compare a substantial impact on a policy which is basically unfavourable to a group with some small adjustments to a policy which is more in line with a group's thinking?'[33] With this point in mind, it would be inaccurate to treat the policy outcome as a dichotomous variable.[34] To judge success on whether or not a policy changed or a vote was won would misrepresent the lobbying process.[35] The winner–loser dichotomy is misleading. The policy process is not a simple game.

8. It can be difficult to separate the closely entwined functions of different professionals who will have a similar brief from the client. Some interest groups employ more than one lobbying consultancy,[36] whilst on other issues (e.g., take-over battles) participating companies hire lawyers, merchant bankers, accountants and financial public relations consultants, as well as lobbyists. Outcomes are usually an amalgam of various factors. It is difficult to distinguish between where monitoring or contact-building ends and where 'lobbying' begins. Furthermore, precise assessment is difficult because some clients, having no discernible policy goal, require only profile-raising. The objectives of

clients often differ, too.[37] Some will want to change law or regulations, whilst others want less tangible services, such as contact-building. Clients can also often have multiple objectives.

9. Effectiveness or success is often a function of expectation.[38] The political consultant may persuade clients to scale down their objectives so they become a 'placebo'. In the end what the client 'wants' may be so limited and unnecessary as not to be worth while. But, by achieving those circumscribed goals, the client perceives the lobbyist as effective. Otherwise, a compromise with government may be forced. Whilst falling short of the client's ultimate objective, the compromise may be favourable to the client.

In essence:

> there is no clear methodology which can enable a clear assessment of group effectiveness. One has to look at policy outcomes ... and then try to assess how far those policies have been influenced by [one group] as distinct from other actors. It is possible to fall back on perceptions of effectiveness, but if a group is perceived to be effective, this may itself be a cause of effectiveness rather than a way of measuring the dependent variable.[39]

The principal problem when assessing 'the effectiveness of the lobbying techniques used, whether by organisations or their consultants, is that it is impossible to tell whether the tactics adopted make any difference'.[40] Customers often find it difficult to show any definite benefit from services provided to them. 'Given the difficulty that political scientists have in measuring influence, it could be expected that there are no standards or criteria for effectiveness accepted by the lobbyists themselves.'[41] Therefore the judgement has to be subjective.

As such, the interview material used in this book, and the subsequent conclusions, are based on actors' perceptions of influence rather than *actual* influence. However, 'if groups act on this perceived reality then the perception is just as important as an objective assessment'.[42] Whilst it may be impossible to be precise about the effects of actions, we may draw general conclusions about the attributes which might help towards effectiveness. Given the pitfalls, the best one can offer is generalisations and illustrations drawn from a period of participant-observation.[43] Whilst the effects of lobbyists' actions may, strictly speaking, be unmeasurable, interviewing relevant actors and obtaining their subjective assessment is the most appropriate means of judging effectiveness.

Measuring effectiveness

Attempts to assess effectiveness have included surveys of MPs by polling companies, client surveys and efforts to establish a causal link between lobbying and legislative votes.

The trade association sector has undertaken research to improve its political effectiveness. The former Department of Trade and Industry (DTI) Secretary of State, Michael Heseltine, attacked the complacency of trade associations that 'believe they are effective, when it is all too brutally clear they are not'.[44] In 1996 the DTI, launching a Trade Association Initiative, published a best-practice guide and funded a study into effectiveness.[45]

To be effective a trade association should externally: represent the whole industry; be aware of changing policy; form coalitions; maintain contact with key officials and politicians; respond to formal consultation; be regarded as credible by decision-makers; maintain an active media-relations programme; maintain contact with academics, think tanks and other opinion formers. Internally, a trade association should have resources; provide quality services; satisfy members and clients; have a long-term strategy; and have a high-calibre secretariat and management team.

In a survey in 1996 MPs were asked their impression of the 'overall effectiveness of various lobby consultancies in *providing advice* to their clients'. For about 60 per cent of companies the majority of MPs felt unable to express an opinion. In those 40 per cent of leading companies where the majority of MPs did express an opinion, 53 per cent of MPs felt the consultancies in general were 'very' or 'quite effective'.[46] The survey did not ask MPs if they felt lobbying consultancies were effective in helping their clients meet their objectives. A further reason for viewing these data with scepticism is that one can argue that MPs rated firms effective if they 'liked' them, so the firms rated most effective may be those run by the most amiable people.

Some consultancies (e.g., Shandwick Consultants) employ polling agencies to survey their clients to see whether they believe they are obtaining an effective service. Other methods of self-assessment are used. Shandwick argues that if press coverage shifts from describing an outcome from 'being possible' to 'being probable' it might be considered successful repositioning. Similarly, 'positive mentions … in the House of Commons could be another measure of success'.[47]

However, these assessment criteria are dubious. Press comment is often imprecise, especially on mergers and take-overs. Second, unless the *raison d'être* of the client is to be mentioned in Hansard, this measure is futile.

For example, Hansard references are irrelevant to a manufacturing company with a solid customer base; whilst to a public utility company, avoiding negative parliamentary comment may be crucial to preventing local newspapers running with hostile stories.

Grant Butler Coomber (GBC), a London public affairs consultancy specialising in technology policy, leads the assessment of performance and effectiveness. Between 5 and 10 per cent of its fees are set aside for the measurement of effectiveness. The measurement of performance has been client-driven. GBC's business philosophy is to seek to prove to clients that they receive a clear return on investment. GBC charges clients according to whether targets, which are set and agreed to in advance by the client and consultancy, have been achieved. Assessment is undertaken by focus groups, surveys and interviews.

Further efforts to improve lobbying effectiveness draw on American management consultancy techniques.[48] Advocates of benchmarking argue that effectiveness demands lobbyists quantify and qualify their goals.[49] Benchmarking concentrates on internal process and not external independent variables, though it may improve an organisation's ability to react to external shocks. Miller suggests that those who deal with government 'should be regarded not as an overhead but as a profit centre'.[50] However, it is often difficult for lobbyists to link their activities to those issues deemed most important by their clients' senior officers.[51]

Benchmarking involves comparing the actions of one organisation to a high-performing neighbour. It encourages quantum rather than incremental learning. Benchmarking forces a lobbyist to define a client's objectives and requirements and set achievable goals. Its principal utility is as a check against complacency built on past successes.

Other tools that are used to measure or improve effectiveness are quantification (this applies a monetary value to lobbying, i.e., the value of legislation adopted or defeated); client surveys; broader opinion-former surveys; process maps (diagrams that identify unnecessary steps in procedures); and measuring results against objectives.[52]

How to judge effectiveness

Given all the difficulties in measuring the influence of lobbyists, the design presented here cannot resolve all the aforementioned problems. The best it can hope for is to suggest options to mitigate some of the pitfalls.

Analysing the directly observable attempts by lobbyists and their clients to influence policy is sensible. Whiteley and Winyard argue that the most appropriate way to assess effectiveness is to interview policy-makers and other actors to obtain their perceptions.[53] Different respondents see the process from different perspectives and have different conceptions of 'effectiveness'. Therefore, it is important to gain the perceptions of as many players and from as many angles as possible, including lobbyists, their clients, their opponents, the administrative and political executive and legislators, in order to obtain some form of balance.

This book examines policy outcomes. Its methodology looks backwards from the outcome to the inputs of various actors and the impact of contextual variables. Policy outcomes, not lobbyists, will be the focus of analysis. It uses self-reports of lobbying activity by lobbyists to assess their own perceptions, but will limit the risks inherent in such a methodology by interviewing lobbying opponents and other key actors. A shift of emphasis allows the question to be broadened to include other factors that impact on policy. A question asking what circumstances allow for effectiveness enables the research to pay closer attention to the independent variables.[54]

In examining effectiveness the book identifies the key decision-points in the policy-making process. It investigates what lobbyists did, what they wrote and said to whom and when, and whether lobbyists influenced a decision or helped create an environment in which the decision could be made.

Any study should clarify the clients' objectives to establish whether or not their aims were achieved. Researchers should interview clients to discover what strategy the lobbyist advised (which the client had not envisaged). The study distinguishes between the publicly-expressed objectives and the private objectives of the client, and assesses whether the lobbyist down-graded the initial objectives. Only once this framework is clear is it possible to judge what influence lobbyists had. The book measures effectiveness by how successfully lobbyists meet their clients' targets. The salient task is to judge what effect lobbyists' techniques or services had on achieving the goals of the client whilst accounting for external factors.

Therefore, this book assumes lobbyists to have been effective if they have had some effect on a policy outcome that can be traced to their input into the policy process whilst controlling for external factors.

Effectiveness depends on a combination of factors, which can be split in two: factors beyond the control of the lobbyist and factors within his or her control. Measuring effectiveness can realistically be undertaken only in the context of those factors within the lobbyist's control.

Whilst all the internal variables may be operating efficiently, they may have little impact on policy because of the intervention of external variables. So assessment of effectiveness will need to be subtle. On occasions, the failure to achieve a desired policy outcome might not mean the lobbying was ineffective. It may at times be important to disentangle effectiveness from the policy outcome and activity of the lobbyist. Survival may often be the key to success. 'The outcome of any particular issue will be less important than that the group lives to fight again. Given the surrounding circumstances, therefore, success might be defined in any number of ways. It will not necessarily mean that the group "won".'[55]

Lobbyists can set an objective, run an effective campaign, fail to achieve that objective, but achieve an acceptable subsidiary outcome such as inducing decision-makers to think again about an issue. Even if the policy outcome was not the one desired, it may be possible to conclude that the lobbyist performed effectively if the contextual variables were hostile and obstructive.

Variables influencing effectiveness

Lobbyists can be effective, but their influence has limits. With sensitivity to context acknowledged as an essential requirement in studying effectiveness, this chapter examines the existing literature and draws out the external variables and the internal variables that act as determinants of effectiveness.

External variables

Sensitivity to context

Interests are shaped by context: social, economic and governmental.[56] An important gap in group literature is the lack of attention to contextual factors such as economic growth, government action and political conflict.[57] A broad range of factors affects decisions.[58] External factors and government officials are significant contextual variables.[59] Heinz *et al.* conclude that whilst 'Groups and their representatives are often influential ... so are other actors including government officials, academicians, and journalists.'[60]

Political science has suffered because effectiveness and influence have been portrayed as a game that produces winners and losers. Salisbury suggests the process is continuous with no clear resolution, and recommends closer attention to context.[61] Some academics have advocated a population-ecology perspective that places emphasis on the environmental, social and political factors rather than on internal factors.[62] Biologists would not explain the population and behaviour of an animal species 'without taking into consideration environmental factors such as the amount of food available, the climate or the presence of competitors'.[63]

Researchers must seek to demonstrate the effectiveness of a lobbyist when controlling for rival factors that may have influenced the decision. The conventional approach is to 'estimate a baseline of expected behaviours using a set of measured variables such as ideological predisposition, direct interest, committee assignments, and party, then to ascribe any deviation in voting patterns to whatever lobbying activities might have been measured'.[64] However, attempts to measure effectiveness depend on all the other influential variables having been identified; to try to do otherwise would be based on the 'chimeral promise of measuring the unmeasurable'.[65]

It is necessary to pay attention to the exogenous variables that could provide other explanations for a similar policy outcome. Exogenous forces may affect a community by opening or closing a 'policy window' of opportunity. The ability of lobbyists to exploit a policy window depends on the willingness of government officials to modify their behaviour. Because to a large extent policy outcomes depend on exogenously-determined factors rather than the explicit behaviour of actors, successful lobbying is largely dependent upon contextual variables.[66]

Some commentators recognise the importance of evaluating the activity of lobbyists in a wider political context. Eckstein notes the pattern of policy is an important determinant of effectiveness because 'it is one of the situational elements which selects among the objective attributes of the group those which are of special account'.[67] In discussing the problems of studying lobbying, Baumgartner and Leech quote various scholars:[68]

> The fact that scholars have tended to debate how important lobbying is might not be because one person is right and another is wrong but, rather, that *influence is conditional*.[69]

> The most important point, however, is that so much of the variance in success is not explained by these analyses. This suggests that the determinants of success are usually situation specific. The outcomes appear to turn less on the presence of broad variables ... than on much more particular factors that vary from issue to issue.[70]

> The kinds of issues that become salient, how they are defined in policy debates, and the different institutional arrangements for making policy choices all have a powerful impact on group fortunes.[71]

Macro-political events and high political actors influence effective-ness.[72] Berry recognises that 'Regardless of how hard lobbyists work, policy outcomes will often be determined by factors out of their control.'[73] These external variables are the cause of the discrepancy in effectiveness studies. Issues of effectiveness can be explained only in the context of policy issues.

Profile of the case

An important contextual variable is the salience or profile of an issue. The type of issue will usually determine its profile and the campaign style, although the profile of some issues can be raised by campaign techniques. A technical issue can be made high-profile by lobbyists.

Lobbyists may be more effective if the issue they are concerned with is low-profile, non-political and technical. Jordan recognises that 'the less open the lobbying the less complaints there will be'.[74] Baumgartner and Leech argue: 'Focusing only on those cases with little or no public controversy is incomplete and can be misleading, just as would be a focus on highly salient issues.'[75] This book examines four issues at dif-ferent levels of salience.

The lower the profile the less likely government is to have a fixed view. Lobbyists dealing with low-profile, non-controversial issues are likely to deal with the bureaucracy, whilst those dealing with contro-versial issues concentrate on the legislature.[76] The task of lobbyists is more difficult on high-profile issues.[77] The more important the issue, the more likely both sides of the argument will mobilise, which may mean cancelling one another out.

The higher the profile, the broader the issue network and the more likely it is that players begin to lose control. Government can lose con-trol. Lobbyists lose control too. The presence of more groups compli-cates issues and presents a wider range of choices. The more players in the game, the more restricted lobbyists' effectiveness. Lobbyists have to work harder on higher-profile issues. It is also more difficult for com-mentators to establish a causal link in high-profile issues because there are more variables.

Quality of the case

Arguably the most effective technique has remained unchanged: a well-founded case that pre-empts all counterarguments.[78] Miller suggests that in an average decision the merit of the case accounts for 70 per cent of influence factors.[79] The case must be accurate, reasonable and politically attractive. Miller's assertion could imply an over-confident assumption that there are both objective criteria of evidence and of policy choice, and that all fully informed and intelligent people would agree with one another once all the facts were available. In fact, Lord Tebbit has argued that whilst it may be necessary to have a strong case, it is not necessarily sufficient.[80] One person's well-founded argument is another's dogmatic nonsense. The ideological, doctrinal, or policy culture may be receptive to some arguments and not to others. The quality of the case cannot be divorced from political circumstances.

Lobbyists can mould the case put to decision-makers. They can emphasise themes that connect with politicians. Briefs sent to Whitehall policy officials need to be well-researched. If there are evidently negative consequences, the civil service would prefer lobbyists to state them openly. Lobbyists should anticipate arguments and deal with them: 'do not try to sweep inconvenient information under the carpet: assume that officials will find out, so get your rebuttal in before they draw the wrong conclusion'.[81]

Whilst some groups are treated seriously and acted upon, others will be 'politely received, but mainly ignored'. One minister, Joel Barnett, found it difficult to treat representations seriously when they made an unbalanced case.[82] So how the case is presented, as well as its objective merits, is important. Baumgartner and Jones propose that effectiveness depends on whether the client's objectives destabilise or reinforce the existing policy communities, and whether the issue is on or off the political agenda.[83] The decision to lobby will depend on perceptions of the chances of success.[84] Miller says lobbyists should ask themselves: 'Is this a "yes-able" proposition; and if not, can we make it so?'[85]

Government

Democratic government is a key explanatory variable in its own right. Lobbyists tend to be effective only if their client's case is in line with government thinking. Government can ignore a lobbyist if contextual factors are hostile. Similarly the strength of politicians or officials affects policy actors.[86]

To leading practitioners the autonomy of government is central. Government officials do not see themselves as a part of a wider audience; they are part of a self-contained system with its own rules and sensitivities. Miller says:[87]

- the cart rarely pushes the horse: the system expects you to know which institution to deal with and who to approach;

- the system is the boss: it hates people who crow about their successes … it checks everything and suspects all arguments/views from outside the system;
- politicians want themselves and their institutions to be appreciated and respected;
- the system is more important than those on whose behalf it is run (it decides what it wants to do and then asks us if it is ok);
- the system's daily/weekly/annual rhythm will not change for you. It expects you to work within the timetables for MPs, assembling EU Presidency priorities and bids for UK legislative slots;
- lobbying should be focused because the system has limited patience. Unnecessary contact is disadvantageous.

Not only can a change of parties in government influence effectiveness, but also changes in personalities at the top of parties. There were substantial differences in the way the Heath and Thatcher governments approached some interest groups.[88] Wilson surmises: 'circumstances change, and as circumstances change, interests find it necessary to form groups or to adopt different tactics. An interest protected by a favourable ideological climate may not find that it is so protected for ever.'[89] Ministers matter. Government actors have autonomy. These factors have unintended effects that can benefit or injure the client.

Lobbyists' effectiveness can be determined by government structure.[90] Eckstein notes three factors: first, whether power is concentrated or dispersed. Where power is widely dispersed groups are given multiple entrées into the system. Second, effectiveness may depend on the electoral system. For clients the ability to mobilise sheer weight of numbers is more important under proportional representation, whereas breadth of support is important under the plurality model. Third, the administrative structure may be a determinant of effectiveness: 'Administrative systems are not merely tools for executing policy, but are themselves structures of power; they influence (often make) policy, and within them different departments carry different degrees of weight depending on the political position of their heads, the broadness and significance of their functions and their traditions.'[91]

Another important contextual factor is government officials' concept of the public interest. Because the public interest is not codified, it is a nebulous and indistinct notion.[92] A working definition often used by officials is that policy is in the public interest if it is likely to be approved by Parliament. However, most officials tend to balance the client/consumer interest against supplier/producer interests. Officials will subject submissions to a range of questions: Can the ideas work? What is wrong with their case? Is the case in line with government policy? Will government look negligent if it ignores the submission? Is the case built on sound data? Where did the data come from? Will their case be attacked by other lobbies? Have they acknowledged the weaknesses in their own case?[93]

Scope of change

Effectiveness depends on the scope of change. Jordan suggests lobbyists are more likely to be effective if they are attempting to change existing legislation. He has termed this factor the 'piggy-back' approach.[94] He notes that a campaign will be more effective if influencing an existing Bill rather than attempting to raise new interest. However, it is unclear if Jordan is correct, and it may often be easier to introduce change before issues become legislation.

Many issues are delegated to civil servants, thereby allowing politicians to avoid choosing between conflicting interests.[95] Lowi recognised the importance of the scope of change by noting the difference between substantive legislation and legislative evasion (decisions made by administrators).[96] Lobbyists tend to be more effective on policy developed by administrators. Hayes argues that the scope of policy change – whether it is discretionary policy (symbolic and structural) or explicit policy (material and allocative) – influences the effect of lobbyists.[97]

Type of change

The type of policy change required may determine the effectiveness of the lobby. Issues may be at the margins of the legislation, but central to the client's concerns. Minor changes to legislation are more likely to be effective than objections to manifesto commitments: for example, the utilities' opposition to Labour's windfall tax.[98] The British Airports Authority (BAA) was initially included in the tax; its strategy was not to oppose the tax, but to seek to prove to government that BAA did not fit its own criteria, leading to BAA being taxed less than other utilities.

Hayes draws on the typology of Salisbury and Heinz to distinguish between structural and allocative policy.[99] Structural policy changes establish rules for future allocation. Allocative policy confers direct material or symbolic benefits. Clients of lobbyists may seek to obtain tangible benefits rather than just changing the rules. It is possible that the nature of a policy change – allocative or structural – may affect the likelihood of success.

Extent of lobbying

There might be an occasion when organisational lobbying is diluted through over-use.[100] As a consequence of the growth of public relations in the 1970s, professional lobbying became synonymous with its intellectually inferior neighbour. Miller suggests business has concentrated too much on providing information rather than building a well-constructed case, and warns that it is mistaken to equate power of delivery with the strength of the argument.

Too much lobbying can be ineffective. Lobbyists should do less, but do it better by concentrating on fewer activities with greater care.[101] It has been argued that the British Airways parliamentary lobby was so big that decision-makers expected it and discounted accordingly.[102]

There may be occasions where different lobbyists work for different clients within the same sector (e.g., telecommunications). The agendas of the various lobbyists may not be in direct competition, but a degree of overlap would reflect the different competitive pressures and may lead to decision-makers receiving confused signals from a sector. A policy area lobbied from all sides by lobbyists may create more freedom for the politician or official to act.

The presence or absence of active opposition is significant.[103] Opposition may be more important than a range of broad supportive and co-operative interests. Interest groups and lobbyists will be more effective if opposition is absent.[104] Lack of opposition means the demand pattern is consensual. Opponents shift the demand pattern so it becomes conflictual. If the issue is conflictual, groups may still be effective but their influence is harder to recognise.

Public opinion

The electoral consequence of policy is an important factor for politicians. Effectiveness can depend on 'the "attractiveness" of the client group in terms of its electoral influence and the degree to which it was seen as deserving'.[105] Ainsworth's model states that lobbyists provide politicians with intelligence about constituent preferences; 'the lobbyist signals electoral salience'.[106] Though lobbyists may seek to campaign to change public opinion, they are more likely to be effective if public opinion is already favourable. Public opinion depends on how the client's case chimes with cultural values and emotions.[107]

Six relationships between public opinion and the objectives of interest-groups have been listed by Rose.[108] They are:

- harmony between pressure group demands and general cultural norms

- a gradual increase in the acceptability of political values supporting pressure group demands
- bargaining with fluctuating support from cultural norms
- advocacy in the face of cultural indifference
- advocacy in opposition to long-term cultural trends
- conflict between cultural values and pressure group goals.

Public opinion is an important contextual variable that can either help or hinder a lobbyist. If the structure of the issue at hand allows it, lobbyists tend to be more effective if they can keep the issue out of the public domain and deal with it in the confines of Whitehall.

Economic circumstances

Economic factors affect the likelihood of success. Grant notes: 'Against a background of continued pressure on public expenditure, demands for increases in service provision – or other changes in policy requiring more expenditure – are unlikely to be met.'[109]

Internal variables

Several academics have examined the influence of internal variables.[110] Although they used different methods, most of their findings have proved cogent. One American author, Jeffrey Berry, lists five internal factors that can impact on a lobbyist's effectiveness; credibility, quality research, retaining friends, compromise and dependency.[111] Grant suggests the following internal factors influence effectiveness: internal organisational structure, marketing skills, membership mobilisation capacity, financial and staff resources, sanctioning capacity and choice of strategy.[112]

On some occasions the 'capacity of lobbyists to shape policy [can] be explained by their particular characteristics'.[113] Although Heinz *et al.* found evidence of influence of a 'general sort', they were largely unable to explain self-reports of policy success, and concluded that success on particular events was not well explained by individual characteristics. The organisation type, career path, and political ideology and activism did not explain success; although a long-term track record and contacts improve reputation, it is unclear which comes first.[114] It proved possible to identify effective lobbyists, but 'the characteristics of these elites, and the occasions on which their influence is effective, vary by domain, by issue and by historical period'; in other words, external variables.[115]

Credibility

Lobbyists need to be credible. The analogy of a village community is applied as easily to Capitol Hill as to Whitehall. Reputation is important because a lobbyist's task is to convince decision-makers of another party's case. Effective lobbyists tend not to lie or mislead politicians.

The emergence of a professional status along with the requisite snobbery was charted by Jordan and Moloney. They attempt to debunk the myth that lobbyists can be effective only if they have experience of working in the system, and conclude effective lobbying is something that can be learnt.[116] Whilst experience is important, the most important attribute is credibility.

Credibility is principally a function of other attributes: knowledge, insider status and honesty. Lobbyists should cultivate a relationship of trust with decision-makers. Miller terms this relationship, the 'call back factor' (based on credibility and amiability), or the ability of a lobbyist to have politicians or officials return his call.[117] Trust is essential in maintaining good professional relationships with decision-makers.[118]

To be perceived as honest seems to be regarded as an essential attribute.[119] It may be important for lobbyists to establish a consultative relationship with government departments, because some issues may be the subject of subordinate legislation. The literature suggests that effective lobbyists tend not to spring surprises on government.

In addition to being trustworthy, there are other characteristics an effective lobbyist should possess. According to Milbrath they are 'extrovertness, gregariousness, confidence, sincerity, enthusiasm, energy, forthrightness, thick skin, slowness to frustration and anger, patience, persistence, determination and physical attractiveness'.[120] Jordan and Moloney argue that lobbyists manufacture an empowering and legitimising discourse to mask private dealings with politicians and officials.[121]

Some lobbyists revel in their public profile and enjoy promoting what they perceive as their glory and successes. However, revelling in victory harms reputation. Lobbyists tend to be effective if they are reserved and cautious. It is incumbent on lobbyists to be discreet. Indiscreet lobbyists are ineffective because decision-makers perceive them to be exercising their influence improperly and exploiting friendships. Because the 'system' lobbyists operate within is founded on discretion, judicious behaviour by lobbyists is indispensable.

Available tactics and avoidance of politics

Most lobbyists use a wide range of tactics. Reliance on a single strategy is uncommon. The characteristics of the issue often determine what tactics will be used, but the effective lobbyist knows which tactics to deploy from his armoury.[122]

If the issue is low-profile, effective lobbyists tend to target actors and institutions inside government. If the issue is high-profile, effective lobbyists tend to target Parliament, the media, the general public as well as ministers and civil servants. However, choice of tactics is also a function of internal variables.

The most effective lobbyists 'may not be those that are best at a given strategy but rather those that have the greatest repertory of strategies available to them and who are most skilful at choosing the right strategy for the issue at hand'.[123] Tactic choice depends on a host of internal factors such as human and financial resources, contacts and knowledge of procedure.

This book pays attention to visible and invisible tactics. Visible tactics include face-to-face meetings with policy-makers, correspondence and submissions. Invisible tactics incorporate agenda setting, 'shadow lobbying' and recruiting 'parliamentary pushers'.[124] The process is amorphous, and 'some of the most effective strategies of policymaking may involve much more general efforts at issue definition'.[125] Lobbyists can be effective if they de-politicise a policy issue to avoid it being dealt with as a matter of party political principle.[126]

Burned bridges

Long-term relationships are important. Lobbyists can be more effective if they maintain regular contact with decision-makers and cultivate politicians and officials over time.[127] Lobbyists must be non-threatening and avoid the 'public exposure and humiliation' techniques employed by some pressure groups.

As lobbyists are long-term players, they cannot afford to vent their anger at their failure to achieve their client's objective.[128] It is also important to retain a sense of proportion. They need to keep relationships friendly. The minister or official who refuses to help on one occasion will probably be of help in the future. Effective lobbyists put their collective clients' interests above any one policy failure and tend to be 'non-emotional'.[129] Legislators and their staff 'prefer dealing with contract lobbyists, believing that the penalties for misleading information are so great as to deter the contract lobbyist from telling untruths or half truths'.[130]

Professional lobbyists lack any sanction to punish opponents in government. Contacts would disintegrate in the face of threatening behaviour or unreliable information. Therefore lobbying tends to be persuasive rather than coercive. Effectiveness depends on the actions of others whom lobbyists cannot offend. Some public-interest lobbyists do not care much for those in the system they see as 'sinners and backsliders'.[131]

Lobbyists are unlikely to have these moral objections because they represent others in return for a fee.

Threats and intimidation

At times it may be necessary to sacrifice future co-operation for an immediate return, but to threaten or intimidate is especially high-risk because lobbyists are long-term players. However, there is no reason why a lobbyist cannot pursue a quiet insider strategy and a low-profile outsider strategy simultaneously. A lobbyist can offer a velvet-gloved hand to decision-makers, whilst holding a flick knife concealed in the other.

Compromise

Effective lobbyists tend to be able to persuade their clients of the advantage of compromise or to persuade clients to limit their objectives in the first place. Berry says: 'the difference between success and failure is achieving an acceptable compromise'.[132] The effective lobbyist is constantly seeking acceptable compromises and is searching for solutions. Within the policy game, lobbyists will seek to bargain with those elements of the client's demands that are least important. The client's case can shift from being 'special interest' to 'public interest'.[133] They look for 'sweeteners'. Effective lobbyists cut deals. They can judge positions because they know the personalities and backgrounds of other players.

The concept of Allison's bargaining game has been extended by Jordan.[134] Bargaining enters discussions between lobbyists and decision-makers when terms such as 'trade-off', 'fall-back' and 'sticking point' are used.[135] The concept of bargaining (log-rolling, etc.) seems to contradict the view that lobbyists have no ultimate sanction since, in order to bargain, both sides must have a degree of power. The literature may be skewed because groups in America are arguably in a stronger position than UK groups, where the power relationship favours government.

It is also important to take care when incorporating 'compromise' into measurements of effectiveness. As defined earlier, effectiveness is the ability of lobbyists to achieve clients' objectives. It may be easier for a lobbyist to scale down a client's wishes than to influence government. It may be that the most intelligent (or 'effective') lobbyists encourage clients to pick 'winnable' targets, as opposed to accepting the client's initial brief. So, in certain circumstances, achieving the 'client's' objectives can mean little.

Dependency

Lobbyists have greater potential to deliver clients' objectives if policy-makers depend upon them for credible information. Effective lobbyists drop the right information into the process at the right time. They build up relationships. 'This familiarity in time gives lobbyists the advantage of repeated opportunities to interact with policy-makers to display their expertise.'[136] The restructuring of the civil service means officials have less time to undertake original research and are more dependent on outside information and more open to dialogue.[137] It is possible that lobbyists, like professionals, possess knowledge allowing them to play a part in policy-making.[138]

Smith claims the National Consumer Council produces reports of high quality: without such experience and independence the Council's lobbying would be less effective.[139] 'Lobbyists increase their effectiveness as they increase their knowledge of their policy area.'[140] As civil servants move, and companies enter and leave the policy process as issues change, the lobbyist often holds a wealth of knowledge. What appears technical to others becomes routine for the lobbyist. Some lobbyists are hired to be industry representatives and to manage trade associations. Their expertise makes them valuable to those in government.

The pre-legislative stage

The key to effective lobbying is monitoring. Passive monitoring of Hansard is not enough; effective lobbyists tend to monitor actively. They obtain the views of officials about policy development and feedback on representations.[141] Those organisations that hire lobbyists receive advance warning of policy thinking and are therefore advantaged. 'Potential' and less-organised groups lack this basic monitoring resource and are less effective.[142]

The most effective lobbying is done at the pre-legislative stage when policy is germinating in Whitehall offices.[143] Berry suggests that 'influence is achieved through continuous work in the trenches'.[144] Miller notes: 'the great proportion of administrative judgements ... are made by officials' early in the legislative process.[145] He suggests officials become disposed against lobbyists who concentrate on Parliament. By the time legislation reaches the House of Commons it has been months in drafting. Interest groups must invest time and resources early on, other-wise the campaign is likely to be considered opportunistic or even lazy. Parliamentary fire-fighting tends to be less effective than pre-emptive lobbying.

Client–lobbyist relationship

Effectiveness can be judged only if a client's lobbying strategy has a clear focus. Lobbyists might help secure a favourable operating environment for their client.[146] How the client is perceived by decision-makers is an important factor. It is important to understand whether the client takes the lobbyist's advice. If the client acts contrary to the advice of consultants, it is difficult to judge effectiveness. The brief of the client and the services required and provided are important factors to understand when examining success. The effective lobbyist is not forced by the client to react to developments, but plans in advance of the political agenda.

Effective lobbying is dependent upon the understanding and support of top executives in the client organisation. Support for the lobbyist must be consistent. Understanding of the lobbyist's strategy must be realistic.[147] Eckstein suggests organisational cohesiveness is important for effectiveness and is a function of other variables, notably the degree of client commitment.[148] Effective lobbying requires the involvement of key employees of the client organisation. The point Grant makes about membership mobilisation by pressure groups is relevant to lobbyists since a lobbyist must be able to mobilise his client: the actions, whilst possibly intrusive and time-consuming to the businessman, are inclined to be low-cost politically, such as attending meetings and preparing research.[149]

Effectiveness depends on how 'open' or honest the client can be with the lobbyist and whether the client will share with the lobbyist the construction of the case. If the lobbyist is asked simply to 'communicate' an organisation's policy, the lobbyist's impact may be restrained. Researchers should be aware that much of the lobbyist's work is advisory. If lobbyists' advice is not taken, commentators cannot judge effectiveness.

Timing

Timing is a factor in any political campaign. Timing a campaign or an approach effectively can be the consequence of luck. It may also be down to skill. More effective lobbying may occur in the later stages of government. Greer argues that a government's parliamentary agenda is crammed with manifesto commitments in the first two to three years of its life, so for big issues it is wise to wait until later in the Parliament.[150] However, it is also possible to argue that the bigger, more controversial issues need to be grasped in the first years of a new government – the honeymoon – when the government's popularity can carry issues forward.

Quid pro quo

'Mutual aid' implies lobbyists should be able to offer decision-makers something positive or at least neutral (certainly not negative) in return for being granted insider status. Rhodes argues that: 'all actors in a particular policy area need one another'.[151]

Even if a deal is not self-evident, an effective lobbyist tends to recognise that government will be more likely to deliver policy change in exchange for concessions. Concessions may involve making a policy change more in line with the government's conception of the public interest.

Coalitions

More groups usually mean increased conflict.[152] Effective lobbyists mobilise other interests, so the messages politicians receive from their constituencies or centrally are supportive. As there is more diversity and more interests active in policy-making, the potential for coalition-building increases. Lobbyists can help form connections with other organisations based on shared interests.

As technology and the nature of a competitive market ensure increased conflict within the business community, the nature of divisions and shared objectives changes constantly. For example, the changing nature of the telecommunications business has transformed group relations and the policy community.[153] Coalitions form and break down constantly. The perceived benefits to potential coalition members may be distributed unequally, making coalition less likely.

If there is conflict within the business community there is the possibility of vicarious representation. Collective groups are often unorganised. An issue that leads to powerful actors on both sides offers collective groups the opportunity of representation by one of the active interest groups.[154]

Coalitions allow lobbyists and their clients to share resources and improve effectiveness. Coalitions enhance credibility.[155] Grant argues that to be effective, interest groups must reduce external competition. Any coalition and interest group improves its effectiveness by constructing an internal structure that involves a variety of viewpoints in the decision-making process. The risk of tensions breaking apart a coalition or group is real, and breakaways are damaging.[156] The coalition must take account of its members' views and be flexible with regard to contextual factors.

If consensus proves impossible, then Miller suggests lobbyists get their retaliation in first by pre-empting the points the opposition might make.[157]

Contacts

The 'unique selling point' of the professional lobbyist is his access to parts of the decision-making system that an in-house lobbyist cannot reach.[158] Lobbyists tend to be effective if they are well connected. Contacts bring intelligence and inside information which, in turn, bring status and policy expertise.[159] Contacts facilitate access, deliver intelligence and amplify advocacy. Kooiman has suggested that no actor has the over-view necessary to dominate or be successful.[160] It is possible that the lobbyist has the best vantage-point. He can weave between the players, talk to all sides and take an objective standpoint.

Various scholars have pointed to the importance of contacts for effectiveness.[161] The American literature shows that contributions to politicians buy access to representatives rather than their votes.[162] Lobbyists could be the 'highly knowledgeable policy-watchers' that Helco wrote about.[163]

Though 'perceived political neutrality' can be essential to effective lobbying,[164] circumstantial evidence suggests ties with parties are important. Most political consultants are party-political, helping the lobbyist gain access to closed political circles and the information that circulates within them.

Procedure

Lobbyists are effective if they understand the procedures of Whitehall and Parliament. Procedure is how the system ought to operate. However, knowledge of the process is as valuable: not just the formal rules, but the informal rules and understandings that govern everyday procedure. They can be as simple as an appreciation of how the working days of officials and politicians are structured. Lobbyists understand the 'language' of Whitehall. The similarity of characteristics displayed by civil servants and interest-group leaders (and lobbyists) is striking. They are alike in 'their official personalities, modes of operation, language and perception of the policy process... Such skills have to be developed... if they want to be effective.'[165]

Resources

Resources are important because they allow interest groups to buy the goodwill of influential persons, to advertise, to hire prestigious lobbyists and to buy in technical expertise.

Conclusions

Important contextual variables have been often omitted from analyses of effectiveness. Many independent variables influence policy outcomes.

The interests of government actors and the wider political, social and environmental context impact on effectiveness. Government will demand public-interest requirements. If the external factors are held constant (Eckstein leaves them out altogether, including the pressure of events and conditions, social values, political attitudes, government mandates and autonomous government departments), then it is possible to show that interest groups (the British Medical Association, in his example) and lobbyists have an impact.[166] If the external environment is friendly, then internal variables become important.

Internal variables, within the control of lobbyists, help explain their effectiveness. The effective lobbyist understands the operating procedures and how to 'play' the 'policy game' within the pre-established rules. In the informal negotiations and bargaining process lobbyists are likely to be more effective if they monitor developments and establish contact at an early stage, before ideas begin to set. Effective lobbyists tend to be able to spot and construct coalitions. The relationship with the client should be close and supportive. Long-term relationships or contacts in Whitehall or Westminster make for enhanced effectiveness. A *quid pro quo* is helpful, as is the ability to compromise. A range of tactics to choose from is also helpful. Effective lobbyists deploy their resources in a skilful manner likely to realise their goals.

Following the unwritten rules on internal variables does not guarantee effectiveness or influence. Lobbyists are constrained, and their effectiveness is in large part determined by contextual variables. But when the context is favourable, these factors enhance effectiveness.

3
The Effect of Lobbyists: A Political Science Framework

This chapter builds a framework for analysing the effectiveness of lobbying. It reviews the political science literature and deduces eight propositions within the context of a multi-level framework. It examines the macro-level, an overall view of the policy process; the meso-level, which concentrates on networks; and the micro-level, concerned with personal interactions.

At the macro-level there are three propositions:

1. Lobbyists tend to be effective if they are lobbying on low-profile, technical and non-political issues.
2. Lobbyists tend to be effective if there are no disadvantageous external or contextual constraints beyond the control of government players.
3. Lobbyists tend to be effective if the beliefs of political decision-makers, pre-existing policy and previous experience of government players are congruent with the lobbyist's objective.

The effectiveness of professional lobbyists can best be understood if their activity is set in the wider context of two 'theories of the state': pluralism and government autonomy. This book contends that pluralism and government autonomy are indistinguishable. Effectiveness is variable, relative, and depends on context. This macro-level perspective proposes that in certain arenas government agencies or actors can act autonomously. The effectiveness of the lobbyist is also constrained by external contextual factors, such as economic factors and the salience of 'public interest' issues.

At the meso-level the policy network approach is best applied.[1] Lobbyists can be facilitators and managers, but also actors in their own right. At the meso-level two propositions are relevant.

1. Lobbyists tend to be effective if they can include their client in the policy community and manage their client's activity within that network.
2. Lobbyists tend to be effective if they pursue a multi-faceted approach and facilitate access to multiple points in the decision-making process.

At the micro-level the chapter examines Allison's governmental politics and organisational models and Rhodes's work on resources. Lobbyists must be aware of the dominant games being played. The effective lobbyist will know the procedures and rules of government, and how to deploy the resources of the client.

Three propositions apply at the micro-level.

1. Lobbyists tend to be effective if they are familiar with routines and standard operating procedures and know when and where to intervene in the policy-making process.
2. Lobbyists tend to be effective if they have good contacts and can spot connections to potential allies and can construct coalitions.
3. Lobbyists tend to be effective if the client has abundant resources and is skilful in deploying them.

Macro-level

Profile, technicality and politicality

Lobbyists tend to be effective if they are lobbying on low-profile, technical and non-political issues.

Furlong suggests that policy type does not make a difference in terms of influence. In other words, interest groups are just as likely, or unlikely, to influence policy tightening a clean air standard as they would attempting to increase social security benefits.[2] Similarly, Whiteley and Winyard argue that a 'quiet insider strategy does not pay off any better than an open promotional strategy. Since the era of consensus politics described by Beer and Eckstein, policy making has become more conflictual, but also more fragmented.'[3]

However, others argue lobbyists will be more effective on issues of low visibility, high technicality and low politicality. Eckstein concluded that: 'the influence of groups certainly is enhanced by the lack of any wide public interest in an area of policy, simply because such lack of interest, apart from minimizing group competition tends to neutralize some of the more important centres of influence which compete with private groups as such'.[4] Furthermore, Stewart notes that 'the situation faced by groups is in part reflected in the general nature of their aims'.[5] As such, on low-profile issues lobbyists will deal with government actors (officials and ministers) rather than with the political process as a whole, thereby increasing their chances of being effective.

Though not directly applicable to the UK, American studies examining the impact of contributions by interest groups on votes of legislators are relevant because they seek to assess the effectiveness of pressure. The literature plays close attention to external factors as key explanatory variables. Various groups of researchers have claimed groups were more effective when issue visibility was low,[6] when the issue was technical[7] or when the issue was politically neutral.[8]

Profile

The influence of lobbyists increases when there is less publicity. This statement echoes the 'distributive' policy noted by Lowi.[9] High-profile issues are more likely to be controversial, forcing external factors into play. Politicians are more likely to be forced to vote in line with their party, with their constituency interests or with their ideology on high-profile matters.

Lobbying is traditionally most successful when it is least overt, and goes largely unnoticed by the public.[10] This conclusion is supported by Schlozman's and Tierney's identification of the most effective tactics being low-profile, including testifying at hearings, contacting officials directly and engaging in informal contact with officials.[11] The least effective tactics are public endorsements of candidates and contributing to electoral campaigns.

On high-visibility issues the party background of legislators is an important determinant of policy outcome. High-profile issues 'require a greater adherence to party and constituent desires. Low-visibility issues allow greater freedom' and 'more behind-the-scene maneuvering [is] possible'.[12] Neustadtl found that the effect of party is greater on high-profile than on low-visibility issues.

The less publicity there is on an issue, the less likely there will be organised opposition. It follows that officials and politicians will have more freedom of movement.[13] Therefore the impact of lobbying varies inversely with the visibility of the issue; similarly, on legislative lobbying the influence of constituents and the media varies with visibility.

In addition, low-profile issues are often dealt with in low-profile settings (arenas in which lobbyists are more likely to be effective). Lobbying is more likely to be effective at the agenda-setting stage of policy-making. As Sabato argues, 'Press, public, and even "watchdog" groups are not nearly as attentive to initial legislative proceedings.'[14]

Technicality

The nature of the issue is a significant variable in explaining effectiveness. Welch suggests research should concentrate on comparing the impact of variables on both obscure technical amendments and highly visible issues.[15] Frendreis and Waterman found that constituency pressure, party and ideology displayed variable relationships with policy outcome, depending on the technicality of the issue under consideration.[16] Sabato also lists technicality as a variable that can affect the dependent variable, arguing that contributions have more of an effect on narrow and specialised issues.[17] Technicality of issues limits the degree of conflict.

Politicality

Interest groups may be most influential on issues that do not arouse controversy within or between the parties. Conway argues: 'the interest group concerns it represents may prevail only on the less visible issues where the influence of party ideology, or constituency are not important'.[18] Malbin also reports that groups can be more effective on nonpartisan issues.[19]

Ideology and party also display a variable relationship with voting; the dominant variable depends on the issue: for example, on high-profile matters constituency concerns can be important.[20] When an issue is non-partisan, legislators often found it difficult to assess the issue's relevance to their constituents, so other variables (such as lobbying) could tip the balance.[21] Although many variables impact on policy outcome, party stance is important.

The more fragmented and open the process, the more likely there is to be an array of access channels available to a range of actors. The wider an issue, the more interest groups are able to hunt for other supporters, thereby destabilising the system. As new players are attracted to an issue when it is redefined and broadened, both government actors and lobbyists are less able to control events. They cannot direct actors on political and controversial policy, and the likelihood of coordinated opposition increases. On high-policy issues the public, the media, the courts and senior politicians become involved. The autonomy of all players, including government, is eroded and control over the game is lost.

Lobbyists can be more effective if the policy community is closed, dominated by civil servants, unconstrained by political involvement, and rarely considered by the national press. The lobbyist can be more effective if the issue does not become 'political'. Subdued pressure is more effective than forceful pressure.[22] Lobbyists are more effective on 'consultation politics' than on 'electoral politics'. If an issue is shielded from public and media scrutiny and does not arouse 'deeply felt convictions, lines of party cleavage, or particularistic constituency needs', lobbyists can be more effective.[23]

Lobbyists are most influential on 'official legislation'.[24] Technical legislation developed by civil servants and interest groups is often a continuation of earlier legislation. 'By interview, deputation, letter or telephone the affected groups keep continuous contact with the administering department ... And out of such two-way consultation on administration new policy often emerges.'[25]

There is often a 'search for predictability' whereby both parties encourage a symbiotic relationship.[26] This search is more evident on small, technical issues. Lobbyists help their clients enter these policy niches. The lobbyist knows the participants in technical communities, and the lobbyist is better able to influence the client's activity in a smaller community.

The salience of an issue can determine how far lobbyists can be effective and whether government actors can act with autonomy. On most issues the salience, technicality and its political nature will determine the type of campaign and the impact of the lobbyist.

External factors

Lobbyists tend to be effective if there are no disadvantageous external or contextual constraints beyond the control of government players.

Government is structured by a range of political and economic constraints which are beyond its control, including the financial markets, the EU, judicial decisions and the world economy. The compatibility of an interest group's objectives with society's values make success likely. Skocpol *et al.*, recognising the importance of contextual factors, suggest that the degree of industrialisation, urbanisation, workforce composition and level of economic development may have been important determinants of pensions reform in the USA.[27]

Changing social, political and institutional environments affect policymaking. Policy change can be 'strongly influenced by the economic, political and ideological context within which the network operates'.[28] Many domestic public policy issues are interlocked with global issues. The government's power and the influence of lobbyists can be restricted by exogenous and contextual structural factors. The international economic environment, supra-national bodies, technological changes and fiscal constraints all limit the autonomy of government actors and affect outside groups.

So lobbying may be peripheral to 'other' significant influencing factors.[29] Smith notes the following contextual factors: 'economic conditions, policy success/failure, world events, level of popular support and
parliamentary support'.[30] Contextual factors can constrain and facilitate players. Lobbyists cannot be effective if the broader context is
antagonistic.

Policy can be structurally determined. Structure identifies winners and
losers. External factors may open or close avenues of opportunity.

Experience and existing policy

*Lobbyists tend to be effective if the beliefs of political decision-makers, pre-
existing policy and previous experience of government players are congruent
with the lobbyist's objective.*

There are several constraints within the government's, but outside the
lobbyist's, control. They are often political constraints, including ideology,
perceptions about limits to government action or acceptable behaviour.
The government has autonomy and, if this constraint is favourable,
lobbyists are likely to be effective. But, as Stewart writes, when a campaign
'runs contrary to the main policies of the political party in power it is
almost bound to fail'.[31]

It is important to move away from examining interest-group
demands to recognising the willingness and the capacity of government
to follow its own objectives. Campaigners tend to be effective when 'the
lobbyist is most closely meeting the needs of those that are being lobbied'.[32] Previous policy choices and past political bargains partly determine current policy. Skocpol *et al.* conclude: 'pre-existing policies, the
institutional arrangements of governments, and the organizational
characteristics of political parties may also influence the goals, access,
and alliances of officials and social groups active in politics'.[33]

Pluralism and government autonomy

This book places group–government interaction in a pluralistic framework. However, to understand the effect of lobbyists, a recognition of
government autonomy is helpful. Pluralism is a resilient policy perspective which concentrates on the interactions of groups with government. Pluralists adopt a behaviouralist methodology and recognise that
groups can mobilise political pressure to their advantage.

Pluralism has been criticised by various scholars and has been modified over the years.[34] A stereotype of the pluralist perspective has been
attacked as being simplistic and holding a benign view of power distribution.[35] Baumgartner and Leech suggest that, in classical pluralism,

'The role of the state was not to dictate outcomes, but rather to arbitrate among various interests.'[36]

Classical pluralism, model I, has evolved into model II (neo) and model III (reformed) pluralism. Neo-pluralists accept business is the most powerful group and can dominate a policy arena.[37] Business inducements are often necessary for a healthy economy, and in a market economy government–business collaboration is needed to make the system work.[38] However, one flaw in neo-pluralism is that it understates government's ability to act autonomously. More useful in explaining why and how lobbyists can be effective is reformed pluralism, because it recognises the autonomy of government actors.

Groups can be excluded from policy-making. Perfect competition between groups does not exist in practice.[39] Reformed pluralists recognise that certain policy arenas are open, whilst others are institutionalised and closed. Since usually only a limited number of groups are either interested or have access, government actors may depend on them for information.[40] Reformed pluralism manages to account for both institutionalised relationships and the exclusion of some groups.

Recognising the autonomy of government actors suggests in some circumstances lobbyists will be ineffective because their client's objectives and those of government clash. Lobbyists depend on government autonomy predisposed in their favour. On routine technical issues government autonomy is theoretically high because changes usually have a narrow impact, but in practice it is more common for government to have no fixed views and be open to persuasion. Conversely, the more high-profile the issue, the less autonomy government has. If the issue becomes highly political, government autonomy can be curbed by a coalition of affected interests and public and political pressure.

Government as a whole does not have a single set of objectives: departments, directorates and units have their own goals, which are loosely tied to the general political drift of the government.[41] Because of this fragmented agenda, Jordan argues, policy communities are 'not compatible with a state autonomy view of politics' because no single state view exists.[42] However, since Jordan accepts sub-governmental autonomy, it follows that the disparate nature of the core means different government actors can act autonomously. While government's interests can be contradictory and might clash, different government organisations can take autonomous action within their policy communities. Because of this disaggregation it is essential to take a disaggregated view of the government, looking at different levels: micro, meso and macro.

'State theorists' argue the pluralist approach views government as a dependent variable: an arena within which interest groups contend or ally with one another to shape policy decisions.[43] Jordan, commenting on Polsby, notes: 'there is an unspoken notion in pluralist research that at bottom nobody dominates'.[44] So government is allegedly no more than a weather vane. Pluralism it is said does not take government seriously as an independent actor, and pluralism supposedly expounds society-centred reductionism.

The 'government autonomy' thesis is founded on four blocks.

1. Public officials can form their own policy preferences depending on the government's internal variations.
2. The government may act on its preferences despite the opposition of powerful societal interests.
3. Governmental institutional contours and procedures can affect government–group relations.
4. Government can use its autonomy to identify important interest groups.

Nordlinger's work – which is empirical, positivist and arguably pluralist – asserts the autonomy of government but does not exclude the power of societal factors.[45] He defends pluralism, but urges recognition of the ability of government players to assert their independence. His focus is on emphasis.

Nordlinger defines different degrees of government autonomy where the preferences of government actors condition policy outcomes. The 'strong state' thesis sees societal–state preferences diverge. The government deters opponents from exploiting their resources, sanctions interest groups or uses its coercive powers to threaten opponents. In the 'medium state', preferences initially diverge but then align once society's preferences alter. When government autonomy is 'weak', government subtly guides policy because its own and society's preferences align.[46]

The government autonomy and reformed pluralism perspectives both recognise that access is not always open and that relationships change over policy areas. Lobbyists may be effective because the government's and client's objectives coincide. Government actors can decide on policy which, in their view, best fits their objectives. Similarly, policy options are often constricted by institutional possibilities.

Various factors suggest that government actors can act autonomously. These factors include: turnover of government actors, centralisation, autonomous policy leadership, unconscious application of rules and the content of ideas.

Turnover in government.   Jordan argues that the initiative is with the groups because civil service turnover means 'the new civil servant relies on the group for policy history'.[47] However, he argues elsewhere that 'not all parties are equal: the governmental department is an actor with special resources (legitimacy, prior knowledge, staff) not available to other actors'.[48] The latter statement is congruent with this book. Ministerial and civil service turnover endows advantages on government. It allows government to change its stance as personalities change and bring some issues to a close and others to the front. Government agencies can be more autonomous if they have a clear conception of their role, distance between themselves and client groups, clear regulations defining responsibilities of social groups and an ability to generate their own information.[49]

Centralisation.   The centralisation of decision-making authority is another variable that affects lobbying.[50] Centralisation precludes other bodies, by formal procedure, from influencing policy. Centralisation can allow lobbyists to be more effective by reducing the number of competing government interests and concentrating authority in units sharing industry's preferences.[51] Changes in the structure of government can alter the capacity of government officials, thereby allowing them to achieve their preferences.

Autonomous policy leaders.   'Autonomous policy leaders' (APLs) are able to 'overcome a range of social, governmental, economic and secular factors which tend to structure policy choice in order to introduce important policy innovations'.[52] For the APL electoral considerations come second to a policy quest: to do the 'right thing'. Again, context is important. Wallis and Dollery conclude it would be wrong to study APLs outside the social context that makes it possible for them to exercise their style of leadership.

Unconscious application of rules.   Government can make policy without groups. The cost of developing policies without the involvement of certain groups will almost certainly be higher, but it is possible. In practice there is a functional need for civil servants to consult.[53] However, groups may be excluded without conscious decision by the institutionalised nature of relationships.[54] The influence of government actors may be exercised in an unconscious manner through the application of operating procedures, repertoires and routine behaviour. McFarland notes:

> Government decision-makers enter politics with their own preferences, which they then promote ... Lindblom implies that, more often

than not, it is government decision-makers who start a policy process. Interest groups react to governmental measures, but do not control government policy-making, which is continually redefined by policy-makers, and perhaps taken in new directions in response to group reactions.[55]

Content of ideas. It is important to take account of the content of ideas: the quality of the case. Lobbyists can help frame the idea within a broader framework.[56] They help clients weave their objectives into government plans. Government may redefine specifics of policy to pacify lobbyists, but the general drift of policy usually remains in line with government objectives. Effective lobbyists identify political and ideological trends and 'surf' the 'waves of enthusiasm'.[57]

* * *

Government does not act as a 'cash register' balancing inputs, and the majority of pluralists have not portrayed it as such.[58] Pluralism does not see the government as neutral: government procedures often 'handicap some efforts and favour others'.[59] Modern commentators, such as Jordan and Richardson, are close to Dahl and Truman in this respect.[60] Although critics of pluralism have been 'more right' in some of their comments than others, much of their criticism is misdirected. In the early pluralist literature 'autonomous government agencies were frequently part of the pluralist descriptions of politics'.[61]

Any perspective seeking to explain how and why lobbyists are effective must take account of autonomous actions by government departments. The debate on the distinction between the two approaches seems tautological.[62] In some arenas lobbyists will be effective because government actors are open to persuasion, whilst in others they will be ineffective because government has fixed objectives. Policy-making should be seen as set in systems of 'structured inequality'. Analyses of lobbying have to recognise the context within which government actors and lobbyists operate and the partial autonomy that government actors exercise. Eckstein argues: 'governmental institutions do not simply ring up the outcome of group conflicts like mere cash registers but themselves make decisions'.[63] McFarland terms this approach 'critical pluralism', which 'admits that government agencies often act autonomously and do not simply reflect the group balance of power within an issue area'.[64] Nordlinger's argument has been paraphrased thus: 'it is just as reasonable to maintain that the state guides policy outcomes as for pluralists to claim that groups do so'.[65]

Almond argues about pluralism: 'Autonomous government agencies are present and important throughout this literature. The pluralist "paradigm" is not the one-sided one of Skocpol, Krasner, and others but rather a two-directional one with the "state" influencing society, as well as the society influencing the state.'[66] Almond says that 'The policeman can stop traffic; drivers cannot stop the policeman.'[67] The effectiveness of lobbying depended on the structure and objectives of government.[68]

Governments have the power to act unilaterally even if political costs of arbitrariness make it unlikely. Richardson and Jordan recognise implicitly the autonomy of government by defining legitimacy as 'acceptance by government departments that the group is making "reasonable" demands which deserve attention'.[69] Such a definition, as Dowding notes, makes the government the source of legitimacy. The government 'allow[s] only those groups with which it sympathises institutional access to policy spheres'.[70]

Since Britain has strong parties and a powerful executive, the autonomy of government institutions and players are key contextual explanatory variables.

Meso-level

To account for the difference of sectoral policy-making this section examines the meso-level concept that includes both external and internal variables. Parsons notes: 'meso analysis is a middle-range or bridging level of analysis which is focused on the linkage between the definition of problems, the setting of agendas and the decision-making and implementation processes'.[71]

The policy community

Lobbyists tend to be effective if they can include their client in the policy community and manage their client's activity within that network.

Policy networks concentrate on the informal policy process rather than on conventional institutions. This book examines policy networks peculiar to policy issues at the sub-sectoral level. Policy communities are networks 'characterised by: stability of relationships; continuity of a restrictive membership; vertical inter-dependence based on shared delivery responsibilities; and insulation from both other networks and, invariably, the public (including parliament)'.[72] Networks stretch across a spectrum from wide issue-networks to narrow and controlled policy communities. Because the form of network relationship differs, policy networks can also explain and account for more corporatist associations.[73]

Marsh and Rhodes are mistaken when they assume issue networks are more likely to exist when the policy area is relatively unimportant for macro-policy.[74] In fact, the technical micro-policy issues are more likely to have a small, homogeneous and stable community.

The policy community approach of co-option and consensual style accounts better for policy outcomes than do examinations of party stances, of manifestos or parliamentary influence.[75] The model assumes policy-making is complex and suggests that focusing on Parliament alone does not explain outcomes because many important decisions are made with little or no party political involvement.

Policy networks can be centred around and directed by a government agency, person or central department, or around specific problems, policy issues and legislation. A core assumption of the network concept is that institutionalised relations develop between governmental and non-governmental organisations to facilitate policy-making.[76] Influence is based on dependence. Jordan notes that, in a policy community, 'a specific item of business is transacted in a context where the participants already have mutual needs, expectations and experiences'.[77] Policy communities are dynamic; they change as policy progresses.

All central departments hold databases of 'interested parties' associated with specific issues. This list may be characterised as the policy network. On particular policy issues a select few will be 'relevant' and asked for their views. Those who return substantive comments are likely to be members of the policy community. Thus, whilst networks may be forces of stability, communities are usually transient because they emerge to deal with policy issues and dissolve once the issue is finished.[78] Nevertheless, the interests continue over the longer the term of their 'policy network' relationship with the departments.

The network approach reconceptualises government–group relations. Richardson and Jordan see 'state autonomy' and policy networks as mutually exclusive.[79] However, government actors and agencies have the potential to act autonomously, and the policy network model fits neatly into the government autonomy/reformed pluralism paradigm. Since there is no single governmental view, different players have their own perspectives, departments have their own styles, units within departments have 'lines', civil servants have personal preferences and ministerial styles differ. Relations between government actors and interest groups vary in a fragmented process. Salisbury argues that the 'use of multiple representatives, each concentrating on a specialized set of policy concerns, surely must intensify the fragmenting, disaggregating tendencies in public policy'.[80] Consistent with government autonomy, access may be denied to groups not in clientelistic relationships. Lobbyists help manage clients' involvement in decision-making relationships.

Policy communities take civil servants to be key decision-makers. Policy is made at lower levels; senior political actors often accept the broad thrust of policy. Many policy areas will be attended to by only a handful of civil servants (possibly an under-secretary, a principal and an assistant secretary) reflecting the complexity and specialisation of policy. This 'linoleum' level is cultivated assiduously by lobbyists because they have a predominance of influence.

The policy community model assumes trust between participants. The lobbyist must develop a reputation as a discreet and reliable source, using a common expert language. Since the Whitehall village is small and professional lobbying is concentrated in a few sectors of government, to be effective in influencing policy, lobbyists and their clients should build long-term relationships through which they should supply reliable information. Professional lobbyists act as channels between clients and officials. Given this information exchange, the civil service might become dependent on, or even obligated to, the lobbyist.

Civil servants usually have stable relationships with outsiders, but a minister may wish to destabilise the community by introducing new actors. Lobbyists can help by pushing clients forward. Communities exist often because government wills it so; and, by locking groups in, the autonomy of government actors can be enhanced.

Civil servants can freeze groups out, but lobbyists can help by suggesting other routes to overcome or avoid obstructive officials or ministers. They can prise open established relationships. New players can enter as the agenda shifts. The type of network and its permeability will vary depending upon the macro-political institutions and the policy issue. Some groups will be outsiders by virtue of their objectives: either way, insiders and outsiders are consulted. Consultation, discussed next, can be unimportant, and interest groups that are consulted can be ineffective.

Lobbyists might be effective because they are of a similar 'political culture' to civil servants and politicians. They have worked in parties, Parliament and Whitehall. Lobbyists learn to 'exploit shared cultural, social and educational backgrounds as well as to play by the Whitehall mores of trust, responsible behaviour, secrecy, compromise and gradualism'.[81] Lobbyists are effective because they 'understand the mentality and processes at the heart of the machine'.[82] They are the ultimate insiders.

Consultation is an everyday part of the policy process. However, the implication in the literature is that consultation and 'insider' status imply influence.[83] But consultation is not influence. Government now engages in preconsultation with a select group, so that formal consultation has less impact on policy. Government actors have their own preferred options. Dudley and Richardson note that long-drawn-out consultation rarely overturns the main lines of public policy.[84] Being on a consultation list does not secure clout. Government decides whom to consult and topics of consultation. It decides what action to take. Although issues of access have implications for power, it is important not to be too concerned with ostensible behaviour because to do so would be to conclude that consultation equals access, which equals influence. The relationship is unlikely to be causal. The British government sees the majority of interests as legitimate. All are invited to participate in consultation. Even opponent groups often enjoy warm relations with civil servants and MPs. They meet officials, are consulted regularly, are suppliers of data and are informed of policy thinking. Despite this access, these groups have little effect on policy.

The notion that insider status is conferred on a few has been found by some to be a myth. Page assumes regular contact with departments and group–government policy coincidence is commensurate with the prestige of insider status.[85] However, the survey on which his findings are based focused on Statutory Instruments. It was undertaken during a 'honeymoon' period, and relied heavily on the perceptions groups held about their own influence. Furthermore, Christiansen and Dowding consider Amnesty International has 'insider status' with the Foreign and Commonwealth Office because Amnesty provides information, attends meetings and maintains formal and informal contact with officials.[86] However, it is doubtful whether Amnesty has affected policy. It has simply been an easy source of information. These examples illustrate how important it is to break the chain that links 'insider' with 'influence'.

The reformed pluralism framework portrays these relationships as ones in which government departments use groups for their own ends as a source of quality information. Insider status does not lead to influence; it is a necessary ingredient but not sufficient. Lobbyists know how to introduce their clients and their new ideas and knowledge to challenge a prevailing process. Groups without professional advice might find access difficult, but the real advantage of lobbyists is that they manage activity within the community.

Multi-faceted lobbying

Lobbyists tend to be effective if they pursue a multi-faceted approach and facilitate access to multiple points in the decision-making process.

Evidence presented by Furlong challenges this proposition since his results 'suggest that organizations may prove more effective in influencing regulatory policy by focusing their efforts on one form of access'.[87] However, many forms of lobbying activity are often positively associated with effectiveness, and 'the general pattern is that doing more of anything produces greater success than doing less, regardless of strategy'.[88] Truman noted groups' effectiveness required access to one or more points of decision in government.[89]

A multi-faceted approach is a product of both internal and external factors. Externally the salience and the political and technical nature of the case, and the stance of government, may determine whether a variety of approaches is exploited. However, if external factors allow a multi-faceted approach its effectiveness is determined by the lobbyist's characteristics, such as skill and contacts. One reason for believing effective lobbying is difficult to measure is that lobbyists may concentrate on those who are already convinced.[90] However, more recent research has challenged this conclusion by finding that lobbyists target a range of players, including friendly and unfriendly legislators.[91]

Access may be a key objective, but it is rarely the ultimate goal of the lobbyist. Access is the 'facilitating intermediate objective' of lobbyists.[92] Access 'structures the success or failure of the lobbyist, all of which come[s] after the access is achieved'.[93] Lobbyists practise low-cost political actions such as involvement in day-to-day discussions, responding to consultation, commissioning research and meeting government. Hansen suggests that lobbyists and their clients can gain access if they have a competitive advantage over rivals in helping the re-election of politicians, and if the issue is likely to recur.[94]

An important resource available to groups is their degree of acceptance by government, and whether this acceptance allows for an informal and friendly relationship. '[G]roups which do not gain legitimacy remain outside the policy-making process and hence are "effectively" mute.'[95] It may be that if access to policy communities is restricted, groups will adopt a high-profile campaign strategy. They will certainly be forced to pursue a multi-faceted approach. Lobbyists provide technical guidance about the most effective manner in which to approach decision-makers. Even for groups with good relations with government, a multi-faceted approach is more likely to be effective.

Micro-level

Following the discussion of networks, it is important to recognise the significance of different layers, spheres, individuals and rules, and their impact on policy outcomes. Institutions, organisations, rules and procedures have profound effects on lobbyists and provide a partial explanation of effectiveness. This chapter has suggested the impact of lobbyists depends on the interests of government actors because they make rules and have the potential to act autonomously. But different agencies have different standard operating procedures (SOPs) and structures that configure relations with interest groups. The effectiveness of lobbyists therefore also depends on those structures and those personalities.

Routines and procedures

Lobbyists tend to be effective if they are familiar with routines and standard operating procedures, and know when and where to intervene in the policy-making process.

Organisational process model

In regarding government actors as an independent variable, analysts invariably focus on recurring directives, procedures and institutional features. Rules and procedures are of key importance. Statutes, conventions, executive orders and culture determine rules. In some networks rules will be explicit, in others implicit; some are stable, others change regularly. But rules define the game. The procedural and cultural aspects of the relationship between the formal and informal rules and the actors impact on whether lobbyists can be effective.

Government administrators are socialised by their experiences, procedures and programmes. There are established rules for resolving disputes and gaining information and advice. Sub-governmental organisations have their own preferences, and officials with narrow responsibilities develop predictable routines and practices when they formulate policy. Organisational needs and rivalries, policy frameworks, decisional criteria and policy options' ramifications all mould preferences.

Institutions enjoy double-barrelled explanatory power because the resources of officials are institutionally derived, and institutional norms and procedures mediate their effective use and impact. A government agency is able to alter interest-group preferences by 'fragmenting, neutralizing and countering the deployment of private resources'.[96] The government's 'recurring directives and activities, internal processes, structural arrangements, and symbolic accoutrements help shape political beliefs and norms; levels and strategies of participation and opposition; the political crystallisation and alignments of ethnic segments, classes and interest groups; and the latter's organisational contours, inclusiveness and specialisation'.[97] Without undermining the concept of reformed pluralism, government actors can be accorded an analytical distinctiveness.

Complex problems are fragmented into component parts, and explanations of policy outcomes must account for government's sub-units.

Government is a disparate set of administrative agencies, which are often governed by their own organising principles. Interaction with groups is conducted within the constraints and opportunities defined by procedures. The government has regulatory and selective functions to define interests and to select legitimate interests. Actors behave in structured contexts that influence outcomes. To judge the effectiveness of lobbyists it is necessary to recognise the organisation of the policy process.

Government and departments have been described as a conglomerate 'of semi-feudal, loosely allied organisations, each with a substantial life of its own'.[98] Each department and sub-governmental unit has responsibility for particular tasks and acts in a quasi-autonomous manner. Because boundaries are blurred, several bodies, co-ordinated by a minister or senior civil servant, will frequently have input into important problems. These leaders impact on, but do not control, the behaviour of organisations. Problems are resolved by SOPs largely because of time pressures and workload. The behaviour of organisations is determined in large part by established routines.

Games and routines explain how decisions are made. Institutional arrangements, pre-existing policies and organisations of parties can affect the influence of lobbyists. The key to effective lobbying is knowledge of the rules of the game and how best to play the game within those rules. Rules differ in each network and community. Effective lobbyists are knowledgeable about the rules of the dominant games played in each arena. In different policy settings there will be different clusters of players with their own rules and operating procedures. A lobbyist must know the rules of the game in each network.

Even though events rarely arise from purposive choices, many theories of organisational decision-making use the concept of rationality. Limits to human capacity suggest that bounded rationality is more appropriate.[99] Perfect information does not exist in practice. Complex problems are disaggregated and passed to different units. Each option and its consequences are not considered by decision-makers; the action considered 'good enough' is often applied. Under comprehensive rationality the search sequence for all available choices is unimportant because all are considered while, under bounded rationality, the order of search is crucial because the first 'good-enough' option is accepted.[100] Organisations do not consider broad consequences of all possible actions. They have certain procedures with short-run feedback mechanisms to ensure prompt corrective action and prevent crystal-ball gazing. Organisations have SOPs that constrain effective choice in recurring issues. Responses are often steps learned by previous experience.[101] Decision-makers have to deal with the problem of uncertainty. To control uncertainty actors respond only to information processed by channels.

Allison presents a paradigm of organisational process that can be applied to lobbyists' activity.[102] The basic unit of analysis is governmental action not as deliberate choice, but as organisational output. Whilst actual occurrences are organisational outputs, some of which may be altered by government actors, most behaviour is determined by previously-established procedures. Organisational procedures constitute a range of choices open to decision-makers. Cybernetic theory rests on a decision-maker having 'a repertory of operations which he performs in sequence while monitoring a few feedback variables'.[103] Organisational outputs structure issues within constraints within which leaders must decide; they rarely write on a clean slate.[104] Peculiar to central government is that each department runs its policy in a quasi-independent way: 'factoring' permits specialisation.[105] Since factoring also encourages parochialism, lobbyists can be effective because they range across institutions. They hold information about the stance of institutional players and they understand that the structure of the issue is determined by organisational output. The lobbyist can be well co-ordinated on issues. Because established groups and government sometimes galvanise parochialism, thereby ensuring high-entry barriers to policy-making, lobbyists can be useful facilitators as well as players in their own right.

SOPs and repertoires of organisations may be affected by the intervention of senior government actors, but complete control is not possible. Lobbyists can encourage ministers to break procedure. If senior politicians are unable to force changes in standard operating procedures they may still be able to decide which organisations are involved in which games and at what level. Lobbyists may also introduce new issues to certain organisations.

The descriptive power of this model for lobbyists is based on them understanding organisational routines that produce outputs. Reaction to problems is rarely the consequence of far-sighted and flexible analysis. It is determined chiefly by operating procedures. Procedures and routines allow bureaucrats to deal with similar policy matters day after day with little thought. To business, these procedures seem complex and formal, but they are the lobbyists' stock in trade. Effective lobbyists are familiar with those routines. They know when and how to intervene.

Contacts and coalitions

Lobbyists tend to be effective if they have good contacts and can spot connections to potential allies and can construct coalitions.

Governmental politics model

The governmental politics model is principally dependent upon internal factors such as the lobbyist's contacts and knowledge. However, the behaviour of other players also affects the ability to form coalitions; therefore, to some extent, external factors are present. Graham Allison developed the governmental-politics model,[106] building on the work of Richard Neustadt.[107] Although Allison applied the model to policy crises, it can be used to explain routine policy development. The model understands events as neither choices nor outputs, but as outcomes. What happens is the consequence of various bargaining games, compromises, coalitions and competition. Allison poses the question: 'Which results of what kind of bargaining among which players yielded the critical decisions and actions?'[108] This model concentrates on perceptions, motivations, positions, power and manoeuvres of the actors. The model has been little applied since Allison's seminal study.[109]

Viewing an action at the micro-level as the product of bargaining between actors in the game helps our understanding of how lobbyists can be effective. Events can be explained when it is discovered who did what to whom and when. The governmental-politics model denies that players plan their moves rationally and accepts that players have imperfect information. Lobbyists can matter because they know the personalities. Heinz *et al.* suggest that lobbying representatives 'who have frequent contact with influential representatives [decision-makers] are themselves likely to be influential'.[110] This 'knowledge' allows lobbyists to understand the history and personal preferences of actors. Their contacts allow them to devise effective tactics. Lobbyists are detached players who can stand back and plan strategy.

The Allison model has pluralist roots. Since he recognised government organisations are not monolithic, the model is compatible with reformed pluralism where different sub-units of government can have different preferences. The governmental-politics model argues that policy is an outcome of bargaining between actors within bureaucratic procedures, but it is usually the government actors who are the more powerful actors and provide strategic direction.

The 'governmental actor' can be visualised as a host of individual players. Only issues of supreme importance attract the attention of the busiest players. Individuals are players because of their occupation; their position often defines their impact. The resolution of problems also depends on personalities. Many lobbyists have worked in government and the parties: they know the personalities within government. This information cannot be gleaned in any other way. Knowledge of the stance, mannerisms, beliefs and convictions of key players endows privilege.

Governmental politics is messy. Actors negotiate and bargain. Government actors have one set of preferences and interest groups another. Lobbyists act as a bridge: they bring the players closer together by identifying common ground. The need to secure effective representation 'is a motivating force in the formation of alliances and the recognition of a common interest'.[111] Lobbyists spot connections with potential coalition partners in order to present a 'broad front' to government. To be effective, lobbyists rely on coalitional lobbying.[112]

Constructing coalitions is an important determinant of effectiveness. The ability and willingness to form coalitions influences the ability of lobbyists and interest groups to influence policy. In addition to the importance of personal contacts, 'the more coalitions that an organisation builds with other groups, the greater its success at influencing public-policy decisions'.[113] Coalition-building is a cause of policy effectiveness.

To explain why a certain decision was made or why a certain pattern of activity emerged it is necessary to identify the games, the players, the coalitions, and the operating procedures. Effective lobbyists can be the locus of initiative, elevating ideas and identifying links and connections. As substantive problems make disagreement likely, consensus-building becomes more important, and lobbyists are more valuable because they can spot themes in their client's case on which they can play with a reasonable chance of success.

Effective lobbyists help knit actors into action-channels, which structure the game by pre-selecting major players.[114] Lobbyists, because they have navigated these channels countless times before, confer advantage on their clients.[115] Each player will 'pull and haul' with the power at his or her discretion for outcomes that advance his or her interest. Effective lobbyists tend to know at what point to play to avoid being over-powered by others. Lobbyists help clients find other options and arguments to put to decision-makers.

The explanatory power of the governmental-politics model opens up to scrutiny the game that yielded the action: the players and their preferences, their positions and action channels. Lobbyists are at the centre of planning the client's strategy, policy and location. Lobbyists are neither 'of government' nor 'of the client'; they can take a detached view of the game.

Allison identifies several relevant factors:

1. The stance of actors has a significant effect on governmental action. The advantages of each player will differ depending on the action-channel, the mix of players.

2. Action does not presuppose government intention. Players with different intentions will contribute to a policy action. Policy emerges from games where players perceive different facets of an issue.
3. Players do not focus on the grand strategic problem but on immediate decisions that must be taken. Lobbyists apply knowledge of previous experience.
4. Diverse demands on players shape perceptions, priorities and issues.
5. Vertical and horizontal demands on actors are distinct. Problems are framed and options specified by lowly actors. They compete to attract the attention of senior actors.
6. The rules of the game affect the strategy of the players.
7. There is no perfect information in games; misperception is a part of bargaining and allows cooperation among people who, had they full knowledge, would not cooperate. Miscommunication between players is also likely in fast-moving games.
8. Multiple games allow limited attention to individual games.
9. Involvement in multiple games means reticence is advantageous. Reticence reduces the likelihood of harmful leaks and gives opponents an ill-focused target of attack.
10. Players have different styles. Officials will adopt a code of conformity to withstand a change of administration. Political actors and lobbyists are more interested in policy.[116]

Information about perceptions, priorities and personalities is not available through documents. Indeed, documents obscure such information. Because lobbyists know actors, they can gather intelligence and disentangle preferences. Their contacts are crucial, and their clients enter the game with an advantage. Policy choices emerge not from rational choice, but from negotiations undertaken within SOPs. The two models presented here to explain the micro-level are complementary since the organisational model analyses the routines of bureaucracy and highlights the aggregate behaviour of organisations, whereas the governmental-politics model emphasises the actions of individual players and the politics between them.[117]

Resources

Lobbyists tend to be effective if the client has abundant resources and is skilful in deploying them.

The significance of resources is widely recognised. Clients can influence policy to the extent to which they can afford. Resources influence group strength.[118] The size of the membership, internal discipline, financial support, the potential for mobilisation and how seriously an organisation is viewed by officials are important resources influencing effectiveness. Political resources are not limited to one group: their distribution takes the form of 'dispersed inequalities'. '[N]o group of more than a few individuals is entirely lacking in some influence resources.'[119] However, the larger, better-organised and well-financed groups are likely to succeed at the expense of smaller less well-resourced groups.

The level of resources is often an ingredient of successful lobbying. Smith argued for 'the availability of the requisite resources for the acquisition of information about the consequences of various positions on a proposal and the presence of creative, experienced people who can transform information about consequences into interpretations that are appealing'.[120] Similarly, Schlozman and Tierney note the importance of finance as a variable that affects an interest group's ability to participate in, and influence, policy-making.[121] Low-profile lobbies require resources because of the need to undertake research, hire skilled staff, and to build up expertise. Langbein and Lotwis suggest resources are a determinant of effectiveness, pointing out 'that relative wealth does not determine overall effectiveness but rather affects how groups chose to exercise influence'.[122]

The amount of time available to the lobbyist is another variable, and the transformation of resource advantage into policy effectiveness is conditional upon the time for lobbying. 'Because of the lack of time available to develop advocacy efforts, the advocate will find it difficult to use its resource advantage effectively.'[123] Lobbyists need time to turn their resource advantage into policy effectiveness.

Skill in deploying resources and knowledge might be more important than the quantity of resources. This conclusion may explain why some well-resourced groups are defeated by interest groups with limited resources. Groups with small resources can have a greater impact on events than those with large resources because 'The use of resources depends on context and strategy.'[124] So 'looking at these resources is not enough to measure their [actors'] capacities, for those resources will only allow actors to bring about outcomes under certain conditions'.[125] Some interest groups have developed a degree of expertise in lobbying greater than the expertise of professional lobbyists. It is not always the case that the more wealthy groups are the most effective.

The skill of players in deploying resources influences policy outcomes. A client with limited resources might be disproportionately effective because its lobbyist uses resources in an adroit manner. Rhodes's work on policy-making and bargaining concentrates on resources. His model of resources available to actors in a game can be merged with Allison's models and set in the context of reformed pluralism. Rhodes suggests five resources are central to effective bargaining and negotiation. They are constitutional and legal, hierarchical, financial, political and informational.[126] The definition of resources is subjective because resources are variable, depend on actors' perceptions and their value is relative over time.[127] The impact of resources depends on the rules governing the exchange relationship and the skill with which they are deployed. Power dependency means the lobbyist depends on the resource commitment of his client. Rhodes seems to support the concept of government autonomy when he argues that one body (government) can be dependent on another (group) for information and services, yet still have power over that organisation.[128] But his theory of power-dependence does not adequately recognise that certain resources decide others. Legal powers determine finance, access to information and hierarchical relations.

Resources make winning more likely, but do not guarantee success; however, neither do deficiencies spell doom.

Conclusions

The risk of a multi-theoretic approach is that it becomes 'descriptively comprehensive but theoretically incoherent, and incapable of being generalised to apply to different issues and decisions'.[129] However, because politics is a multi-level, multi-arena game, adopting a macro-, meso- and micro-level framework is necessary to understand the effectiveness of lobbyists.

Attention to context is important. To explain the context within which lobbyists can be effective, it is valuable to utilise a macro-level concept (recognising external constraints on government, factors internal to government, and government autonomy), a meso-level concept (policy networks) and a micro-level analysis (the merged Allison and Rhodes models examining rules, actors and resources). This framework recognises the complexity of decision-making.

Government action and social context are important in explaining how, why and when lobbyists are effective. If the external context is favourable, then lobbyists have the opportunity to be effective. Effectiveness then depends on internal factors, such as tactics, contacts, knowledge of rules, and the amount and deployment of resources. At the macro-level this framework presents the wider context and government autonomy as key external factors. Both lobbyists and government can be restricted by external constraints. Merging reformed pluralism and weak government autonomy presents a more sophisticated approach. Government players with their own objectives can steer groups, develop their own policy and mould their environment. There is no over-arching single government interest; the interests of government actors do not develop in isolation from groups, and it may even be that government initially responds to groups. However, effectiveness is curbed if the aim of the lobbyist is to achieve change which 'goes against the grain' of current political, ideological, societal or organisational trends. The reformed pluralism model allows influence to be conceptualised in the policy-network model. Policy communities are a source of influence for officials because they limit the options for change. The book will test whether within the policy community lobbyists use their resources to manage their client's performance to improve its effectiveness. Effective lobbyists also adopt a multi-faceted approach.

Within the policy community options are limited by standard operating procedures, which for government actors are more important than rational assessment. Organisational activity is, more often than not, the execution of pre-established routines. Effective lobbyists understand and empathise with the organisational tendencies and standard scenarios used by policy-makers: they know, and can anticipate how, the 'official machine' works. Lobbyists are effective if they ascertain who the key players are, their motivations, their public position and their private objectives and their relative influence. The effective lobbyist comprehends how 'the process' works informally within the formal routines and can predict how the games will be played. They have this information because they are 'close to the ground' and know the players, often because they are associated with parties and consequently trusted by politicians. The lobbyist seeks out connections and affiliations with third parties. During the game the level and the deployment of resources might prove decisive. Lobbyists know how to use resources effectively. An effective lobbyist uses his or her skill and experience to 'punch above his [or her] weight'.

4
Church Bells versus Shop Tills: The Campaign For and Against Sunday Trading

Sundays are special. The right to trade on a Sunday was a high-profile issue fought over the long term at many different levels by two main interest groups, one lobbying for deregulation and the other campaigning for a day of rest and religion. This chapter examines the effectiveness of lobbyists campaigning for both sides. Before 1994, Sunday trading laws were embodied in the Sunday Fairs Act of 1448 and the Sunday Observance Acts of 1627 and 1677. These Acts were updated by the Acts of 1911, 1928 and 1936, which in turn were consolidated as a 'temporary measure' in the Shops Act 1950.

The 1950 Shops Act was riddled with anomalies leading to inconsistencies. It was subject to many attempts at reform, including three Departmental Committees and nineteen Private Member's Bills. Until the 1980s governments believed the Sunday trading law should be changed by Private Member's legislation. The Thatcher government favoured public legislation. However, ministers were shaken by the loss of the government's Shops Bill (1985) at Second Reading, which disrupted its deregulatory agenda.

The subsequent inability of successive Home Secretaries to liberalise Sunday trading was embarrassing. This chapter examines the interest-group activity on the issue from the Government's 1986 parliamentary defeat to the enactment of the Sunday Trading Bill in April 1994. There were two campaigns. The first began with an attempt to reintroduce immediately the Shops Bill, and involved lobbying government, which accepted the principle of the desirability of change, but lacked a parliamentary majority to pass this legislation. Government feared another defeat. The pro-liberalisation lobby was included in the real centre of policy-making whilst the anti-liberalisation lobby was excluded. The latter was disproportionately weak. As a peripheral player it was consulted but had little impact on the policy outcome.

The second phase was the Lloydian period (1992–94, which coincided with Peter Lloyd MP's tenure as Parliamentary Under-Secretary of State at the Home Office). A government majority of 21, continued interest-group intransigence, and a Sabbatarian rump of Tory MPs forced inventive thinking by officials. Consequently policy-making was devolved to key interest groups to produce an options Bill. The process was made transparent to an unprecedented degree as Parliament was presented with a choice of different regimes. Lobbying focused on Parliament as the ultimate arbiter. The final outcome was close. The regulatory option was defeated by 304 votes to 286; a majority of only 18. The partial deregulation option was later approved by 333 votes to 258, a majority of 75.[1]

Interest groups and lobbyists

Conflict between the groups was intense and sharply defined. Two groups dominated the campaign. The Keep Sunday Special Campaign (KSSC) opposed the Shopping Hours Reform Council (SHRC). Three satellite groups circled on the fringes: Outlets Providing Everyday Needs (OPEN), Retailers for Shops Act Reform (RSAR) and Sort Out Sunday (SOS).

Keep Sunday Special Campaign

The Jubilee Trust, a charitable organisation, housed KSSC. It pursued collective objectives. Its priority was to ensure the Shops Act was enforced without creating a backlash, which would deliver liberalisation by default. It had no reforming intentions; it simply wanted to keep shops shut. However, later it was forced to create an alternative to deregulation, and the REST proposals (Recreation, Emergencies, Social Gatherings, and Travel) were launched.[2]

The KSSC was a bizarre 'alliance of Seventh Day Separatists: Labour MPs for the shop-workers, Tories for the family unit and churchgoers from all quarters'.[3] It portrayed itself as the voice of middle England.[4] KSSC was not solely religious, and it also represented national retailers, trade unions and trade associations.

KSSC's intellectual and religious elements were torn between an anti-liberal socio-economic analysis on the left, and conservative moral commitments pulling to the right. KSSC tried to keep these two themes in parallel, but it continued to be caricatured as Sabbatarian. Subsequently, as employment rights became important, KSSC's tradition of one-nation conservatism, which developed into communitarianism, meant Christians and Socialists found a common denominator in dislike of exploitation.

KSSC used a political adviser, and while most work was managed internally, he contributed strategic guidance, political intelligence, drafted documents, and advised on resource prioritisation. The adviser undertook no advocacy. KSSC 'made a conscious decision not to employ professional lobbyists...because the image of the campaign was grass roots up'. KSSC did not want to 'come over as a bunch of smart-arsed lobbyists...[and] cherished its homely, amateur approach'.[5]

Shopping Hours Reform Council

Following the defeat of the Shops Bill in 1986, the Sunday trading lobby disintegrated. In 1987 the do-it-yourself (DIY) groups and the garden centres reconstituted.[6] Although initially a splinter from die-hard retailers, the SHRC became the main pro-deregulation group campaigning for the right for all shops to trade on Sundays.[7] DIY businesses and trade associations supported SHRC. Food retailers joined later, when a loophole in the law allowed them to trade on a Sunday.

GJW and Burson-Marsteller were SHRC's lead lobbyists. GJW was described by the SHRC as 'our eyes and ears wherever they went'.[8] GJW focused on national politicians and civil servants.[9] The campaign was also advised by Lowe Bell Communications, independent consultant Des Wilson, and a Labour consultant.

SHRC harmonised the lobbying of its member companies, using Ian Greer Associates (which worked for Kingfisher), Political Profile (which worked for WH Smith) and Charles Barker (which worked for Tesco). Lowe Bell provided public relations and strategic advice to SHRC. The lack of progress between 1986 and 1990 and Lowe Bell's high cost meant it was removed whilst GJW was retained.[10] SHRC believed 'it was like having a Rolls Royce sitting in the garage. You didn't need it. All you needed was a Mini Cooper.'[11]

Burson-Marsteller was hired in 1993 and Des Wilson continued the public communications brief and focused third-party support by adding a strategic overview, pooling resources of SHRC members, and advising on a grass-roots campaign.[12]

Outlets Providing Everyday Needs

OPEN sought to protect the interests of the small store sector. It wanted the law to allow small retailers to open, but keep the large traders shut. OPEN's aim was to 'minimise the damage that would accrue if SHRC [won] on one hand or KSSC kept us closed on the other. Both were disaster scenarios'.[13] OPEN represented small retail outlets, including over

10 000 small shops, occupying the 'middle-ground'. The group was a very minor player.[14]

Burson-Marsteller was hired in 1986, but OPEN moved to Rowland Sallingbury Casey (RSC) in 1990, supported by a public relations team. Two lobbyists ran the OPEN secretariat.[15] There were no permanent staff.[16] The executive council agreed general policy and funding. A lobbyist said: 'All the campaigning was done by us, including drafting letters, meeting MPs, meeting civil servants, putting out press releases, and talking to the trade press. We did everything. We ran it'.[17]

Retailers for Shops Act Reform

RSAR was a late entrant into the debate, aiming to prevent large out-of-town stores from opening. It campaigned to stop SHRC because of the potential damage to RSAR's members' town-centre businesses.[18] RSAR was a cover for Marks & Spencer.[19]

RSAR used Market Access (now GPC International) for political research and intelligence. The lobbyist 'did not lobby on RSAR's behalf, because RSAR did its representations and its own lobbying'.[20] The consultancy provided 'strategic advice on campaign management and advice and guidance on who the key players were'.[21] Shandwick, a public relations firm, undertook media work because RSAR 'needed to get stories into the newspapers at every opportunity'.[22]

Sort Out Sunday

SOS advocated total deregulation. Chaired by Lord Boyd-Carpenter, it was the guerrilla campaign of the DIY, garden-centre and video rental sectors. It shared members with the SHRC, and 'did not run a whole-hearted campaign because ... there was a risk of upsetting the apple cart of the SHRC'.[23] SOS's strategy was to 'appear to be wanting to change the law, but in fact to render the current law unenforceable'.[24]

SOS remained a fringe group, its natural constituency being the Conservative Party. SOS hired the Public Policy Unit. The lobbyist's 'feeling was to lie low. Government was not going to do anything for quite a while.'[25] SOS lawyers stimulated test cases. The PPU lobbyist said SOS 'decided it was going to do everything but lobby government'.[26]

Macro-level

Profile, technicality and politicality

Sunday trading was a big policy issue. Public interest was great. There were thousands of written representations to the Home Office and MPs, acres of press coverage and hundreds of interest groups agitated. Between

1986 and 1992 campaigning was directed at government. After 1992 lobbying was directed at Parliament, based on letter writing, petitions, demonstrations and the media. As the Sunday trading campaign evolved, its profile increased. Government lost control of group politics, and policy was contracted-out to interest groups. The government's role was passive.

Dozens of lobbyists were active on Sunday trading. By and large they remained in the shadows and were a minor influence on the debate. They briefed MPs and the press, and helped to mobilise constituency support. But this issue was decided on conscience and other factors such as ideology, morality, constituency, and the views of peers. Lobbyists had no direct effect, though they had some indirect influence. Their strategic approach was valuable, but their contribution was limited.

Decisions on non-controversial issues tend to be made within small groups which lobbyists can permeate, but in Sunday trading lobbyists lacked control over events. The game was big, and influence over players and knowledge of personalities was difficult. This case was about ideological conflict between the two main groups. Although SHRC possessed financial and organisational advantages, enabling it to 'shape' public opinion, and it had media support, it still could not win quickly. These advantages made little difference because the context was hostile. A former minister believed the most effective SHRC lobbying was parliamentary assistance, providing MPs with intelligence, briefs, speeches and lists of people for MPs to contact.[27] Lobbyists knew how to put the information into palatable and consumable packages for Members of Parliament.

Lobbyists judged their effectiveness prudently. They qualified their 'successes'. The OPEN lobbyist said he was 'Not totally effective. We had a partial success. We got the best we could out of the final deal … We got a concession.'[28] Contextual variables were important: 'it's arguable whether we did that or whether it would have happened anyway'.[29] The lobbyists were effective in providing the small-store sector with a voice louder than it would otherwise have had.

The deregulation lobbyists believed they were effective. The GJW lobbyist claimed effectiveness because of client satisfaction, arguing that: 'we were working with hard-headed commercial people and if they had not thought we were doing a reasonable job they would have had us out in no time'.[30] His colleague was forthright, claiming the SHRC 'would never have got it without us. We started it. We educated them politically – they were terribly naive.'[31] GJW provided contacts, knowledge of parliamentary procedure, advocacy services and strategic advice to SHRC and lobbied MPs directly to confront KSSC. The risk of an intense parliamentary campaign is over-kill. A former Home Office Minister argued lobbyists were 'regarded by many Members of Parliament as a nuisance, constantly ringing them up to ask them to commit themselves to one side or the other, which would then produce letters from supporters of the other side complaining about the position they took'.[32]

A former minister argued that KSSC was 'remarkably effective ... [in] representing the inchoate fears of a large number of people'.[33] However, one lobbyist from another group considered KSSC to have been 'extraordinarily ineffective', arguing that its 'all or nothing approach' meant it was unable to compromise.[34]

Conclusion

This issue was high-profile, general, and political. A civil servant suggested 'the whole point about the Shops Bill – the absolute agony – was that everyone is their own Home Secretary'.[35] Consequently, the Home Office dealt with a range of views, from the Lord's Day Observance Society to Sort Out Sunday. Everyone had an opinion, and no one felt obliged to justify their views. There was little to be gained from attempting reform because it encouraged protest and won little support for government. The issue became non-political after 1992 because of contextual changes, notably the reduced Conservative parliamentary majority. Lobbyists were relatively unimportant and were minor players. They did not influence policy directly. They were, however, valuable in the communication of policy externally and internally within the coalitions. They helped explain policy to Parliament and the media and helped groups refine their objectives.

External factors

External factors affected lobbying. Advice and action were influenced by external circumstances. A good example is SHRC's view that it got 'no value for money whatsoever' from Lowe Bell because lobbyists 'cannot make government do things government does not want to'.[36] There are several important factors: retailers; a changing society; business profile; parliamentary change and ministerial turnover; and the Labour Party's modernisation.

Retailers

Consumers increasingly shopped on Sundays. Change to the law was easier following social changes. The Conservative government aimed to decriminalise Sunday shopping, while leaving regulation to the market. The SHRC argued 29 per cent of shops opened on a Sunday in England

and Wales compared to 25 per cent in Scotland (in Scotland shops could open legally).[37] The majority of shops trading every Sunday were small shops.

There was cross-ownership between the different retail sectors.[38] A key moment came in winter 1991 when food retailers opened, thereby undermining the 'regulation' groups. One participant argued: 'once people got used to shopping on a Sunday the battle was almost over'.[39] The retailers' illegality changed the status quo. In 1986 KSSC had defended the status quo, but by the early 1990s the status quo had changed. SHRC was portrayed as defending people's right to shop, whilst KSSC wanted to turn the clock back.

A changing society

The workforce was changing. Whilst the 1975 Labour Force Survey found 3.4 million people worked regularly on Sundays (15 per cent of the workforce), by 1987 the figure was 5.6 million working at some time on Saturday and Sunday, or on Sunday.[40] Staff in catering, leisure and transport sectors had also worked on Sundays for decades.

Consumers had a different set of priorities from those in the 1950s. In 1950 only 26 per cent of married women worked outside the home. The figure in the early 1990s was 70 per cent.[41] In fact, 73 per cent of unmarried women worked full-time. By the 1980s the UK was the most irreligious country in Europe. Church attendance was 20 per cent.

'The reason SHRC was more successful is that the tenor of its campaign and the message it preached was more in line with reality.'[42] The SHRC's messages were closer to people's material instincts. KSSC tried to save a society that no longer existed. Public support gave government the credibility to back Sunday trading since it could argue it was not going against the grain.

The UK's business profile had also changed. The Auld Report noted that in the 1970s small businesses closed at a rate of 45 a day.[43] The four leading supermarkets served 3.5 million customers each, and increased their market share. The big retailers controlled the food market. The consequence of the 1990s recession was fierce competition between larger retailers for diminishing consumer disposable income, and some retail chains opened on Sundays to increase turnover.

Parliamentary change and ministerial turnover

The 1992 General Election delivered the Conservative Party leader John Major a parliamentary majority of only 21, and with many Conservative MPs actively supporting both sides, Sunday trading could not be resolved by a whipped Bill. Therefore government devolved the process to the groups, which benefited SHRC. SHRC was able to shift its campaign to Parliament and broaden its coalition. KSSC remained stuck in an 'opposition mindset' and failed to hold its allies together or widen its appeal.

Ministerial turnover irritated interest groups because they were forced to begin again from 'square one'. A reshuffle propelled David Waddington (as Secretary of State) and David Mellor (as Minister of State) into the Home Office. SHRC hoped the Waddington–Mellor team would be dynamic but, despite having 'friendly' ministers, SHRC was ineffective because the ministers were restricted by Parliament. Government acted when circumstances changed. A civil servant argued: 'Peter Lloyd was not more effective than his predecessors. In a sense he was lucky. Circumstances were more favourable.'[44]

The Labour Party's modernisation

KSSC was the natural home for old-style Labour MPs, but Labour's modernisation and ideological realignment drove it to attract the southern, middle-class voter and businesses more likely to sympathise with SHRC.[45]

KSSC lobbied the sympathetic parliamentary body, whilst SHRC concentrated on the head. SHRC companies learned their way around the networks of party-modernising apparatchiks. 'KSSC concentrated on backbench people who were individually sympathetic, rather than working out who were the coming people.'[46] Labour was 'lobbied tremendously by SHRC, they were taken for meals ... and functions were held. They received a barrage of propaganda from SHRC.'[47]

In 1989 both Labour and the trade union Union of Shop, Distributive and Allied Workers (USDAW) opposed deregulation.[48] But as modernisation progressed, Shadow Cabinet members no longer defended existing law. Labour MPs aired their support for Sunday trading. SHRC hired a consultant to lobby Labour because 'the traditional lobbying companies had expertise dealing with technical issues, civil servants and government ministers, but were less developed on Labour lobbying'.[49]

The former KSSC president and Labour peer, Lord Graham, broke ranks in 1992, arguing that out-of-town stores should be allowed to open.[50] When the Labour MP, Roy Hattersley, retired from the Home Office brief, and broke free from the constraints of collective responsibility, he publicly supported Sunday trading.[51] If retailers were to back the European Social Charter protecting workers' rights, Labour stated it could support liberalisation.[52] Tony Blair's appointment as Shadow

Home Secretary moved Labour further towards liberalisation. Blair showed himself as a moderniser and consumer-friendly and, whilst being 'assiduous in not hitting a lobby [KSSC] which had Church support',[53] his Home Office team refused to support old-style Labour backbencher Ray Powell's KSSC-drafted Private Member's Bill.[54]

In preparation for a Labour government, SHRC sought a Labour figurehead.[55] Margaret Jay was ideal: she was at the heart of the Labour Party being former Labour Prime Minister Lord Callaghan's daughter, a key moderniser, close to Blair and a working woman.[56] SHRC meetings between Blair and Baroness Jay, as SHRC president, produced indications of support. SHRC acted as an informal channel of communication between Blair and the Home Secretary, Kenneth Clarke. Furthermore, GJW was acceptable to Labour because its lobbyist, a former adviser to James Callaghan when Prime Minister, was close to John Smith, the Labour leader, and 'knew all the people well. She was well liked and well respected.'[57] SHRC attached itself to the right-wing, modernising, feminist element which included the Emily's List network.[58] The Parliamentary Labour Party's shift, driven by modernisers, Scottish MPs and a wish not to have to deal with Sunday trading when in government, was confirmed by a survey in 1992.[59] Labour offered to 'co-operate positively with the government to get legislation through the House'.[60] Supporting deregulation was arguably the first act of 'New' Labour.

KSSC hoped backbench Conservative Sabbatarians would ally with old-Labour MPs to hold the conservative retailers in their coalition. However, only the old-Labour majority stayed solid, whereas the aspirant payroll vote was implicitly directed to the modernising agenda. Short-term concessions to the SHRC business alliance, however, were a politically-astute long-term strategy to re-position Labour.

The shift in Labour ideology was critical. Modernisation split the Labour vote. Elements of the Labour Party were managed effectively by SHRC. Lobbyists used the modernisers to exploit the party's desire to be perceived as pro-business and pro-consumer. They understood how the elite teams operated. Labour broke from the top-down, not bottom-up. KSSC believed 'nothing, at that point in political history, could have over-turned this balance of forces'.[61]

Conclusion

Despite SHRC lobbying, the Conservative Government could not introduce legislation in the 1987–92 Parliament because the context was unfavourable. Failed lobbyists believed their ineffectiveness was the consequence of factors beyond their control. One lobbyist said, 'I wish we had been able to do more, but in the end you can only do as much as circumstances and your client allow you to.'[62] The EuroShop lobbyist said: 'one can never be sure one has done a brilliant job. Whether you were effective or not depends on so many other factors.'[63] The KSSC lobbyist was 'relatively ineffective when faced by the external circumstances with which we had to contend'.[64]

By the early 1990s regulationists were hampered and the deregulationists aided by social and economic factors. The deregulationists were with the 'spirit of the times'. SHRC lobbyists were effective because of contextual factors. Although KSSC's post-modern call for a break in the weekly rhythm was powerful, it was ineffective because of broader changes beyond its control (retailers opening, changing society, changing business profile, the government's majority and the modernisation of Labour) which all undermined KSSC. Developments could only weaken KSSC.

Experience and existing policy

Group objectives

KSSC launched proposals to challenge the Conservative Government to clarify its manifesto pledge, and to attract broader support (REST).[65] However, the proposals to restrict Sunday trading to a limited range of shops were as complicated and irrational as the 1950 Shops Act.

The SHRC agenda amounted to the privatisation of the Conservative Government's electoral programme.[66] The central theme was to distinguish between small and large traders. Retail units over 3000 sq. ft would open between 10 am and 4 pm, whilst shops of less than 3000 sq. ft were to be allowed to open all day and workers would be protected.[67]

OPEN wanted its retail sector to be allowed to trade longer than others by restricting trading to shops under 3000 sq. ft. Independent retailers only made profits when the multiples were shut, and competition on Sundays would destroy them.

RSAR's objectives were more liberal than those of KSSC. The size of retailer allowed to open was 3000 sq. ft and the conditions small shops had to satisfy in order to open were more vague than KSSC's proposals. Large shops, with some exemptions, would remain closed.

SOS favoured total deregulation.

Government objectives

The Conservative Government was divided and never overcame the paradox of supporting a deregulationist free-trade agenda, whilst supporting the family and church. The party's 1987 Campaign Guide read: 'The

Government remains committed to the principle of liberalising Sunday shop opening hours, but sees little purpose in introducing a Bill until clear support for change can be guaranteed in the House of Commons.'[68] Under Margaret Thatcher free trade generally triumphed over family and religion, except over the 1985 Shops Bill.

The Conservative Government's third term was characterised by a commitment dating back to before 1985, which was entangled with memories of burned fingers. The loss of the Shops Bill at its Second Reading made government wary of reintroducing reform. The late 1980s were spent hunting for a solution. By the 1990s the debate shifted to the need for compromise.

Deregulation was the fashion in the late 1980s and early 1990s. Michael Heseltine, President of the Board of Trade, launched a crusade against red tape in 1992. Deregulation of Sunday trading hours fitted this policy backdrop. A civil servant suggested the SHRC was the 'strongest deregulatory group at a time when the initiative was a deregulatory one'.[69]

Conclusion

Given the ideology and pre-existing policy commitments of government, it was more difficult for KSSC to achieve its objectives than SHRC. In the pre-Lloydian period the government's free-market ideology supported Sunday trading. Regulation and restriction were excluded from its agenda. The Prime Minister, John Major, and Home Secretary, Michael Howard, like many of their parliamentary colleagues, supported total deregulation. The preferences of government and SHRC were non-divergent. They shared a similar 'world view'.

The government objected to KSSC policy. Ministers opposed the REST proposals. One former minister argued that an effective lobbyist should have a case 'within the thrust of government policy. If you're going with the flow of government policy, you are all right.'[70] However, opposition to Sunday trading had become so out of step with the mood of the time that continued, assertive support for opposition was a barrier to political elite decision-making. KSSC swam against the political tide by 'moving against a government machine that had positively decided it wanted this [reform]'.[71] OPEN's case was disadvantageous and their argument anti-competitive and anti-deregulation. OPEN's lobbyist admitted, 'We were starting on the back foot.'[72]

In most cases lobbyists tend to be effective if their case is congruent with government beliefs and pre-existing policy. SHRC was close to government in the pre-Lloydian period because of its access and intelligence. However, government lacked the power to deliver deregulation. Success is authorised by government players except when the government's majority is small, or when the issue is a matter of conscience.

Meso-level

The policy community

Lobbyists follow rules of the game to enter the policy network. There were two networks: a closed policy community, and a secondary broader network which changed over time.

After the 1986 defeat SHRC presented its strategy to the Home Office. 'The government made clear if a policy was going to be delivered it was up to [SHRC] to deliver it and sell it. They would have nothing to do with promoting it.'[73]

In the first phase ministers were the fulcrum of the small and tightly integrated primary community. Government restricted entry to those players who shared its views. KSSC and OPEN were overlooked. SHRC was authoritative and its relationship with government was institutionalised. Relations with the Home Office were 'sometimes in conflict, often in agreement, but always in touch and operating within a shared framework'.[74] The relationship fits the Marsh–Rhodes typology of a policy community.[75]

Secondary groups had sufficient resources to be included in policy-making but their ideas were disconsonant with government. KSSC was part of this sub-sectoral network that was neither cohesive nor integrated. Gaining access to this network was not difficult, but participants had little influence on policy. There was often outright hostility between members. KSSC was excluded from a Home Office working party looking for workable solutions, but it lobbied for inclusion and argued that the consensus sought by government was precluded by its exclusion. Though KSSC spent considerable time in the company of Home Office civil servants, in an attempt to win serious support for its proposals, policy was clearly established and consultation constituted little more than procedural etiquette.

The Home Office Minister, Tim Renton, in February 1989, failed to convince a Cabinet committee that the SHRC option would command parliamentary support, and the Prime Minister was forced to accept defeat. The pre-1992 liberalisation campaign died when the government refused to include the Bill in the 1989 Queen's Speech. There was no prospect of reform between 1990 and 1992 because of the proximity of a General Election. Another 'palliative' consultation round was subsequently launched to keep the two main lobbies quiet.

After Mrs Thatcher's resignation as Prime Minister the issue became less a matter of doctrine and more a problem of governance. Support for deregulation continued under the new premier, John Major. He said: 'Experience in Scotland does suggest that a suitable consensus is possible. I hope one can be found south of the border.'[76] Yet another session of round-table talks with ministers began in Spring 1991, leading Major to pledge that reform of Sunday trading would be included in the Conservative Party manifesto.[77] The pledge was not the consequence of effective lobbying but a rolling commitment, and the new Prime Minister continued his predecessor's policy.

The second period of the campaign, which started after the 1992 General Election coincided with Peter Lloyd's tenure in the Home Office.[78] Lloyd was a respected parliamentarian, widely liked across the parties, and less partisan than his predecessors. The modest Conservative victory at the General Election confirmed full deregulation was impossible. Under Lloyd the policy community was broken apart. As external circumstances changed, government recognised it could not negotiate a settlement. The imperative of the Lloydian period was to create a policy to deliver a choice between effective and workable, but wholly different, reform options.[79]

The insider–outsider distinction dissolved. Officials needed partners in interest groups with whom they could talk formally and informally to construct choices. Government demanded Parliament make a positive choice rather than a negative one. The object of the exercise was to ensure the Bill reflected what the groups required. Civil servants did not question the views of groups or whether the options were workable. The Home Office found a willingness to negotiate in OPEN, RSAR and the SHRC, irrespective of under-pinning political differences. Lobbying ministers became irrelevant because government had opened the door. Civil servants were working for the main groups. It was the first Government Bill where officials and parliamentary counsel were loaned to interest groups to design law. Ministers wanted deregulation, but they wanted the issue settled even more.

KSSC focused on government too long after the focus had shifted to Parliament. It saw conspiracy everywhere. It did not believe the Home Office tried to put a workable regulatory option in the Bill. KSSC had become accustomed to opposition and wasted energy worrying about the politics being played by government when, in the second stage, there was none.

Conclusion

Before 1992 government undeniably provided SHRC with privileged access to the policy community in exchange for it leading the public campaign for liberalisation. There was an inner and an outer circle (a primary and a secondary community). The primary community was small. The secondary community was bigger and involved consultation, but little influence. In the Lloydian period lobbyists were unnecessary for access to the primary community because the government was open. Lobbyists cannot take credit for SHRC's position during the policy community core in phase one either, because SHRC was in league with government.

The history of closeness and exclusion in the pre-Lloydian period conditioned players' expectations in the Lloydian period. SHRC and ministers formed bonds before 1992 because their goals converged and KSSC was actively excluded because of its aims, in a way that was less true subsequently. After 1992 KSSC preferred to think of itself as the downtrodden victim of conspiracy. Its failure to compromise or develop a workable solution (and its unwillingness to let anyone help) was fatal. Lobbyists played little role in helping their clients access the network but did manage their clients' activity effectively. Groups are more effective if they are in the policy community.

Multi-faceted lobbying

Parliament

All sides targeted Parliament. Sympathetic MPs initiated Early Day Motions (EDMs), questions and debates. Up to 1992 SHRC concentrated on Tory MPs, whilst KSSC held together an influential coalition of backbench Labour and Conservative MPs. SHRC's campaign to broaden its appeal led it to a multi-party lobbying strategy.

A backbench Labour MP tabled a Private Member's Bill in January 1993 which re-introduced an earlier KSSC-drafted Ten Minute Rule Bill.[80] The Bill presented a challenge to SHRC, and SHRC-friendly MPs tabled over 100 technical amendments at report stage, some drafted by the lobbyist, GJW. Angela Rumbold, MP, led the campaign and co-ordinated SHRC's 'parliamentary pushers', and the Bill was defeated. Lobbyists relied on procedural knowledge to achieve this, and the retailers' concern that the campaign was too low-profile proved unwarranted.[81] A public campaign would have unsettled the Home Office. Lobbyists knew that parliamentary procedure provided them with the opportunity to defeat the Bill without delivering KSSC publicity.

KSSC also lobbied MPs and it benefited from feedback from informal discussions between members and ministers. 'An enormous number of MPs were willing to go to the wall' for KSSC.[82] However, whilst it might not have lacked 'heavy-weight' support on the backbenches, it did lack the support of party elites.

Political parties

KSSC held over 500 constituency meetings and supported the Christian Election Forum, which pressured candidates on religious issues such as Sunday trading. Some vulnerable candidates committed themselves, if elected, to vote against Sunday trading.

Retailers had a strong presence at party conferences. A senior retailer argued that: 'the purpose [of being there] is not necessarily to influence MPs; you have dinners and lunches with MPs but you can do that easily in Westminster. It is to create the right climate amongst party members and local councillors.'[83] If one group attended, the others felt obliged to. OPEN found attendance a 'soul destroying experience' but being there was important because 'if everyone else is there you have to be there'.[84] The GJW lobbyist argued: 'if you are involved in a campaign, a healthy presence at party conference shows you are on the map. We knew if we weren't there KSSC would be.'[85] Attending conference seemed to be worthwhile to raise profile and to influence grassroots party opinion.

Media

The media enthusiasm for deregulation cannot be credited to SHRC lobbyists. Support dated back to Baroness Trumpington's 1981 Bill and had been strong during the 1985 Shops Bill. SHRC pushed at an open door. The journalistic support for liberalisation created a context in which it was easier for politicians to make SHRC-friendly decisions.

Support may have been the consequence of journalistic work patterns, or pressure on editors from proprietors and retailers.[86] Newspapers supported liberalisation because it was popular with the public. The tabloid press supported Sunday trading. The *Sun* wrote: 'The government must immediately legalise Sunday opening. Religious fanatics and stroppy unions preventing us from shopping when we want must be ignored.'[87] Similarly, the *Sunday Mirror* published the names of all 144 MPs who voted against an SHRC-sponsored Private Member's Bill and encouraged readers to complain.

KSSC struggled to get its agenda adopted by the national media. Whilst the *Daily Telegraph* and *Evening Standard* were supportive, KSSC would have been helped by an education campaign by professionals in the media. The media was biased against KSSC and it was portrayed as a collection of killjoys. KSSC found the local press more amenable because 'a local newspaper struggles to find material...to fill the pages. If we prepared articles and sent them to the local newspapers, they were delighted to publish them.'[88]

Lobbyists' contacts helped them place stories, but the media represented the 'new consumerism' and reflected opinion polls showing the popularity of Sunday shopping. The press linked its agenda to social trends and the shift of opinion within Labour.

Public opinion

Public opinion was the most valuable and difficult form of support to generate. Lobbyists stirred up support in the constituencies; however, there were no 'real' grass-roots organisations, despite the term being widely used. This campaign activity has been characterised by US observers as 'astro-turf' lobbying; it is artificial and manufactured but looks like the real thing.

SHRC established a variety of front bodies, including the All-Party Group on Sunday Trading; Council Leaders in Favour of Sunday Shopping; and purported grass-roots organisations such as Working Women for Sunday Trading, Consumers for Sunday Trading and the Sunday Shopping campaign. These campaign groups exaggerated the issue's electoral salience. However, SHRC was out-manoeuvred by KSSC which used its Church network, circulating draft sermons, parish newsletters, correspondence and signature campaigns. It leafleted customers about stores that broke the law and wrote to clergymen to encourage their congregations to write to MPs, causing SHRC to mail Britain's 18 000 clergymen.

SHRC established a network of regional organisers, and constituencies were targeted to buttress the London-focused campaign. The regional campaigners, a group of amateur politicians, were assisted by over 400 local voluntary co-ordinators. A 'Sunday Shopping Bus' toured the country and a 'sign-up' campaign collected one million signatures. SHRC companies orchestrated their employees and customers to write to MPs, with store managers helping their staff to write letters that looked 'diverse and heart-felt'.[89]

Retailers were advantaged by their closeness to the consumer with whom they built an alliance. There was an extensive programme of getting MPs in the stores. GJW lobbied prospective candidates in key seats and invited them to local stores. KSSC, RSAR and OPEN all wrote to MPs in whose constituencies they had a presence and invited them to members' stores.

SHRC commissioned 37 polls, and found consistent majorities of two-thirds favouring Sunday trading. In the run-up to the government Bill's Second Reading the media were bombarded with polls. A final crescendo of lobbying culminated in National Sunday Shopping Day in September 1993.[90]

Lobbyists helped mobilise public opinion, and MPs were sensitive to opinion polls.[91] The tactical value of polls was not lost on the deregulation lobby; they provided a peg on which to hang news stories. Surveys helped form and lead public opinion and were mutually reinforcing.

Conclusion

Lobbyists were active on several fronts. However, effective lobbying, especially on issues of conscience, was built outside London in the constituencies. KSSC used the church network and invited MPs, whilst SHRC used its stores to lobby MPs. SHRC also ran a media strategy based on opinion polls, the uneven application of the law, and consumer demand. A multi-faceted approach was used by all groups in this campaign and was a pre-requisite for an effective campaign. Whilst one route may be pre-eminent, such as constituency lobbying, other avenues were pursued concurrently.

Micro-level

Routines and procedures

Rules and procedures are learned through experience. Informal rules and the rhythm of policy-making are difficult to learn by simple observation. A premium was placed on those who had worked within government. After the 1986 defeat and until 1992, a knowledge of civil service and government procedures was important. Civil servants were involved in formal consultation with groups and drafting the legislation. Government was the focus of lobbying. SHRC had the advantage in the first phase because it hired advisers with knowledge and experience of the civil service procedure.

After 1992, knowledge of parliamentary procedure became important as the focus shifted away from government. Civil servants were 'used to a situation where they advise the minister and they drive through legislation on a three-line whip. They were not very good at understanding the mood of the House – what would work and what would not.'[92]

It is useful to distinguish between lobbying aiming to shape 'political policy' and that focusing on technical points. Different types of lobbying require different techniques. Officials are amenable only to intellectual argument about issues of probability and risk, especially exposure of their minister. Despite the fact that SHRC's lobbyists knew the rules and were effective in delivering the perception of widespread support, the Home Office could not deliver legislation because it risked exposing the government. For Home Office ministers to accept political risk in proposing Sunday trading they required lobbyists to 'deliver': to lobby other ministers, MPs and others to build support. Though GJW and SHRC knew their way around Whitehall, they could not deliver support.

SHRC's greater resources allowed it to buy a greater level of expertise than KSSC. Knowledge of procedure allowed SHRC lobbyists to operate with confidence, but there is little evidence to suggest the lobbyists' knowledge of rules helped their clients. The issue was so general, and (later) the process so transparent, that effective lobbying did not require knowledge of technical or complex procedures.

There was little that was arcane or mysterious in the work of officials, but understanding the internal mechanisms of organisations was important. Miller argues that 'friends in high places are no match for an understanding of the mechanics of the decision-making process' because government must justify its decisions and prove it has consulted widely.[93] SHRC's knowledge of procedure, rules and rhythm was essential during the first phase, allowing it to maintain pressure on ministers. These rules were either learned through insider experience, or developed by lobbyists as they dealt with the system.

Conclusion

SHRC lobbyists knew the personalities and the informal rules. Many had worked within the system, which enhanced their effectiveness. KSSC lobbyists did not 'work the system' as effectively as their opponents. With some exceptions their staff and advisers had not worked in the civil service or the political arena; they were outsiders in experience and contacts.

Contacts and coalitions

Contacts

Contacts are an additional research attribute for lobbyists: they deliver information. They are the lobbyists' unique selling point. Government contacts were valuable between 1986 and 1992. Parliamentary contacts became more important after 1992. Contacts were insufficient to persuade decision-makers of the merits of a case, but they provided the intelligence necessary for effectiveness.

SHRC had access to the people who were making the decisions within the political parties. Lobbyists' contacts helped SHRC access the Labour Party. Lobbyists organised contact-building programmes, acted as an introductory service, picked off key individuals, built relationships and explained internal party politics. SHRC networked furiously: it 'worked hard at developing a contact list. Everywhere we went, they appeared. It was like Hitchcock in his films.'[94]

SHRC had a good relationship with the Conservative Party, and to many looked like a Conservative club. Conservative insiders (the Party's Treasurer and former Central Office employees), advised by Conservative strategists, were managed by a steering committee of Conservative businessmen led by a chief executive claiming to be on first-name terms with two-thirds of the Cabinet. Information rarely came from officials, but more often from ministers at social occasions. Intelligence was 'good because there were quite a few ministers that were sympathetic and they were helpful in keeping us in the picture'.[95] This Conservative bias became a liability after 1992, when SHRC donned a Labour cloak provided by Baroness Jay. GJW claimed Labour spokesmen contacted the firm of lobbyists. Party spokesmen would allegedly call and ask, '"I want to learn very quickly about X; have you got someone I can have a meeting with?" If they trust you to do that, it proves you are effective.'[96]

However, access to ministers was not the consequence of effective lobbying. Ministers 'never refused to see anybody'.[97] A civil servant suggested: 'Peter Lloyd was very available to the groups – he would see all of them.'[98] Similarly, other lobbyists argued access to ministers was 'easy'.[99] But KSSC's relations with ministers remained frosty. KSSC described Home Office ministers as like 'Rottweilers being tamed'.[100]

Civil servants were anxious to know the internal politics of the different lobbies. The civil service was active in dealing with interest groups, so the groups did not have to fight for access. SHRC was locked into the civil service and had excellent intelligence. Civil servants briefed SHRC in off-the-record discussions away from the Home Office. However, when SHRC set up meetings with civil servants, it 'always used to take the GJW lobbyist with us, or [he] would set up the meeting and he would go. He would be instrumental in setting them up.'[101] The relationship between SHRC and Home Office paralleled the relationship between the farmers and the Ministry of Agriculture, Fisheries and

Food. Producer interests, claiming to speak for the public interest, were permitted easy access to policy formulation.

KSSC's access to Whitehall varied. It was good during the Powell Bill and KSSC believed it was given a 'fair hearing' by civil servants, but never believed the civil service was neutral. KSSC was tolerated rather than having a real impact. One KSSC adviser argued meetings with civil servants 'were always unpleasant. It was never an equal meeting of minds.'[102] OPEN developed a more effective rapport with Home Office officials. Their lobbyist spoke 'on a daily basis with the Home Office drafting team ... [the official] felt he could have an impartial conversation with [the lobbyist] about the issues. There was a two-way flow of information.'[103]

Good contacts were essential. Closed networks were difficult to enter. Conservative and Labour contacts allowed access to the key party networks.

Coalitions

The debate over whether lobbyists should focus on allies or adversaries continues.[104] SHRC lobbyists undermined KSSC by recruiting those initially opposed to SHRC, such as trade unions. Groups manoeuvred to strengthen themselves, undermine their opponents and jockeyed to build alliances. For either side to emerge victorious it had to persuade a parliamentary majority that it was representative of mainstream thought. That meant constructing a broad coalition. SHRC was more effective at portraying its option as a quintessential compromise.

Trade unions. SHRC split the trade union USDAW away from KSSC. Whilst the Labour front-bench supported SHRC, backbench support was disparate. USDAW would deliver enough Labour support for SHRC to ignore the obstructive Sabbatarian Conservative MPs. SHRC turned USDAW by:

- portraying KSSC as religious extremists and separating the goals of KSSC and USDAW (the religious and the social case);
- convincing USDAW leaders they could trust SHRC;
- exerting pressure on USDAW;
- mobilising the workforce against the union;
- opening stores to 'prove' demand for Sunday trading.

USDAW was never comfortable with its association with KSSC's religious element. KSSC needed USDAW to avoid perceptions of religious extremism. However, KSSC's separation of the Biblical and labour

elements paid insufficient attention to employment issues, thus opening a chink in KSSC's armour. In February 1992 KSSC abandoned
employment provisions in the Powell Bill to broaden its parliamentary
appeal and made overtures towards RSAR. KSSC's move threatened
USDAW's interests.

SHRC used support from the General and Municipal Boiler-Workers'
Union, the Transport and General Workers' Union and the Manufacturing, Science and Finance Union to convince USDAW to leave KSSC. SHRC
opposed the Employment Bill to protect its coalition-building with
USDAW. It feared Sunday trading could be seen as part of a strategy that
left workers vulnerable. The Department of the Environment (DoE)
refused employment concessions necessary to secure USDAW support.
To compensate, SHRC offered voluntary employment protection whilst
KSSC ignored the issue.

Tesco's role in USDAW's volte-face was vital. Tesco was asked 'to
have a go at USDAW'.[105] Tesco co-operated closely with USDAW and
helped it recruit. In 1993 USDAW needed Tesco's support to conduct a
re-authorisation exercise to guarantee its income. Although there was
no direct threat of non-cooperation, USDAW came under indirect pressure: 'It was said to us as a caution, there was never anything specific.'[106]
Because USDAW had a large percentage of its assets (union members) in
one company the leadership was susceptible to pressure.

Tesco informed employees that USDAW was not representing their
interests. Staff petitions flooded the union. USDAW's leadership met its 96
Tesco shop stewards in mid-1993 and was told its policy was untenable.

Finally, USDAW realised its policy of opposition to liberalisation
would lead to total defeat. Workers were keen to work. Consumer
demand was evident and stores were trading. The leadership formalised
its support for SHRC weeks before the government's Bill appeared.

Whilst the votes of USDAW-sponsored MPs were not affected by the
union's new policy, the Parliamentary Labour Party (PLP) more generally moved to support SHRC. A mixture of stick and carrot turned
USDAW. The union's capture was a political coup for SHRC and holed
KSSC. It was the most important development of the campaign.

Coalitions between groups.   SHRC made limited compromises by drop-
ping full deregulation early on, then moving from eight to six hours.
These compromises broadened the number of SHRC supporters, but did
not allow for alliances with other groups. One interest group described
the SHRC as 'Mafia hitmen', arguing that the principal 'could have got
people to do things to our business ... He was just that sort of person.'[107]

In spite of these skirmishes, the key developments in inter-group politics took place within the 'regulation lobby'.

KSSC was forced onto weak ground by contradictions in its proposals, and at every stage it acted too slowly to prevent its support haemorrhaging. In December 1991, under commercial pressure, KSSC retailers opened their stores on Sundays. The coalition began to crack as KSSC retailers fled to RSAR. There was also pressure on KSSC to compromise from government and its business supporters. Aware of its diminishing support, KSSC began formal talks with RSAR in July 1993 and later abandoned its central policy by accepting pre-Christmas Sunday trading. Despite these discussions, the Sunday Trading White Paper contained four options: deregulation, SHRC, RSAR and KSSC.

Having danced and spat at one another for so long, only days before the government's Bill was published KSSC, OPEN and RSAR merged. Their options would be presented as one. OPEN and RSAR moderated KSSC by pulling it away from an extreme position. At the time the move was seen as a masterstroke, but it produced a fudged policy. By merging, the groups conceded their proposals could not individually secure a majority, and they hoped an amalgam of their ideas could muster support to defeat deregulation. The late concessions destroyed the regulators' integrity.

Conclusion

Contacts with MPs were important because there was a scramble for the last available vote. Personal friendships were used to gain access, to obtain information, and to ask questions. SHRC hired lobbyists who understood the parties' policy-making systems. The SHRC's Conservative bias, initially important, changed as it needed to influence opinion within Labour. KSSC's political contacts were less effective. Contacts with civil servants and government were less relevant.

Whilst coalitions were important, lobbyists played little role in building coalitions. Groups sought to attract the support of MPs who were predisposed to opposition. SHRC was more successful than KSSC at lobbying its opponents. KSSC was ineffective in protecting and broadening its constituency. The regulators' coalition came together too late and in desperation. The regulators' lack of will, expressed in their dilatoriness in coming to a deal, their lack of drive, and their reluctance to provide adequate resources, prophesied their defeat.

Resources

Resources, whether financial, human or geographical, were important. *The Economist* noted that 'millions are being spent on lobbying. The alliances are waging fierce campaigns.'[108] The imbalance in financial resources between the two interest groups was significant.

The John Lewis Partnership, USDAW and Milwards were the main funders of KSSC. KSSC was a charity run on a shoe-string: 'It never had the resources or the management skills to construct the sort of lobbying campaign that might have had an effect.'[109] Though KSSC thought it could do without lobbyists, a more convincing reason for the lack of professional assistance was insufficient resources. KSSC 'got reasonable funding from retailers and trade unions and more from the churches. But it takes a lot of £5 donations from members of churches to compare with the millions [of the SHRC].'[110]

KSSC relied on part-time volunteers who were not driven by the motivations and management techniques of the corporate world. Because KSSC was based on charity, voluntarism and faith, inefficiency and mental rigidity were the price of these staff. Despite most staff working on a semi-volunteer basis, SHRC's private investigators estimated that KSSC staffing and occupancy costs for two offices exceeded £800 000 per annum. A more likely figure was a peak of £350 000 a year with a norm of £2–300 000.[111] Although high-calibre volunteers offset KSSC's financial weakness, as the campaign moved into a war of attrition the lack of funds undermined its effectiveness.

Multiple retailers spent millions of pounds funding SHRC, hiring lobbyists, forming front organisations and sponsoring legal challenges. GJW acknowledged high funding levels were important because 'we needed to do a lot of polling to track attitudes...We needed to have campaigns in the stores and a high visibility because...the people in favour of doing something are the worst people at bothering to be counted.'[112] Resources helped motivate people. SHRC lobbyists used the internal resources of the retailers and their managers. Their strategies depended on the resources of huge commercial organisations. The companies ran grass-roots campaigns, devised by lobbyists in London. Store managers lobbied MPs locally. 'There was a sea change the moment the retailers began to devote internal resources, both in terms of a campaign manager, funding for materials and a determination that they were going to involve people on the ground.'[113]

SHRC's resources allowed it to raise its profile. Its lavish campaign was down-graded at times to avoid offending Labour politicians. KSSC estimated 25 per cent of the time of retail branch managers was dedicated to promoting Sunday trading, which 'adds up to millions of pounds worth of man hours. I have privately estimated that they spent at least £60 million on that campaign.'[114] SHRC estimated it spent £6 million.[115]

Even if SHRC accounts existed, they would not reflect the true cost of its campaign.

SHRC, unlike KSSC, could purchase professional specialists. OPEN retained close links with its members to ensure funding.[116] RSC charged a below-market rate because the food-retail sector was an area they could exploit. They serviced OPEN as a 'loss leader' to win new business.[117]

RSAR resources were low compared to the SHRC. Marks & Spencer 'made a contribution of between £100 000 and £200 000',[118] but its campaign lasted only a few months. The RSAR coordinator argued that: 'effectiveness does not depend on resources. Of each hour spent I would like to think lobbyists are as effective over one hour, as they are over 25 hours. But, you can do very little in one hour. If you have money you can buy more hours.'[119]

The economic power of the big retailers was significant and intimidated ministers. One minister said: 'Dick Greenbury was frightfully rude to me and... [asked] why I was being so stupid?'[120] Similarly, Tesco's Chief Executive 'used bully-boy tactics of shouting'.[121] After their conversations with ministers, senior retailers:

> picked up the telephone and rang someone further up the line and said 'that bloody person is getting in our way'. To what extent I was supported I have no idea. The big boys try and trample over government to get their own way. Does it work? Sometimes it does, yes.[122]

Conclusion

The financial resource disparity was significant, whilst the human resource disparity was less obvious. SHRC hired professional advisers whilst KSSC could not. SHRC's strategy utilised the considerable resources of client companies, allowing it to fight on several different fronts. KSSC used the Church's support and the network of congregations to counter the SHRC's regional campaign. Until 1993, USDAW also provided KSSC with a national reach. KSSC's ineffectiveness was caused by the lack of large-scale financial backing and enforced and purchased human resources. SHRC's greater resources aided its effectiveness.

Low-profile outsider tactics

Lobbyists will tend to be effective if they pursue low-profile 'external' tactics.

Another proposition, not discussed in Chapter 3, reflects the failure of the existing literature to recognise the use of low-profile external tactics. Both the main groups pursued low-profile external strategies to increase pressure for action. The SHRC, frustrated at government impotence, supported its retail members in breaking the law. KSSC, enraged by its 'exclusion' from the real centre of policy-making, turned to Europe.

'Legal lobbying'

SHRC retailers, as a corporate policy, coordinated opening times to orchestrate a legal challenge. They launched a comprehensive assault on the Shops Act 1950 based on spurious defences.[123] It was more economic for retailers to open and pay fines rather than obey the law. Their disregard for the law made the Shops Act unenforceable.

The challenge was a sham. It was, however, effective because the complex and fast-moving legal position allowed large retailers to manufacture a 'culture of normality'. SHRC hoped to reform the law by ensuring it was vigorously enforced, thereby mobilising the dormant public majority. But, there was no 'vigorous enforcement' of the Shops Act because legal challenges caused chaos, allowing *de facto* deregulation and the more conservative food retailers to enter the fray.

From November 1991 the Sunday trader was effectively free from prosecution pending an European Court of Justice ruling. The legal process was neutralised. There were various themes to the legal campaign.

First, retailers appealed to the European Court of Justice (ECJ), alleging Section 47 of the Shops Act 1950 was a measure having an equivalent effect to a quantitative restriction on imports within the meaning of Article 30 of the Treaty of Rome.[124] In three years there were two references to the ECJ on Sunday trading. The first judgement in November 1989 was unclear.[125] The ECJ passed the issue back to national courts to decide.[126] Since UK courts reached conflicting judgements, retailers found guilty were encouraged by uncertainty to appeal. A Crown Court ruling in February 1990 stated local authorities had a duty to prosecute but, only months later, companies successfully argued that the Shops Act contravened the Treaty of Rome.[127] The final decision in the 'Euro-defence' confirmed the Act did not conflict with the Rome Treaty.[128]

Second, enforcement agencies, aware of the impotence of criminal law, resorted to civil injunctions. However, because an ECJ ruling was pending, local authorities risked having to compensate retailers if the Shops Act were subsequently found to breach the Treaty of Rome. In January 1989 injunctions were rejected until the ECJ ruled on the

Article 30 defence. Prosecution was effectively held in abeyance. In July 1990 a permanent injunction was granted against B&Q, which spurred a resumption of injunction applications.[129] However, retailers retrieved their principal weapon – cross-undertakings in damages – in April 1991. Thereafter, because local authorities were required to set aside funds for cross-undertakings, enforcement became financially hazardous. One year later the House of Lords overruled the Court of Appeal, ruling that local authorities seeking injunctions would not be liable for compensation. The matter was referred back to Europe.

Third, local authorities became pawns in the battle between the two main groups. Local authorities were under a duty to prosecute.[130] However, some were reluctant to prosecute because it was unpopular.[131] KSSC threatened local authorities with writs to force prosecution, whilst SHRC criticised strict law enforcers for wasting public funds and threatening jobs. Local government had two concerns: first, the legal costs. Retailers called for lengthy trials to hear evidence, knowing local authorities could ill afford expert witnesses. Local government spending was under ever closer scrutiny because of the Community Charge. The second concern was the risk of cross-undertakings. There was pressure not to seek temporary injunctions if they risked exposing the authority to damages for lost trade. By 1993 around 90 per cent of local authorities had adopted a passive or inactive stance to enforcing the law.[132]

Despite undermining the law, SHRC lobbyists enjoyed good relations with Home Office ministers and officials even though they aided and abetted law breaking. The Euro-defence delayed the administration of justice, allowing traders to trade in breach of the criminal law. This low-profile external strategy produced a procedural quagmire disproportionate to the likelihood of its ultimate success. The tactic was effective: the legal chaos was deliberate, planned and resourced. Breaking the law was perceived to be more effective than lobbying.[133] Legal procedures were used to keep stores open to encourage latent demand. The tactic was a means to an end. It was never likely to succeed, but it created political pressure on government.

Europe

KSSC wallowed in its 'outsider' status and liked being an irritant to government. As a consequence of its 'exclusion' KSSC turned to Europe, where it found the 'issue more in line with Brussels's thinking than Westminster's'.[134] The European Parliament harboured a supportive climate of opinion for KSSC which, with its European allies, sought to outlaw Sunday working through an amendment to Article 4 in the Social Affairs Committee of the European Parliament (EP). The Social Affairs Committee did not adopt the amendment but in December 1990 it advocated that member states should adopt the necessary measures to ensure each worker was, 'in principle', entitled to a free weekend.

The Commission published a draft Directive in October 1990 recommending a minimum one day off in every two weeks. The German delegation proposed the 'weekly day' be Sunday.[135] The compromise read that 'as a rule' the weekly day off should be a Sunday. The following year the Netherlands and Germany proposed that the mandatory 36-hour continuous rest period include Sunday. Though the proposal was included at German insistence, KSSC believed it was its doing: 'we fought like tigers to get the Sunday issue in the working time directive and succeeded'.[136]

The then Employment Secretary, Gillian Shephard, MP, reported: 'there was general acceptance of the proposal that Sunday should "in principle" be the weekly day of rest but should not be obligatory'.[137] The Ministers' meeting in May 1992 agreed Sunday need not be an obligatory day of rest as proposed initially in the Working Time Directive. The phrase 'in principle' allowed the UK leeway. Despite supra-national lobbying and a broad-based coalition transcending national boundaries, the British government neutralised KSSC at the EU level.

Similarly, KSSC's strategy did not have an adverse affect on its relations with the Home Office but weakened its parliamentary support because many Conservative Sabbatarians were Euro-sceptics. Europe was a weapon KSSC was 'forced' to use. Most participants believed the tactic was part of the 'game' to keep pressure on government. KSSC's 'outsider' strategy did not exclude it from the policy process. The European strategy was to be expected and groups used Europe whenever it suited their short-term advantage.

Conclusion

A spectrum of tactics was employed by the interest groups, ranging from insider to outsider. Insider techniques included negotiation and the provision of research data and services for officials. Outsider techniques included lobbying European institutions and the campaign to undermine an Act of Parliament. It may be that low-profile external tactics are only effective if the interest group enjoys good relations with government. Low-profile external tactics are ineffective when deployed by outsider groups, but effective when employed by insider groups.

Conclusions

External variables

A sense of history was important. SHRC was on the crest of the ideological wave: the 'spirit of the age' worked in its favour. There was a gradual erosion of KSSC's ideas. Party ideology also played a significant role because SHRC did not have to lobby government for its case to be accepted. Deregulation was fashionable to Conservatives, and SHRC linked its policy to liberty and freedom whilst, for Labour, SHRC promoted consumer sovereignty. The government grew in confidence as memories of the 1986 defeat faded. A turnover in backbenchers gave government more confidence. As a consequence of the government's smaller majority after 1992, policy-making was devolved to the interest groups, and government became a broker. Government was weak and strength lay with the groups. SHRC effectively promoted its solution, whilst KSSC was more effective in its oppositional mode; it was ineffective in an inclusive process. The Labour Party's shift was also significant. Eighty-nine Labour MPs helped to pass the Sunday Trading Bill in 1994. Labour modernised itself, and Tony Blair as Shadow Home Secretary portrayed the party as consumer-friendly and 'modern'; he supported SHRC. The high number of Labour Scottish front-benchers, and the 1992 intake of modernisers, helped SHRC. The workforce and society had evolved. Millions of people worked on Sundays, the majority of married women worked and the UK was irreligious.

Internal variables

Within the interest groups professional lobbyists were not dominant. Full-time officials ran the campaigns. Industry leaders were policy drivers. Lobbyists were strategic advisers. Lobbyists facilitated SHRC's access to Labour, and lobbied MPs directly as well as facilitating contact with MPs and providing intelligence. After 1992 government contacts became less relevant because the policy community was made transparent. Because SHRC consisted of staff who were also professional politicians and campaigners, it is difficult to separate their closely-entwined roles. The lobbyists' understanding of procedure was somewhat important in Parliament, but civil servants were open and ready to help groups, so this resource became less important.

KSSC's inability to form a broad front was deleterious. It failed to maintain and expand its coalition. SHRC's success lay in compromise which, although appearing to be a concession to Sunday sensibilities, was congruent with what retailers suspected the market would tolerate.[138]

USDAW's turn was a political coup. Top-down and bottom-up pressure coordinated by SHRC, Tesco directors and employees coincided with customers shopping. USDAW delivered SHRC Labour backbench support. SHRC deprived KSSC of middle-ground support from trade unionists, Labour MPs and shop-workers.

Lobbying was complex and multi-faceted, but in the Lloydian period it concentrated on the constituency link. Therefore although one approach was more effective and dominant, other tactics were used. The companies mobilised their staff and customers to contact MPs.[139] There was a campaign to get MPs into stores and use the media and opinion polls. The mail-bag was important on a free vote. The ability to stimulate hand-written letters to MPs was potent.

The disparity between the resources of the groups was notable. Though KSSC had volunteer workers, the resources of SHRC clients enabled it to run an effective regional and national campaign, hire lobbyists, advertise, and fund ECJ cases. The legal challenges were important. Opening stores whetted consumers' appetites. SHRC aided and abetted law-breaking by adopting a strategy designed to undermine the law, which spawned *de facto* deregulation, changing habits and expectations. Once retailers had started trading, KSSC could not put the genie back into the bottle.

Lobbying on Sunday trading was atypical. The issue was initially intensely political. The focus of lobbying shifted from government to Parliament as circumstances changed. Government moved from searching helplessly for a solution in a web of interacting groups to a passive role where policy development was handed to interest groups. Parliament was given a genuine choice.

The issue was long-fought and high-profile. *The Times's* sketchwriter wrote: 'In the public galleries sat legions of professional lobbyists. Talk about shopworkers' rights, but what about lobbyists' rights? *Any* outcome to this debate doomed hundreds of these to unemployment'.[140]

Lobbyists were not important; they were minor players. External variables determined the outcome, including social change, government majority, Labour Party modernisation, and new unionism. Context was key. Internal variables (including resource disparity, the ability to construct and maintain coalitions, the ability to mobilise wider opinion and the media, contacts, knowledge of procedure and low-profile external measures) mattered, but operated within a wider environment in which contextual factors held sway.

Lobbyists consistently over-estimated their impact. A civil servant believed: 'lobbyists always claimed success even it if was in the natural course of events. You can claim anything as a lobbying success.'[141] In the 1987–92 Parliament KSSC was successful in preventing change, but it failed in the long-term largely because it was politically naive. Though it was tenacious and built up ferocious loyalty, KSSC could not extend its reach outside its minority parliamentary and public supporters. Because of its earlier exclusion, KSSC's lack of objectivity and its inflexibility infuriated potential allies. The rickety concordat, which existed for a brief moment in April 1986, could not be maintained over the longer term. That government had to wait seven years to legislate, and then do so with a free vote on an 'options bill', does not prove KSSC's influence but rather shows that government and SHRC had to wait for the context to change.

After 1992, external factors favoured SHRC and disadvantaged KSSC. Changes within Labour, a changing society and a narrow government majority helped SHRC. It negotiated with decision-makers, and was engaged in a partnership. Its policies were congruent with government objectives, so government readily accepted SHRC's use of external tactics. SHRC adapted to changing circumstances by compromising and broadening its appeal.

5
The Failure of CrossRail

This chapter examines a middle-profile policy issue. CrossRail was a proposed railway under central London to link Paddington and Liverpool Street Stations. After a tortured birth CrossRail was rejected by Parliament. This chapter focuses on the initial decision to approve the scheme and the subsequent battle to stop it. It examines the stop–start nature of CrossRail's progression, and explains that whilst government's policy did not change, in practice Treasury hostility, weak political commitment and ineffective lobbying undermined the flagship scheme.

To understand the policy-making process, it is necessary to set the period in context. London Regional Transport (LRT) became a nationalised industry in 1984 when control was transferred from the Greater London Council (GLC) to the Department of Transport (DTp).[1] The DTp had grown rapidly, and faced intense pressure over transport infrastructure.[2] It was keen to prove itself. After years of decline, the population of London unexpectedly began to grow in the 1980s; thus, public transport congestion became a policy problem. There was a 'dramatic mood for change'.[3] The DTp's glib answer was to instruct London Underground Limited (LUL) and British Rail (BR) planners to identify cost-effective improvements to relieve congestion.[4] So panic, a need for information, and the desire to avoid spending money motivated the Central London Rail Study (CLRS). One Treasury official admitted it was 'an excuse for not being able to do something now, which is a common response in government'.[5] CLRS bought short-term peace at the expense of increased medium-term pressure. CrossRail's profile was subsequently heightened when ministers published the study.

CLRS articulated the case for transport improvement more effectively than either BR or LUL alone could have: 'It helped their position because a reputable group had come up with these conclusions and this information was in the public domain.'[6] The study was in effect a quasi-consultation paper; it proposed an upgrading programme and three schemes to ease east–west axis congestion, one of which was CrossRail.[7]

Interest groups and lobbyists

Those promoting and opposing CrossRail used lobbyists. CrossRail used public money to employ a lobbyist to help it make its case in Parliament and public and to get around the Treasury. Ian Greer Associates (IGA) was hired to assist the in-house public affairs team. The parliamentary office accounted for half the entire project. It included petition managers, lawyers and draftsmen. Around seven staff lobbied politicians and government at every level. The remit of the in-house team was unclear. One recalled: 'when I arrived they did not know what public affairs or government relations was. They wanted me to do reactive work.'[8] Their IGA lobbyist concurred: 'public affairs people were brought in whenever there was a problem or a crisis and were told what needed to be done'.[9] There was, however, a need for assistance because of the lack of support from key opinion formers within government. The minister recognised the value of the lobbyist: 'The professional lobbyist was there to advise an organisation which are [sic] (London Transport is an example) good at what they do, but they are not necessarily adept at identifying which MPs would have an interest and who ought to be brought on'.[10]

CrossRail's lobbyists were required to maintain a high-profile for the project as well as provide basic services such as 'intelligence gathering and monitoring at European, national, regional and local level as appropriate [and] advice on parliamentary procedure and convention'.[11]

CrossRail demanded 'a specialist consultancy with an understanding of major public service infrastructure projects and the empowering legislative procedure. This is targeted at the parliamentary field.'[12] Following a competitive pitch IGA was hired to:

- have CrossRail designated a scheme of 'national significance' by the Secretary of State for Transport;[13]
- minimise opposition to the project at both national and local levels;
- progress through the Transport & Works Act (TWA) process;
- build public and private support from the Treasury for CrossRail;
- build confidence on the part of the potential financial backers that there was sufficient parliamentary and Government support.[14]

IGA was hired because it seemed to have good credentials, and knew the relative importance of people who needed to understand what the project offered.[15] Charles Barker provided public relations support. Burson-Marsteller ran the CrossRail Coalition. Shandwick advised the City of London Corporation (supporting CrossRail was part of its survival strategy). Tower Hamlets, which opposed CrossRail, hired GJW and later Market Access (now called GPC International).

Macro-level

Profile, technicality and politicality

The CrossRail concept had lain dormant in London Transport's archives for years, but was reactivated by the six-week CLRS. It was a technical proposal, but had wider political implications. It had low-profile and high-profile elements. Overall, lobbyists had little impact. Apart from undertaking a basic political audit of CrossRail's supporters they were invisible to civil servants and ministers. A former minister said: 'I was not even aware of who was lobbying for London Transport. They certainly played no part in any of the machinations I was involved with.'[16] He argued: 'nobody in the department was interested in who was lobbying for what. We were all entirely consumed with what the economics were and what the logistics were.'[17]

The minister believed IGA 'failed to anticipate the dangers that I too failed to anticipate. I do not regard that as dreadfully culpable.'[18] Lobbyists helped their client by advising them on parliamentary machinations, but had no impact on policy outcome. A senior Treasury official argued that lobbyists had no impact on CrossRail.[19] Another felt lobbyists were 'utterly unimportant' and 'did not impinge' on policy.[20] Lobbying DTp ministers and officials was 'froth' because they were convinced of the case. IGA's parliamentary-based campaign did not challenge the influence of the Treasury. An official closely involved with CrossRail concluded: 'IGA, because of its style, was unhelpful to London Underground. I don't think they did anything for them.'[21] CrossRail was a clumsy campaign. It was unsubtle. 'There were things that were said and done that grated with government. If you annoy the Treasury and the Department of Transport it is not the best way to get the result you want.'[22]

The CrossRail public affairs team was ineffective because 'it had the wrong skills and was drawn from the wrong sources. It made the wrong contacts with decision-formers.'[23] Ministers perceived CrossRail as controversial and did not feel obligated morally.

Whilst decision-makers questioned the value of lobbyists, the client was satisfied with IGA. CrossRail's manager says: 'the lobbyists we used provided value for money'.[24] An in-house lobbyist argued that IGA effectively monitored Parliament, and they helped CrossRail to understand the mood of MPs and provided general advice.[25] CrossRail believed IGA provided 'eyes and ears and manpower. They were able to go out and talk to people. It is too grand a statement to say "they influenced public policy". They helped us put our case.'[26] IGA's remit was to 'identify opinion formers and discreetly lobby them ... their brief was to influence'.[27] When asked whether IGA achieved that brief, the manager replied: 'No, I do not think they did. I am not sure they were the right firm. I was not particularly impressed. The project manager did not know enough to check whether they were really being effective.'[28] The lobbyist was ineffective, and the client incapable of judging its activity.

When asked whether he achieved his client's objectives, the IGA lobbyist answered: 'No. It was impossible to change Treasury's mind.'[29] The lobbyist blamed his ineffectiveness on his client's management structure and competing agendas. His advice was ignored. He produced:

> proposals for CrossRail all of which were read and very little of which was acted upon ... It was the one account where we could never get to see the people at the top, never get to have a frank discussion and never get them to agree the forward strategy.[30]

Conclusion

CrossRail was a technical, low-profile and non-political policy, but lobbying on that basis was ineffective. Lobbyists did not impinge on day-to-day policy-making. They were partly effective in organising limited media and third-party support to engineer short-term political support. CrossRail was initially advantageous to government. The impetus for CrossRail came from within government. However, there was no organised and continuing high-level support for CrossRail. DTp looked for outside assistance.

The lack of a champion doomed CrossRail. To persuade the Treasury to fund a project of this size, CrossRail lobbyists needed to show there was more at stake than the comfort of commuters to the east and west of London. Its technocratic approach crumbled when faced by fickle political fashion. CrossRail and IGA failed to raise CrossRail's profile within government. Its fortunes followed a familiar pattern: initial political enthusiasm, which waned as the focus of political attention moved to other priorities. The absence of a determined champion, and IGA's failure to link CrossRail to government's broader themes and to raise its profile to broaden its appeal, meant that the weight of advocacy fell almost entirely on DTp ministers who lacked influence and, later, interest.

It is possible that lobbyists could have been effective had they taken the low-profile, technical and non-political proposals and found high-profile messages understandable to a wide audience.

External factors

Economics

The squeeze on public expenditure, the battle against inflation and the recession of the early 1990s weakened the case for CrossRail. CLRS was undertaken against a background of financial deregulation and London's blossoming international status. It assumed the growth of the 1980s could be sustained. However, the recession's impact in south-east England was severe. Over five years growth was 0.8 per cent, and rail commuting fell sharply.[31] CLRS's employment projection of 100 000 additional jobs in central London by 2000 was replaced by a 150 000 fall.[32] The economic context reduced the requirement for additional transport capacity. Despite the 1990 Autumn Statement providing for CrossRail, the Treasury hinted the plans would be delayed because of financial uncertainty.[33] In the post-General Election Public Expenditure Survey round the Chancellor admitted there was blood on the carpet because of the recession and the need to restrain the pre-Election spending boom. Although £200 million was earmarked for CrossRail, rail and LUL improvements were dropped.[34] BR's spending plans were cut by half and London Transport's budget was cut by 10 per cent.[35]

Transport expenditure was low priority and an easy target. There was a preference to deflect pressure for spending cuts to capital projects. 'The PSBR [Public Sector Borrowing Requirement] was out of control', recalled one senior official; 'the hunt was on to find money everywhere. We kept saying to ministers "if you want to save money then stop this project".'[36] Whilst the Treasury publicly extolled the project's virtues, it undermined it in private. The 1993 Budget Statement reflected this approach by reaffirming the Treasury's commitment to CrossRail, but announcing a review to determine private-sector finance potential.[37]

CrossRail lobbyists were impotent when faced with government reviews. A review of project cost and opportunities for private-sector involvement in 1993 concluded that CrossRail had no 'fatal flaw' and was well-conceived, being an attractive project to the private sector.[38] Simultaneously, SG Warburg examined options for privatising Cross-Rail, and claimed that around 40 per cent of the capital cost could be privately financed.[39] The Treasury bombarded the promoters with questions about cost and technical details.[40] A Railway Operators' report concluded that CrossRail 'attains a range of benefits going beyond its stated purpose as a transport function', and validated the project for the third time in 12 months.[41] Nevertheless, weeks later the Treasury demanded another study, which aimed to improve cost-effectiveness and reduce public-sector cost.[42] The report played into Treasury hands by noting that CrossRail was 'a visionary project which may be ahead of its time in view of the change in employment and commuting patterns'.[43] It called for CrossRail to be delayed.

These reports were an attempt by the Treasury to stop the policy. 'No matter how good these consultants were, the idea that in 4–6 weeks they could work magic, and find truths that the Secretary of State's agents would not have found in years, is unconvincing.'[44] Although DTp officials described the reports as 'a bit of silliness', they delayed the project long enough for circumstances to change.[45] Treasury ministers, although guilty, were left with no blood on their hands. For the Treasury, 'it was hard to kill CrossRail cleanly when you had public statements from John Major. Given what the Prime Minister had said to the CBI [Confederation of British Industry] it was jolly hard to get a minister to stand up in public and say "we have the authority to kill the CrossRail project"'.[46]

The case for CrossRail, initially strong, weakened as the economy dipped into recession and congestion faded. There was inevitability in the argument against CrossRail: employment in London had been falling for decades and the 1980s were a blip.

Politics

The 1990 local elections took place in remarkable circumstances, because 'the poll tax fiasco was at its full intensity'.[47] The poor state of London's transport system was a factor in the Conservatives' unpopularity. In the 1990 London borough elections the Conservatives and Labour were roughly neck and neck. John Major's intervention to secure CrossRail's Second Reading in Parliament was made against a backdrop of government unpopularity. Senior ministers feared outright rejection would damage Conservative candidates in the May local and June European elections in 1994, and harm the City of London's reputation. The decision enabled the Bill to enter its Committee stage in July 1993. The government supported CrossRail up until these elections.

Disarray in the Conservative parliamentary party caused by Europe, weak leadership and low morale threatened parliamentary business. Withdrawal from the Exchange Rate Mechanism undermined popular and market trust in the government, and the coal-mine closure programme triggered media and popular opposition. The Prime Minister's determination to ratify the Maastricht Treaty convulsed the parliamentary party. Its right wing blamed the Exchange Rate Mechanism for magnifying the recession and, as the party splintered into factions, it grew increasingly nervous because falling unemployment and economic growth failed to deliver political rewards. John Major was wounded and his government vulnerable.

An early sign of Major's fight-back to reassert his authority over a divided Cabinet and party was the decision to reject the pleas of leading right-winger Michael Portillo, Chief Secretary, and to press ahead with CrossRail despite Treasury resistance. The decision indicated a tougher stance in settling Whitehall disputes.

Conclusion

One part of government wanted CrossRail stopped, whilst others promoted it. Despite broad support and DTp advocacy, lobbying by the CrossRail team and other third parties was undermined by the recession. The context changed: the fall in employment challenged CrossRail's rationale. Only one external variable – concern about Conservative performance in local and European elections – reprieved CrossRail temporarily.

Lobbyists did 'not have a lot of power up against the wheels of government ... [and] the Treasury. They were on a hiding to nothing.'[48] IGA was hamstrung. Lobbyists were ineffective because there were disadvantageous contextual constraints beyond government's control.

Experience and existing policy

Before the Treasury rearguard action, CrossRail was approved not because of effective lobbying but because of partisan advantage. In 1988 the Prime Minister chaired a meeting, attended by the Transport Secretary and civil servants, to decide on CLRS priorities. Several reasons explain CrossRail's prioritisation.

First, it was the least bad option because it gave both BR and LUL a 'pet project'. London Transport (LT) alone would have found it difficult to promote an additional scheme, but BR could share the burden. However, CrossRail was the priority of neither: in fact LUL favoured the Chelsea–Hackney Line (CHL) whilst BR favoured ThamesLink. Second, CrossRail was cheaper than CHL. CrossRail cost £870 million, whilst CHL was estimated at £1 billion. Benefit-cost analysis established CrossRail as the stronger project.

Third, party advantage is a convincing explanatory variable. A junior DTp official presented CrossRail to Thatcher rather than the Secretary of State. One official explained: 'She would have been interrupting the Secretary of State all the time. It would have been a barrage of complaints that he had not thought things through.'[49] The discussion progressed:

> Margaret Thatcher just dismissed Chelsea–Hackney with one sweep of her hand, and said, 'Hackney! Hackney! Do you know what sort of people live out in Hackney? They are not Conservative voters! Who wants to go to Hackney? These are not our people! No! Tell me about CrossRail'. And that was it.[50]

LT believe CrossRail was not imposed from politicians or the Cabinet.[51] However, the decision was taken at the highest political level and was based on political calculations. An official commented: 'it is a classic example of where a year's work boiled down to a ten second political prejudice'.[52] Consequently CrossRail was prioritised over the Chelsea–Hackney Line, and then faced competition with the Jubilee Line. The 1980s dilemma of 'Which one first?' had, by the early 1990s, become 'Which one?' The 1980s 'was a happy time in the Department of Transport. We had an enormous roads programme and we had every conceivable railway as a candidate. In our naivety we thought CLRS was additional to Jubilee Line.'[53] Supporters hoped to build the two schemes sequentially.

The 1990s were less happy. CrossRail was introduced only once the Jubilee Line Extension (JLE) Bill had completed its parliamentary stages. DTp then faced the challenge of progressing CrossRail, in the face of Treasury opposition.

Treasury

Understanding the interaction between the Treasury and the DTp is central when assessing the effect of lobbyists. Several factors explain the Treasury's role. First, the dominant operating assumption (that once a project or activity was approved the Treasury would find the required resources) changed. The key objective for departments and lobbyists was to have projects approved. A Treasury official argued: 'once you get an announcement, come hell or high water, you are tied in'.[54] There was a belief in Whitehall that projects which 'could not be afforded one year could be put in the budget in one or two years' time'.[55] The reward system focused on approval and announcement, not on delivery. It encouraged over-emphasis of benefits and under-emphasis of costs and risk.

Whilst there was an assumption that announcements became self-fulfilling, in reality departments would be unwise to claim success until a project was complete because the Treasury could find ways to over-turn decisions. 'Treasury knows, and have been proved right, that many things get announced but not everything that is announced happens. There is no reason why they should give up hope.'[56]

When CrossRail was approved there was no apparent fiscal crisis. Public-sector debt was being repaid. Pressures for flexibility in the planning total and for increased spending were accommodated within a growing GDP. But in the following months, the Treasury, under intense pressure to control public expenditure, moved to block CrossRail. The Treasury's power deepened and widened after 1990. A new planning total was effective from 1989 to 1990. Top-down totals were made to stand, and additional departmental bids ruled out. This new approach reflected the new personalities and priorities of government. John Major was the first ex-Chief Secretary, and one of the few ex-Chancellors, to become Prime Minister. He worked with the Treasury to exclude opportunities for ministers to appeal from one to the other.

The New Control Total meant that the Public Expenditure Survey became more sophisticated and a new Cabinet committee, the Cabinet Committee on Public Expenditure (EDX), imposed decisions upon ministers. When the Transport Secretary appeared at EDX, the Treasury sent 'briefings – not only for our ministers, but also for the other ministers – saying "if you want to save money, here is something to get rid of".'[57] There was an institutional opposition within the Treasury to mega-projects. There was also a clear 'Treasury view'. The Treasury was shielded from, and consequently irritated by, lobbyists. It believed it assessed issues objectively and that ministers decided the 'incommensurables'. Officials saw this 'institutional view' as an aversion to 'bad economics'.[58] The Treasury believes it has no pressure groups, allowing it to act as a catalyst spurring on the spending departments, which resist change because of special interests snapping at their ankles.

The Treasury's relationship with the DTp was arm's-length and mutually suspicious. The Treasury characterised the DTp as producer-led, soft and in its operators' pockets. A Transport official commented: 'Treasury said to me "the problem is that Transport has been the voice of BR in government, as opposed to the voice of government in BR".'[59] The affliction was diagnosed as the 'Today Programme syndrome', which Treasury officials defined by its cure (any problems with government policy could be solved 'by a little bit more of the same and a little bit more money').[60] The Treasury deployed several counter-lobbying tactics.

It pitted DTp projects against one another, by hinting that competing schemes were more viable.[61] It tried to push the DTp past the annual deadline for submitting Private Bills, to buy time to undermine the project. It also used assessments as delaying mechanisms.

The Conservative Government wanted to involve the private sector in major projects. In 1992 a private–public mix was proposed to fund CrossRail. The Autumn Statement changed the rules about public–private cooperation. Norman Lamont, Chancellor of the Exchequer, said: 'the Government will actively encourage joint ventures with the private sector, where these involve a sensible transfer of risk to the private sector. We may be prepared to consider such an approach, when the time arises, for projects such as east–west CrossRail.'[62]

CrossRail became the centrepiece of a strategy to involve private money and expertise in major projects. Although the Private Finance Initiative was floated by the Treasury in 1988, it was officially launched in 1992.[63] PFI abandoned the Ryrie Rules and sought new ways of financing worthwhile public investment outside the Public Expenditure Survey.[64] Whilst DTp projects were promising for PFI, they presented two difficulties. PFI undermined a strategic approach in the pursuit of private money because private-sector cherry-picking weakened government's ability to shape coherent policies. Second, PFI allowed the Treasury to intervene on any significant capital project in the public sector. Because capital projects were easier to postpone than current spending, political priorities dictated that demand-led programmes took precedence. Indeed, the 1992 policy of protecting capital projects 'in the pipeline' was abandoned in 1994.

Departmental agendas

By the early 1990s railway privatisation had moved up the political agenda and had become a higher priority for the deployment of political and financial resources. Privatisation disrupted CrossRail because it was conceived as a publicly-funded scheme; consequently it soon fell outside government's agenda.

The Railways Act (1993) vertically separated the BR network. Following the 1992 White Paper, BR's planning capability was wound down. The privatised network did not provide a framework in which major projects, such as CrossRail, could be identified, developed, planned, financed, implemented and managed. Privatisation prevented systematic consideration of new investment. Thereafter no single railway authority was responsible for developing new projects.

CrossRail complicated privatisation because it linked separate franchises and threatened Railtrack. CrossRail jeopardised Railtrack's flotation because it would have cost more to build than the paper assets of Railtrack. Because asset value affected track charges, Railtrack was desperate to abandon CrossRail. IGA's political communication strategy was challenged because its advice 'had to go through Railtrack's privatisation lawyers to be cleared. Approval or rejection would take days. There was no ability to react swiftly.'[65]

Civil servants neglected new rail projects because the political priority was to produce a workable privatisation schedule. One senior official recalled:

> it was a busy time at the department. There was the biggest ever road building programme, railway privatisation under way, the Channel Tunnel was still not open, the CTRL as well as aviation and shipping issues. There was not the focus on one scheme as there perhaps would be now.[66]

'Departments shift not only numbers of people but also quality of people into interesting areas.'[67] By the early 1990s privatisation had become the 'interesting' area: the talent pool working on new projects was diluted. One former civil servant recalls: 'There was a colossal number of civil servants working on privatisation. The privatisation side was weighed down, and it was very light on new projects. Each was headed by a Deputy Secretary, but one had constant access to the Secretary of State and the other did not'.[68]

The labour-intensive and politically-sensitive privatisation process ran to a tight parliamentary timetable and faced anti-privatisation publicity so that even Conservative MPs had to be dragged kicking and screaming into the lobby to support the Bill. Privatisation coincided with John MacGregor replacing the public-transport-friendly Secretary of State, Malcolm Rifkind. MacGregor, from a country constituency where mobility meant roads and cars, was less willing to fight for CrossRail in the annual public expenditure rounds.

Conclusion

CrossRail began life congruent with government objectives and pre-existing policy. IGA was unable to highlight CrossRail's connections with the government's programme. The Prime Minister and DTp ministers did not have the political arguments to allow them to challenge the Treasury. Treasury intransigence is a key determinant of the policy outcome. The Treasury fought a war of attrition on CrossRail. It 'doggedly fought it all the way. It jumped on every opportunity to cut back

CrossRail's resources. It was not a glorious fight, but Treasury officials believe it was right.'[69] Tension between the DTp and the Treasury increased because of informal and institutional changes in the Treasury, and conflict with political priorities. CrossRail lobbyists were ineffective because political considerations and previous experience impinged.

Meso-level

The policy community

Both 'client' and the 'policy community' were part of government. This case exposes the fiction of a single government view. The CrossRail policy community, centred on the DTp, numbered around 20 government actors. It included officials in grades 7, 5, 3 and 1, and two ministers in the DTp, Treasury and DoE, the Prime Minister and key advisers from the No. 10 Policy Unit.

Not all was well at the DTp. Parkinson, rather like the old lady who witnessed road accidents when out driving, found in 1989 'a department that had felt under siege waiting nervously for the next disaster and the next bout of criticism'.[70] The DTp was not a visionary department: 'the vision came from ministers. Privatisation was their idea. The department was not really in favour of privatisation.'[71] Neither was the department much interested in new railways. One former official argued:

> Transport has never been interested in new rail development or had a great role in it. DTp never really had a transport planning capability. They did on the highways because they are in charge of the national road system, but in terms of other infrastructure, it never had a transport planning capability.[72]

Big public transport projects were also politically unpalatable because they usually took over a decade to deliver, were costly and the electoral rewards were difficult to quantify. The DTp also had two structural weaknesses: limited budgetary autonomy and even less political influence. Its projects became second-best compromises, the outcome of squabbles with Treasury. Outsiders and lobbyists played little role in these machinations.

Although the CrossRail Bill was introduced in November 1991, it did not receive its Second Reading for another 18 months.[73] Lobbying helped the DTp deliver the Second Reading, but failed to see the Bill through Parliament. CrossRail lobbyists worked to a tight deadline to mobilise the policy community. Private Bill legislation delayed after

June 1993 fell under the untested Transport and Works Act (1992). Lobbyists feared it would take five years to pass legislation under this procedure. The objective of the campaign was to discourage the Treasury from opposing CrossRail in Whitehall, or to persuade the Cabinet Committee to overrule the Treasury.

DTp relied on business and local authority support to keep CrossRail alive. John MacGregor appealed directly to the prime minister. Ministers discussed CrossRail in the London Cabinet Sub-Committee (EDL[L]), chaired by the prime minister. An intense political campaign, focused on the prime minister, guaranteed his support despite Treasury opposition. However, a Treasury proviso required 'the private sector be fully involved' and, whilst the full Cabinet approved the prime minister's decision, the victory was hollow because it left unanswered the question of funding.[74] The Treasury had ensured CrossRail proceeded as a joint venture, and the DTp did not at that stage realise was how perilous a joint venture was.

Nevertheless, orchestrating the policy community to pressure Major to deliver his backing was 'a triumph because it raised the political stakes and tied him in. Steven Norris (Minister for Transport in London) used it ruthlessly again and again and directly to John Major.'[75] An alliance of MacGregor, John Gummer (Environment Secretary), Tim Sainsbury (Industry Minister) and Steven Norris defeated the Treasury in the short term. 'It was that committee which kept the commitment going and stopped CrossRail being pushed out. It was a battle between everyone on the sub-committee and the Treasury.'[76]

Among the personalities of the policy network LUL had few friends. Ministers and officials believed LUL demanded many resources but delivered only aggravation. One former minister felt LT 'spent money like water, expected billions from taxpayers, and always gave you a cost over-run in return'.[77] There also was 'a combined view that London Underground was run by a bunch of comedians' and 'as individuals they are second rate'.[78] Even their own ministers lacked confidence in them, arguing: 'Whitehall was jaundiced about London Underground. With justification. They were hopeless.'[79] Treasury ministers in particular were irritated by LUL. 'Kenneth Clarke [Chancellor of the Exchequer] believed London Underground were just a bloated bureaucracy full of lefty do-gooders. He was personally enormously hostile.'[80] A senior LUL executive, probably correctly, believed that Conservative ministers thought his team was 'a bunch of wankers who could not make it in the private sector'.[81]

CrossRail did not lobby civil servants directly, and was reluctant to encourage third parties to lobby. In IGA's 15-page strategy programme, officials merited only two paragraphs. Those paragraphs refer to junior ministers and special advisers. At no point in the document are senior civil servants mentioned. DTp officials dealt only with senior BR and LT managers.

Another significant factor explaining the splintered nature of the policy community was that central government distanced itself from LUL after the 1987 King's Cross fire to emphasise that operational responsibility lay with LUL. LUL recognised it was not well liked. 'It took a long time to build ourselves up. We were the bad guys. We killed thirty-three people. Ministers were happy for us to be distanced on an organisational level.'[82] LUL was found to have been derelict for not bringing to the government's attention its full requirements. Thereafter, because private channels were blocked, LUL presented its case publicly and forcefully, which irritated government.

Conclusion

Lobbyists played little role in policy-making. LT and BR had access to the policy community by virtue of their public-sector status, but their clout and activity were circumscribed. They did not deal with Treasury officials or ministers. Only Transport officials dealt with the Treasury. CrossRail was one place removed from the decisive policy arena. Its case was filtered through BR and LT, then through Transport officials to the Treasury. IGA did nothing to help CrossRail in this environment and did not manage its activity; it was even unable to offer advice on how to act. Whitehall networks were anathema to IGA. Its expertise lay in the personalities and politics of Westminster. The lobbyist was ineffective. It played no role in installing its client in the community, and failed to manage CrossRail's activity in that network.

Multi-faceted lobbying

Parliament

LT asked the DTp to promote CrossRail as a Hybrid Bill, which implied government commitment; but government refused. The Treasury's script was evident from the Private Bill introduction in November 1991. The Deputy Speaker framed the debate around an instruction so the Committee had:

> particular regard to the financial justification for CrossRail in the light of the proposals for the privatisation of British Rail, to the proposed method of financing CrossRail in the light of the Government's announcements that it should be substantially funded by the private

sector, and to its interrelationship with other rail projects across London which have been put forward since the Central London Rail Study was completed [i.e., JLE].[83]

CrossRail targeted MPs on the route and classified them by 'their ability to approach ministers and Opposition spokesmen as individuals with a legitimate interest in CrossRail's success'.[84] Though the network of important Whitehall players was small, IGA recommended a target audience of:

- route MPs;
- Greater London MPs;
- members of pertinent backbench and select committees: Transport, Environment, Trade and Industry, and Treasury;
- other MPs with an appropriate interest: e.g., the M25 Group;
- Parliamentary Private Secretaries to ministers in the four key departments, particularly Transport and the Treasury; similarly, Special Advisers, including those to the Chief Whip in the House of Lords and the Leader of the House of Commons;
- Opposition spokesmen for the four key departments and their research teams;
- Government and Opposition Spokesmen in the House of Lords;
- 63 interested non-route MPs;[85]
- London-based peers, as well as those with an interest in the four key issues;
- councillors on the route, and in London and the south-east more generally.

Parliamentary lobbying was straightforward. The in-house team simply 'dealt with letters and went to public meetings to talk about the project. The project director went to see MPs and other interested groups.'[86] A damning verdict of CrossRail's lobbying was that it admitted most MPs remained 'relatively ignorant' about the scheme and 'did not know anything about it'.[87] IGA briefings and presentations to backbench committees and interested peers and MPs started late, after the Bill's introduction. IGA suggested that after a formal lunch briefing most MPs would refuse to spend time being updated, so IGA urged CrossRail managers to make themselves available in the Commons for 20–30 minutes 'to conduct informal conversations ... on one of the Committee corridors'.[88] Following CrossRail's briefings IGA would verify the effectiveness of its client's lobbying by speaking to MPs briefed by CrossRail to 'identify shortcomings in the briefings'.[89]

CrossRail's internal lobbying guidance recommended MPs be presented with a one-page written brief as an *aide-mémoire*. When encouraging MPs to speak, IGA counselled that 'bullet points [need to be] provided, if not speeches written'.[90] IGA recommended CrossRail organise a reception at the Palace of Westminster to allow discreet selective lobbying of a targeted audience. IGA also recommended 'telephone canvassing to establish likely voting patterns'.[91] It later suggested CrossRail establish a parliamentary 'hotline number' to help MPs answer constituents' problems. During the Bill's parliamentary stages IGA led a 'War Cabinet' to coordinate activity, to little effect. The Bill Committee members were mavericks at odds with the leadership of their respective parties, and the Committee eventually concluded the preamble to the Bill not proved.[92] The MPs were unconvinced by the evidence, irritated by the minister's cavalier attitude, and disturbed by the government's lack of commitment. When it gave its judgement, the committee provided no reasons for its decision.

Although there was a fierce parliamentary campaign to relaunch the project, since the Committee had not acted outside procedure and there had not been a material change in circumstances, the Bill was killed on 5 July 1994. Cabinet decided soon after that CrossRail should proceed through the Transport and Works Act Order, yet in January 1995 CrossRail was delayed indefinitely.[93]

Public and party

There were formal consultation exercises, but no attempt to build a strong public campaign. There was no endeavour to fire public imagination or to build a groundswell of support. IGA believed mobilising public support was dangerous because of the project's nature, arguing with some justification that 'it was difficult for a nationalised organisation to prompt the public to write to government to get something for itself'.[94] IGA did, however, consider party conferences to be an opportunity to 'consolidate the support ... built up over the previous year and to generate post-Summer Recess enthusiasm'.[95] IGA advised that MPs needed their memories refreshed and their resolve inured to support the project. CrossRail had stands and receptions at Labour and Conservative conferences in order to raise its profile, foster high-level political contacts, reach 'target audience' MPs, maintain a position on the political agenda, and meet new MPs and peers.[96] IGA held its own reception at party conferences, where it showed off its contacts to clients. CrossRail was encouraged to attend, because the reception afforded 'a useful opportunity to meet senior politicians in an informal setting'.[97]

Media

LUL's managing director was an ardent briefer of London's newspaper, the *Evening Standard*. The media campaign aimed to persuade the prime minister and ministers of the political advantages of the scheme. IGA's Media Unit claimed to 'assist' CrossRail by pre-empting ill-informed speculation and agreeing a 'line-to-take'.

A press conference was organised to campaign for Second Reading. Material was distributed and journalists briefed in advance. Transport correspondents from national broadsheets were lobbied in writing and by telephone. 'Pegs' were found to hang stories on. London First, which was formed to represent London's businesses (made up of 59 companies), secured a promise of support from the *Evening Standard*'s editor.[98]

The weekend before the Cabinet sub-committee met, stories were placed in Sunday broadsheets, setting the political agenda. London First leaders wrote to *The Times*, and the CBI increased pressure by publicly criticising government, accusing the Cabinet sub-committee of behaving secretively.[99] It is unlikely, however, that positive media coverage was the consequence of effective lobbying. The *Evening Standard* particularly promoted London issues, and its transport correspondent was a supporter in his own right. In fact, the *Evening Standard* campaign may have backfired because it riled Treasury ministers and officials. A senior Treasury official said LT:

> conducted a lobbying campaign, not just on CrossRail but on all their activities, through the *Evening Standard*. Ministers took the view that we are not prepared to reinforce bad behaviour. If people think they can win by slagging us off in the *Evening Standard*, everyone will slag us off in the *Evening Standard*. We don't want that. We want to see people lose if they start slagging us off. If LUL think they can roll us over by hacking at us through newspapers they have got another think coming.[100]

Though this 'Treasury view' appealed to non-Transport members of EDX, DTp informally approved of CrossRail's media campaign. One former political adviser argued:

> If you were me in the Department of Transport wanting to do CrossRail you were thrilled there were people on the bandwagon. You could say in a note to the Prime Minister and copied to the Treasury 'Prime Minister, I am inundated. It is awful. The pressure is relentless.'[101]

LUL recognised that its media strategy risked irritating officials and knew 'it made the Treasury apoplectic'.[102] But, it believed, 'ministers sought to minimise opposition. If you do not heap pain on them they do not notice. The *Standard* helped heap pain.'[103] Ministers read their press cuttings and leaders every morning and were influenced by what they read. The campaign bought a stay of execution; the Treasury was temporarily defeated and the Second Reading assured. The *Evening Standard's* support raised CrossRail's profile, delivered public, local authority and elite political support and isolated the Treasury further.

Conclusion

Parliamentary lobbying for CrossRail was the least difficult form of lobbying, but also the least effective. It was the easy option to tell the client to undertake briefing of MPs and party conference stalls, rather than face the unpleasant task of recommending difficult, low-profile and tedious, but potentially high-influence activity such as research, case-building with Treasury officials and the orchestration of senior political support. The important policy activity took place inside Whitehall. CrossRail lobbyists did not pursue an effective multi-faceted campaign. But, at moments of crisis (Second Reading and before Committee Stage) the DTp, CrossRail and London First did manage to build a coalition of interest groups and media to pressure the Cabinet. At these times the strategy was multi-faceted, involving elite-centred lobbying, media, and third-party support. However, the role of the professional lobbyist was limited, as effective short-term activity was coordinated by London First under the umbrella 'CrossRail Coalition'.

Whilst the Treasury never changed its mind, the CrossRail Coalition bought a stay of execution by effectively heightening the profile of the issue. Had it remained a technical matter confined to the policy community, the Treasury would have won earlier. A multi-faceted campaign helped CrossRail, but a misdirected effort and poor advice meant the CrossRail lobby was ineffective.

Micro-level

Routines and procedures

'Lobbyists can do an important job. Never underestimate their ability to say to an organisation that believes it wants to see the minister – "You do not want to see the minister – you want to see the grade 7 or grade 5".'[104] Civil servants believe important lobbying targets are middle rank officials: 'the thirty-somethings who are the basic policy analysts – get hold of them and persuade them'.[105] CrossRail failed to do that.

CrossRail's Bill Team planned to defend the Bill by preparing to nego-tiate minor amendments to pacify objectors without increasing costs (a procedure that had worked successfully in the past). This approach depended on government support and a satisfactory committee chairman. Given IGA knew that elements of government were ambivalent, commit-tee membership was crucial, and the appointment of a sympathetic, or at least impartial, chairman was central. The chairman, Tony Marlow, MP, had his own maverick agenda and during the Committee stage became the first MP for 54 years to call from the floor of the House for his own leader and prime minister to resign.[106] Transport ministers knew Marlow was a risky choice. One commented: 'I tried to nobble him as hard as I could.'[107] If there was one point where CrossRail and its advis-ers failed it was the selection of committee members. IGA prided itself on its behind-the-scenes contacts at Westminster, and it must have known there was a problem. It had time to help as well as the support of DTp ministers. CrossRail either failed to recognise the danger, or failed to find a better candidate.

Civil servants were not explicit; they gave clues and, because some lobbyists had worked in government, they could 'read the tea-leaves'.[108] A senior official argued that knowing process is important: 'meeting and greeting is counter-productive particularly post-Nolan'.[109] CrossRail's routine lobbying was ineffective because it was unfamiliar with routines and procedure and continued to focus on meeting MPs. Officials tended to be more comfortable with lobbyists who had experience of the sys-tem. They were more open if 'they knew they were not going to get embarrassed and were not going to be put into an awkward position by some ill-informed lobbyist asking questions'.[110]

There was an increase in 'shadow lobbying'. Supportive MPs were used as 'secondary lobbyists', and the Bill's promoter, David Lidington, was a conduit between ministers and promoters. IGA met MPs alone in addition to the client's meetings. IGA proposed parliamentarians be briefed 'in groups over lunch at 55 Broadway, within walking dis-tance of the Palace of Westminster'.[111] IGA advised some formal meet-ings: 'Labour Members, in particular, tend to prefer this approach.'[112] They were less willing to be 'wined and dined' and IGA suggested CrossRail 'play down references to Labour bugbears – tourism, the City, Canary Wharf, markets, stuffy economists' terms, London's status and prosperity'.[113]

IGA attempted working with parliamentarians to:

- raise CrossRail at relevant Questions and in debates and, informally with Ministers;
- put down Parliamentary Questions, EDMs and seek an Adjournment Debate;
- take a delegation to the Prime Minister and/or the Chief Secretary to the Treasury or Transport Secretary;
- speak in support of the project in parliamentary debates as part of the TWA procedure.

Conclusion

All of IGA's knowledge was directed at the processes and personalities of Westminster. CrossRail believed IGA had an excellent knowledge of parliamentary procedure. However, the evidence suggests IGA did not understand the technicalities of its client's policy and neither did it understand civil service procedure. 'IGA – all they ever did was wine and dine MPs. What is the point? It was mind bending in its simplicity.'[114] IGA may have understood informal rules, such as the need to tell MPs something new on each occasion and Labour MPs' unwillingness to be wined and dined, but this 'knowledge' was irrelevant to the arena where CrossRail was really decided, namely Whitehall. IGA's links into Whitehall were not strong, and its lack of technical knowledge of both its client's case and official procedure hampered its client's lobbying.

Contacts and coalitions

Contacts

IGA believed it had 'an extremely effective network of contacts among Ministers, Opposition Spokesmen, Members of both Houses, Civil Servants and Party officials'.[115] This network supposedly provided clients with timely political intelligence and access to policy-makers. IGA was hired because of its contacts with Conservative ministers.[116] The lobbying company portrayed itself as a collection of insiders with access: 'Everybody knew IGA'. Senior CrossRail managers believed: 'You had to be able to be continually whispering in ministers' ears at every function they went to, particularly the private ones.'[117]

Contacts allow lobbyists to know 'who are the right people to hit and when to hit them'.[118] IGA focused on MPs. Greer was able to get 'names' to attend meetings. But IGA ignored the civil service. An official recalls: 'I spoke to a number of official colleagues. IGA had never been anywhere near them. That is their brand of lobbying – parliamentary based. But in that case it was wholly inappropriate.'[119] IGA arranged for CrossRail directors to meet 'ministers and … route MPs that we normally would not have been able to get hold of'.[120] CrossRail was impressed by IGA's access to MPs, its ability to arrange meetings, and its conduct at party conferences. One said: 'They were fantastic at party conferences. They got us into lots of events. They had a huge lunch and we would be put on a table with route MPs and council leaders and people from London First'.[121]

It is unclear why CrossRail did not expect to achieve this level of access as a matter of course. CrossRail believed that 'Greer in person had access to the Prime Minister. He used it only sparingly. There is no doubt whatsoever the fact that we were allowed to proceed into Committee was a result of Ian Greer seeing John Major.'[122] There is little evidence to support this contention. This chapter shows that the stop–start progress of the Bill was the consequence of several variables, not least the prime minister's determination to reassert his political authority. Yet the client believed:

> Ian Greer was seeing John Major on behalf of his clients at least once a week. It was amazing. He would ask if we felt that the time was right for him to speak to the Prime Minister. There is no doubt that man had tremendous access. Greer could move amongst virtually the whole of the Cabinet how he wished, and he did.[123]

There is no real evidence to suggest IGA's access influenced policy. Hints of privileged access, which were later to lead to Greer's downfall, over-awed clients and were a valuable marketing tool, but there is no proof they played a part in CrossRail's fate.

Coalitions

There was no initial coalition for CrossRail because it was unnecessary, since there was political support early on. As political support waned a coalition would have helped, but outside the times of crisis no broad support existed. Whilst there was a sense of approval, the support was intangible.

There was a lack of Conservative MPs in London to support the scheme publicly. There was also no political consensus in London. Parties were beset by factionalism. CrossRail campaigners 'could not get Tories and Labour to work together. You could not get Bromley Tories and Westminster Tories together and you could not get Labour in Hounslow and Labour in Camden together.'[124] 'Labour versus Tory versus Liberal Democrat. We tried to get them together. It was hopeless. Even the Tory MPs split between inner and outer London.'[125]

The 29 affected local authorities supported the project. The Labour Association of London Authorities and the Conservative London Boroughs' Association issued a rare joint statement attacking government's lack of commitment. The commuter counties were also supportive. Although IGA proposed liaison with local authorities, there was poor communication. IGA admitted that 'nothing was being coordinated on a political level'.[126]

Tower Hamlets, the City of Westminster and the City of London Corporation were the most important local authorities because of tunnelling impact. Tower Hamlets opposed CrossRail. Westminster was supportive, as was the City of London Corporation in order to protect the City against Docklands. The Corporation lobbied for CrossRail, in part, because it owned land at each of the four proposed central stations, which presented enormous redevelopment opportunities.[127]

The 1992 Conservative government magnified the voice of London. It instituted a Cabinet Sub-Committee for London and a London Transport Minister. London First chose CrossRail to cut its campaigning teeth. These organisations had limited impact on policy. Whilst ministers 'made a habit of lunching in the City and hearing what groups of people thought, London First was not a particularly influential lobby in this case'.[128] An official recalled: 'the City was not particularly noisy'.[129]

When the Treasury attempted to block the Second Reading of the CrossRail Bill, a 'CrossRail Coalition' was organised to shore up the DTp. A broad front was presented to promote the scheme. Letters to decision-makers were followed by orchestrated parliamentary questions. DTp officials and ministers were provided with evidence and 'would be offered every encouragement to press on'.[130] The CrossRail Coalition was also 'an attempt to persuade Londoners, London business, local authorities, pressure groups and government'.[131] It effectively amplified 'third party noise' to make it easier for key government ministers to ally together to overrule the Treasury. This said, apart from key moments of effective campaigning, broad external support for CrossRail drifted.

IGA identified targets and advised on briefings. Groups that could endorse private-finance proposals were particularly important. However, the coalition was weak since members did not deliver anything in exchange for a favourable policy output. Officials believed coalition members did not bring 'something to the table': 'Ministers always listened politely but the CrossRail Coalition was not particularly influential.'[132] A senior Treasury official said that 'for lobbyists to say things which are demonstrably in their self-interest cuts little ice'.[133] Officials rejected the coalitions using a Whitehall colloquialism: the 'Mandy

Rice-Davies dismissive'.[134] Officials, especially those at the Treasury, were used to lobbies pursuing selfish objectives.

Opponents. A collection of interest groups opposed CrossRail. 'There was an informal Mafia out to kill CrossRail. [Members] all stayed in touch with each other.'[135] Perceptions of opposition made the scheme less attractive politically. Steinbruner labels this perception an 'assumption of sensitivity to pertinent information'.[136] Politicians' perceptions of construction 'horror stories' were deleterious. A former Cabinet Minister believed that 'CrossRail floundered because of the weight of objection against it which made it unreasonable to proceed with'.[137] A minister recalled: 'the idea of digging up Oxford Street was daunting. We had been badly scarred in Kent with the Channel Tunnel Rail Link.'[138] A political adviser continued: 'I cannot begin to tell you the problems. You had people screaming, particularly all the posh folk in Belgravia and Mayfair.'[139]

The route alignment took little account of political reality and, as the Opposition Transport spokesman noted, the alignment passed 'the doors of just about every influential interest group in the country and, as everyone knows, many of them do not like it'.[140] A former Cabinet minister believed 'CrossRail was ill-thought out. It went from nowhere to nowhere. No sane person has ever wanted to go to Shenfield.'[141] It is evidence of CrossRail's lack of political sophistication that, when the congestion case weakened in the early 1990s, it resisted switching its case to emphasise connections to Heathrow, the Eurostar terminus at King's Cross and Docklands, which would have broadened its appeal.

Although 314 petitions were lodged against the Bill, there were two main opponents. The Residents' Association of Mayfair (RAM) was run by a retired businessman who devoted significant time to its campaign. RAM was supported and financed by local residents and business. Public meetings were organised, a regular newsletter was published, and petitions and letters to MPs arranged. It placed stories in the local and national press and met ministers.

The second, the London Borough of Tower Hamlets (LBTH) Council, took a parochial stance towards CrossRail. LBTH bordered the City and Docklands, but had gained from neither, and decided costs outweighed benefits. LBTH's opposition was based on anticipated disruption; it felt 'LT looked at east London and thought "low value – good place for a work site".'[142] LBTH's policy was driven by its new devolved structure. Politicking between neighbourhoods and the pockets of minority communities complicated matters. Experienced officers resigned as a consequence of a chaotic reform programme, and relations between government and councillors deteriorated. One former Cabinet minister recollects that Tower Hamlets councillors 'were appalling people. Dreadful. So bad as to be almost indescribable.'[143]

However, the Treasury connected with LBTH to promote their shared agenda, to disrupt the progress of the scheme. LBTH's lobbyist dealt directly with officials and sought to undermine the scheme with civil servants and the press.[144] LBTH's advisers persuaded the Treasury to insist on a study comparing the costs and benefits of the northerly surface routing with CrossRail's preferred tunnel. But, the lobbyist said, '"that meeting" from the Treasury's perspective never took place, but they nevertheless found the information incredibly helpful'.[145]

Conclusion

Whilst there is no evidence to suggest Ian Greer's supposed access to the prime minister was effective, it would be facile to suggest contacts were unimportant. IGA's contacts were one-dimensional, and were party based. Some argue lobbyists may be effective for business, but they are not valuable to public bodies because 'people like BR and LUL have good links into Whitehall and also into the Department which owns them and whose role in life is to take the ambitions of their nationalised industry and translate them in a way to win the day'.[146]

However, public bodies increasingly need lobbyists because their contacts in Whitehall are not sufficient to push a policy. As Whitehall is often a mess of conflicting interests, lobbyists help their clients appeal to senior politicians. Had IGA really had influence and access to Major, it would have been useful in these circumstances.

The coalitions reflected the divisions within government, and groups formed around both Treasury and Transport. Proving to decision-makers there existed support, and consensus was not sufficient to secure success. Whilst coalition support is useful, campaigns can succeed without it provided there is political commitment. CrossRail believed opponents presented little threat. However, whilst they were small and poorly resourced they had a powerful ally in the Treasury, which used the flaws exposed by the groups to attack CrossRail.

CrossRail's support, although broad, was shallow and hazy. It failed to create a tight group of supporters. The CrossRail Coalition rescued the project twice: yet it was short-term and reactive. CrossRail needed a long-term proactive group of supporters. IGA and CrossRail were ineffective because they lacked a broad range of contacts and long-term allies.

Resources

Financial resources

Financial resources are important for long-term campaigns. A minister argued that: 'to indulge in a long-range "five-years-before-you-put-a-spade-in-the-ground" type project you need deep pockets'.[147] Cross-Rail devoured money: by 1998 it had absorbed £123 million. Given its stop–start nature it spent 80 per cent of the total budget on external consultants. IGA charged CrossRail a reasonable £5000 per month for consultancy services. This figure fell as the campaign progressed to £4000 then £2500. The fee for monitoring, a separate activity, was £1000 per month. Although a former Transport minister argued that 'London Transport would have been better advised to put more resources into lobbying rather than less', CrossRail was constrained from launching a comprehensive lobbying campaign because of its public-sector roots.[148] Indeed, the *Evening Standard* reported ministers were 'livid that LT has spent £250 000 on professional lobbying through a public relations firm that they believe is designed to discredit the Government'.[149]

Managerial resources

The lack of a real champion had important consequences for the way CrossRail was managed. Management was weak, uncoordinated and divided. The BR and LT chairmen had agreed to promote CrossRail jointly, but they soon both lost interest.[150] A committee managed CrossRail poorly. Its stewardship was 'debilitating. It lacked focus and it lacked agreement. There was no one person in charge.'[151] The two organisations soon lost control. Furthermore, CrossRail was not a natural team and there was no loyalty or commitment from staff who often had diverse backgrounds and were either consultants or temporary secondees.

Poor management and a lack of client commitment undermined the effectiveness of the campaign. If the client fails to provide commitment to the project and is unresponsive to the advice and work of the lobbyists hired, then it is almost certainly doomed to fail. IGA had difficulty 'because we did not know our client's strategy. CrossRail did not know themselves what the agendas of BR and LUL were.'[152] An internal paper warned of:

> [the] heavy constraints in the marketing of the scheme, i.e. it must be low-key and subject to the sensitivities of all three promoters, but the control of the information supporting the CrossRail case is also in the hands of the promoters. Where evidence emerges to support CrossRail

but conflicts with existing interests it is not unreasonable to assume it will be suppressed. The project cannot bite the hand that feeds it.[153]

So, even had CrossRail been well resourced and managed, its lobbying would have been cautious. An official said: 'it would have worried me if the CrossRail project team had been lobbying hard. Campaigning for a project when funded by departmental expenditure is extremely doubtful.'[154] The CrossRail account was atypical 'because being a public-sector organisation they were not happy for IGA to be seen to be working on their behalf in the House. They were quite happy to be directed by us, but they did not want it done by us'.[155]

Some CrossRail managers believed using lobbyists to their full potential was difficult. 'We were not allowed to use lobbyists in the way we wanted to. We wanted them to be much more active than they were. They did provide advice, most of which we were not allowed to act on.'[156] Therefore, in many respects, CrossRail prevented IGA from lobbying effectively.

Conclusion

Despite the substantial financial resources possessed by the supporters of CrossRail, the campaign failed. Financial resources alone do not guarantee effectiveness. In two senses CrossRail was resource-poor: it had poor managerial resources and lacked a sense of ownership. Jealousies between the promoters were debilitating and injured CrossRail's policy and momentum. Lobbying was ignored or tolerated by management. Only too late did management recognise that selling the project politically was more important than design or engineering. Second, CrossRail lacked autonomy. It was inflexible and could not deal with officials. The lobbyist's advice was ignored and it was fearful of encouraging third-party support.

Conclusions

External variables

The economy was the most influential external variable on this policy issue. CrossRail was conceived as the economy entered recession. By the early 1990s CrossRail's imperative vanished, and tax revenue dried up. The dispassionate observer witnessed falling employment and congestion, and other projects increasing east–west capacity. The case, initially strong, weakened over time.

The consequence of the changing economic circumstances was the fingerprints of the Treasury's 'hidden hands' being found all over CrossRail's defeat. The real campaign was one within government. Though the Bill Committee was the vehicle for CrossRail's death, the real assassin, which killed the project by a thousand cuts, was the Treasury. Lobbyists were unable to overcome the Treasury. Despite being overruled by the prime minister, the Treasury damaged CrossRail at every opportunity. Major's public statements were mood music to disguise Treasury mischief. Spending departments became weaker and more dependent on Treasury patronage. The DTp could not publicly blame the Treasury for CrossRail's demise. A civil servant argued: 'once there is a collective decision, you have to go with it. You cannot blame the Treasury, tempting though it is'.[157] However, there was no collective decision against CrossRail. In fact, the opposite was true. The Cabinet Committee approved CrossRail. Treasury officials carried their public expenditure powers very far indeed.

The bizarre nature of London politics also played a role. There was no political consensus in London: not only did different political parties in London disagree, but there was disagreement within parties. CrossRail also lacked heavy-weight advocates. There were no senior Conservative MPs in London to promote CrossRail.

Finally, political preferences were important. First, ministers took a complacent view of the City of London, viewing it as successful and preferring to leave it alone; consequently, they felt no moral obligation to deliver CrossRail. Second, there was also a (mostly inaccurate) perception of broad opposition, making CrossRail politically unpalatable. Third, the project was conceived as a public-sector funded scheme just when the trend was in the opposite direction. The scheme clashed with railway privatisation and failed to find a private-sector partner.

Internal variables

Whilst most ministers and officials interviewed discounted lobbyists, the client believed the lobbyist was effective. Indeed, IGA claimed to be 'committed to achieving a satisfactory resolution to the campaigns that it conducts for its clients... [o]ur clients can be confident that by purchasing our services they are subscribing to the outcome rather than to a collection of individual actions'.[158]

Although IGA was working for a fragmented client, whose components had different agendas, it found it hard to understand its client's problems and was unable to advise the client sensibly. Its standard approach of briefing MPs and attending party conferences was inadequate in this case. No serious effort was made by CrossRail, DTp or London First to build wider support to counter the Treasury's wholly negative influence. No major project would ever succeed were cyclical downturns used to argue against them. Though some events were held to broaden support, internal failings prevented effective lobbying.

Coalition support for CrossRail was weak and transient. The diffuse support for CrossRail was not transformed into political capital. Furthermore, there was poor coordination. One lobbyist recalled that the campaign 'was not coordinated at all'.[159] There was a lack of direction and enthusiasm.

At moments of drama IGA did help convey messages to the key people. Its access, through its existing client base, to the CBI and big business helped orchestrate letters to *The Times*, which kept alive political perceptions of the project. However, the strategy was superficial because it attended to the symptoms rather than the causes of the problem, and as a consequence the political commitments which London First and IGA engineered were not durable.

The scheme was not sold effectively to politicians. The project team was engineer-led and politically naïve. Lobbyists failed to emphasise CrossRail's structural and regional benefits and its general quality. In addition, the promoters had different corporate objectives and competing priorities. A multi-headed directorate made cohesive management difficult. CrossRail was the first priority for none of the clients. Joint advocacy weakened promotion. There was no institutional champion for the scheme.

* * *

External and internal factors both affected the policy outcome. Whilst the context was disadvantageous to CrossRail, the client and lobbyist were ineffective. They failed to achieve their objectives. The most important variable was the Treasury, not outside interest groups. The battle was trench warfare between the Treasury and the DTp. The irony of this case is that IGA was employed by a branch of government to lobby government in support of government policy, and it still failed.

Lobbyists were relatively unimportant. The best they can claim is partial credit for having helped engineer a stay of execution, but even then contextual variables explain the outcome. The lobbyists were ineffective when their achievements are judged against their objectives. They failed to achieve their objectives; failed to have CrossRail designated a scheme of national significance by the Transport Secretary; failed to minimise opposition to the project; failed to see the project progress through the TWA process; failed to gain Treasury support; and failed to organise financial backers.

6
The Success of the Jubilee Line Extension

Government transport decisions in the late 1980s were based not on socio-economic benefits and costs but on political factors which overruled the Department of Transport's own studies. This chapter examines the JLE as a middle-profile issue which became political as its profile heightened. The influence of the developers of Canary Wharf, Olympia and York (O&Y), and its lobbyists distorted policy. Their effective lobbying and political factors meant that solving central London's transport crisis was postponed to build JLE. Ministers admitted that by the benefit-cost ratio JLE did not meet the established criteria for approval. The JLE outcome is testament to the effect of a well-researched and well-executed lobbying campaign. This case shows the defeat of the lead government department and the success of O&Y and Lowe Bell (now Bell Pottinger).

This chapter refutes Fanstein's assumption that 'government's reluctance to shoulder the full cost of the Jubilee Line extension and build it in advance of development reflected a half-hearted commitment to Canary Wharf'.[1] In fact once O&Y arrived, contrary to the popular myth, government did not respond tardily.[2] Whilst for CrossRail government studies were a delaying ploy, in the JLE case government-commissioned research was moulded to legitimise O&Y's demands.

Interest groups and lobbyists

In his role of inner-city saviour Michael Heseltine (when Secretary of State for the Environment) attempted to re-orient London's development to the east. Heseltine wanted to create an eastern corridor – echoing the M4/Heathrow corridor – focused on the Thames Gateway. The London Docklands Development Corporation (LDDC) was established to encourage private-sector and development-led regeneration. Docklands was designated an enterprise zone in an attempt to remove local authority obduracy.[3] Ministers believed London's eastern local authorities had neither the wherewithal nor the political will to act. A former cabinet minister believed that: 'it was not the money that was the problem. It was the statist psychology of Tower Hamlets. We had given up any chance of working with these boroughs.'[4]

Regeneration depended on transport. However, an inevitable consequence of market-led development was the absence of strategic transport planning. LDDC enhanced the local road network and built a light rail transit system: the Docklands Light Railway (DLR). Between 1981 and 1985 LDDC's achievements were modest. Olympia and York rescued it. O&Y's high employment predictions forced LDDC to re-evaluate transport provision. O&Y moved to tie the DLR into the transport network, contributing £69 million to extend and upgrade the railway and £25 million to Canary Wharf Station. Second, it lobbied for an underground line to ensure Canary Wharf's success. LUL's lack of interest in the line to Canary Wharf forced O&Y to develop its own scheme. O&Y drafted and referenced a parliamentary Bill for a stand-alone line and offered to plan, construct and pay for the entire railway, estimated at £700–800 million. Although DTp rejected O&Y's offer, the company bounced back with another idea: the Jubilee Line Extension.

O&Y hired Lowe Bell Political to provide political strategy advice. O&Y required assistance handling the media. Given the policy implications of the development for London in general, O&Y had a broad requirement for access to politicians to promote not just Canary Wharf, but regeneration in general. Although the DoE was responsible for Docklands, the scale of the development implied more extensive political interest. One O&Y executive recalled:

> it seemed to us that the issues we faced stretched from Environment, to Transport, to Trade and Industry. We understood from the beginning there was the need to access politicians at the right level and as foreigners, new to this country, it seemed sensible to work with people who had access already, rather than us trying to create them.[5]

O&Y described the brief for the lobbyist: 'It was none of this fancy business, "Can you?" It was "How do we get it?", "What do we need to do?", "Who do we need to meet?", "How do we go about it?", "What is the strategy?", "What are the tactics?" The objectives were clear'.[6]

Lobbying by O&Y and its consultants sent shock waves through government. Lowe Bell helped plan and execute an elite-focused lobbying campaign, which overruled the policy community. O&Y executives were in regular contact with senior politicians and advisers, and ignored or sidelined unhelpful civil servants and public-sector bodies.

Macro-level

Profile, technicality and politicality

Large infrastructure policies have both technical and public-interest elements. The cost of constructing new railways automatically increases the issue's profile, as does construction impact. The issue's importance was intensified by the status of London and later by the Millennium celebrations. The Central London Rail Study was based on employment projections which ignored Docklands, so an East London Rail Study (ELRS) was commissioned. The ELRS subsequently legitimised the political approval of JLE, and attempted to make a political issue technical. LT believed government was 'saying to us "You do not have a choice. Build the bloody railway and write a report that justifies it".'[7] Because the government had rejected O&Y's earlier offer to build, finance and operate its own railway, O&Y needed its JLE idea 'approved' by government research.

ELRS was undertaken by the private sector under pressure from O&Y. O&Y shaped ELRS, so that the JLE alignment followed almost exactly O&Y's recently rejected line. The ELRS sanctioned O&Y's earlier proposals. The only difference from O&Y's plan was that civil servants' rejection of the first proposal had cost the public sector £500 million because the taxpayer would now pay for most of the scheme. O&Y lobbied furiously for a Bill to be introduced to Parliament, and even offered to pay government's drafting costs. DTp rejected its advances, but in 1989 a joint O&Y/LRT/LUL team was set up to manage further design and Bill preparation.

O&Y recognised the fact that JLE competed against the CLRS CrossRail option favoured by LT and DTp. To O&Y it was clear the chances of getting both funded were very low for both budgetary and practical reasons. It was important for O&Y 'to ensure ministers in the respective departments understood the strengths and weaknesses of both cases';[8] in other words, to ensure JLE was pushed ahead of CrossRail because the project approved first was more likely to succeed. Consequently O&Y adopted 'reverse tactics' and sought to raise JLE's profile within government, from being a technical policy to one regarded as high-profile, general, and political. O&Y recognised government wanted it at top level; it was the lower, technocratic levels that opposed JLE. 'The Prime Minister wanted it and London Underground did not. This is where lobbyists came in. Tim Bell's [from Lowe Bell] job was to keep it on the agenda and go to Margaret Thatcher.'[9] O&Y's lobbyists targeted senior politicians.

O&Y recognised it had the support of the DoE and the Prime Minister, Margaret Thatcher. It overcame DTp reticence and institutional inertia by harassing officials. O&Y directors 'would be on the telephone two, three, four times a day. They would not let go.'[10] A former political adviser argued that moving the issue so it became high-profile within government was effective because 'if you are irritating you are winning. If you do not irritate, they are not listening and they will not do it.'[11] O&Y certainly irritated DTp officials. It 'irritated government and transport providers. Its only mode of operation was to be contentious.'[12] Officials complained about O&Y's discourtesy. 'Officials would come screaming to me saying "That man is so rude"', recalled one special adviser.[13] Lowe Bell helped smooth relations with officials and ministers.

Michael Portillo, then Minister for Transport, announced that government was minded to approve JLE, even before DTp had received ELRS, but with full knowledge of CLRS. Despite recognizing central London congestion Portillo argued curing it was expensive, complicated and disruptive. He said government wanted to 'see a new underground line to Docklands and east London' to help O&Y.[14] JLE was approved in principle before the Commons rose in 1989.

Cecil Parkinson was appointed Secretary of State for Transport in July 1989, and in a bilateral meeting the Prime Minister was convinced of the case for JLE. It would be built, he argued, only if 'sufficient contributions are forthcoming from property developers and other landowners who would benefit'.[15] In principle negotiations over the contribution did not prevent legislative approval. However, in reality Treasury was dissatisfied with O&Y's offer of money and tried to stall the process until after the November deadline. A former Cabinet minister recalled: 'the Treasury's game was to spin it out beyond [Bill introduction] and there would be another year lost – another year for arguments for not having it'.[16] Parkinson recollected that an 'argument had been under way for many months and little progress had been made, so I decided to invite Paul Reichmann, the head of Olympia and York, to meet me to see it we could negotiate an agreement'.[17] Reichmann made his offer, but the Treasury again rejected it.

Tim Bell, of Lowe Bell, learned through his contacts that the Transport Secretary was attending a party at the Chancellor's constituency home. There the Transport Secretary received:

a dispatch rider carrying a House of Lords envelope from Keith Joseph saying Paul Reichmann was absolutely horrified at the cavalier treatment Treasury had given his final offer. Because it was a Friday evening (he is an orthodox Jew), he got another not orthodox

Jew, Keith, to write in his place. It was a brilliant move. I read the letter, then showed it straight to John Major. So Reichmann got his point of view straight into the hands of the Transport Secretary and the Chancellor of the Exchequer in the same day.[18]

Reichmann refused to increase his offer during a meeting with the Transport Secretary the following week, although terms were relaxed. The matter was finally settled on the day of the Autumn Statement. The Transport Secretary informed the Treasury that no more private-sector money was available and, predicting the Chief Secretary's rejection, the minister 'arranged for both to see the Prime Minister that night'.[19]
An attendee at the meeting recalled its progress:

> It was an amusing meeting. She started in a wonderful way. She said to Norman Lamont (Chief Secretary), 'You have never made any money, have you, Norman?' It was wonderful – you knew the result at that point. 'How much did *Paul* offer?' Note *Paul*. I said, '£400 m in cash'. And she said, '£400 m! Have you any idea, Norman, what a large sum of money £400 m is? £400 m of your own money! It is amazing'. Then she said, 'You are not really rejecting this offer, are you, Norman?'[20]

The Treasury was overruled by the Prime Minister. 'It was dragged kicking and screaming by a combination of the Prime Minister, Secretary of State for Transport and the Secretary of State for the Environment.'[21] On 16 November 1989 Parkinson said: 'I welcome this contribution, which is of an unprecedented scale. This is a further example of public- and private-sector contribution to the mutual benefit of both.'[22] *The Times* recognised the outcome was 'the result of intense Whitehall lobbying by Olympia & York'.[23] LDDC admitted O&Y's effect on governmental decision-making, stating: 'without O&Y's initiative in campaigning for and part funding for the new line, there would not have been such strong government support for the proposal'.[24] A representative from the City Corporation argued: 'Tim Bell in those days had the ear of the Prime Minister and he was a hired gun for O&Y. He did his job successfully.'[25]

DTp officials were rightly sceptical about JLE. In hindsight, some argued its choice was the 'right decision for the wrong reasons', noting 'there may have been some serendipity'.[26] Other officials believed that 'O&Y and their lobbyists were pushing at an open door'.[27] One minister believed lobbyists had 'no impact whatsoever' because JLE 'did not require lobbying'.[28] Likewise, a former political adviser says of the Prime

Minister that lobbyists:

> did not have much impact on her. She had no hesitation about see-
> ing Paul Reichmann or other major outside investors. I would only
> have had to say to her that Paul Reichmann wanted to see her for her
> to have agreed to it. I do not recall the request came from Tim Bell.[29]

However, whilst some officials regarded lobbyists as overrated, they
believed that because they 'were close to Margaret Thatcher they might
have got the door of No. 10 opened to Paul Reichmann'.[30] But Paul
Reichmann was an effective lobbyist at all levels of government. O&Y
drove the policy process. Without O&Y the JLE would not have happened. The idea would not have come from Government.

A Cabinet minister believed lobbyists 'had a catalytic effect. They
helped their client be more effective. If the client had not been impressive they could not have made the difference.'[31] Another Cabinet minister said that whilst:

> Tim Bell knew how the system worked – he could talk to people and
> soften people up and make sure a point of view was heard – there was
> a limit to what lobbyists could achieve. They were not decisive. I do
> not think they would pretend to have too much influence. I do not
> recall Tim ever coming to see me about the Jubilee Line.[32]

O&Y's strategy was direct lobbying, mainly by senior directors, with
door opening by Lowe Bell, based on hard facts or researched opinion.
O&Y worked hard. It is an example of where professional and informed
lobbying made a substantial difference. Lobbyists may have had an effect
on the policy-making because they got the policy on to the political
agenda: 'Without lobbyists O&Y would never have been able to keep the
Jubilee Line on the agenda until it got approved. Without professional
lobbyists an outsider would not have been able to get it on the agenda.
O&Y were outsiders.'[33]

O&Y believed lobbyists were the key to achieving their objectives.
A former O&Y executive argued that the campaign 'would not have been
successful without them'.[34] Lowe Bell were 'able to get us an audience
with, and a hearing by, the key people at the right time. There is no merit
in life being right too late.'[35] A colleague adds: 'I do not think we could
have done it without them. They could not have done it without us. It
was a great team.'[36] O&Y had vision, it had money, it had a project close
to the heart of government and dear to the leader of the party. It was a
golden combination.

Conclusion

The Treasury fought the project, and DTp officials opposed JLE. Both departments were overruled by the Prime Minister and the Transport and Environment Secretaries. The decision was a leap in the dark, which required political risk. One former official argued: 'the initial decisions on JLE were taken when there was not that much constructed in Docklands. O&Y could have backed off and government been left with an embarrassing building site.'[37] The issue was initially highly political and controversial. O&Y encouraged government to dampen political controversy by having JLE approved by an official study. JLE subsequently became a technical, non-political issue legitimised by experts. But JLE would have died at Treasury and DTp hands had it remained a decision for technocrats. O&Y and Lowe Bell recognised this; they took the technical recommendations and heightened the issue's profile and political nature within government by emphasising the project's political benefits and its connections with the government's programme. Lobbyists are effective if, when facing 'blocking players', they take a low-profile, technical and non-political issue and heighten its profile, and its general and political case *within* government.

External factors

There were disadvantageous factors affecting the approval of JLE, but effective lobbying and political commitment mitigated their impact. Other constraints disrupted its progress, most notably a recession which caused O&Y's collapse.

From canary to albatross

O&Y entered the London property market hoping to repeat its recent success at the World Financial Center in New York. But Canary Wharf was completed at the low point of a recession and, though O&Y had planned a cash cushion to survive two recessions, the internationalisation of property investment meant the markets in London, New York and Toronto moved together. The recession's depth and length meant there was no counterbalance, and this precipitated O&Y's collapse. Despite government officials trying furiously to bring the deal to a close, when O&Y went into administration it had not completed a funding agreement for its contribution to JLE. Although government gave the impression of a public–private partnership, it had committed itself to build JLE without a binding contract.

The Treasury jumped at this window of opportunity to kill JLE because it was under pressure to cut public expenditure. The Treasury: 'did not care about JLE. It wanted to pull the plug. It was hundreds of millions of pounds of ringfenced money that could come back into the public expenditure programme.'[38] In the middle of the 1992 General Election campaign O&Y failed to deliver the seed-corn £40 million payment, and JLE was halted on 1 April 1992. Consequently, the government and the banks played a game of poker. Government warned in stark terms that JLE would not go ahead unless the contribution were forthcoming. The Transport Secretary, John MacGregor, said: 'I see no prospect of my authorising a start on construction until and unless the agreed contributions are assured.'[39] The Prime Minister reinforced the message: 'our policy at the moment is to build the Jubilee Line when we have the contribution of a stated sum from the private sector.'[40]

The banks remained unconvinced. The receivers thought government was bluffing and there followed a grotesque dance, after which the banks eventually realised their asset would either be the subject of a fire sale or they would have to find £400 million. Government restated that public money would be released only when the private-sector contribution was guaranteed. The Treasury opposed any form of 'lame-duck' rescue of Canary Wharf. A Treasury official said: 'we thought JLE was dotty. When Canary Wharf went down we were quite keen to pull the plug on it.'[41] The private-sector contribution became the albatross that the Treasury attempted to hang around the Department of Transport's neck. By this stage DTp was fully committed to JLE, and LT's chairman, who was also a director of HSBC (a major funder of Canary Wharf), was convinced of the importance of the scheme. DTp officials recognised that 'if the JLE were allowed to go down the plug hole no private-sector partner would ever come in with government again'.[42] The DTp minister:

> outrageously stressed our commitment to the Jubilee line at every public opportunity. I had a right to do it because it was part of our manifesto commitment. I felt strongly that my job was to fight for the project and to move so far ahead that it would be inconceivable that I could have the ground cut from underneath me.[43]

There was a terrific Whitehall battle to keep the JLE. The Treasury came under pressure from 'general City interests' and the Cabinet Office to rescue JLE, but the Treasury's response was '"Absolutely not. We had a deal. £400m or we are not shifting a bucket of sand". Most ministers were saying we should give them it.'[44] In 1993, as tenants began to move into Canary Wharf, the banks agreed to commit £400 million. However, one month later DTp, supported by the Treasury, refused the 'drop dead' clause demanded by the banks, which would have ensured the return of their contribution if the line were delayed. As momentum sagged, the Treasury threatened the banks that if they did not sign up to the deal it would withdraw its support. However, a deal was eventually agreed in the summer of 1993, allowing the Transport Secretary to approve JLE. In September Canary Wharf was financially reconstructed and emerged from administration in October. The arrangement provided for a £98 million payment immediately, and a further £300 million over 25 years. The Transport Secretary gave his:

> approval for London Underground Ltd to let contracts for the construction and equipment of the Jubilee Line extension. This reflects the fact that in anticipation of their release from administration, and with the permission of the Court, Olympia & York as the developers of Canary Wharf have entered into agreements to make a contribution of some £400 million towards the cost of the extension as previously envisaged.[45]

Conclusion

This case study shows up the divisions within government and the external constraints impacting on policy-making. The effectiveness of O&Y and Lowe Bell was hampered by the recession and O&Y's collapse. JLE's survival is testament to senior political commitment and effective lobbying in the face of hostile external variables. When O&Y collapsed, LDDC hired Lowe Bell to ensure continuity of the campaign. The political commitment in No. 10 and DTp resisted and overpowered the Treasury. The presence of hostile external factors did not prevent lobbyists from making a difference. Though lobbyists are most likely to be effective when contextual factors are advantageous, they can be effective when there are disadvantageous contextual variables, but their impact depends on having a good case and an impressive client.

Experience and existing policy

Redevelopment

Government in the early 1980s made a decision to promote Docklands rebuilding. Thatcher wanted redevelopment of London's Docklands to succeed to vindicate the notion that the private sector would invest on the back of pump-priming by government, and that her government could succeed where Labour local authorities failed. The government and O&Y needed one another. O&Y's development was to be a monument to the vitality of Thatcher's free-market philosophy.

In 1990 the Minister for Transport wrote that JLE 'will assist regeneration of the area in line with our Inner Cities policy and improve the labour supply to Docklands further assisting regeneration there'.[46] His successor argued: 'the case for the Jubilee Line extension depended not just on the measurable benefits but to a significant extent on the regeneration benefits which are not captured in the conventional cost benefit procedure'.[47] Ministers wanted the Urban Development Corporation(UDC) 'to fly. They did not want it to be a failure. It had to succeed. O&Y was coming to make a Tory policy a success.'[48] UDCs were an ornament to Thatcherism. Mrs Thatcher began the 1987 General Election at Canary Wharf and hailed it as ensuring the future of London as a world financial centre. When she officially launched its construction, she said it was a 'bold', 'ambitious' and 'far-sighted' scheme.[49]

Michael Portillo, Minister of Docklands Transport, was ordered personally by Thatcher to resolve the problems of Canary Wharf, and he wanted to encourage Londoners 'to focus on a new centre of population and business'.[50] The political commitment was obvious. He said: 'there must be more work per square mile being done on transport infrastructure in Docklands than in any other area in the country'.[51] Ministers were under pressure to deliver because 'what was happening there was a triumph of our policies. Right across the whole of government, we were keen on regeneration, business success and a strategy for east London.'[52] Michael Heseltine, reappointed Environment Secretary in 1990, built on earlier programmes by launching a plan to regenerate the area east of London. He said: 'there is no urban project in the world that should command more notice and imagination'.[53]

Private-sector involvement

A private-sector donation to the DLR extension established an important precedent. However, O&Y's contribution added a new dimension to government's efforts to involve the private sector in public projects. Its agreement to provide £400 million provided for a step-change in the government's programme to involve private-sector expertise and finance. The contribution was an essential lever in delivering JLE, and although not the clinching argument, JLE would not have proceeded without it. The contribution made the benefit-cost ratio more acceptable. There was also a belief within government that, because it was 'bending over backwards to make a success of Canary Wharf, the developers ought to cough up'.[54] The contribution was a quasi-commercial deal in which both parties got something they wanted. 'O&Y put millions of pounds on the table. Reichmann put his entire business on the table.'[55] Nevertheless, the contribution was good value for O&Y and a bad deal for government. O&Y may have been politically naïve, but it recognised JLE would be built for political reasons. Although forced to contribute, it avoided paying a significant proportion of costs. Whilst initially thought to be 40 per cent of total cost, the net contribution was worth between £120 and £150 million to the project, around 5 per cent of the out-turn costs.[56] It is possible that the costs incurred by the delay caused by the private-sector renegotiation were greater than the contribution, and that the relatively small offer caused 'a disproportionate diversion of public funds from projects which would be of more general benefit'.[57]

Officials rightly regarded the contribution as notional. It would have been difficult 'for government to justify the JLE had they not had the fig leaf of a private-sector contribution'.[58] Ministers talked of the contribution only in cash terms, and 'smoke and mirrors' were used in Parliament. The contribution allowed ministers to 'refute the suggestion that this was a private favour for a bunch of Canadian Jewish millionaires'.[59]

Despite being trumpeted as a *laissez-faire* triumph, Canary Wharf represented central government intervention on a huge scale. Docklands was never really a private-sector development. Developers were enticed by tax breaks. LDDC consumed £1.37 billion of the £1.8 billion paid to UDCs between 1981 and 1992. It received £3.5 billion more in government grants to meet infrastructure costs, excluding JLE. Add the JLE, and the public sector has paid well over one-third of the total £12 billion investment. Docklands was one of the most intensively subsidised 'private' developments in Western Europe.

Symbolism

Although Harold Macmillan once said, 'if people want a sense of purpose they should get it from their archbishop. They should certainly not get it from their politicians', some politicians operate viscerally.[60] Margaret Thatcher and Michael Heseltine both operated on political emotion. Government, embodied by the Prime Minister, believed Docklands would propel London into the twenty-first century. She was personally committed. She argued: 'where there is no vision, the people perish. And we started to provide the vision.'[61] Ministers 'recognised that we had potentially a success on our hands which if we were not careful we would convert into a disaster'.[62] The Prime Minister enthused about the 'biggest commercial development in the world' and congratulated:

> Mr Reichmann and Olympia & York for their vision. We have to thank them for their faith in Britain. ... And I hope that won't be the end; that this new spirit of enterprise, of adventure, will continue in

this country, because I believe that with the renewal that we have seen in Britain, we should be in perhaps the best position to lead Europe.[63]

There was huge enthusiasm to demonstrate that the Docklands project could work. Canary Wharf was a flagship. 'There is a point in politics when all barriers break down. The sky's the limit – we will go for it. Forget the benefit-cost analysis. It becomes a political gesture.'[64] Ministers and advisers recognised that Reichmann offered government a vision, and consequently political passion created momentum behind JLE. 'Passion is very important. If politicians become passionate about a particular project, it does not matter what it is, they have the ability to talk directly to the people.'[65] O&Y gauged government's mood successfully. The contribution was important psychologically and symbolically. Government had much to play for. The appeal of the Reichmanns to governments everywhere was noted by *Business Week*:

> Perhaps the most distinctive Reichmann trademark is the brothers' willingness to take huge gambles that only pay off way down the line. That's what endears them to governments. In massive public–private partnerships like the World Financial Center, they put up the financing, the government provides cheap land, and together they create whole new urban centers.[66]

Conclusion

Tying a proposal into the government agenda is crucially important. JLE was not justified by its objective merits, but succeeded because of its connections with the government's programme and experience: redevelopment, private-sector involvement and symbolism. O&Y based its lobbying on how its *entire* development delivered broad policy objectives. Redevelopment was a long-standing objective of the Conservative governments. Ministers were eager to assist O&Y because it made their policy a success. The private-sector contribution proved public–private projects could succeed. Although ministers misrepresented the value of the contribution, JLE would not have been built were not private-sector money forthcoming. Finally, O&Y's commitment to the UK was important symbolically. Rational decision-making was replaced by gesture politics. Almost everything about O&Y fitted the government's agenda.

Meso-level

The policy community

In 1992 modifications to London's governance built a policy community around a Cabinet committee,[67] below which was a policy community for

London's transport, which revolved around the Minister for Transport in London.[68] For JLE a transient community of players was established, access to which was restricted. A formal network existed around the minister, who chaired an action committee of all the key players.[69]

DTp initially blocked the O&Y proposals because they did not fit with the Department's schemes and ran counter to the views of policy officials. The effective lobbyist moves immediately to the Treasury and often to the No. 10 Policy Unit. Lowe Bell did that; and because of DTp's views, O&Y approached others. There were three relevant political camps outside DTp (No. 10, the Department of the Environment, and the Treasury), and all were cultivated assiduously by O&Y and Lowe Bell. O&Y lobbyists did not focus on civil servants because they believed them to be immune to their arguments. A former official said: 'the most important thing was to make sure that ministers were getting access to alternative views that they would not normally have got from the traditional method of LUL briefing civil servants and civil servants briefing ministers'.[70]

O&Y and Lowe Bell found established networks impenetrable, and changing the officials' agendas proved impossible. This intransigence led Lowe Bell to contact politicians directly. For several months JLE occupied the attention of the Prime Minister intensely.[71] Even officials in ministers' private offices were unaware of some of the confidential briefings Transport ministers received from O&Y. Lobbyists provided information to ministers that they were unable to obtain from civil servants. One official recalled:

> In the run up to the decision on JLE [lobbyists] focused almost exclusively on politicians. I think they came to the conclusion that civil servants were not the right audience for the particular issue in question which was about getting political backing for a project that the system did not want and had not thought of. They had to get political commitment.[72]

Reichmann enjoyed a personal chemistry with Thatcher. There was empathy between the two because Reichmann was a risk-taker, self-made, an outsider and Jewish. She undoubtedly afforded Reichmann greater access than the chairmen of nationalised industries. A political adviser recalled: 'Thatcher was pushing it like hell. She just loved the Reichmann brothers.'[73] Paul Reichmann circumvented the policy community to obtain an informal oral commitment to link the development to the Underground network personally from Thatcher. Such a swift agreement to major public expenditure was uncharacteristic of her. Her 'authority was very much behind it and it lingered on into 1992. It was seen as a done deal.'[74] This informal understanding was not specific. Whilst the deal may not have been a 'cast-iron copper-bottomed guarantee that a particular project would be finished by a particular date', Reichmann would have left his meeting with Thatcher 'confident that he had engaged her attention and would regard it as a case of very successful lobbying'.[75] O&Y and 'Paul Reichmann did rely on government commitment and it would have been a verbal commitment. He decided "if the Prime Minister gives me that sort of assurance that is good enough".'[76] JLE was cemented into the government's programme only because the conventional policy-making process was subverted.

The Treasury suspected a deal had been struck with Reichmann. One official thought: 'there probably was a deal. Reichmann would have been barmy to go ahead with Canary Wharf without it'.[77] The deal was eventually formalised and a 'heads of agreement' letter was sent to ministers which 'was then handed to lawyers and the half dozen sentences that were acceptable to Reichmann and ministers were subject to an amazing amount of work by lawyers'.[78]

Department of transport

Senior officials in the DTp disliked O&Y. LT's reaction to O&Y was one of outright opposition. DTp was wedged in CLRS's furrow and did not wish to be forced on to other issues such as the JLE and the East London Rail Study. Because Transport officials relied on LT for analysis upon which subsequent policy decisions were made, the Department was reluctant to challenge the CLRS's findings. O&Y believed the DTp 'did not want to do anything that might involve them taking responsibility for the operators. There was a tendency to be palmed off to LT.'[79] O&Y grudgingly recognised LT was a key audience. Senior LT managers loathed O&Y because O&Y ruined its own agenda and threatened its monopoly over London's railway. An O&Y executive commented: 'LUL were opposed to JLE at the beginning. They fought it all the way. They fought it not because they did not want the Jubilee Line but because they had their preferred options.'[80]

Whilst the majority of civil servants were antagonistic, a minority welcomed O&Y, believing it to be a 'breath of fresh air' after having to deal with LT. One senior official concluded: 'I had no respect for LT. They were incompetent.'[81] O&Y and its lobbyists benefited from the support of this handful of key officials and advisers in DTp. They acted as informal pushers of the O&Y case inside government. A former political adviser stated: 'I would certainly help them in meetings [and advise

O&Y] how they should approach meetings'. The flow of information was two-way. The political adviser recalled that O&Y provided:

> intelligence about what they were up to, which meant I could sit in meetings and I could contribute to those meetings, helping my boss. At the end of the day, it is your boss versus officials. Just my man and his juniors versus officialdom. The officials would line up in legions around the table.[82]

Department of the Environment

DoE, as Docklands' sponsor department, supported O&Y and was a lobbyist on its behalf inside government. A former cabinet minister said:

> in the Environment ministry we thought it was very important because it seemed to us that this was a restatement of the importance of London as a centre. London was beginning to have its day again and we were beginning to win the battle internationally. Docklands was crucial for that.[83]

DoE had a different agenda from DTp. DoE had part-funded DLR to aid regeneration, and supported the railway because it would not be funded from the DoE budget but from DTp's. O&Y's lobbyists ensured DoE officials were comfortable with the arguments, presentation and logic of its case. Having the DoE 'on side' was critical in the campaign with DTp officials.

HM Treasury

The Treasury often refused to examine new projects. Those improving existing services were more likely to receive attention. However, in the late 1980s the Treasury was not hostile to DTp bids for new schemes because of intense pressure on the transport system. The Transport Secretary submitted to the Treasury an outline for a 20-year programme of investment in LUL. By October 1989 the Treasury had told DTp to halve its £3.5 billion bid for rail schemes and its £12 billion for road schemes, because they exceeded long-term spending targets. The Treasury refused to approve the rail Bills due for introduction in November 1989. To proceed with the JLE, the DTp sidelined (it believed temporarily) the other schemes. *The Times* explained: 'The Department of Transport has been told to choose between the proposed Paddington to Liverpool Street rail link [CrossRail] and the extension of the Jubilee Line from Green Park to Stratford, because the Treasury cannot afford both schemes.'[84] The Treasury refused to fund both projects because of fiscal constraints. Parkinson launched a counteroffensive following the 1989 party conference to protect JLE, and the JLE gained Treasury approval only because of the Prime Minister's involvement.

Conclusion

The number of influential government players was small: the Prime Minister, Secretaries of State and ministers in Departments of Transport, Environment and Treasury, and the relevant Permanent Secretaries, Deputy Secretaries and Assistant Secretaries in each department. The DTp made it clear the JLE decision was not its own. A *Times* editorial noted: 'The transport department has never denied that the Jubilee Line queue-jumped the London investment list on Margaret Thatcher's instructions, only to help make Canary Wharf viable.'[85] O&Y and Lowe Bell were effective because they were not members of the closed consensual network. They went around the policy community to the Prime Minister to force change. Lobbyists can sometimes be more effective if they extract their client from the policy community. Lowe Bell was effective because it did not include its client in the policy community. O&Y ignored the London and transport policy communities, and took its campaign to a political level to overrule the traditional policy-making streams and target the top political executive.

Multi-faceted lobbying

Parliament

O&Y's tactics emphasised the wider political benefits of JLE and targeted the Prime Minister and some ministers. However, O&Y pursued a limited multi-faceted campaign and did lobby Parliament. It targeted MPs on relevant committees, other advisers and decision-makers. When lobbyists briefed interested MPs on the Canary Wharf project it included in those discussions information about JLE. O&Y brought MPs, decision-makers and journalists to the development to lobby them. O&Y seconded key personnel to the LUL Bill Preparation Team. The Bill received its first reading in January 1990. The legislative process was made easier by O&Y's earlier lobbying, and its decisions about alignment limited opposition. In committee the Bill attracted only 96 petitioners: consolidation meant only 24 were presented to the Committee. In general, Parliament was not important because most MPs were uninterested in JLE and parliamentary lobbying concentrated the Bill to ease its passage. Parliamentary approval was seen as a technicality.

Local government

O&Y briefed affected local authorities to ensure 'all relevant officials and councillors are aware of the implications and benefits of the rail line so that during the parliamentary passage they are able to provide informed support'.[86] The City of London Corporation opposed JLE because it threatened its interests. It preferred to see JLE re-routed or killed.

O&Y lobbied Tower Hamlets, and the company's regeneration, employment and training contributions helped 'oil the wheels' of support for the whole project. O&Y attempted to convince local people of its case. It financed a construction training college and established a £2 million fund for local schools and colleges. O&Y's contractors were required to employ 10 per cent of their workforce from the local community. O&Y's community outreach programme and training commitments were in the original 'master building agreement' signed before JLE was conceived. O&Y believed detailed consultation with local authorities and community groups would help it 'sort out who will be obstreperous and oppose the line under any circumstances, from those who have legitimate concerns'.[87] O&Y did an enormous amount of work with community groups, and this support was repaid in their active support for the JLE.

Conclusion

Some politicians and advisers in Downing Street, DoE, DTp and the Treasury believed JLE was the right policy. There was an informal grouping, constantly thinking, 'Who else are we going to talk to? What meetings are we going to facilitate?'[88] These internal advocates worked closely with O&Y and their lobbyists. O&Y were effective because they dropped the idea in several different places in government. In addition to No. 10, O&Y talked to DoE and the Cabinet Office, as well as the DTp. O&Y did not really run a multi-faceted campaign, though it did put effort into lobbying key MPs and sections of the media. JLE was really decided by senior ministers. O&Y lobbied MPs, journalists and local government not because it had to, but because it wanted to minimise opposition. Lowe Bell and its clients were effective because their campaign was multi-faceted, but it is possible to speculate that they would have 'won' without that extra effort.

Micro-level

Routines and procedures

A civil servant described O&Y as 'peculiarly bloody-minded' with 'little idea how to handle us. They believed a bit of North American "know how" would fix it'.[89] To prevent this perception spreading, O&Y hired lobbyists who understood the system. Knowing informal rules was important.

Lowe Bell helped O&Y avoid defeat at an early stage. Lobbyists had learned from DTp that LT was about to present its 'priority list' of ten schemes, which did not include JLE. The lobbyists advised: 'you must accept that if you do not do something you will lose because they will have made the decision. You have to change it and stop it now.'[90] Lowe Bell recommended O&Y send a cash offer directly to the minister. The lobbyist cautioned: 'If you send a letter to the department you may find it is not reviewed until after the meeting with ministers.'[91] Paul Reichmann agreed a letter offering a £100 million contribution. O&Y in London 'had it signed by Reichmann who was in Canada, and had it hand-delivered to the Transport Secretary at a dinner that night. I would never have done that myself because I would have thought I had time. But Tim advised we would have lost it.'[92] This intervention ensured JLE was discussed when officials briefed ministers. Whilst this bypassing of the civil service annoyed officials, the lobbyist's understanding of individuals and policy-making in practice prevented O&Y from losing at a very early stage. 'It was tactical nous, a knowledge of individuals, knowledge of process and knowledge of people, which kept us in the game.'[93]

Lowe Bell took a foreign client, unfamiliar with British politics, and ensured it performed at the standard of its home environment. It was important for O&Y not to commit errors. It was important, in order to make O&Y seem serious, that it had a thorough understanding of the local environment, including its politics. Lobbyists brought an understanding of how government worked and an understanding of government policy.

LUL remained obstructive even after DTp ministers had approved JLE and the Bill was introduced. DTp policy officials relied almost exclusively on LUL for information, but LUL was a 'reluctant promoter of that Bill and that project'.[94] In Parliament, at the Second Reading of the Bill, lobbyists briefed 'MPs and made sure they understood what the issues were and how important the scheme was'.[95] O&Y and the DTp made sure appropriate MPs were approached for the Bill Committee and appropriate 'suggestions were made to [the Chairman of the Committee of Selection] about how important it was to get the selection right'.[96] O&Y believed that: 'On the Jubilee Line we fixed our Bill. We fixed it. You put a safe Tory MP in the chair, and we knew if you did not your Bill may fail.'[97]

DTp felt LUL 'dealt with petitioners badly and slowly. They were dragging their feet.'[98] O&Y also believed LUL were not managing their legislation effectively. Lobbyists used their knowledge of parliamentary processes to act as a channels of information to inform DTp officials about what happened in Westminster. Whilst government remained technically neutral on Private Bills, 'clearly it was a Bill that ministers wanted to see pushed through'.[99] A senior official recognised the fact that, 'if the lobbyists had not been involved, and I had not known the lobbyists well by that stage, I think government could have been seriously embarrassed on one or two occasions. We needed information to know what was going on. The lobbyists were very effective.'[100]

Conclusion

One former adviser argued: 'It is useful for lobbyists to know the system, but they can have someone to tell them how it works – someone from inside the system. Lobbyists do not have to be *of* the system.'[101] One lobbyist said: 'One has seen politics, so you understand what makes these people tick. There is nothing new there ... [I] understand how the system operates, how to frame your arguments, how to prepare yourself, and how to communicate what you are trying to do.'[102] This knowledge of informal rules and a knowledge of parliamentary process helped ensure JLE progressed though important stages.

Contacts and coalitions

Contacts

Lowe Bell's Conservative contacts were legendary. A former Cabinet minister recalls: 'A friend of mine who worked for Lowe Bell and was representing O&Y, said "Would you mind coming to a presentation given by these two people?"'[103] The minister attended the meeting and recalled about O&Y: 'I have never seen such a slick performance before – absolutely astonishing. These people had their act together. It was like a tornado that arrived in town.'[104] Lowe Bell 'had contacts at every level. They believed in working at every level. That is something O&Y never could have done ourselves.'[105] Lowe Bell organised lunches to meet decision-makers. One senior political adviser commented:

> Lowe Bell and the team was trusted by all of us. We knew they were good guys. When they said we must see these people we said 'okay'. Because of the status of Tim Bell and the team it was a third-party endorsement that O&Y needed. Lowe Bell would not work for third-rate people so you felt you were safe.[106]

Ministers and special advisers were comfortable working with Lowe Bell. Friendships delivered information. One lobbyist suggested: 'Contacts were important to pick up intelligence about the way things were moving, which influenced strategy significantly.'[107] Another lobbyist commented: 'a lot of people I was at the Department of Transport with are my chums. They are friends of mine.'[108] Having a network of friends allowed lobbyists to be in the information loop: 'you come across it in the course of day to day events. You get a sense of it. You just pick it up...You keep in touch with people.'[109] Lobbyists knew decision-makers personally. One official recalled: 'The real trick that one lobbying firm brought to the party was they knew people like Michael Portillo personally. They were very effective at lobbying Portillo and myself when I became the responsible official.'[110]

O&Y had substantial political influence. It was an outsider in two senses and an insider in another. It was an outsider because it was a property developer and not a developer of urban railways; it was also a Canadian company, perceived as a 'foreigner in a foreign land'.[111] But O&Y was an insider because it had high-level access to ministers and political support. Whilst executives in London had easy access to senior decision-makers with lobbyists' help, much contact was undertaken personally by Paul Reichmann. An O&Y adviser said of Reichmann's access: 'I have never seen anything like it. He would ring up Thatcher from his portable phone driving around in his limo.'[112]

Civil servants thought O&Y believed 'they could get in anywhere' and thought they could 'bang the table then God help you'.[113] Officials had the Prime Ministerial deal 'thrown' at them by O&Y when obstacles arose. O&Y directors 'had a great "card" which they would play whenever there was a problem: "you and us have a deal and we should be pulling in the same direction".'[114] The Reichmann–Thatcher deal gave O&Y credibility. An LT manager said of the Thatcher–Reichmann connection, 'I rather despised it all and I did not like Reichmann's personal style.'[115]

Coalitions

There was no broad coalition of supporters for JLE. O&Y's campaign focused on three central departments (DTp, DoE and DTI), the Cabinet Office and No. 10. Some civil servants thought O&Y was 'ghastly' because everything about them alien. DTp officials were shocked by O&Y's aggressive attitude. Relations between LT, DTp and O&Y remained tense after government had approved JLE. Ministers, however, sided with O&Y and believed their own officials to be 'bloody-minded';[116] they became impatient with the bureaucracy and lack of vision. O&Y 'were given the minimum possible assistance' by DTp and LT.[117]

Some opponents of JLE lobbied government. Docklands threatened the City of London, and as a consequence the Corporation relaxed planning guidelines, allowing a further 20 million square feet of office space within the City.[118] The Corporation believed JLE was built only as a tax break for Docklands.

Conclusion

Effective lobbyists distinguish between those who decide and those who inform. Lower down the hierarchy are those with no power of assent, but significant power of dissent and the ability to block. In a stereotypical North American approach 'the Olympia & York philosophy was whatever barriers you come across you either go around them, under them, over them or finally, through them'.[119] O&Y had a reputation for success, which was shared by their lobbyists. 'Lowe Bell's contacts in the Conservative world were superb', and they were hired because 'they were deemed to be the best'.[120] O&Y's two lobbyists – Lowe Bell and GJW – complemented one another. O&Y recalled: 'Tim Bell did not know the process very well. GJW would give us papers on the process. Bell just knew how to get in to see people.'[121] Bell understood Thatcher: he understood what made her tick. His role was to introduce ideas and his clients to the system. Conventionally third-party endorsement is regarded as essential to an effective lobbying campaign. This campaign was atypical: a quasi-commercial deal, senior political commitment and its centrality to the government's political agenda cemented JLE. Coalitions were not important in O&Y's lobbying. Contacts were important and lobbyists effectively spotted allies in government; allies outside government and broader coalitions were not important.

Resources

The economic might of O&Y was overwhelming. O&Y was run with obsessive secrecy by three brothers. It moved into property development in 1965, and developed Toronto's First Canadian Place in 1974. The project was massively profitable, and the family soon became the world's largest property developer and was listed amongst the ten richest in the world. The company reputedly had assets worth $25 billion. The Reichmanns' reputation for trustworthiness enabled them to 'consummate deals with a handshake and to obtain non-collateralized loans from usually wary bankers'.[122] Bankers jockeyed to lend O&Y money, allowing the company to obtain funds whilst it provided minimal financial information. O&Y had an established record in speculative development, including the World Finance Center in Manhattan. It was the largest single office landlord in USA, owning 40 million square feet of office space. Canary Wharf was the largest development in Europe.

O&Y was not only the biggest; it was the best. It pioneered new construction and financing techniques. Its commitment to quality design and public amenities, together with innovative building techniques, encouraged good relations with host governments. The company had the Midas touch. Its economic might was awesome. O&Y invested more in Britain 'than all the Japanese automobile manufacturers put together'.[123] Lobbyists were helpful, but the economic power of O&Y and Paul Reichmann's prestige meant they had access to No. 10 and ministers in their own right.

The cost of the lobbying campaign

O&Y spent many millions of pounds developing and presenting their proposals. A senior businessman argued that the cost of services of lobbyists and specialised consultants over two years was 'well into a seven figure sum'.[124] LT had never experienced 'a scheme which had so much political lobbying and tactical meetings about who to lobby next. O&Y had a whole unit to influence government and decision-makers.'[125] O&Y paid LT for technical research and hired a transport consultancy to examine the available options. '[W]ork was largely funded by them. They paid LT to look at their schemes. It was positive lobbying. LT could not refuse to do it.'[126] A former Cabinet Minister noted: 'They were coming out with an idea a day. London Transport were running to catch up.'[127]

Managerial resources

JLE was given top priority within O&Y. A senior O&Y executive devoted his entire time to lobbying for a transport link. A political adviser cautioned: 'If you want a successful campaign, there has to be a massive investment of time from the top people in any organisation. You have to do that for something of that size. Paul Reichmann was back and forth across the Atlantic like a yo-yo.'[128] The resources O&Y committed to the campaign were 'very significant'; a former Cabinet Minister argued:

> There was such a lot of momentum and drive and vision, much of which depended on resources. Every day you saw that they had a new idea, that they had moved the debate forward. Personally I found it very impressive. It could not have been generated without resources and not without quality people.[129]

Conclusion

To be effective clients must resource a lobbying campaign sufficiently. One lobbyist argued: 'if a client is committed to achieving a particular outcome on a particular project it has got to resource it properly. O&Y certainly did.'[130] Lobbyists focused O&Y's activities and made O&Y's lobbying more effective. O&Y's structure and devotion of substantial financial and managerial resources to the JLE campaign was an important factor in its success.

Conclusions

External variables

O&Y and their lobbyists had a case that was in line with the government's agenda at the highest level. O&Y was making the government's Docklands policy a success. JLE delivered other parts of the government's agenda, principally private-sector involvement in public projects and regeneration. Whilst JLE was not approved because of the private-sector contribution, it would not have gone ahead without it. The money was essential to justify the decision. But the developer was astute enough to recognise JLE would be built for political reasons, and therefore was unwilling to contribute a substantial share of costs.

The lobbyists fitted their client's policy into the wider political picture and were effective in harnessing the reinforcing supporters and arguments. DTp was averse to new ideas because it was comfortable in the CLRS agenda. This attitude dictated O&Y's *modus operandi* to engage the political level. O&Y's lobbyists effectively forced the issue into the open and on to ministers' agendas. JLE had support at the highest level. The drive from ministers and the Prime Minister, who had invested substantial financial and political capital in Docklands, ensured success.

External economic factors were important and did impinge; however, despite the recession and the collapse of O&Y, the political commitment to JLE remained. Also, the lack of a political consensus in London allowed O&Y to 'divide and rule' by relying on top-level support.

Internal variables

Whilst contextual variables were important in shaping the policy outcome, so were the internal variables within the control of the lobbyist and its client. The client and the lobbyists spent time and money on securing the profile of the scheme and making sure government did not lose sight. The lobbyist helped build political confidence in a decision that required a leap of faith. Lowe Bell's lobbying was important because it concentrated on the 'top' to deliver political support to navigate around 'blocking' civil servants and their public-sector clients. Lowe Bell's activity was largely hidden from officials and LT as the company lobbied No. 10 and senior ministers.

The client and its lobbyists enjoyed top-level access, subverting the normal policy process. The lobbyist acted as a catalyst, introducing information into parts of the system and starting a chain reaction, which it reinforced. Lobbyists helped arrange meetings with appropriate ministers, civil servants and advisers. Lowe Bell helped gain access to the Prime Minister. JLE was the triumph of internal politics and Margaret Thatcher's cosiness with the Reichmanns. Officials and some ministers preferred other policies, but the political elite chose JLE. The oral commitment that Reichmann received from Thatcher echoed an earlier deal struck personally by the Prime Minister. The DTp Accounting Officer *did* express doubts to ministers about JLE, but his concerns were not so grave as to characterise the project a 'bad buy'.[131]

The number of influential policy-makers was limited. No. 10, Environment, Transport and Treasury were the involved departments. The Prime Minister was the most important actor. A small and restricted group of senior politicians took the decision to promote JLE. The role of the civil service and Parliament was limited. O&Y and its lobbyists rolled-over official intransigence and sidelined the wider policy community. They operated effectively within Whitehall to overcome DTp scepticism and Treasury hostility. Lobbyists were effective in advising O&Y to 'go around' the Transport Department. Lobbyists were able to engage the Prime Minister's interest at moments when the process floundered. Lobbyists helped their client understand the frailties of the individuals and the system which, if it did not ensure the client won, at least ensured it did not lose at crucial moments in the process.

The campaign to secure the JLE was well-resourced. In addition to considerable financial resources, it had less tangible resources such as the triumphal mentality of the private sector. It was used to winning. O&Y's golden touch was in contrast to the grey, mundane public-sector bodies. O&Y also had significant managerial resources. Canary Wharf's success depended on JLE, so O&Y devoted substantial time and resources to securing it. The management team were single-minded, committed, well-briefed and effective advocates.

O&Y did not undertake a wide multi-faceted campaign, involving Parliament, the media or the public. It did, however, deal at all levels and branches of government. Lobbying across Whitehall was concentrated, intense and bordered on saturation. O&Y recognised that complex decisions would not be made by DTp alone, and targeted other key players in government, especially actors who were likely to be enthusiastic, such as No. 10 and DoE. Support from other areas of government forced DTp to accept a new agenda.

* * *

Political and business pressures supporting JLE meant the routine policy system was overruled by ministers. A technical government report sought to legitimise the high-level political decision taken earlier to approve JLE. Ministers recognised JLE's transport case was weak, but approved JLE not because of its measurable benefits, but because of intense lobbying and political factors, especially prime-ministerial support. JLE underwent formal appraisal processes, but conventional evaluation did not account for political and economic factors. Political pragmatism ruled. A former minister reflected that: 'the government looked very silly having given the go-ahead to a scheme which even by my assessment had less of an immediate return than CrossRail'.[132] Politicians played a central role in setting departmental agendas. The civil service was over-ridden. Civil servants and some ministers were subservient to a high-level political deal.

7
Limiting Professional Liability

Accountants campaigned to change the law on professional liability to reduce risks for both firms and partners. The issue was technical, non-political and had a low public profile. The campaign to limit professional liability began in 1978, but this chapter focuses on the big firms' involvement since the campaign's concerted yet inconspicuous relaunch in the early 1990s. Though liability was a most important issue for accountants, debate was restricted to journals and technical sections of national broadsheets. This campaign has not previously received attention.

There were two strands to the accountants' campaign: (A) the risk to the firms, and (B) the risk to partners. Auditors claimed they were exposed to unreasonable risk because various financial crises had encouraged plaintiffs to target them. The campaign's ultimate objective was to limit these risks by replacing the law of joint and several (J&S) with proportionate liability. The supplementary goal was to protect the assets of partners. Partners were personally liable to the extent of their personal assets for the firms' liabilities and debts. The desired policy change – Limited Liability Partnerships (LLPs) – would limit liability to the firm and the negligent partner.

On strand A, a legally blameless plaintiff does not carry the risk of a defendant's insolvency when another jointly liable defendant remains solvent. The plaintiff's loss is regarded as indivisible if caused by the combined action or inaction of more than one party.[1] J&S applies only where all co-defendants are equally and fully liable.[2] There were four reform options proposed to change this structure. The first was proportionate liability, which would recognise the difference between legal causation and degree of blame. Reform would limit a concurrent wrongdoer's liability to his proportionate liability.[3] Each defendant would be responsible to the plaintiff only for part of the damage caused.[4] The second option, a statutory cap on damages, would limit liability and protect against 'Armageddon claims'.[5] A cap is easy to operate, and a limit covering the majority of claims would retain the deterrent effect of tort damages.[6] The third option, contractual exclusion clauses, required amending section 310 of the Companies Act 1985,[7] the Unfair Contract Terms Act 1977 (UCTA) and the Unfair Terms in Consumer Contracts Regulations 1994.[8] Exclusion clauses would be enforceable against parties to the contract, and would not protect professional defendants against tort claims by third parties.[9] The fourth option, contributory negligence, would permit auditors to defend themselves by arguing that others contributed to their negligence.[10] Under current law it is difficult for auditors to 'argue contributory negligence in the shape of the company's failure through its directors when the audit function involves just such an issue'.[11]

Under strand B, to protect the partners the principal reform model was Limited Liability Partnerships. LLPs are useful in 'Armageddon' claims because partners' assets would be protected. The assets of the individual would be ring-fenced, but the assets of the firm and negligent partners would remain at risk.[12]

Interest groups and lobbyists

PriceWaterhouseCoopers coordinated lobbying along with other Liability Reform Group (LRG) members; Ernst & Young (E&Y), Deloitte Touche, Arthur Andersen and KPMG. Ian Greer Associates (IGA) won the £120 000 lobbying contract because, according to *The Guardian*, it emphasised its ties with the Corporate Affairs Minister, Neil Hamilton. The lobbyists' remit was 'to achieve limited liability status for the accountancy profession. In order to meet that objective, primary legislation would need to be introduced in the 1995–96 Parliamentary Session, which would begin in November 1995. IGA would then have followed the legislation through parliament, which would have meant another year's work.'[13]

Leigh and Vulliamy claim IGA implied that soundings with the minister indicated he was 'sympathetic' and emphasised that IGA's Managing Director was a 'former researcher to Neil Hamilton'.[14] Hamilton's brief included company law, and IGA was hired 'because of its relationship with Neil Hamilton, on whose desk this lay'.[15] A lobbyist met Hamilton off-the-record to brief him, whilst senior partners met him formally months later. The firms also held a meeting with the Secretary of State. However, IGA's contract was terminated when the company was the subject of *The Guardian*'s investigation, led by David Hencke. IGA's dismissal was described to the Select Committee on Standards and Privileges. The lobbyists:

> attended a meeting with Mr Brindle [of PriceWaterhouse]. There was a copy of *The Guardian* of 20 October on the table in Mr Brindle's office. ... Mr Brindle said that he had had discussions with the Senior Partners in the other major accounting firms and he informed Mr Sweeny and myself that the Big 8 had decided to bring IGA's contract with them to an end as a result of *The Guardian*'s allegations, particularly because they involved Neil Hamilton MP, the Minister with responsibility for their profession.[16]

The minister believed:

> *The Guardian*'s conspiracy theories about this matter were preposterous and could be seriously advocated only by individuals who have little experience or understanding of the workings of government – particularly in a technical area such as this. I was well able to evaluate the representations to me on technical issues and could identify special pleading without difficulty.[17]

GJW was invited to tender for the vacant role. A senior partner recalls: 'we had a beauty parade. GJW came along and within ten minutes of the presentation we knew he was the guy we wanted.'[18] The regulatory body of the accountancy profession, the Institute of Chartered Accountants for England and Wales (ICAEW), acted as a client façade. GJW had two tasks: project management and advising on campaign tactics. A civil servant said that: 'the firms are very clear with us that the political consultant is there to give advice, not to open doors and pull strings'.[19] LRG informed GJW: 'You are paid to tell us what we do when we get inside those doors. There is to be no direct contact between you and the government. We employ you to help us read politics.'[20]

Macro-level

Profile, technicality and politicality

Strand A

Liability reform is technical and non-political. It is also perceived as low-profile, even though it has a wide impact. One official said: 'this is certainly not front page of The *Sun* stuff. I have not seen a lot of comment or articles in the *FT* [*Financial Times*], *Observer* or *Sunday Times*.'[21] The nature of the issue dictated the type of campaign. It was not possible to run a high-profile campaign on liability because 'campaigners will not get tears shed for unfairness against lawyers and accountants'.[22] The *Financial Times* recognised the government was 'unlikely to see much public appeal in an issue that is barely understood within Britain's boardrooms, let alone outside them'.[23] The Liability Campaign Group adopted a low-profile approach, shunning media coverage, as requested by the DTI; yet the campaign was high-profile within a very small policy community. The large firms believed they 'owned' the reform agenda. Government remained disinterested in this policy change and, following several requests by LRG for stays of decision, LRG finally faced the Company Law Review or outright defeat.[24] The Company Law Review was grudgingly accepted because its 'long grass' would stop liability reform being completely removed from the agenda or rejected.

Strand B

LLPs were also low-profile, technical and non-political. Government saw LLPs as low risk and non-partisan, with broad support from interested parties. In the new Labour government's 'arrival pack was a note saying "This proposal is on the stocks. Are you happy with it?" They were.'[25] Labour carried forward a Bill drafted under the Conservative government. LLPs succeeded because they were uncontroversial. Lobbyists were of some value. They acted as translators and brokers. Following the Bill's approval in principle, lobbyists concentrated on finding legislative time and cautioned against controversy. A senior partner recalled: 'The minister told us "If there is something wrong with the Bill I would rather you did not make a lot of noise in public. I would rather you went to see officials".'[26] If the firms made 'noise' in public, they risked losing the legislation.

The effect of lobbyists

IGA fell into the 'Hencke problem'.[27] One lobbyist recalled: 'When I first joined IGA it had a brand value. Politicians and civil servants would trust you. When the Hencke story blew that changed, and that damaged our effectiveness'.[28] One leading accountant said IGA added 'not much value. It is not very clear to me what they did for us.'[29] Another senior partner said 'Greer was pretty useless. I do not think they were highly regarded.'[30] An ICAEW representative argued: 'My view is that IGA added nothing and that the accountants were wasting their money.'[31]

GJW was more central to the campaign. It was less conspicuous, but a central player advising on interaction with decision-makers. The lobbyists scripted things behind the scenes, then pushed the client forward to do it. The lobbyists believed they were 'crucially involved. We had a quite central role in all the documentation that went out from the group. Nothing went out without us looking at the substantial drafting.'[32] Although the lobbyists failed to achieve their clients' policy objectives they added value by advising how civil servants worked, how the Cabinet machinery operated, and providing an insight into ministerial priorities. GJW added a sense of cohesion by establishing a core: it gave the LRG 'vigour and discipline. They were very effective. They had a knowledge of what the papers should look like, and their timing. They understood how government works.'[33]

Civil servants believed the campaign was ineffective. One official argued: 'If you look at the quality of the campaign I would not have paid them very much. I think we know them, but I would expect them to be operating at a political level. I don't trust many people, and I trust lobbyists least of all.'[34] Another agreed, arguing: 'I do not think they have been very effective in dealing with government.'[35] A third suggested, 'the fact that we have said we are not going to do it implies they have not been effective'.[36]

Conclusion

There was no 'public' element to the liability campaign. It focused exclusively on civil servants and ministers. The lobbyist provided management consultancy and tactical advice. A partner said: 'We do not blame GJW for the failure, we have all failed.'[37] Another concluded: 'GJW has done everything we have asked of them. But in the sense of not having achieved our objective then they have not been effective.'[38] The campaign for liability reform was ineffective. Although the issue was low-profile, technical and non-political in a partisan sense, the impact of change has been wide, causing complications for policy actors with public-interest concerns. The two issues were linked so closely that lobbyists could not use higher-profile tactics to raise the profile of the liability issue within government because the success of the LLP campaign depended on a low-profile approach.

External factors

This section examines the impact of external constraints on strand A objectives. Some external factors beyond the control of players should have advantaged the campaigners. The profession suggested it was unfairly targeted, pointing to increased litigation from the recession of the late 1980s.[39] The number of claims against the big firms rose from just three in 1982–83 to 627 in 1992–93, and the size of the average claim increased by a factor of 12.

This increase in litigation gave rise to defensive auditing to avoid risk.[40] Interim reporting was increasingly being given orally and audit advice became hedged with caveats, becoming almost meaningless. The audit firms were also increasingly screening clients, which was having an adverse effect on competitiveness because the innovative sectors were seen to be too risky.[41] The more risk-averse attitude being adopted by the bigger firms, they argued, threatened the 'world-class status' of the British accountancy profession, as did recent reform in the USA.[42] Increased costs to clients were also seen to be problematic because the costs of defending and settling claims are passed to clients; insurance premiums rose by a factor of 37 between 1982 and 1992.[43] Finally, the firms claimed that high-calibre personnel were refusing to become partners.[44]

Despite these external factors supporting the firms' campaign, the effort was ineffective because of other factors, such as the litigation cycle, a Law Commission study, and the lack of acceptable reform options.

The litigation cycle

One explanation of the lobby's ineffectiveness was bad timing. The campaigners never answered the question of why a minister should want to take forward legislation as a General Election was approaching. An official argued: 'the problem with the campaign was they got themselves together and ginnied up at the fag end of a government'.[45]

Furthermore, the campaign reached its full intensity when litigation had fallen away. It was the increase in business failures in the early 1990s recession that had galvanised the big firms to seek reform. However, by the time of the campaign the economy had improved and business failures were low. One senior partner argued: 'One problem we had is that in the economic environment we could not sustain the campaign effectively because the litigation against the firms was low.'[46] Another senior partner echoed these sentiments, noting the firms 'tend to see solidarity when they are at the edge of a cliff. We were not quite at the edge of a cliff.'[47]

Official studies

In 1989 an industry–DTI committee, led by Professor Andrew Likierman, examined professional liability for negligence.[48] The committee failed to reach firm conclusions, allowing the government to avoid making a decision. The Likierman study was followed up by a Law Commission investigation since ministers recognised the auditor claim as 'an issue worthy of proper examination'.[49] However, the Law Commission rejected proportionate liability in practice and principle.[50] The Commission kicked the ball into the long grass and removed liability from ministers' desks, also effectively silencing the accountants. The outcome was seriously damaging to the auditors. However, the Law Commission left the door ajar for the reform lobby by accepting that a strong economic efficiency or public-interest case would justify sacrificing sound legal principle.[51]

Conclusion

A civil servant argued: 'given their case and the political context I think it highly unlikely that they could have got further than they have got on broader liability issues'.[52] The success of LLPs and failure of liability reform were determined by matters separate from lobbyists. The failure of joint and several was determined by political forces. The political realities were negative. Whilst the firms managed to amass evidence to support their case, it was not believed by government. Its scepticism was not aided by the firms' truculent attitude. One significant constraint beyond the control of all actors was that the potential solutions proposed by the firms were equally as bad. One senior official argued: 'If we had thought there was a really good case but they had not made it, we could have made it anyway. We were not convinced the problem was sufficiently serious that another bad solution was better.'[53] On LLPs, strand B, there were no contextual constraints affecting lobbying. Government was sceptical of the accountants' case on liability, unimpressed by its timing, and was restricted by the lack of acceptable options. The presence of disadvantageous external factors limited the effect of the lobbyist.

Experience and existing policy

Since the case was technical and non-political, the views of government players – politicians and officials – were important. A civil servant noted:

> Individuals responsible for policy advice have their own views. Government has a view. It is not simply a reactive body. On an issue like this, which is an important policy area but which is not political, there is a lot of leeway at the micro-level because government is a player in its own right since it stands for the public.[54]

The failure of LRG's strand A campaign was caused by its ineffectiveness in linking its demands into the government's key themes. The lobbyists tried to establish a clear focus and shape LRG's political message because they knew the themes of the government and what messages were likely to work. Ministers wanted the firms to construct a public-interest case, and it was the lobbyists that commissioned Herbert Smith (solicitors) to compile a study of case law and settlements and collect data on public-domain settlements to build a public-interest defence.[55] The lobbyists also discussed with the DTI the requirements of economic research under-taken at the Department's request by an economic research consultancy, London Economics.[56]

However, the firms were unable to look further than the confines of their own commercial desires. The DTI believed the firms failed to provide conclusive evidence. 'They refused to submit evidence for what they had to settle claims for. They presented their case on what might happen.'[57] The firms failed to put themselves in the position of the government. They were slow in submitting papers and were bad at addressing govern-ment's concerns. Civil servants indicated several times the issues the firms had to address, but they failed on each occasion. DTI officials were further unimpressed when they discovered firms had failed to limit liability in non-audit work where they were able to do so. The DTI demanded that accountants act to limit their liability outside statutory audit, through contract and the adoption of aggressive risk-management policies. Only late in the campaign did the firms meet government's demands.

A deal

An official believed accountants portrayed the issue 'in terms of saying "We'll give you that if you give us this." It is not a simple give and take. We do not strike deals or bargains.'[58] But, despite the protestations of offi-cials, government often looks for a package. On the reform of liability the firms could not agree what, if anything, to offer government in exchange for reform of joint and several. An official believed that to have been effective LRG 'would have had to make concessions, which they would have rightly seen as the first step in a negotiating process, which would have led them to be pushed to make further concessions'.[59] A list of con-cessions was drafted and circulated, but some firms refused to consider them, believing they had a right to demand change without offering any-thing in return. Various options were discussed, including expanding the scope of audit to comment on corporate governance,[60] and offering assurances on company information.[61] The firms believed the offer was credible because: 'We get limited liability and the public gets openness and accountability.'[62]

On strand B government *took* transparency in exchange for LLPs; dis-closure rules are the same as limited companies. A civil servant argued: 'We could not give LLPs without added responsibilities. We try to find a benefit in the same area.'[63]

Politics

Strand A (liability reform) was time-consuming and politically unattractive, whilst strand B (LLPs) was quick and involved little political risk. The DTI had important political issues to deal with, including minimum wage, union recognition and welfare to work. Liability reform would not help junior ministers into the Cabinet and risked being perceived by 'public interest' campaigners as a special deal for one group. One factor that disadvantaged the firms was the large salaries received by partners. Ministers were irritated by and concerned at salary levels because they feared they established precedents for industry at large. One official said: 'They are not awake to that. We are conscious of it. They earn three quarters of a million – we think that is sufficient reward to outweigh the risk.'[64]

Conclusion

Government had its own objectives. To be effective lobbyists must 'help' government achieve its aims. The DTI most certainly did not religiously follow the lead of outside groups and had wider public-interest concerns close to heart. In some respects the campaign and its lobbyists were effective in tying their case to government's objectives as they pushed the modernising agenda. However, they were out-manoeuvred by the DTI as the Department used their arguments to justify including joint and several in the review of Company Law, effectively removing the issue from the political landscape. Ministers had more important issues to deal with. Overall, the Liability Reform Group failed to link its case to government because it was unwilling to share information with government, and some submissions were poor quality. Government had to force the firms to act to limit non-audit risk. The firms could not agree what to offer government in exchange for reform; finally, J&S reform was politically unattractive.

Strand B (LLP reform) was so uncontentious and the case so convincing that it was in line with both Conservative and Labour government beliefs. Strand A objectives were not congruent with political beliefs and the previous experience of government players.

Meso-level

The policy community

Lobbying the opposition

For most of the campaign Labour was in Opposition and Stuart Bell, MP, was Labour's accountancy spokesman. He did not share the sceptical view of auditors held by some colleagues and launched a charm offensive to win over the business community. GJW worked with Bell to engineer Labour support for proportionality and LLPs, and to quieten PLP dissent.[65] Margaret Beckett, the Shadow Secretary of State for Trade and Industry, was briefed regularly. GJW wanted the Opposition team to feel involved in policy development. Bell dined regularly with partners from the Big Five firms. In August 1996 Bell offered government the Opposition's cooperation on the 'non-political' reform of joint and several.[66]

Before the General Election the Shadow Minister 'was trying to be approachable and friendly to business – almost bending over backwards. We drafted after the meeting two possible paragraphs for insertion into the manifesto', explained the lobbyist.[67] So the lobbyist drew up paragraphs for the 1997 Labour manifesto: the first on LLPs and the second on liability. A covering letter later formed the basis of two journal articles, under Bell's name, which explained Labour's policy.[68] The lobbyist said that when 'Bell submitted the two paragraphs we wrote speculatively; we did not assume that he would get them past the manifesto editor'.[69] However, Labour published a *Manifesto for Business*, which included the following paragraph:

We will ensure there is a framework of independent regulation for the accountancy profession. We will review the laws on joint and several liability so that incorporation in this country provides accountants with adequate protection.[70]

The outcome was a jumbled mess and as a consequence of pressure of space, two paragraphs were merged into one. The second sentence confused the risks to the partner and the firm. The Business Manifesto was not put before the PLP, unlike in 1992. One Labour MP said: 'I do not know how it got there. ... The whole thing was a shoddy, concealed back door business.'[71] Bell's detailed policy articles could not now be taken as Labour policy because they pre-dated the Manifesto. Bell was forced to claim that the muddle demonstrated 'the complexity of the issues involved', and he restated the broad principles underlying Labour's approach.[72] However, despite this mistake the lobbying firm was effective in including and managing its client in the Labour Party network, the consequence of which was a manifesto commitment.

Policy community

The transient liability policy community was built around a DTI minister responsible for accountancy. The potential or dormant community included the following actors:

- Secretary of State for Trade and Industry;
- Minister of State for Corporate Affairs;
- Minister for Trade and Competitiveness in Europe;
- 3 DTI civil servants in Company Law Directorate;
- DTI special advisers;
- Chancellor of the Exchequer;
- Chief Secretary to the Treasury;
- 3 Treasury civil servants in the Finance Regulation and Industry and Financial Management Reporting and Audit Directorate Directorates;
- Treasury special advisers;
- Lord Chancellor;
- 2 Lord Chancellor's Department (LCD) civil servants;
- LCD special adviser;
- 1 Department of the Environment, Transport and the Regions, civil servant;
- 2 advisers in the No.10 Policy Unit.

Non-government actors included the professional bodies, the Big Five, the small firms networks and European-level groups. However, the number of *influential* players was smaller.

Officials

Middle-ranking DTI officials were the key government actors. Three people in the DTI were actively involved. No other departments were active on liability, although some were interested. The circle of those who could have been influential was wide, but their involvement was conditional on other factors. DTI's Company Law Directorate listed approximately 1500 organisations, of which several hundred were invited to respond to its LLP proposals. Only 114 did so, and of this number many had no substantive comment. The 'real' policy community was very small. Interest groups were active only when an issue concerned them directly; otherwise they lay dormant. Communities emerged and dissolved over specific issues. The big firms did not struggle to be involved. They had good links to government. Ministers invited them to participate. Lobbyists were irrelevant. One former minister recalled:

> I visited many individual firms of accountants as 'their' minister and invited many individuals to participate in the generation of policy. For example I invited a senior tax partner to chair a tax deregulation

taskforce. I alighted upon him because of an article I read in *Accountancy Age*.[73]

The big firms worked closely behind the scenes with the government, offering technical advice. An official argued that the community included interest groups who sought out civil servants, but noted: 'the Accountancy profession is incestuous – the same people crop up all the time. We try and make it as broad as possible.'[74] Rather than exclude interest groups, civil servants were desperately trying to increase the range of representation:

> Consultations are important because government wants to be open and ensure everyone is consulted, so that by the time you get legislation everyone is cleared. Anyone who rings up with an interest will be added to the consultation list and will get a copy of consultation papers. That is the limit of our powers. It is important for us that people comment on the draft.[75]

Even substantive interest groups, such as the Institute of Directors (IoD), were invited to participate but had no substantive comment. Many responses from groups:

> were unhelpful. On a few questions the answers were useless because they misunderstood the point. It just shows how little outside groups understand. When we dealt with LLPs we held a range of meetings with the accountancy profession, the legal profession, investors and clients. We tried to get the people who would be interested.[76]

Since the issue was technical and low-profile, DTI officials went out looking for commentators. They alerted groups and encouraged them to give their views, but found it difficult to motivate them.

Ministers

Labour DTI ministers 'had no set answers. There was a genuine attempt to try and work out what was best.'[77] The manifesto commitment allowed LRG to ask for clarification. The lobbyist argued: 'It is amazing that we got the commitment when the issue did not matter. That is our saving grace.'[78] In the event Bell was not appointed to the DTI.[79] Bell was so anxious to please that he was perceived by many as having gone too far in placating the accountancy profession. The lobbyist argued: 'One does not see the problems when a senior spokesman is turning your way. You think that is an element of success. In retrospect he was trying too hard.'[80] Bell's old brief was divided between Ian McCartney and a Blairite appointee and former businessman, Lord Simon. The lobbyist drafted a submission on joint and several in June 1997 to coincide with the minister's post-election review of departmental priorities. McCartney, a leftist former party activist, was less friendly and less willing to bend over backwards than was Bell. Furthermore, it became clear that the Secretary of State, Margaret Beckett, had no interest in accountancy.

The lobbyist drafted a letter to the DTI asking for a 'council of war' to discuss matters with ministers in October 1997. Partners met officials after the October meeting to clarify the conclusions of the ministerial meeting. However, a second 'crunch meeting' was held with ministers in July 1998, which confirmed the failure of the liability campaign. In a summer reshuffle Peter Mandelson, MP, became Secretary of State for Trade and Industry and in that year announced a Draft LLP Bill.[81] However, on the real prize of joint and several liability reform he said:

> no sufficient basis had been identified, of either principle, commercial or economic interest, for a fundamental reform of the law affecting professional liability. ... A convincing case has not been made for fundamental change. We will keep the situation under review in case new evidence emerges. In the meantime I would encourage the accountancy profession to contribute to the fundamental review of company law that is now underway including on the question of the relative responsibilities of auditors, investors and directors.[82]

Conclusion

The client did not need lobbyists to access the policy community because they were firmly ensconced in the DTI. Though LRG dominated the policy-making arena, the department fulfilled its commitment to give 'full consideration to the views expressed by all interested parties' to broaden interest.[83] The lobbyist helped build contacts with Labour and, by luck rather than good judgement, delivered a manifesto commitment. The lobbyist was also useful in identifying the players who needed to be contacted in order for the LLP Bill to proceed. The real policy community was transient and small. The influential number of players numbered no more than a handful.

Multi-faceted lobbying

GJW's brochure says: 'the best government relations practice operates at all levels – from the grass roots right up to the national and pan-national parliaments'.[84] The DTI recognised that the firms were playing the game at various different levels in different arenas. However, LRG had to win the argument first with civil servants and ministers. Parliament and the media were largely absent from policy development. On strand A LRG focused on civil servants exclusively, whilst strand B lobbying targeted Cabinet Committees and some MPs.

Cabinet committees

On strand B (LLPs), once the LLP Bill was approved in principle the lobbyist targeted the Queen's Speech and Future Legislation Committee (QFL) and the Cabinet's Legislation Committee (LEG) to ensure a legislative slot. This activity was covertly supported by the DTI which was concerned that a Bill would not be prioritised. QFL demanded that the LLP Bill be judged uncontentious in order to secure parliamentary time because, whilst the Commons was occupied with complex constitutional legislation, government hoped to busy the Lords with uncontentious Bills. The lobbyist coordinated the accountants' approach with the legal profession, which was also affected by LLP legislation, to ensure that the Lord Chancellor, the Attorney General and the Lord Advocate were briefed. The lobbyist also briefed special advisers and junior ministers at LCD, special advisers in the Treasury and the Head of Financial Services in the Treasury. LRG representatives also lobbied No. 10 Policy Unit advisers.

LEG examined draft bills and considered parliamentary timetabling. The lobbyist examined the LEG membership, picked the influential people and targeted their special advisers. The lobbyist focused on advisers to the Leader of the House, the Treasury and the Cabinet Office, because of their overarching roles, as well as the DTI.

Parliament

The firms barely campaigned in Parliament. MPs were unimportant. The few questions raised in the House were largely arranged by whips to announce government action. One LRG member said: 'We never got to the point of cultivating the MP in the street.'[85] The backbench Labour MP, Austin Mitchell, initiated the only public scrutiny of LLPs and liability. Mitchell attacked the 'lovely little arrangement' operated by the firms.[86] His opposition did not concern the accountancy firms because they found him a comical figure. One senior partner argued: 'The advice we were getting was that having Mitchell against us was a major plus point.'[87]

Few MPs understood the issue as it was too complex to invite any substantive scrutiny. Whilst No. 10, the Cabinet Office and the Treasury supported the business agenda, lobbyists were concerned at parliamentary hostility. As part of Labour's drive to 'modernise' Parliament, draft Bills were published to encourage lobbying and more thorough parliamentary scrutiny.[88] The lobbyist briefed all parties' spokesmen about the LLP Bill as the seven-page Draft Bill's public consultation ran concurrently with a Select Committee investigation. The DTI warned LRG that criticism from the accountants would mean the loss of the Bill from the timetable, effectively preventing the group from recommending amendments.

The lobbyist also prepared LRG for the Select Committee Inquiry by briefing Select Committee members, involving Stuart Bell and selected PPSs. The lobbyist established contact with the Select Committee Clerk and received assurances that the Committee would not interfere with the Bill's principles. The campaign also 'squared' selected third parties to ensure the evidence was predominantly consistent and supportive.

Opponents

As LLPs were low-profile, technical and non-political there was little opposition. On liability (strand A), because the issue was complex, detractors used 'the *Sun* headline' approach. The issue was presented in simple terms, such as 'secretive fat cats lining their own pockets'. Officials bemoaned the lack of an active articulated contribution from the public interest angle. Opponents characterised the firms' objectives as 'anti-consumer' and argued that the campaign was ill-considered, bad-tempered and selfish. Concerned about possible opposition, LRG lobbied the DTI to publish only firm proposals because their lobbyist believed that if 'industry, business and parliament did not have time to look at it and if it was not properly scrutinised, it would go through quickly'.[89]

Media

The campaign eschewed a media campaign because they wanted to avoid controversy. The LRG used the media carefully. The DTI official said: 'It is not something we would encourage.'[90] The lobbyist placed articles in the *Financial Times* but, significantly, the articles were shown to, and approved by, DTI before publication. DTI clearance was judicious because one senior partner recalled: 'There was a very clear message to us that if we had concerns, we should tell them [DTI] directly rather than through the columns of the *Financial Times*.'[91] The lobbyist cultivated contacts in the *Financial Times* and *The Times*, but coverage outside the specialised press was limited. Both lobbyist and client were happy having a low-profile media strategy.

Conclusion

There was no need for a multi-faceted approach. Indeed, it would have been counterproductive. The LLP campaign was effective because it concentrated on one element of the policy-making system: Whitehall, namely officials and Cabinet Committees. There was limited briefing of MPs on the Trade and Industry Select Committee. On the liability issue, LRG pursued a low-profile campaign, directed exclusively at civil servants and (through them) ministers. Though tempted to raise the profile when defeated in September 1998, it did not, because to have done so would have jeopardised the LLP legislation. A multi-faceted campaign may be ineffective on low-profile, technical and non-political issues.

Micro-level

Routines and procedures

The lobbyist's role was to guide clients 'through the procedures of government consultation so that you make your case with maximum effect'.[92] The brochure noted that the lobbying firm had worked with politicians and some of its staff were former officials; consequently they had 'a comprehensive and inside knowledge of the processes, procedures and etiquette of government'.[93]

The lobbyist 'put in effort, time and resources into identifying what the department wanted and what it didn't want'.[94] An official argued that: 'Lobbyists were much clearer about the processes the civil service goes though.'[95] The lobbyists assisted officials with their brief, and then were able to ask for help in return. It was a reciprocal process. A civil servant argued that the lobbyists came:

> to us and said 'We guess you are going to do *X* next. What is the best way in which our clients can approach you?' That allowed us to focus their effort. We did not have to deal with a campaign that lobbied ministers and MPs. Such a campaign takes valuable resources away from dealing with the subject matter, to dealing with correspondence. A lobbyist brings advantages for civil servants.[96]

On technical issues the conviction, vigour and perceptions of officials are central. A strong and respected supportive official makes success more likely. Understanding inter-departmental relations was also important because 'Ian McCartney and Lord Simon [the junior ministers] saw the Treasury as more important than their Secretary of State. The Secretary of State would go along with the advice of his junior minister on this.'[97] The degree of trust between the lobbyist and the six clients was substantial. Each firm entrusted individually to the lobbyist confidential financial data about its business. No other co-campaigning firm saw the data passed by the others; only the lobbyist and the lawyers saw everything.

The lobbyist also used a BBC journalist and E&Y adviser, Nick Ross, to lead a 'brain storming session' on repositioning after Labour's victory. Ross was valuable because of his knowledge of the sector and his contacts with Lord Simon and Geoffrey Robinson. Just as GJW used Ross as 'an independent source to verify what we were saying',[98] the DTI sometimes used GJW to reinforce its advice to LRG. Contrary to the conventional responses of civil servants, one official said:

> You can say to GJW 'this is the message we gave them [LRG]'. Having it come from the lobbyist reinforces it. You may think you have given a clear message, but the accountancy firms can misinterpret your advice. They are more likely to take the advice of the lobbyist because they are paying them.[99]

Shadow lobbying

The IGA-led campaign failed in part because lobbyists dealt directly with decision-makers. 'Greer was fronting with ministers.'[100] IGA adopted a high-profile approach. A former minister recalls: 'there were one or two meetings with the representatives of the Big Eight accompanied by their lobbyists, IGA'.[101] Although lobbyists were present:

> No-one from IGA contributed to the substantive discussions – indeed, as the subject-matter was extremely technical it would have been absurd to expect that of non-expert lobbyists in the presence of experts on both sides of the table. The lobbyists had no impact whatever on the policy-making process on this issue.[102]

GJW lobbyists did not attend meetings with ministers, although they were involved in every aspect of their preparation. They stayed in the background. A senior partner said: 'Virtually all the representation we would do ourselves.'[103] A civil servant interpreted the relationship: 'GJW have been more active with LRG who have then played with us on the basis that contact was already established.'[104] The lobbyist set up the meetings and briefed the officials or advisers in advance. Most of the meetings the lobbyist attended were with special advisers. One official argued: 'It is fatal to use lobbyists as an intermediary, because ministers and their advisers want to hear from the people on the ground – from those who have actually experienced it.'[105]

Lobbyists did brief officials and special advisers for several months following the 1997 election, when ministerial responsibilities were unclear. Also, four firms were distracted by merger proposals, so it was the lobbyist who sent policy papers to the Treasury, and dealt with its officials on an off-the-record basis and communicated frequently with special advisers.[106] Although not at the front-line, GJW was central. The lobbyist noted:

> We were the origin. Everything that was sent out was put through other people in the chain. There was a cumulative effect. We were the genesis of most of the argument but we were rarely the delivery mechanism. We dealt with officials directly and they always knew we were behind activity. But officials were cautious and more comfortable dealing with the client. We were not about to embarrass them. We assisted them in their agenda.[107]

Conclusion

The lobbyist was pivotal to the campaign's management and structure. Its knowledge of rules and procedures underpinned its ability to draft submissions and arrange meetings. Though its impact on the policy outcome was marginal, the lobbyist played a central role within LRG, and without the lobbying consultancy the campaign would have been less coordinated and lacked the confidence to operate effectively in Whitehall.

Contacts and coalitions

Contacts

A key element in the lobbyists' efforts was the relationship developed with Labour in Opposition. The firms seconded staff to Labour. Stuart Bell's association with the wife of a Big Five senior partner, who was his literary agent, also facilitated access. The lobbyist noted that relationships with Labour were 'always friendly. We had no real need for any lobbying.'[108] When Bell did not become Corporate Affairs Minister, he joined Ernst & Young as a parliamentary adviser and lobbying firm Bell Pottinger as a consultant. He advised on New Labour themes and, more importantly, he reminded 'civil servants and ministers of their manifesto commitment, because he wrote it. He also helped keep us up to date.'[109] The firms regarded him as 'a friendly MP who whispered in the ears of Derry Irvine and others to remind them'.[110]

Limiting Professional Liability   175

Formal contact with ministers was infrequent. LRG formally met ministers twice in twelve months after the election, but the firms held individually and jointly a series of lunches with Margaret Beckett. She was content to leave policy in the hands of her ministers.

GJW's brochure claimed it could put clients 'in touch with the right people in the right places and at the right time'.[111] The lobbyist dealt with politicians and advisers directly mainly at social gatherings, despite the clients' 'back room role' instructions. There is a discrepancy between what the lobbyist actually did and what the clients admit to. However, direct contact was usually undertaken when the target was known personally to GJW lobbyists. For example, staff from the lobbying consultancy attended the 'right' social events. At the Labour Party Gala Dinner, the lobbyist 'was on a table with [the Chief Secretary to the Treasury], so I broadly floated it across his agenda in so far as saying, "is it okay, Chief Secretary, if I go and brief your special adviser about accountants' liability?" He said yes.'[112]

Furthermore, the lobbyist explained the most effective way to approach the Secretary of State for Trade and Industry:

to get to the Secretary of State, I will have lunch with his special adviser. At the same time I will invite the Treasury's special adviser. The next step is to encourage both of them to brief the DTI Secretary of State to get him to meet directly with the accountants. There are lots of informal situations where you can raise the possibility.[113]

The firms had good contacts with politicians – often better than those of the political consultant. 'If you look at the list of who's who in British politics and you ask the auditors to tick off who they know, you'll have ninety-nine per cent of the people there.'[114] Partners were 'on the A list for No. 10 dinners because they are movers and shakers'.[115] A senior partner argued the firms did not need the lobbying consultancy to arrange access to ministers, because 'we know them. You take this firm, every Cabinet minister will be known on Christian name terms by someone here. We do not need GJW.'[116]

The large firms supposed they were important players and were taken seriously by government. Another senior partner said: 'I would be staggered if we could not get to a minister that we wanted to get to. It may take us three months. We can roll them in usually.'[117]

Contact with officials depended on seniority, section and department. The lobbyist had good relationships with officials, arguing 'We are locked into the DTI.'[118] A senior partner noted: 'DTI officials told me they are very comfortable with the use of GJW. They liked us doing it because officials normally criticise us for not understanding politics.'[119]

GJW dealt directly with middle-rank officials approximately every week by telephone or by letter to deal with detailed questions.[120] The client held a series of meetings with officials, and access was never problematic. LRG members also enjoyed good relations with officials; contact was 'very regular'.[121] Letters and submissions to DTI were proof-read by policy officials and returned to the lobbyist, allowing them to be amended before being sent to ministers. 'DTI officials strangely agreed to review the letter and the accompanying appendix in draft form. That helped, but there were few changes.'[122] This degree of trust was a consequence of the firms' long-term links into DTI. One official argued that because 'the Big 5 are involved in government, I do not think the strategy firms are valuable. Any of these people could get in to see people from the DTI this week if they wanted. ... Civil servants are quite open about the issue.'[123] Civil servants believed they were 'generous to the point of opening doors and giving advice on how to do it'.[124]

The firms had excellent contacts with politicians and civil servants. Their contacts assisted the firms. GJW added an extra layer of contacts, particularly with New Labour ministers and special advisers.

Coalitions

Changes to liability affect common law. The accountants could never win alone on strand A issues. Government told the accountants they needed a broad coalition. 'The point had been made to them many times that they would need some support, off-the-record of course.'[125]

There are several elements to the coalition, consisting of five rings: at the centre is (*A*), made up of the Big Five firms. *A* is surrounded by the ICAEW (*B*), which has sought to build alliances with other accountancy associations and smaller firms (*C*). The firms have also tried to ally with other professions (*D*), and to the wider business community (*E*).

On strand A, a rootless coalition existed on the causes of, but not the solution to, the liability issue between *A, B* and *C*. The coalition within *A* was weak: 'they tried to conduct a tight campaign and argue the agenda was specific, but when it got to the nitty gritty it fragmented'.[126] In *B*, although ICAEW claimed to be a professional body dedicated to the public interest,[127] in practice it reflected and promoted the Big Five's interests. Notionally a regulator, the ICAEW is the profession's defender and advocate.[128]

Many groups in *C* did not support liability reform because it was 'a big firm problem, and to middle-sized firms it does not really matter'.[129]

LRG was ineffective because its coalition did not include *D* and *E*. Organisations in *D* and *E* did not recognise a problem. LRG 'did not understand that civil servants had to look at this issue in relation to architects, lawyers and other professionals. We were not just dealing with accountants.'[130] The ICAEW organised a 'Professional Liability Group' to build bridges to other interested groups.[131] A senior partner admitted that the Big Five 'have not done a good job rallying the support of the lawyers and the consulting engineers. You cannot expect just the auditors to do it. If I were government I would put two fingers up. It looks like a special interest lobby.'[132]

Lawyers were slow to organise, and the Law Society's opposition complicated matters.[133] Lawyers had academic and legal objections.[134] City law firms used the City of London Law Society as a mouthpiece to bypass the Society's national policy of opposition. Coordination with the accountants was poor because 'the accountants were blinkered. They did not make a great effort to talk to other professions.'[135] The coalition was weak and ephemeral.

Interest groups in *E* were essential to success. An official argued: 'If you cannot persuade your clients, you are going to have great difficulty persuading government.'[136] LRG obtained support from some audit clients such as the CBI, IoD, 100 Group, London Investment Banking Association (LIBA) and National Association of Pension Funds (NAPF). The lobbyist believed that 'part of the skill of what we have done is to get them [business] to sign up to broad concepts and not detail. Proportionality is a nice concept.'[137] An official argued: 'That was quite clever. It did not go beyond fairness. There was a high level of generality. The devil is usually in the detail.'[138] Outside the Big Five there was no agreement on what the answers were. It was even unclear whether there was a question.

In Strand B a broad coalition extended across *A, B, C, D* and *E*. The coalition was not difficult to construct for a low-profile non-contentious issue. The lobbyist admitted: 'Once we have the shape of the [LLP] Bill, we can jettison the rest of our consortia. We have to carry them with us on the basis that they will not object to the Bill.'[139] The clients of professionals had few concerns about LLPs.[140]

Conclusion

Though the lobbyists had good contacts, they were matched (if not bettered) by the clients. The accountants had friends in Whitehall and the parties. The firms hired GJW because 'It is more efficient for GJW to tell me who I should contact and their phone numbers. It is better than using our own resources. It is a question of time and money.'[141] GJW was especially effective in providing access to Labour.

On LLPs the lobbyist effectively built a coalition which minimised dissent. However, on liability GJW and LRG were ineffective in building a coalition. There was no agreement on policy. They failed because of 'a lack of clarity about objectives and the people who need to be picked off. They have not done those things effectively.'[142]

The coalition was accountant-led, and its policy objectives did not invite broad and stable coalitions. The firms' inability to build an effective coalition was the cause of their ineffectiveness. Contacts were important, but the failure to spot and cement connections with other interest groups was debilitating.

Resources

The campaign to limit liability was not restricted to the UK. The Big Five campaigned globally. In Jersey two firms contributed over £1 million to the drafting of the Jersey LLP law, which even acknowledged the 'contribution of PriceWaterhouse, Ernst & Young and others ... to the structure and detail of the draft law'.[143]

The Big Five in the USA used their massive resources to run television-advertising campaigns to secure the support of politicians, businesses, journalists and academics.[144] The profession pumped millions of dollars into the campaign funds of key politicians. In the 1994 Congressional cycle it donated US$3.6 million.[145]

The chairman of the ICAEW Audit faculty argued in 1996: 'this is just the start – it took the Americans four years to effect change ... We have completed the first mile of a marathon – and this is a marathon we intend to finish and finish strongly.'[146] The IGA account was worth £120 000. An IGA lobbyist argued that money is important 'not because it buys you access, but it gets you basic resources, it buys you focus, it buys you expertise'.[147]

The ICAEW has an annual public relations budget of approximately £500 000.[148] The public 'line' was that the firms worked 'in support' of ICAEW. In reality the firms ran the show and a senior partner argued: 'Any campaign of this kind has a cost to it in terms of intellectual energy and a financial cost as well because we employ people to do analysis. The firms have the resources that the Institute does not have.'[149]

GJW's contract was worth over £300 000 a year.[150] This figure ignored the time spent by senior partners making representations and attending meetings. It excluded the legal advice, the research costs and fees of counsel.

Economic importance

The money spent campaigning is not always a significant determinant of effectiveness. The big firms are massive multi-national businesses. Their economic value and the number of employees affect how intently government listens to their arguments. The UK accountancy/audit market was estimated at £7.3 billion.[151] UK fee income was estimated at £3.5 billion a year.[152] Britain has over 250 000 qualified accountants: 'the highest number of accountants per capita in the industrialised world and more than the rest of the European Union put together'.[153]

Managerial resources

Though firms devoted time to the campaign, the managerial resource has been poor because commercial pressures made it difficult to obtain agreement. The firms were often unwieldy, and had competing interests. As a consequence LRG was lethargic. Partners found it difficult to relate to the political environment.

Officials regarded inability to cooperate as LRG's principal weakness. One argued: 'They do find it difficult to work together. ... Their inability to get together and share information has delayed reform considerably.'[154] The lowest common denominator became LRG policy: 'they could never agree what it was they really wanted'.[155]

The firms had an informal network. The most senior partners dined informally each month to discuss important matters. Below them audit, tax, law, and risk partners also dined regularly. LRG was the driving force and policy originator, rather than ICAEW, because senior partners lacked 'confidence in the ability of the profession, through its trade association, to get its act together'.[156] A City lawyer argued: 'The accountants fight like tigers amongst themselves.'[157] In fact solidarity among the group disappeared when the government demanded evidence.[158] The collection of information caused them difficulties because they could not work together as a group.

Conclusion

The firms threw money at the campaign. Their ability to hire top-quality political, legal and economic advisers enhanced their effectiveness. However, managerially the campaign was weak. GJW was unable to coordinate the firms' activities effectively. They failed to act in harmony. Rivalry prevented the adoption of a common policy. The campaign would have been more effective had managerial resources been stronger.

Low-profile outsider tactics

Frustrated at the glacial pace of policy-making, some firms pursued an insider and a low-profile outsider strategy concurrently. The outsider strategy had two themes: a threat to move off-shore, and an attempt to play governments off against one another. Some firms were unwilling to pursue the time-consuming strategy necessary to persuade government of their case. They moved to register outside UK jurisdiction as offshore centres engaged in a race to provide attractive regulatory environments.[159]

Professions considered registering in the Channel Islands. E&Y and PriceWaterhouseCoopers offered, at their own expense, to draft a law in Jersey.[160] Amid controversy the Jersey States approved a LLP law. A Jersey Senator who championed the law was accused of a conflict of interest for using his influence to speed up the drafting of the law.[161] The law politicised Jersey politics and the process was investigated by a Committee of Inquiry.[162] The law was enacted in June 1998.[163]

The move off-shore can be understood only if observers are aware of the motives of the firms. Some firms saw Jersey as a viable alternative to the UK. One partner argued: 'We went to Jersey because we thought it was the place to go given the UK situation.'[164] Partners believed ministers were unwilling to act.[165]

Sceptics argued Jersey was never a viable option, but was planned strategically as a lever. One senior partner said: 'We would be mad to go to Jersey.'[166] Mitchell argued: 'the real intention behind the Jersey flight is to hold the British Parliament and public to ransom and blackmail the UK into extending similar concessions'.[167]

However, to argue that the move to Jersey was *planned* as a mechanism to pressure the UK government inflates the firms' competence. In reality the firms stumbled to Jersey as a consequence of misreading the UK policy process. After all, had government 'thought the action was inappropriate there are many ways government could have stopped it. It would not have been difficult to make Jersey unattractive to them.'[168] LLPs were not raised with the DTI until the Jersey effort. The concept raised little difficulty for UK policy officials, but it was not something the firms ever asked for. They assumed they would not succeed; 'That was a foolish assumption.'[169] Another official recalled asking a representative of the firms: '"Why didn't you come to us instead of going to Jersey? We would have been happy to run with it." The individual was non-plussed. They simply did not think of approaching us.'[170]

Austin Mitchell's argument is incorrect. However, the *unintended effect* was that Jersey became a political catalyst which engaged ministers. The threat of moving off-shore alarmed and activated government.[171] The Opposition supported the firms.[172] A senior partner described ministers and civil servants as 'all running around like space cadets'.[173] An official put it more benevolently: the threat 'meant ministers decided this area of law reform was a priority, which they had never previously seen it as'.[174]

Michael Heseltine's proposed quick-fix option, based on secondary legislation to be operational by 1998, was dropped because it was unworkable.[175] A civil servant said that: 'ministers, who never really understood how legislation worked, seemed to think that with a bit of goodwill they would get the whole thing through in 2–3 months. That talk was totally uninformed.'[176] Roger Freeman, junior Cabinet Office minister, recognised the case for protection against suits, but warned it would require primary legislation.[177] So an LLP consultation paper was published in January 1997.[178]

Jersey helped the DTI put an LLP Bill in the queue for legislative time. 'The prospect of a perceived loss of business to Jersey was a powerful jolt. ... Jersey supplied an argument we could use when competing for scarce legislative time.'[179] By recognising the fragmented nature of government, it is possible to understand why the DTI welcomed the higher profile of LLPs because it helped the department promote its legislation. The government was not a helpless bystander observing the overtures of powerful international accountancy practices.[180] In reality, Jersey reflected the audit profession's ignorance of British government.

Playing governments off against one another

The Big 5 are global players and sought to marshal their arguments internationally. The firms: 'exercised a campaign that keeps pressing on one country and saying "We are talking to another country and they are doing this, that and the other." '[181] A number of countries have introduced some form of reform, including Australia, Canada and Switzerland. In Canada a Senate Committee recommended modified proportionate liability be introduced. The DTI was aware of the firms' tactic. 'The accountants and the audit profession operate on a worldwide basis very effectively, so we seek the views of the Australian and American governments as well as the European Union.'[182]

The USA is an important jurisdiction. Following a major litigation crisis in the early 1990s American firms sought a safer legal framework.[183] When the company-friendly State of Delaware recognised LLPs,[184] the big firms reorganised themselves as LLPs.[185] Currently 46 states have LLPs and are able to provide an inshore 'offshore' solution.[186]

By 1995 proportionate liability was on the legislative agendas of approximately half the states.[187] At least 33 states have either abolished or substantially limited joint and several liability.[188] Against the wishes of the President, who vetoed the Bill,[189] Congress passed the Securities

Litigation Reform Act in late 1995.[190] In 1995 the Senate approved legislation that established damages (non-fraudulent) proportionate to their degree of liability.[191]

The civil service did not want Britain 'to get into legislative arbitrage', although it recognised the need to ensure a competitive environment.[192] But the civil service was 'always being told that other countries did this and that and the other. Half the time it was found not be true, or the circumstances were limited. You were always being told that other people had solved the problem and it was not true.'[193] In fact the firms' tactics were:

> not effective because we talk to our counterparts in other countries, which neutralises their activity ... We are not out of line globally. The firms try to play off governments, and the first one to fall will put the rest at a disadvantage. So we do keep in touch. That is a totally informal network.[194]

Conclusion

The Jersey threat was an unintentional success. The firms had not approached government about the possibility of UK LLP. They began the move offshore on the assumption they had failed in the UK. The threat heightened the issue's profile, leading to pan-government pressure for a solution. The DTI used this pressure to progress legislation. A senior partner argued: 'If we made a reasonable amount of progress quite quickly, it has got bugger all to do with the cohesiveness of the profession or GJW.'[195] The low-profile outsider tactic to take business offshore had the unintended effect of spurring new and powerful coalitions within government, allowing LLP legislation to progress.

Conclusions

The accountants failed to achieve their primary goal of reforming the liability regime, but were effective with the subordinate objective of limiting risk to partners.

The ineffectiveness of the liability campaign had been obvious for some time. Ever since the Law Commission's report the accountants had been losing. The policy outcome was determined principally by external factors. Factors within the lobbyist's control had little impact. An official argued: 'I do not know that a lobbyist would have been able to change anything by doing anything differently.'[196] Table 7.1 summarises the external and internal variables that affected the policy outcome.

Table 7.1 External and internal variables affecting the policy outcome

External Variables	
Joint and Several (risk to the firm – Strand A)	**Limited Liability Partnership** (risk to the partner – Strand B)
Technical issue, but one with broad public-interest, legal and commercial implications. More variables made success less likely.	Technical issue – excited no interest. It bored MPs, allowing it to slip by.
The issue could be characterised politically as a concession to a privileged special interest.	The issue was non-partisan.
Low-profile, but to raise the profile risked weakening the fragile coalition, mobilising the opposition and jeopardising LLPs.	The issue had a low-profile, which was raised effectively within government to engage ministers. If the issue had remained low-profile it would not have been effective.
Complex and lengthy legislation. Ingrained common law concepts apply to the whole of tort and contract law, not just accountants.	Short and straightforward legislation taking little parliamentary time.
Likely parliamentary opposition.	No parliamentary opposition.
No broad coalition of support. Narrow coalition built on weak foundations.	Broad and committed coalition of support.
No consensus on the causes of the problem. Being targeted as a 'deep pocket' affects only the bigger firms, inviting opposition from smaller partnerships. The people who want it appear to be those who deserve nothing.	Consensus on the problem. All partners from partnerships of all sizes are subject to unlimited personal liability, inviting wide support.
Big legal change. There is no agreement on the appropriate reform. Lawyers do not want section 310 reform, business does not want compulsory Directors and Officers insurance, investors and venture capitalists do not want a statutory cap.	Consensus on the solution.
Potentially some important opponents, including British Venture Capital Association, Association of British Insurers, British Bankers' Association, and Institute of Directors. 'A lack of clarity and opposition to it by the rest of industry signed its fate.'[197]	No significant opponents.

184

Table 7.1 (Continued)

External Variables	
Joint and Several (risk to the firm – Strand A)	**Limited Liability Partnership** (risk to the partner – Strand B)
Not politically attractive. No electoral reward. Manifesto commitment was fudged; a review will meet the pledge. One senior partner said, 'It is of absolutely no interest to anyone, which is a recipe for a political disaster'.[198]	Not politically attractive, but the legislation delivers another manifesto commitment that can be 'ticked off'.
Bad timing – fag end of a tired government that was not interested.	Good timing. Non-controversial legislation could be slotted into the legislative timetable around the time consuming complex constitutional legislation.
Have not proved case. Government not convinced 'UK Plc' is disadvantaged by law of joint and several.	Case proven. Partnership Act dates back to 1907 and required modification. 'Powerful arguments of greater flexibility and competitiveness.'[199]
The alternatives are just as bad. Auditors are campaigning to shift the balance of responsibilities, shifting liability to other actors.	Change is relatively simple and does not adversely affect third parties.
In no other common law jurisdiction have the accountants been successful in achieving their objective on proportionate liability.	International comparison. The business vehicle existed in other jurisdictions, creating pressure on UK government.
The Law Commission concluded that replacement of joint and several with proportionate liability was not desirable.	No official committees have opposed LLP reform.
Reform could be characterised as a concession to a privileged vested interest. The smaller firms want to retain J&S because litigation is deflected to the larger firms.	LLP reform can be characterised as modernising the business environment, providing a new trading vehicle.
Reform was out of step with government policy. The salary levels of senior partners concerned Labour ministers and DTI officials.	LLPs can be portrayed as being in line with government policy.

Table 7.1 (Continued)

Internal Variables	
Joint and Several	**Limited Liability Partnership**
Unwillingness to work closely with government and provide data.	The little information that was requested was presented.
Poor managerial resources. There has been a constant dilemma over tactics. DTI was exasperated with the failure of the five audit firms to agree a common position. They have found it difficult to work together to produce an all-embracing campaign. They had differing objectives.	Good managerial resources. The Big Five, bar KPMG, were at one over the benefits of LLPs. They had a single objective.
The risk to firms is cyclical: campaign geared up when litigation was low.	The risk to partners is cyclical, but it did not affect the effectiveness of the campaign.
No serious consideration, and no agreement on what concessions the accountants could offer government.	Government demanded public disclosure requirements and creditor guarantee procedures. Most firms favoured openness and transparency.
No burning platform. There were no low-profile external measures for the accountants to use to pressure decision-makers.	Burning platform of Jersey created pressure on government to act.
The joint and several commitment in the manifesto was fudged; government can fulfil the pledge by introducing a J&S review into the Company Law Review.	Good relations with Labour in Opposition. Relations with Bell were instrumental in getting the LLP commitment into the Business Manifesto.
Big 5 had failed to limit their liability by means open to them.	There was no action within the firms' control which could alleviate the problem they faced.
The firms had good access to government.	The firms had good access to government.

8
When Lobbyists Matter: Conclusions

Policy-making takes place in a web of government players, outside interests and often lobbyists. Whilst researchers can usually spot when a decision was taken and by whom, it is more difficult to disentangle the contribution of lobbyists from all the other factors impacting on policy-makers. The difficulty with judging when lobbyists are effective is that policy decisions have been explained on various levels. There is often an element of truth in the various descriptions. The contradictions in the literature are variations that can be explained by attention to context. The impact of lobbyists is variable. Effectiveness depends on context and circumstances. This book has elucidated the contexts under which lobbyists are effective.

Macro-level

Profile, technicality and politicality

Lobbyists tend to be effective if they are lobbying on low-profile, technical and non-political issues.

The lobbyist can be effective on low-profile issues because government can deal with more issues simultaneously. Lobbyists tend to act as interpreters, explaining procedures and rules to clients, and their clients' policy objectives to decision-makers. Lobbyists are likely to be more valuable to their clients on low-profile technical issues because outside organisations are less likely to know whom to approach or how. For the most part campaigns on technical issues do not focus on Parliament or the media. On highly technical matters civil servants want to talk to outside groups and lobbyists. They want information to inform policy-making and lobbyists know how to provide this material to make their client look good. Lobbyists can get a lot more small items dealt with successfully because they persuade the officials in the department to get it right in the first place. The most effective lobbying is often done with officials.

Regulations may be of vital importance to a company or sector, but are rarely of importance in high politics. De-politicisation of issues can help negotiations. Lobbyists have the potential to be more effective on issues on which the government is unlikely to take a firm political stance. In addition, there are less likely to be organised opponents on low-profile, technical and non-political issues. The more visible the lobbying, the more likely it is to produce equal and opposite reactions and bring other groups out fighting. Bandwagons do not roll in low-profile lobbying. Private lobbying is more effective than high-profile lobbying. Lobbyists often underestimate how much more influential they are if they are quieter. As soon as lobbyists leap on to a platform and yell with a megaphone they fail to have the same effect. High-profile games are more complex and there are multiple actors, and only a few issues can be handled at a time, making success less likely.

When an issue is high-profile, civil servants produce for their minister a defence of the options available. Holding arguments are drafted to justify a range of possible decisions. Likewise, if there is a large number of groups ministers will seek to distance themselves from the lobbies. On the more important issues both sides of the argument may employ lobbyists, and their activities could cancel one another out.

Professional lobbyists may be somewhat effective on high-profile 'political' issues where there are significant political pressures for change, and they happen to be on the right side. In these circumstances the decision will turn not only on an analysis of the merits of a case, but on electoral considerations, political priorities, personalities and media interest. But lobbyists have little influence on mega-issues such as foreign policy and big economic changes. On high-profile issues lobbyists are unlikely to be able to provide new information; therefore their value lies in raising political and emotional issues. Success then depends on whether the case is in line with government policy or political beliefs and on favourable external factors beyond government's control.

The merits of a policy may not be the dominant factor in a large, high-profile issue, but they tend to be in low-profile issues. Lobbying on low-profile issues is frequently fact-based and concentrates on civil servants. Lobbying can encourage officials to think about new aspects of the case. On low-profile issues effective lobbyists do not pressure decision-makers; they simply improve their clients' presentation of its case.

On technical, non-partisan issues with a low-profile decision-makers are 'liberated' from other variables such as mass opinion, economic factors and party political influence. On these types of issue decision-makers do not have to choose between competing social groups since the issue usually has a narrow impact. On those issues that begin as low-profile, the lobbyist who faces defeat can be effective by 'jacking up' the issue by adopting high-profile tactics and increasing the issue's profile *within* government. Therefore it might be more appropriate to conclude that lobbyists tend to be effective if they are lobbying on low-profile, technical and non-political issues, but those lobbyists facing defeat can heighten the profile of the issue *within* government.

External factors

Lobbyists tend to be effective if there are no disadvantageous external or contextual constraints beyond the control of government players.

Lobbyists rarely associate the failure of their clients with any error on their part. If policy defeats are beyond the control of the lobbyist, then it is possible to argue that policy victories are also beyond their control. The policy-making system is not a hermetically-sealed box. External factors and institutions, and the outside world in general, structure the options open to government. Various factors affect a lobbying campaign, including changing business and social attitudes, the state of the economy, parliamentary make-up, the EU, courts, party reforms or official reports.

With Sunday trading the principal disadvantageous contextual constraint was the government's narrow parliamentary majority. Lobbyists could do little to overcome the 'blocking' Conservative MPs. External factors can assist a lobbying campaign. The Labour Party's modernisation and social changes in the Sunday trading case helped SHRC and damaged KSSC. Labour and SHRC objectives merged, allowing the Conservative government to deliver liberalisation.

CrossRail lobbyists faced disadvantageous external factors, and were incapable of dealing with the challenges they posed. They were equally ineffective when facing a factor beyond the control of most key government players: Treasury intransigence. The economic context, which began positively, changed and injured CrossRail grievously. However, CrossRail was helped temporarily by a mingling of CrossRail and government objectives. Government continued to show CrossRail its commitment to London in the approach to elections.

However, political autonomy and effective lobbying can overcome disadvantageous external or contextual constraints. Lobbying and political commitments mitigated the impact of external constraints over JLE, which included a recession and the collapse of O&Y (JLE's principal advocate). Whilst CrossRail sank, JLE remained afloat despite a rougher storm. There was a battle within government as No. 10, the DoE and (later) the DTp fought against the Treasury to keep JLE.

In the liability case the economic environment should have helped the lobbyist but did not, because civil servants did not believe the lobby's case. If the DTI had believed the firms' case, it could have ignored the Law Commission's conclusions. The Commission's report was a useful shield to hide behind.

Advantageous external factors provide the environment in which a lobbyist might be effective. Similarly, a disadvantageous environment with external variables hostile to the lobbyist's objectives means success is less likely. The proposition, though mostly valid, does not always hold. Lobbyists *tend to be effective* if there are no disadvantageous external factors. The wider economic, political and judicial contexts affect the effectiveness of lobbyists. But effective lobbying and the autonomy of senior government players can overcome contextual factors. Political actors can overcome negative external constraints. It might be more appropriate to conclude that lobbyists tend to be effective if there are no disadvantageous contextual constraints; but disadvantageous external factors can be overcome by skilled lobbying and the support of senior political players.

Experience and existing policy

Lobbyists tend to be effective if the beliefs of political decision-makers, pre-existing policy and previous experience of government players are congruent with the lobbyist's objective.

Lobbying to achieve an objective that corresponds to what the government wants to do is likely to be effective. Government players are not sponges. Political actors have partisan agendas. Civil servants have public-interest objectives. Both have personal objectives. This book has shown that lobbyists can be helped if their case is congruous with the beliefs of ministers or the policy of the government, or undermined if the case is incongruous with either. Government autonomy and reformed pluralism make a valuable framework for assessing independent variables affecting policy outcomes.

'Bad' ideas are less likely to succeed, but many 'good' ideas are passed over. The quality of the case is supposedly an objective judgement. However, subjective political or partisan issues can overrule objective merits. If the implications of a policy change are extra expenditure, it may be difficult for lobbyists to achieve their goals. Heinz *et al.* found lobbyists pay little attention to the funding implications of their demands, whilst most officials give the highest importance to budgets. Lobbyists are not indifferent to the financial implications, but they do not focus on them. The evidence suggests they should focus on the cost implications of their proposals and that the cost of the policies is often a central issue.

SHRC's objectives were in line with government's pre-existing policy and the beliefs of ministers. KSSC's beliefs conflicted with the views of ministers and the existing policy and themes of the government. Whilst SHRC and its lobbyists worked in support of government – their agenda amounted to the privatisation of the government's mandate – lobbyists had little effect. Despite ministers' emotional commitment to SHRC's objectives, government was restrained by 'external constraints' beyond its control. Thus, whilst SHRC was advantaged, and KSSC disadvantaged, by the relationship between their objectives with government policy, SHRC's leverage could not be translated into victory because of contextual factors.

CrossRail was initially favoured because of the perceived partisan advantage the scheme delivered, as assessed by the Prime Minister. However, it was the strengthened Treasury under John Major's government which saw the scheme fall foul of the Treasury 'view', as its officials and ministers worked to abandon CrossRail by arguing that it was inconsistent with the government's medium-term objectives. Lobbyists were ineffective because the Treasury opposed CrossRail and, despite a formal government commitment, there was no senior political commitment to CrossRail. This vacuum of support can be explained by CrossRail also conflicting with another policy objective: railway privatisation. In comparison, JLE succeeded because of a ten-second political prejudice. There was senior political support for JLE and ministers were encouraged to assist O&Y because the scheme chimed with the government's agenda of redevelopment, private-sector involvement and symbolism. JLE was successful because of its connections to the government's political programme.

The broader liability campaign failed because neither the client nor the lobbyist could link the firms' objectives to government policy. The firms were unable to look beyond their own commercial desires. The issue was of such low-profile significance that there was no association with political beliefs or pre-existing policy, and therefore no partisan advantage to be gained from acting. Thus liability reform failed, whilst LLPs succeeded because they represented such a non-contentious policy that a government of either party would have felt comfortable promoting it.

The permanent civil service prevents lobbyists in the UK from having the degree of influence they have in America. A professional and unbiased civil service means the opportunities to be effective are limited. However, changes to the civil service have implications for lobbyists. The days of the Permanent Secretary being the sole channel of advice to ministers are over. There has also been a reduction in the number of senior civil servants, and they are more often policy managers and implementers than advisers. The move to smaller and more junior teams offers the lobbyist the opportunity to duck and weave in order to outplay the civil service. The decline of the senior generalist policy adviser means fewer officials in Whitehall today take the overall view and examine wider ramifications. Policy advice has been 'privatised'; ministers listen to the wider community for advice, including lobbyists. Because ministers deal increasingly with junior civil servants whom they neither know nor trust, lobbyists known to ministers can promote their client's interests more easily, potentially threatening the public interest and increasing the chances of 'policy disaster'.

Government actors have autonomy depending on context. Lobbyists tend to be effective if their objective is in line with existing policy or political beliefs, unless the issue is of such a low-profile and so highly technical that the political effect of acting is negligible.

Meso-level

The policy community

Lobbyists tend to be effective if they can include their client in the policy community and manage their client's activity within that network.

The policy community is smaller than often portrayed in political science literature. To all intents and purposes the community comprised a consultation list. However, analysts should focus on those groups who are *involved* in policy-making. This book challenges the association between insider status and influence. Many are considered insiders, but few have any real impact. Most interest groups were consulted and enjoyed good relations with government, but many of these interest groups did not have influence. The number of key players was small. Lobbyists are not important for inclusion, because many groups are included. But, because so few interest groups participate actively, lobbyists are effective because they can *manage* and *coordinate* their clients' activity and improve it.

In the case of Sunday trading the policy community was broken open by government. In the pre-Lloydian stage SHRC was included in the policy community, whilst KSSC was excluded. SHRC was granted access and given confidential information by ministers, PPSs and officials whilst KSSC was kept in the dark. Lobbyists did not assist the SHRC in accessing the community, but did help it manage its involvement more effectively. In the Lloydian period the government's slim parliamentary majority meant a whipped Bill could not resolve the issue. Therefore the previously restricted policy community was opened to all interest groups representing the major forces in the debate. Lobbyists played no role in involving the groups but made their actions more effective by skilful management.

CrossRail was 'of' government, and its promoters were part of the official policy community. The lobbyist played little role in involving its client. However, the formal policy community was not where the real decisions on CrossRail were made. At moments of crisis CrossRail – the 'CrossRail Coalition' – mobilised and provided temporary support to the Prime Minister and other ministers in the policy community to defeat the Treasury. The ineffectiveness of the lobbyist was evident in its inability to sustain the coalition over the long-term.

JLE shows that, to be effective, lobbyists do not have to include their client in the policy community. In fact the lobbyist extracted its client from the network and took the issue to Downing Street. The policy community was overruled. Lobbyists and O&Y cultivated No. 10, the Treasury and the DoE, and used them to 'lobby' on their behalf inside government. Lobbyists circumvented the established networks because they found them impenetrable.

The liability policy community was small and transient. It was dominated by three civil servants. The firms already worked with civil servants. Lobbyists were irrelevant to gaining access but helped co-ordinate the activity of the big firms. Lobbyists were also effective in penetrating the closed New Labour network, which helped the firms obtain a manifesto commitment. Lobbyists do not play much of a role in inserting clients into policy communities. The client's status, objectives and behaviour will usually determine if it is included. The civil service is now open to representation and keen to encourage outside participation.

It is a necessary requirement for effectiveness that lobbyists include themselves or their client in the network of interests involved in policy-making. Lobbyists can be effective by inserting their clients, and managing their activity, in the arena where policy is decided. Lobbyists do play a role, which involves helping their clients manage their activity in networks, by coordinating activity and improving the quality of submissions and communication in general. Since lobbyists can be effective when their client is not included in the policy community, and lobbyists play little part in 'including' their clients but more of a role managing their activity, it is more appropriate to conclude that lobbyists tend to be effective if they insert their client in the *arena where the policy is decided*, and manage their activity skilfully.

Multi-faceted lobbying

Lobbyists tend to be effective if they pursue a multi-faceted approach and facilitate access to multiple points in the decision-making process.

In the Sunday trading case a multi-faceted campaign was key for effectiveness, though one element was more important than the others: constituency pressure. Both main interest groups lobbied in government, Parliament, the parties, the press and the public. KSSC was effective in mobilising the public minority hostile to liberalisation, creating the perception of widespread scepticism. Liberalisation lobbyists were unimportant in orchestrating media support because it was already 'onside'. But lobbyists helped create the perception of a grass-roots demand for Sunday trading by assembling 'astro-turf' organisations. Though both sides pursued multi-faceted campaigns, they were focused at one target: Parliament.

CrossRail lobbyists lost the battle inside government and were ineffective in launching a multi-faceted campaign to compensate. This inaction contributed to their ineffectiveness. Their concentration on backbenchers and party conferences ignored the real decision-makers and their 'influence factors'. IGA's role was limited. A short-term burst of activity around the 'CrossRail Coalition' was multi-faceted and effective in buying stays of decision, but it was not sustained in the long-term.

On JLE the lobbyists and client eschewed a multi-faceted approach. Lobbyists concentrated on influential senior ministers and the No. 10 network, because they recognised the policy would be driven forward by politicians. Civil servants, Parliament, the media and the public were excluded. Though O&Y did lobby affected local authorities, MPs and the media, this activity was not in order to see the project succeed, but to ensure its success met with as little organised opposition as possible.

There was no multi-faceted campaign for liability reform. The campaign targeted civil servants. Parliament and the media were absent. Parliamentary activity was often the consequence of government intervention (planted questions) or brief debates inspired by uninfluential but outspoken critics. There was no need for a multi-faceted approach; indeed, it would have been ineffective and was actively discouraged by ministers and officials. Civil servants wanted the issue's profile to remain low. The firms were restricted from adopting a multi-faceted campaign on liability, partly because to have done so would have damaged LLPs.

This proposition may be more relevant to the USA and other federal systems where there are more routes into the diverse centres of power. In the UK power is concentrated at the centre. A multi-faceted campaign is not a requirement of an effective lobbying campaign. Targeting multiple points in the decision-making process can be damaging. There is insufficient evidence to support the view that a multi-faceted campaign is a determinant of effectiveness. In fact, on low-profile, technical and non-partisan issues a multi-faceted approach can be ineffective. It likely that lobbyists tend to be effective if they pursue a multi-faceted approach on high-profile, non-technical and partisan issues.

Micro-level

Routines and procedures

Lobbyists tend to be effective if they are familiar with routines and standard operating procedures and know when and where to intervene in the policy-making process.

Effective lobbyists seemingly know the process. Much of the art of influence involves knowing who to contact, when and how, in a myriad of complex and compartmentalised public services. Even knowing the basics is important, such as whether No. 10 is likely to be involved in a certain issue and how an issue links to the government's wider agenda. It is possible to argue that lobbyists do not need to be knowledgeable about rules and procedure because the system tells them what to do. Procedural information is easily accessible. The market is easily bamboozled: few people realise the *Civil Service Yearbook* is an effective route map to policy-making. There is no magic to understanding procedures, but they are often difficult to understand because the system does not communicate effectively. Lobbyists simply take the initiative to ask. They recycle information.

In the Sunday trading case there was some evidence to suggest that lobbyists provided an advantage to their clients because of their procedural knowledge. SHRC advisers had a greater level of expertise. Although the issue was highly political, requiring no detailed knowledge of Whitehall procedures, lobbyists were effective because they advised SHRC on tactics to defeat a Private Member's Bill. In general, however, the system was unusually open and transparent.

On CrossRail the lobbyist did not understand, or failed to provide a strategy to deal with, the informal procedures of the decision-making system. The lobbyist lacked an understanding of Whitehall processes, and the strategy focused on Westminster. IGA's knowledge of procedure did not extend much beyond the provision of a monitoring service. In contrast the lobby for the JLE was effective because both client and lobbyist understood the way decisions were taken inside government. They manoeuvred around the machine with skill, and side-stepped the civil service to deal directly with ministers. Defeat was avoided at an early stage by dealing directly with ministers.

Likewise lobbyists were effective in briefing the big audit firms concerned with liability on how to draft submissions, when to submit them, whom to call, when to call them, and how to make presentations to ministers. They understood the need to put the client first. Lobbyists attended meetings with decision-makers infrequently but were involved in almost every aspect of their preparation. When necessary the lobbyists participated in the process, and their experience and knowledge of the process were important.

Most lobbyists spend their time advising clients how to present their case, conducting research, being helpful and maintaining cordial relations with decision-makers. But effective lobbyists have a feel for the political process: an instinct as to what will work and what will not. They should know what arguments will influence politicians and civil servants. It is important to understand where political actors 'are coming from' and see them all as players in a game. Effective lobbyists understand how the 'political mind' works. It is the psychology of politics that is important.

Some ministers and officials prefer to deal with lobbyists. However, since the early 1990s advocacy by lobbyists has received critical press interest and has been seen as suspect, and so that form of contact has declined. There has been a growth in shadow lobbying, where lobbyists act as facilitators, providers of contacts and strategic advisers, rather than as advocates. Shadow lobbying is more effective than direct advocacy. Effective lobbying is limited to facilitation. Clients are more effective because they have a real interest in the policy, which delivers credibility.

Effective professional lobbyists are those whose presence decision-makers are scarcely aware of, making it even more difficult for researchers to examine their effect. A good lobbyist should not be seen. All the evidence suggests that lobbyists tend to be effective if they are familiar with routines and standard operating procedures, and know when and where to intervene in the policy-making process.

Contacts and coalitions

Lobbyists tend to be effective if they have good contacts and can spot connections to potential allies and can construct coalitions.

Contacts

Over Sunday trading the SHRC and the retailers had excellent contacts with the Conservative government, and the lobbyists' contacts added a little. Contacts were not important for access, but did deliver information. Ministers often told SHRC and its lobbyists informally of recent developments. The lobbyists were effective in helping SHRC access the networks of modernising Labour MPs. They introduced their clients, built relationships and explained Labour politics. KSSC's contacts were less well developed. It had many supporters in all the main parties but they were detached from the party elites.

In the CrossRail case lobbyists were ineffective in providing introductions to decision-makers *who mattered*. The lobbyists had excellent contacts in the Conservative Party and they lobbied MPs, arranged briefings and dinners, but the lobbyists ignored the civil service. Their lack of contacts in Whitehall was crippling.

The JLE case shows contacts can be extremely helpful in influencing policy-makers. O&Y, an outsider in many senses, was transformed by its lobbyist into a pre-eminent insider. Their access was famed and contacts helped O&Y to enter closed party networks. Politicians trusted O&Y and its lobbyists. Contacts delivered early access to information.

In the case of liability reform the clients had better contacts with officials and Conservative ministers than the lobbyist. They were on the 'A-list for No. 10 dinners' and partners in the firms knew most Cabinet ministers on first-name terms. However, the lobbyists added value because of their contacts with Labour. Their promotional literature boasted of being able to put clients in touch with the right people. They also operated effectively at the official level, being discreet, trustworthy and professional.

Lobbyists claim to know influential decision-makers and to have preferential access. Lobbyists consciously build networks. They persuade their clients to sponsor events at national and local government party conferences; business and political charitable events; political functions at constituency level; political seminars and fringe meetings. Consequently lobbyists can become useful to parties as a source of income. Lobbyists probably have more effective contacts with politicians than with officials. Ministers and their special advisers are more susceptible to lobbyists, particularly with a new government, and especially if they are dealing with friendly faces (people they have worked with in the political environment in the past). Lobbyists have access others would not. In reality, though, a lobbyist's access is, more often than not, the consequence of working for significant clients and is not necessarily based on his or her own importance. Lobbyists do not have preferential influence.

In conclusion contacts are not essential, but they deliver intelligence and allow lobbyists to have issues and procedures explained to them. So it is wrong to claim contacts are not important; but they are overrated. Professional lobbyists portray a familiarity with politicians and those involved in politics. Contacts make lobbyists seem plausible.

Coalitions

Whilst coalitions are neither necessary nor sufficient for effective lobbying, a broad coalition of support is a beneficial attribute. Coalitions can be very important for effective lobbying.

Over Sunday trading coalitions were central, but lobbyists played little role in spotting connections or building alliances. Groups tried to win over opponents and sceptics. SHRC undermined KSSC by moving on to its territory and recruiting the trade union, USDAW. SHRC effectively portrayed its policy as a compromise, whilst KSSC was perceived as intolerant and inflexible. The regulators' merger came too late in the campaign to be taken seriously.

In CrossRail a long-term coalition would have been helpful, but the client and lobbyists were unable to construct one. The transient CrossRail coalition, which was mobilised at critical moments, secured ephemeral victories. The short-term CrossRail coalition was rejected by civil servants using the 'Mandy Rice-Davies dismissive'. The coalitions reflected divisions with government: opponents allied with the Treasury to heighten the profile of opposition.

In JLE there was no coalition; but one was unnecessary. O&Y's campaign was focused, almost exclusively, on three central departments. Opponents were limited. Third-party endorsement was not necessary because the project was in line with government policy and had support from senior ministers.

In the 'liability' case, broad support was fundamental, but eluded the firms. The firms and the lobbyist managed a broad and united coalition on LLPs. On broader liability reform the firms could barely agree between themselves; the accounting profession was divided; and there was no harmony in the wider business community. Government demanded evidence of third-party support, believing that if the firms could not persuade their clients then government was unlikely to be convinced.

Lobbyists' effectiveness depends on the extent of opposition to their objectives. Lobbyists can help build and sustain coalitions in order to convince officials that they have broad support from important actors. Where the lobbyists work for a peak organisation with a sizeable membership or several clients on one issue, the lobbyist may be able to ensure cohesion and prevent divisions. Company directors, ingrained in their businesses, see other companies in their sector as competitors, not potential allies. Lobbyists, as observers, are able to spot shared objectives and connections. Lobbyists can be effective in bringing people together. Coalitions and third-party allies may be unnecessary; therefore it is more appropriate to conclude that lobbyists tend to be effective if they possess the ability to spot connections to potential allies and to construct coalitions in cases where there is no political support from senior ministers.

Resources

Lobbyists tend to be effective if the client has abundant resources and is skilful in deploying them.

Resources can be structural, and include the economic importance of the interest group.

The effectiveness of the retail alliance in the Sunday trading case was enhanced by the size of their businesses, the number of employees and their significance to the British economy. KSSC had few structural resources. It relied on part-time volunteers. Its lack of resources prevented KSSC from hiring professional advisers early in the campaign, whereas SHRC was able to hire experienced lobbyists with contacts and knowledge of the system. The resource disparity was significant. SHRC's campaign utilised the massive resources of client companies, allowing it to fight on several fronts and be more effective.

CrossRail's resources were weak. Whilst it had access to money to hire lobbyists, one minister argued that it would have been better for CrossRail to have spent more on lobbying. Ineffectual management caused CrossRail's frailty. It was weak, uncoordinated and divided. CrossRail was also constrained by its managing companies in regard to what it could do.

O&Y by contrast, in the JLE case, was resource-rich. Its lobbying effort cost millions of pounds. Its management was focused, experienced and committed, and it was not constrained by convention. It was able to hire advisers who recommended unconventional lobbying techniques which O&Y pursued with ardour. Because of the abundant resources lobbyists were able to add value; they helped to make O&Y's lobbying more effective.

Similarly, resource constraints were not relevant to those firms campaigning for reform of the liability regime. The firms were global businesses and immensely powerful. In addition to numerous academic studies and the time of senior partners, the firms paid the lobbyist over £300 000 a year. However, the firms were weakened by a lack of agreement at the senior level between the firms. The Liability Reform Group was lethargic and the firms' inability to cooperate was a principal weakness. Despite their resources, the firms were ineffective.

Financial resources can be important, and allow the lobbyist to use all the tools at his disposal to run a campaign. Financial constraints can limit a programme of action, thereby hindering effectiveness. However, financial resources are not key determinants of effectiveness. Though SHRC out-spent KSSC, the outcome was not determined by the groups' budgets. The Big Five firms spent a large amount of money on the campaign, but were ineffective. Client commitment is an important resource: lobbyists need access to the right people at the right level in the client organisation. The commitment of senior executives is necessary. Weak and uncoordinated management leads to ineffectiveness.

Resources allow for effectiveness under particular circumstances. It is not always those lobbyists with the greatest financial or managerial resources at their disposal that are effective. There are several dimensions to resources, including finance, national structure, number of staff, and the client's influence over the implementation of policy. The skill of the lobbyist is the deployment of these resources in an efficient manner. Whilst context is important, the evidence suggests that lobbyists with more resources are more often effective.

Low-profile outsider tactics

Lobbyists tend to be effective if they pursue low-profile, 'outsider' tactics.

Outsider tactics can be effectively pursued concurrently with insider tactics, but only if the outsider strategy is low-profile. This distinction is not recognised in the literature. Restraints on groups, which encourage them to pursue low-profile methods, break down when groups are discontented, leading them to adopt controversial tactics. Lobbyists pursuing ineffective low-profile insider strategies have several options. They can continue their low-profile strategy in the hope government will recognise their case; they can stop lobbying and lose; or they can choose an 'outsider' strategy. There are two types of outsider strategy, low-profile and high-profile. High-profile outsider strategies involve mobilising electoral blocks (e.g., petitions, a media campaign or demonstrations).

Litigation, activity challenging the law and subtle 'threats' are defined as low-profile outsider tactics. The evidence suggests 'outsider tactics' must be low-profile to be successful. These tactics often run in parallel with tactics aimed at maintaining close 'insider' links with departments. In two of the four cases examined, low-profile outsider tactics were used successfully. Over Sunday trading the pro-liberalisation companies pursued a complex, time-consuming legal challenge that brought UK law into disrepute. Their spurious defences made the law unenforceable. This outsider tactic was deliberate, planned and resourced. Despite causing government embarrassment and civil servants extra work, the lobby maintained warm and close relations with ministers and officials. The evidence suggests low-profile outsider tactics are valuable when the interest group enjoys good relations with government.

In the 'liability' case, the accountants continued to enjoy good relations with government despite engaging in outsider tactics. They attempted to play governments off against one other, and threatened to take their business offshore because they were frustrated with the glacial pace of policy-making. The firms stumbled across Jersey as a consequence of their lack of knowledge about UK policy processes. The unintended effect was that the threat to move to Jersey became a catalyst which engaged senior ministers, who then activated the government machine.

This book challenges the conventional view that insider groups in policy communities will respect informal procedures and will not embarrass the government. The evidence presented here shows that groups can maintain insider relations, be trusted and be given confidential information and yet still pursue low-profile outsider tactics designed to embarrass and pressure government.

The tactic must be low-profile, with the objective being to raise the profile of the issue within government to involve higher-level political players. Lobbyists seek to change elite perceptions about an issue. They deal with the issue at the routine, mundane and conventional 'official' level until the prospect of failure or stonewalling means they have no other options. There is no longer the incentive for those losing the argument to continue abiding by the insider's rules. Then, effective lobbyists raise the profile of the issue within government. Using high-profile outsider tactics is high risk, and usually signals a failure to achieve objectives within the conventional process. They are rarely effective. However, when conventional insider methods have failed lobbyists can be effective if they pursue *low-profile* outsider tactics to raise the issue's profile *within* government.

When lobbyists matter

It would be wrong to conclude that lobbyists never influence policy, because they sometimes do matter. Lobbyists can be a worthwhile investment. It is often rational for organisations to hire lobbyists because they bring economies of scale in services such as monitoring and contact-building, and they bring experience and educate clients. They introduce new ideas and a sense of realism, and on occasions their involvement can overturn established procedures and affect policy outcomes.

However, whilst interest groups may be central to the policy-making system, lobbyists are rarely at the centre of the decision-making process. Lobbyists do not really matter unless the context is right. Effectiveness is often situation-specific and conditional on a host of external and internal variables. The influence of structure and context, and the role of political constraints and government autonomy are all important factors. Lobbyists' influence is constrained by these factors, including economic factors and judicial decisions, and other constraints (ultimately within the control of politicians), such as political trends and perceptions. Lobbyists face internal constraints, including resources, their contacts, knowledge and the quality of their case.

Often lobbyists just run with the crowd. They add or subtract a little along the way. Policy is decided by bigger factors than lobbyists. Though they are active on many aspects of policy, lobbyists rarely affect policy outcomes. Their impact is at the margins of policy. The evidence suggests the 'communications school of lobbying' is more convincing. Unless external circumstances are auspicious, lobbyists usually fail. Although lobbyists believe themselves to be effective, the evidence shows the perceptions they hold about their impact on policy-makers is, by and large, contrary to their real effect. Much of their influence is illusory. Their role is often overplayed by the press. A lot of their work is mundane (either postbox activity, or telling clients whom to write and talk to). Many lobbyists are glorified press officers helping to publicise a client's case. They often 'hold hands', accompanying clients who lack confidence when they approach the government.

These findings do not assume lobbyists do not add value to their clients, because the evidence suggests they do. Lobbyists matter more when working on low-profile, technical and non-political issues; when there are no disadvantageous external factors; and if the issues fits government trends. Lobbyists also matter if they include their clients in the arena where the policy will be decided and manage their activity; if they pursue a multi-faceted approach on high-profile issues and a targeted approach on low-profile issues; if they are familiar with informal rules and SOPs; if they have good contacts and can construct coalitions when necessary; and if their clients have sufficient resources.

Notes

1 Introduction

1. Finer (1966), p. 18.
2. Salisbury (1984), p. 70.
3. Finer (1966), p. 18.
4. Baumgartner and Leech (1998), p. 13.
5. Grant (1995), p. 152.
6. Grantham (1989).
7. S. Berry (1992), p. 227. Cliff Grantham claims the most important question, 'and the most difficult to answer, is what effect do political consultants have in influencing public policy?': Grantham (1989), p. 512.
8. Emphasis added: Jordan (1991a), p. 189.
9. Jordan (1991a), p. 189.
10. Warhurst (1990).
11. S. Berry (1993), p. 345.
12. G. Palast (1998), 'The American Way of Influence', *Observer*, 19 July 1998, citing Larry Makinsons from the Center for Responsive Politics in Washington.
13. Public Relations Consultants Association (PRCA) and International Committee of Public Relations Association (ICO) (1997); Fairchild (1997) and Fairchild (forthcoming).
14. I. Greer (1997); N. Jones (1995; 1999); Mitchie (1998); Moloney (1996); Souza (1998).
15. The *News of the World* declared in their Political Thought of the Week, 'Lobbyists are to government what a dog is to a tree.' *News of the World*, 5 July 1998.
16. Greenwood (1998b), pp. 487–600.
17. Broad surveys have been conducted by Heinz *et al.* (1993); Milbrath (1963); Schlozman and Tierney (1986); Walker (1991).
18. Milbrath (1963); Dexter (1969a); Scott and Hunt (1965); and Zeigler (1964), in Leech and Baumgartner (1998).
19. Lewis Dexter has argued that lobbyists target their friends and leave their enemies alone. See Dexter (1969a and 1969b). Also Bauer, Pool and Dexter (1963).
20. See Leech and Baumgartner (1998).
21. This field of political science has been well ploughed by Ainsworth and Austen-Smith (amongst others) who developed the counteractive theory of lobbying. They claimed, in contradistinction to Bauer, Pool and Dexter, that the interest group more likely to lobby is the one against whose interests the legislator will vote in the absence of lobbying. Supporting groups are then forced to lobby their supporters – counteractively – to offset the approaches from the first group.
22. Baumgartner and Leech (1998), p. 64.
23. Moloney (1996), p. 146.

24. Evidence of Rt Hon. John MacGregor, MP, to The Committee on Standards in Public Life. Transcript of Oral Evidence, 24 January 1995, p. 79, section 395.
25. HC Debates, WA, col. 228, 9/12/1998.
26. See the Cash-for-Questions affair in 1994 and the Cash-for-Access story in 1998 in the UK. There have been various books on the substantial influence of lobbying in the USA; see the following American commentators: Birnbaum (1992); Birnbaum and Murray (1987); Choate (1990); Edsall (1988); H. Smith (1988).
27. 'Labour to sell policy papers to lobbyists', *The Independent*, 9 March 1998; 'Labour spin doctor quits to join Thatcher's PR man', *The Independent*, 8 April 1998; 'Blair woos sponsors for welfare roadshows', *The Guardian*, 28 January 1998; 'Revealed: Labour's links with lobbyists', *The Independent*, 24 March 1998; 'Companies hand out jets and Jaguars as pre-election perks', *Observer*, 23 March 1997; 'Ex-Labour aides selling the inside track on how to block party policy', *The Independent*, 7 September 1998. Also see the cash-for-access investigation by the *Observer* which started with the following story: 'New Labour insiders offer secrets for cash', *Observer*, 5 July 1998. See the quality press for the following eight days, 5–13 July 1998.
28. 'New Labour insiders offer secrets for cash', *Observer*, 5 July 1998.
29. G. Palast, 'The American Way of Influence', *Observer*, 19 July 1998.
30. *Ibid.*
31. The key criticisms were that lobbyists: boasted they made use of Treasury information before it was announced; helped a company save £40 million by persuading ministers to abandon plans for a car park tax; knew in advance the contents of the Chancellor's Mansion House speech and that the Treasury would announce a new housing inspectorate; breached the embargo on a Trade and Industry Select Committee in advance of publication and sent it to a client (in reality an *Observer* journalist); claimed to have privileged access to ministers and key advisers in government; passed inside information about public spending plans to an investment bank; arranged a meeting between PowerGen and Treasury officials; placed clients on advisory committees; and were able to arrange tea with the Paymaster General.
32. 'Cabinet tells Blair: ditch the lobbyist', *Sunday Telegraph*, 12 July 1998.
33. Purnell and Armstrong concluded: 'There is nothing intrinsically improper about the role of political consultants. On the contrary, they have a valuable role to perform in assisting their clients to make proposals and cases to agencies of government in the most effective way.' Purnell and Armstrong (1998).
34. Both Latham and Truman showed decision-makers changing policy to satisfy interest-groups. E. Latham (1952) and Truman (1951). See also Lowi (1969); McConnell (1966).
35. Schattschneider (1935a).
36. Doig (1986a; 1986b; 1986c; 1990a; 1990b; 1991; 1995b).
37. Burns (1963); Chub and Peterson (1989); Lowi (1969); Rauch (1994).
38. Grenzke (1990), p. 144.
39. HC Debates, WAs, 9/3/1999 col. 168; 31/3/1999 cols 684, 712, 758, 842; 13/4/1999 cols 14, 29, 34, 108, 123, 145, 170; 16/4/1999, col. 367; 19/4/1999 col. 415.
40. Baumgartner and Leech (1998), p. 126.

41. Baumgartner and Leech (1998), p. 178. See also Browne (1995); Hansen (1991); Heinz *et al.* (1993); Knoke (1990); McFarland (1993); Schlozman and Tierney (1986); Walker (1991).
42. Grantham (1989), p. 514. Malbin concurs, arguing 'Interest groups tend to be more successful on bills that do not capture the public's attention than on ones that do.' Malbin (1984), p. 249.
43. Frendreis and Waterman (1985), p. 403. Charles Lindblom noted some policy areas received public attention whilst others received no public attention; he argued business will be at its weakest on issues in the public domain. See Lindblom (1984).
44. Milbrath (1963), p. 7.
45. Salisbury (1984), p. 71.
46. Baumgartner and Leech (1998), p. 29.
47. Salisbury prefers the word 'representative' to lobbyist as a description of the individual because it 'connotes a free-standing agent, retained on a fee-for-service basis and often on the assumption that the agent possesses particular skills or credentials of relevance to the advocacy role that are not readily available within the interested organization, whether institution or membership group'. Salisbury (1984), p. 72.
48. Greenwood and Thomas (1998), p. 491.
49. See Milbrath (1963), pp. 7–8.
50. Pross (1991).
51. See Milbrath (1963), p. 8: 'Lobbying is the stimulation and transmission of a communication, by someone other than a citizen acting on his own behalf, directed to a governmental decision-maker with the hope of influencing his decision.'
52. Salisbury (1984), p. 71.
53. Select Committee on Members' Interests: submission by Professors Michael Rush, Philip Norton, Colin Seymour Ure and Malcolm Shaw for the Report on Parliamentary Lobbying, HC 586 Session 1990/91.
54. Association of Professional Political Consultants, Introductory Paper.
55. *Ibid.*
56. Jordan (1989), p. 107.
57. PPU (1991a), p. 1.
58. Grantham (1989), p. 508.
59. Andrew Gifford, evidence to the Committee on Standards in Public Life, 24 January 1995.
60. Parliamentary agents include Dyson Bell Martin, Lewin Gregory, Rees & Freyer, Sharpe Pritchard, Sherwoods & Co and Vizzards. Most of their political work is oriented towards legislation or regulation.
61. European Parliament, *Second Report on Lobbying in the European Parliament*, Committee on the Rule of Procedure, the Verification of Credentials and Immunities, Rapporteur: Mr Glyn Ford, 12 June 1996, PE 216.869/fin.
62. Luff, evidence to Select Committee on Members' Interests cited in Doig (1986c).
63. For example, Walker limited his definition of an interest group to functioning associations open to membership and concerned with policy: Walker (1991), p. 4; Baumgartner and Leech (1998), p. 26.

64. See Crawford (1939); Herring (1929); Key (1964) and Truman (1951) in Baumgartner and Leech (1998), p. 27.
65. Salisbury (1984).
66. Baumgartner and Leech (1998), p. 68.
67. Gray and Lowery (1996a); Heinz *et al.* (1993) and Schlozmann and Tierney (1986), p. 10; and all use broader definitions of interest groups.
68. Association of Professional Political Consultants register of June 1998.
69. Salisbury (1984), p. 73.
70. Martin Smith (1991).
71. A *Financial Times* survey in 1985 of 180 sizeable companies found more than 40 per cent utilised the services of political consultants.
72. Jordan (1991b).
73. Salisbury (1984), p. 74.
74. McSmith and Calvert (1999), 'Look who's coming to the rescue of Augusto', *Observer*, 17 January 1999.
75. Jordan and Richardson (1982).
76. See, for example, Beer (1982); and Middlemas (1986; 1990; 1991).
77. Jordan (1991b).
78. Schlozman and Tierney (1983), p. 367.
79. Humphries (1991), p. 355.
80. Mazey and Richardson (1992).
81. 'Old political foes team up to lobby in new parliament', *Scotland on Sunday*, 5 July 1998; John (1998) 'Devolution encourages new business-politics links', *Public Affairs Newsletter*, vol. 5, no. 2, October; 'Scottish public affairs firm calls for strict new Code of Conduct', *Public Affairs Newsletter*, vol. 5, no. 1, September 1998; 'GJW launches new Scottish political consultancy', *Public Affairs Newsletter*, vol. 4, no. 9, June 1998.
82. Miller (1988).
83. G. Wilson (1991).
84. Norton (1991), p. 62.
85. Doig (1986c), p. 524.
86. Post (1991).
87. Kavanagh (1992).
88. Jordan (1991a).
89. G. Palast (1998), 'The American Way of Influence', *Observer*, 19 July 1998.
90. *Ibid.*
91. Philip Norton (1995), contribution to a seminar on 'Ethical and Effective Lobbying' organised by Bruce Naughton Wade (public affairs counsellors) 21 March 1995.
92. Cited in Jordan (1989).
93. Miller (1991).
94. Rush (1990a), p. 143.
95. S. Berry (1993).
96. See Rush (1990b), especially David Judge's ch. 2 and Michael Rush's conclusion.
97. Grantham (1989), p. 505.
98. Miller (1987), p. 38.
99. Searing (1993).
100. *Ibid.*

101. Doig (1990a).
102. Norton (1991), p. 72.
103. Miller (1987), p. 42.
104. Rush (1990a), p. 143. Approximately 44 per cent of written and oral evidence comes from outside groups.
105. Judge (1992a).
106. Rush (1990b); I. Marsh (1986); and Judge (1990).
107. Judge (1992a).
108. Miller (1988).
109. Finer (1958), cited in Jordan (1991a).
110. Quinlan (1994).
111. Cited in Jordan (1991a).
112. Miller (1987), p. 97.
113. First Report of the Committee on Standards in Public Life, vol. 1, Report, *Standards in Public Life*, p. 35, Cm 2850-I.
114. Cabinet Office (1998).
115. *Ibid.*
116. *Ibid.*
117. *Ibid.*
118. Doig (1990a).
119. Purnell and Armstrong (1998).

2 What Effectiveness Means for Lobbyists

1. Fritschler (1975); Rothenberg (1992), especially ch. 8.
2. Hansen (1991); Schlozman and Tierney (1986).
3. Maass (1951).
4. Heinz *et al.* (1993), p. 313.
5. Glynn, Gray and Jenkins (1992).
6. '[T]he extent to which the objectives of a policy are achieved. The most effective policy is one which achieves all its objectives': Treasury (1988b), p. 28. 'Effectiveness means providing the right services to enable the Local Authority to implement its policies and objectives': Audit Commission (1986), p. 8. 'Ensuring the output from any given activity is achieving the desired result': Price Waterhouse (1990), p. 4. 'The value which society desires from given inputs and outputs of a particular service': Tomkins (1987), p. 49.
7. National Audit Office (nd), p. 5.
8. Glynn, Gray and Jenkins (1992).
9. Unintended effects can be beneficial and intended effects can be undesirable.
10. J. Berry (1977); Milbrath (1963). The studies prove certain types of strategies are more effective than others: for example, face-to-face contact is regarded as more effective than letter-writing campaigns.
11. Heinz *et al.* (1993).
12. For a useful book that assesses influence and tries to predict when groups will attempt influence, see Gamson (1968), chs. 4, 5, 7 and 8.
13. Grant (1995).
14. Wooton (1970) noted it is 'a real Irish bog of a subject that has claimed many victims' (p. 73); and G. Wilson (1990) has concluded it was impossible to measure, in Moloney (1996), p. 34.

15. J. Berry (1997), p. 162.
16. J. Berry (1977), p. 271.
17. Johnson attempts to measure the effectiveness of various independent variables (concentrating on Political Action Committee contributions) on Congressional voting patterns by using a simultaneous equation model. She reaches few firm conclusions, but says PACs (Political Action Committees are cause-related political interest groups) are 'minimally successful in influencing... voting patterns'. See L. Johnson (1985).
18. J. Berry (1977), p. 285.
19. Grantham (1989).
20. Chappell (1981).
21. Salisbury (1975), p. 207.
22. J. Berry (1977), p. 274.
23. Grant (1995), p. 75.
24. R. Smith (1995).
25. Schattschneider noted that interest groups and lobbyists sought to exaggerate their importance: Schattschneider (1935a), p. 225. Heinz *et al.* were aware of the risks of inflation in self-reports of success but stated confidently 'there does not appear too much bias of that kind in these kind of data': Heinz *et al.* (1993), p. 346.
26. Although lobbying companies are sophisticated and professional, there is rarely a tangible end product attributable to their actions. See Grant (1995).
27. J. Berry (1989a), p. 163.
28. D. Evans (1996), p. 291.
29. Dahl (1991).
30. J. Berry (1977), p. 274.
31. Salisbury (1984), p. 71.
32. Grant (1995), p. 129.
33. Grant (1995), p. 129.
34. Studies using probit analyses treat policy outcome as a dichotomous variable assigning 1 to successful and 0 to unsuccessful. For example, D. Evans (1996) and Wiggins, Hamm and Bell (1992).
35. Baumgartner and Leech (1998), p. 135.
36. British Gas hired many of the leading consultancies to lobby for the liberalisation of the gas market. Its rationale was to prevent competitors from hiring the highest calibre advisers.
37. Grant (1995).
38. Heinz *et al.* (1993), p. 352.
39. Grant (1995), p. 152.
40. Miller (1991), p. 63.
41. J. Berry (1977), p. 274.
42. Furlong (1997), p. 341.
43. Richardson and Jordan (1979).
44. Michael Heseltine, cited in Boléat (1996), p. 136.
45. Compass Partnership (1996).
46. Harris Research Centre (1996).
47. *CrossRail Contract – A proposal submitted by Shandwick Consultants Ltd*, London, December 1994.

48. Benchmarking has become increasingly fashionable in public affairs in the 1990s. There has been a spate of articles in public affairs journals, see *ImPACt* published by the American Public Affairs Council; *Public Affairs*, published by the Public Affairs Association of Canada; *Communication World* published by the International Association of Business Communication; *Corporate Public Affairs* published by the Australian Centre for Public Affairs; and the *Public Affairs Newsletter* in the UK.
49. Fleisher (1995), p. 20.
50. Miller (1997).
51. Fleisher (1997).
52. Hawkinson (1997).
53. Whiteley and Winyard (1987), in Grant (1995), p. 129.
54. Such as the ideology of state actors and government institutions, economic constraints, electoral politics, prior policies or the constraints imposed by supra-national treaties.
55. Heinz *et al.* (1993), p. 351.
56. Gray and Lowery (1996b); Salisbury (1984); Walker (1991) in Baumgartner and Leech (1998), p. 7.
57. Baumgartner and Leech (1998), p. 12.
58. McFarland (1987).
59. Gray and Lowery (1996a; 1996b). It has also been shown that contextual factors affect decisions to join groups. See Baumgartner and Leech (1998), p. 79.
60. Heinz *et al.* (1993), p. 57.
61. Salisbury (1984) in Baumgartner and Leech (1998), p. 14.
62. Gray and Lowery (1993a; 1993b; 1994; 1995; 1996b); Walker (1991).
63. Baumgartner and Leech (1998), p. 104.
64. *Ibid.*, pp. 36–7.
65. *Ibid.*, p. 37.
66. Kingdon (1995).
67. Eckstein (1960), pp. 36–8.
68. Baumgartner and Leech (1996c), p. 25.
69. Rothenberg (1992), p. 254.
70. Heinz *et al.* (1993), p. 351.
71. Mucciaroni (1995), p. 26.
72. McFarland (1991).
73. J. Berry (1989a), p. 81.
74. See Jordan (1991b), p. 182.
75. Baumgartner and Leech (1998), p. 40.
76. Bacheller (1977).
77. Grantham (1989), p. 514.
78. Miller (1988).
79. Miller (1997). Political concerns account for 15 per cent, pressure 5 per cent, big battalions 15 per cent, media 10 per cent and the courts 1 per cent.
80. Norman Tebbit, *The House Magazine*, 29 November 1985.
81. Miller (1997), p. 14.
82. Barnett (1982).
83. Baumgartner and Jones (1993).
84. Baumgartner and Leech (1998), p. 140.

85. Miller (1997), p. 10.
86. R. Hall (1996); R. Hall and Wayman (1990).
87. Miller (1997), p. 7.
88. Grant (1995), p. 145. Aaron Wildavsky's book on the American budgetary process notes the House Appropriation Committee was governed by a Treasury norm. However, an influx of Liberal Democrats rejected the existing norms and changed the character of the institution. See Wildavsky (1964), pp. 47–62.
89. G. Wilson (1981), p. 13.
90. Eckstein (1960), pp. 36–8.
91. *Ibid.*, pp. 36–8.
92. Eckstein said: 'I for one have no idea how to determine an objective general interest.' He suggests three questions deal with the situation. Does the policy adopted seem to be what most people want? Would the policy have been more effective if the lobbyists and interest groups had been less effective and less involved? Does a policy, because of special interest pressure, withdraw too large a share from total national wealth relative to other services? (Has the group encroached unduly on the generalisable resources of society?) See Eckstein (1960), p. 160.
93. Miller (1997).
94. Jordan (1991a).
95. Hayes (1978), p. 144.
96. See Lowi (1969, 1971).
97. Hayes (1978).
98. Jordan (1991a).
99. Hayes (1978).
100. Miller (1991).
101. Miller (1997).
102. Miller (1991), p. 59.
103. Salisbury and Heinz (1970).
104. Hayes (1978).
105. Grant (1995), p. 131.
106. Ainsworth (1993), p. 41.
107. Rose (1974), p. 253, in Grant (1995), p. 143.
108. Rose (1974), p. 254–5.
109. Grant (1995), p. 147.
110. J. Berry (1977); Grant (1995); Schlozman and Tierney (1984; 1986); Walker (1983; 1991).
111. J. Berry (1989a), pp. 81–5.
112. Grant (1995), pp. 130–43.
113. Heinz *et al.* (1993), p. 405.
114. *Ibid.*, p. 407.
115. *Ibid.*, p. 408.
116. Jordan and Moloney (1993).
117. Miller (1997).
118. Holbech (1991).
119. Cates (1988).
120. Milbrath (1963), p. 141.

121. Jordan and Moloney (1993).
122. It is also likely that internal variables, as well as external context, will deter-mine what mixture of tactics (strategy) will be used. For example, tactics are likely to depend on financial, time and human resources.
123. Baumgartner and Leech (1998), p. 148.
124. Shadow lobbying describes how professional lobbyists no longer engage in direct advocacy with decision-makers, but remain in the shadows and advise their clients how to deal with politicians and officials.
125. Baumgartner and Leech (1998), p. 155.
126. Jordan (1991a), p. 185.
127. Contrary to this assertion, Heinz *et al.* note that the more time lobbyists spend in a policy domain and have established themselves, the more likely they were to name adversaries and enemies. See Heinz *et al.* (1993).
128. Key (1964).
129. J. Berry (1989a), p. 83.
130. G. Wilson (1991), p. 68.
131. J. Berry (1989a), p. 83.
132. *Ibid.*
133. Jordan (1989), p. 186.
134. *Ibid.*, p. 193.
135. M. Smith (1986).
136. J. Berry (1989a), p. 84.
137. Pryor (1997).
138. Parsons (1996), pp. 153–68.
139. Martin Smith (1991), p. 125.
140. J. Berry (1989a), p. 83.
141. Miller (1997).
142. Baumgartner and Leech (1998), p. 97.
143. Jordan (1991a).
144. J. Berry (1989a), p. 199.
145. Miller (1987), p. 99.
146. Boléat (1996), p. 238.
147. Cates (1988), p. 243.
148. Eckstein (1960), pp. 36–8.
149. Grant (1995), pp. 137–8.
150. I. Greer (1985).
151. R. Rhodes (1996b), p. 657.
152. J. Berry (1989b).
153. J. Berry (1997).
154. Baumgartner and Leech (1998), p. 114.
155. See J. Berry (1989a), p. 194.
156. See Grant (1995), pp. 134–6.
157. Miller (1997).
158. G. Wilson (1991).
159. See J. Berry (1989a), pp. 79 and 185.
160. Kooiman (1993), cited in R. Rhodes (1996b).
161. Heinz *et al.* (1993); Schlozman and Tierney (1986).
162. J. Berry (1997); D. Gopoian (1984); Schlozman and Tierney (1986).

163. Helco (1978).
164. Martin Smith (1991), p. 125.
165. Grant (1995), pp. 138–9.
166. Eckstein (1960), postscript.

3 The Effect of Lobbyists: A Political Science Framework

1. D. Marsh and R. Rhodes (1992).
2. Furlong (1997), p. 340.
3. Whiteley and Winyard (1987), p. 136, in Grant (1995), p. 141.
4. Eckstein (1960), p. 155. Eckstein suggests that in the simplest terms 'group influence is enlarged by anything which restricts the influence on policy-making of anything else. This either is or comes close to being a tautology, but is none the less worth stating.'
5. Stewart (1958), p. 4.
6. Conway (1991); Grenzke (1990); W. Jones and R. Keiser (1987); Magleby and Nelson (1990); Neustadtl (1990); Sabato (1989b); Schlozman and Tierney (1986) and F. Sorauf (1992), cited in R. Smith (1995).
7. Frendreis and Waterman (1985); Sabato (1985); Welch (1982), cited in R. Smith (1995).
8. Conway (1991); Frendreis and Waterman (1985); Magleby and Nelson (1990); Malbin (1984); Schlozman and Tierney (1986); Wright (1985), cited in R. Smith (1995).
9. In his review of Bauer, Pool and Dexter's *American Business and Public Policy* Lowi noted three types of policy issue – distributive (narrow), regulative (middle) and redistributive (broad) – when discussing group–government interaction. Lowi suggested the salience of the issue affected campaign and legislative behaviour. See Lowi (1964; 1972).
10. Schlozman and Tierney (1983).
11. Schlozman and Tierney (1986).
12. Neustadtl (1990), p. 550.
13. Grenzke (1990).
14. Sabato (1990), p. 135.
15. Welch (1982).
16. Frendreis and Waterman (1985), p. 402.
17. Sabato (1990), p. 136.
18. Conway (1991), pp. 211–12.
19. Malbin (1984).
20. Frendreis and Waterman (1985), p. 412.
21. *Ibid.*, pp. 401–12.
22. Stewart (1958), p. 34.
23. Schlozman and Tierney (1986), p. 314.
24. Finer (1958).
25. *Ibid.*, p. 20.
26. Jordan, Maloney and McLaughlin (1992b).
27. Skocpol, Abend-Wein, Howard and Goodrich-Lehmann (1993).
28. D. Marsh (1995b), p. 3.
29. S. Berry (1991), p. 21.
30. M. Smith (1995a), p. 111.

31. Stewart (1958), p. 111.
32. Bennett (1997), p. 62. The author suggests the problem with a voluntary business association sector is that it promotes fragmentation; therefore he suggests 'a level of state organisation or "support" is required to assure association effectiveness from a *public policy perspective'*.
33. Skocpol, Abend-Wein, Howard and Goodrich-Lehmann (1993), p. 692.
34. Various scholars critiqued pluralism as an inaccurate description of policy systems, including Cater (1964); Fritschler (1975); Lowi (1969); Maass (1951); McConnell (1966), in Baumgartner and Leech (1998), p. 57.
35. Some authors argue that pluralism sees the state as neutral, and say that policy-making is accessible to all, and that outside groups are equal to government in their influence. See Dearlove and Saunders (1991); and Jessop (1983).
36. Baumgartner and Leech (1998), p. 48.
37. Various scholars have noted bias in favour of the business community, notably, Heinz *et al.* (1993); Schattschneider (1935a, b); Schlozman and Tierney (1983; 1986); Walker (1983; 1991).
38. Lindblom (1977), p. 175.
39. Richardson and Jordan (1979).
40. M. Smith (1990).
41. Departmental autonomy is increased when the political head and official torso of a department work together; when they are founded on a functional mandate rather than around a clientele; when their actions involve applying fixed regulations and laws; and if civil servants are able to generate information and data internally. See Atkinson and Coleman (1989b).
42. Jordan and Maloney (1997), p. 565.
43. P. Evans, Rueschemeyer and Skocpol (1985); Krasner (1984); Skocpol (1980; 1982).
44. Jordan (1981) p. 101, citing Polsby (1963). Similarly Helco notes it is difficult to identify the dominant actors: Helco (1978).
45. Nordlinger (1981; 1987). McFarland also notes the autonomy of US state institutions, using the term 'elite pluralism' to describe a triadic theory of power where policy can be dominated by groups, but opposing groups also emerge. He recognises that government agencies are assumed to have some autonomy. See McFarland (1987).
46. Christiansen and Dowding (1994).
47. Jordan (1990c), p. 332.
48. Jordan (1981), p. 106.
49. Atkinson and Coleman (1989b), p. 52.
50. Cortel (1997).
51. Cortel (1997) p. 269 says 'an interest group's influence can increase when an institutional network links the group's representatives to a centralised desision-making structure'.
52. Wallis and Dollery (1997), p. 2.
53. Jordan, Maloney and McLaughlin (1992a).
54. M. Smith (1993), p. 72.
55. McFarland (1987), p. 138.
56. The term 'policy discourse' was used to describe the interactions of individuals and institutions in policy-making. Within this discourse, the

concept of 'framing' was used to set the idea in context and to explain its underlying rationale. See Merin and Schon (1991).

57. Baumgartner and Jones (1993), p. 5.
58. Schlozman argues 'government is no mere punching bag registering the relative strength of the pressure group blows to which it is subjected.' Schlozman (1984).
59. Truman (1951), p. 322.
60. Jordan and Richardson (1987a; 1987b); Richardson and Jordan (1979).
61. McFarland (1987), p. 139.
62. David Marsh notes:

> contemporary pluralism recognises an increased role for the state. This is particularly clear in the work of Nordlinger who emphasises the autonomy of the democratic state and views pluralism as much in terms of conflict between the different interests of sections within government as in terms of conflict between interest groups within civil society.

See D. Marsh (1995b). Jordan argues 'those wishing to bring the state back in also want to decompose the state. The weak state is fashionable. There is no longer a homogeneous state.' Jordan (1990b), p. 484.
63. Eckstein (1960), p. 153. He says earlier that 'it is always the interplay of governmental structure, activity and attitudes which determine the form of pressure group politics.' (p. 17).
64. McFarland (1991), p. 270.
65. Christiansen and Dowding (1994).
66. Almond (1988), p. 866.
67. *Ibid.* Almond later concludes that 'overwhelmingly the pluralist literature has been shown to be one in which governmental autonomy is recognised.'
68. Eckstein (1960). Herring (1936) also recognises the autonomy of government actors and their pursuit of the public interest in the face of competing group demands.
69. Jordan and Richardson (1987b), p. 29.
70. Christiansen and Dowding (1994).
71. Parsons (1996), p. 85.
72. R. Rhodes (1997), p. 38.
73. Jordan (1981).
74. D. Marsh and R. Rhodes (1992).
75. Richardson and Jordan (1979), pp. 73–4.
76. Jordan, Maloney and McLaughlin (1992a).
77. Jordan (1990c), p. 326.
78. See Jordan and Maloney (1997), p. 574.
79. Richardson and Jordan (1979).
80. Salisbury (1984).
81. Doig (1991), p. 149.
82. Miller (1991), p. 58.
83. Grant (1978; 1989).
84. Dudley and Richardson (1998).
85. Page (1998).
86. Christiansen and Dowding (1994).

87. Furlong (1997), p. 340.
88. Heinz *et al.* (1993), p. 348.
89. Truman (1951), p. 437.
90. Bauer, Pool and Dexter (1963).
91. Austen-Smith and Wright (1994; 1996).
92. Truman (1951).
93. Ainsworth (1993), p. 43; Christiansen and Dowding (1994).
94. Hansen (1991).
95. Christiansen and Dowding (1994).
96. Nordlinger (1988), pp. 883–4.
97. *Ibid.*, p. 884.
98. Allison (1971), p. 67.
99. Comprehensive rationality involves organisations choosing the best option taking account of consequences, their probabilities and utilities. Bounded rationality recognises the physical and psychological limits of man's capacity as option generator, information processor and problem solver. These limits require simplified models to extract the main features of the problem without capturing all its complexity. Allison (1971), p. 71.
100. Steinbruner says in reality the decision process 'proceeds sequentially to examine a set of alternative actions until one with an outcome valued as acceptable is found' (p. 62). He says that the 'cybernetic theorist doubts that decision-makers engage in sophisticated outcome calculations with any degree of regularity or consistency': Steinbruner (1974), p. 66. Dowding argues the contrary. He suggests rational choice provides the mechanisms to explain policy development within policy networks. See Dowding (1995a).
101. Steinbruner mimics Cyert and March who term the application to a problem of an option currently in use elsewhere 'mating': Cyert and March (1963), in Steinbruner (1974), p. 75.
102. Allison (1969; 1971); Allison and Halperin (1972); Allison and Szanton (1976).
103. Steinbruner (1974), p. 55.
104. Incremental decision-making was defended against the rational comprehensive model. See Lindblom (1959) and Wildavsky (1964).
105. Allison (1969), p. 700.
106. Allison (1969; 1971).
107. Neustadt witnessed first hand the bargaining games entered into by the US President. Holding power was not enough to achieve objectives. Neustadt (1963; 1964; 1970).
108. Allison (1971), p. 7.
109. See Dunleavy (1995b); Parsons (1996); E. Rhodes (1994).
110. Heinz *et al.* (1993), p. 350.
111. Stewart (1958), p. 46.
112. The ability to present a broad coalition improves effectiveness. See J. Berry (1989b); Furlong (1997); Herring (1929); Salisbury, Heinz, Laumann and Nelson (1987); J. Wilson (1973).
113. Knoke (1990), p. 208–9.
114. Allison (1971), p. 171.
115. Karl Deutsch refers to these channels of communication as the nerves of government. Whilst other political scientists are concerned with the muscles (power) or skeleton (institutions), Deutsch examined the nerves. He

suggested government is a problem of steering, and that steering is about communication. Deutsch (1963).

116. Allison (1971), pp. 167–80.
117. Allison (1971), p. 275.
118. Dahl (1961); Lindblom (1977); Truman (1951).
119. Dahl (1961).
120. R. Smith (1984), p. 49.
121. Schlozman and Tierney (1986).
122. Langbein and Lotwis (1990), p. 434.
123. R. Smith (1984), p. 51.
124. M. Smith (1999), p. 53.
125. Dowding (1991), p. 5.
126. R. Rhodes (1992b).
127. *Ibid*.
128. R. Rhodes (1980).
129. Dunleavy (1995b).

4   Church Bells versus Shop Tills: The Campaign For and Against Sunday Trading

1. Total deregulation was defeated by 404 votes to 174, a majority of 230: 'MPs pass six-hour Sunday shopping for stores', *Financial Times*, 9 December 1993.
2. The REST proposals were based on exempt shops rather than exempt goods, unlike the Shops Act 1950 which forbade the sale of specific goods. Outlets offering services covered by the acronym REST were to be allowed to open. *Recreation* 'Sports, outings visits and fun. Certain goods might be allowed which help the main activity, such as fishing bait, tennis balls and ice-cream'; *Emergencies* 'Emergencies can happen at any time, and to anybody. Legislation must make allowances for situations where pain or hardship occurs. Goods such as medicines, petrol and vital car parts need to be available'; *Social Gatherings* 'Sunday is a day for people to relax, to meet with family and friends, to talk and share a meal or a drink, to spend time together. Goods such as restaurant meals obviously enhance special gatherings'; and *Travel* 'We all have to travel some time on Sundays, for recreation, in emergencies or to attend social gatherings. It seems sensible that goods which aid a journey should be made available.' See KSSC, 'Consensus on New Sunday Principles', 20 May 1987 (KSSC, 1987c).
3. 'Commons Sketch: Rumbo buys time in shopping row', *Daily Telegraph*, 28 November 1991.
4. William Oddie, 'Never Ever on a Sunday', *The Spectator*, 14 December 1991.
5. KSSC director, interview, 17/3/1997.
6. B&Q, Wickes and Homebase. B&Q estimated sales of £168 million (23 per cent of turnover) were carried out on Sundays. Because companies costed themselves on a six day basis the marginal turnover of 23 per cent accounted, arguably, for the whole of the company's profit.
7. SHRC (1991).
8. Principal of SHRC, interview, 5/5/1997.
9. Chairman of SHRC, interview, 22/7/1997.
10. Principal of SHRC, interview, 5/5/1997.
11. *Ibid*.

12. 'B-M is called up in Sunday trading war', *PR Week*, 3 June 1993 and Des Wilson, 'Diary', *The Spectator*, 6 May 1989.
13. OPEN Chairman, interview, 24/3/1997.
14. OPEN lobbyist, interview, 17/3/1997.
15. The chairman was impressed that the senior lobbyist was a Conservative Prospective Parliamentary Candidate (PPC) in the 1987 General Election, 'worked in Conservative Central Office and was well connected – speech writing for various top ministers'.
16. The chairman used colleagues from member businesses for meetings with ministers.
17. OPEN lobbyist, interview, 17/3/1997.
18. Most M&S, Budgen and House of Fraser stores are in town centres. The SHRC retailers were based mainly in out-of-town complexes.
19. It also included Budgen, Burton Group, Iceland, Next, Gateway, House of Fraser, Aldi, Sears, and Wm Morrison amongst others.
20. RSAR Co-ordinator, interview, 3/6/1997.
21. *Ibid.*
22. *Ibid.*
23. *Ibid.*
24. *Ibid.*
25. PPU lobbyist, interview, 7/3/1997.
26. *Ibid.*
27. Former Home Office Minister 2, interview, 10/6/1997.
28. OPEN lobbyist, interview, 17/3/1997.
29. *Ibid.* The lobbyist argued he was successful by giving OPEN 'a role and an influence far in excess of their actual importance, because we were lobbying on their behalf'.
30. GJW lobbyist, interview, 9/5/1997.
31. GJW Labour lobbyist, interview, 9/7/1997.
32. Former Home Office Minister 2, interview, 10/6/1997.
33. Former Home Office Minister 1, interview, 26/6/1997.
34. OPEN lobbyist, interview, 17/3/1997.
35. Former senior civil servant 8, interview, 22/04/1998.
36. Former SHRC Research Director, interview, 28/10/1996.
37. SHRC Sunday Shopping Update, *The Case for Change*, (nd), SHRC archives.
38. Between DIY chains and food retailers. Sainsbury's owned Homebase, whilst Woolworth and B&Q were part of Kingfisher.
39. OPEN lobbyist, interview, 17/3/1997.
40. Lord Caithness, Committee Stage of Sunday Sports Bill, House of Lords, 5 November 1987.
41. SHRC Sunday Shopping Update, *The Case for Change*, (nd), SHRC archives.
42. Deputy General Secretary of USDAW, interview, 9/6/1997.
43. The Shops Acts, Late-Night and Sunday Opening, Report of the Committee of Inquiry into proposals to amend the Shops Acts (The Auld Committee), Cmd 9376, November 1984, para. 291. The committee was established by the Home Secretary in 1983, chaired by Robert Auld, QC, to consider what changes were needed to the Shops Act.
44. Former senior civil servant 8, interview, 22/04/1998.
45. Radice and Pollard (1992; 1993; 1994).
46. KSSC adviser, interview, 17/3/1997.

47. Deputy General Secretary of USDAW, interview, 9/6/1997.
48. There was an USDAW-inspired NEC proposition.
49. Labour Public Affairs Consultant, interview, 19/3/1997. He talked directly to Labour MPs 'to present arguments in a way that would appeal to Labour MPs'.
50. Lord Graham was formerly KSSC's leading Labour supporter. 'Sunday switch by Graham', *Retail Week*, 21 February 1992.
51. 'Hattersley's trading places', *Sunday Express*, 12 July 1992.
52. 'Toughening of the Law', *Retail Week*, 12 April 1991.
53. OPEN Chairman, interview, 24/3/1997.
54. 'Labour can update policies without losing its roots', *USDAW Today*, June 1993.
55. Principal of SHRC, interview, 5/5/1997.
56. GJW lobbyist, interview, 9/5/1997.
57. Principal of SHRC, interview, 5/5/1997.
58. Emily's List was an informal network of female Labour MPs. Chairman of SHRC, interview, 22/7/1997.
59. 'Sunday trading', *Retail Week*, 11 September 1992; 'Scot MPs have vital role in shopping vote', *The Herald*, 1 November 1993.
60. Offers of cooperation were made before and after the 1992 Election; Labour was keen to forge an agreement between retailers and shopworkers. 'Labour Shifts on Sunday Law', *Retail Week*, 5 May 1991; 'Labour moves towards deal on Sunday trade', *Retail Week*, 3 July 1992.
61. KSSC adviser, correspondence, 27/2/1998.
62. PPU lobbyist, interview, 7/3/1997.
63. Chairman of EuroShop, interview, 14/5/1997.
64. KSSC adviser, correspondence, 27/2/1998.
65. REST – Keep Sunday Special Press Conference on 20 May 1987 at Charing Cross Hotel, transcript.
66. Diamond (1991a).
67. Worker protection included a right to premium pay and protection against being forced to work on Sundays.
68. Conservative Party, *General Election Campaign Guide 1987*, London.
69. Former senior civil servant 8, interview, 22/4/1998.
70. Former Home Office Minister 2, interview, 10/6/1997.
71. KSSC adviser, interview, 17/3/1997.
72. OPEN lobbyist, interview, 17/3/1997.
73. GJW lobbyist, interview, 9/5/1997. The Home Office Minister, Tim Renton, said 'we have no intention of riding into the valley of Parliamentary death again' although he regarded Sunday trading as 'important unfinished business'. 'As you are on Sundays', *East Grinstead Courier*, 24 November 1988.
74. Helco and Wildavsky (1974), p. xv.
75. R. Rhodes and D. Marsh (1992b).
76. HC Debates, Prime Minister's Questions, 7/5/1991, col. 621.
77. 'Sunday trade law reform planned', *Daily Telegraph*, 12 September 1991.
78. Lloyd's official statement read: 'we have been given a mandate for reform by the country and we are keen to get that reform right and in place as speedily as we can'. 'Minister pledges to update Shops Act', *Sunday Express*, 19 April 1992.

79. The formula of mutually exclusive options had been used before on the Second Reading of the Human Fertilisation and Embryology Bill (HC Debates 2 April 1990, cols. 914–1005) offering a choice between 36, 38 or 40 weeks. The Sunday Trading Bill offered totally different regimes.
80. The Shops (Amendment) Bill (Bill 14) presented by Ray Powell was based on KSSC's proposals. A second, the Shops Bill (Bill 25), presented by James Couchman, followed the policy of the SHRC.
81. SHRC retained the bulk of amendments for the Third Reading because amendments introduced at Committee stage cannot be tabled during the Third Reading.
82. OPEN Chairman, interview, 24/3/1997.
83. Senior retailer, interview, 4/6/1997.
84. He likened it to 'pushing water uphill'. OPEN Chairman, interview, 24/3/1997.
85. GJW lobbyist, interview, 9/5/1997.
86. DIY and electrical and food retailers advertised heavily in the tabloid press. B&Q spent £16 million on advertising in the press; other DIY chains (such as Do It All spent £3.2 million during the campaign.
87. 'Ring the Bells', *Sun*, 15 December 1990. The *Sun* established a Sunday Opening database and provided its readers with a telephone number to call for them to find out if stores in their area opened on Sundays.
88. John Lewis Partnership representative, interview, 4/3/1997.
89. A letter to branch managers from Boots HQ recommended giving staff 'pens of assorted colours, a range of notepaper but not company headed notepaper and guidelines on writing letters'. 'Boots tells staff how to lobby for Sunday trading', *The Independent*, 6 November 1993.
90. 'Sunday lobbyists put pressure on', *Super-Marketing*, 3 September 1993.
91. Former Home Office Minister 1, interview, 26/6/1997.
92. Senior retailer, interview, 4/6/1997.
93. Miller (1991).
94. Deputy General Secretary of USDAW, interview, 9/6/1997.
95. GJW lobbyist, interview, 9/5/1997.
96. GJW Labour lobbyist, interview, 9/7/1997.
97. Former Home Office Minister 1, interview, 26/6/1997.
98. Former senior civil servant 8, interview, 22/4/1998.
99. PPU lobbyist, interview, 7/3/1997.
100. KSSC Barrister, interview, 23/5/1997.
101. *Ibid.*
102. KSSC Barrister, interview, 23/5/1997.
103. OPEN Chairman, interview, 24/3/1997.
104. Austen-Smith and Wright (1994; 1996).
105. GJW Labour lobbyist, interview, 9/7/1997.
106. Deputy General Secretary of USDAW, interview, 9/6/1997.
107. OPEN Chairman, interview, 24/3/1997.
108. 'Sunday shopping – Day of unrest', *The Economist*, 27 December 1993–3 January 1994.
109. *Ibid.*
110. KSSC director, interview, 17/3/1997.
111. Deputy General Secretary of USDAW, interview, 9/6/1997; Principal of KSSC, interview, 4/2/1997.

112. GJW lobbyist, interview, 9/5/1997.
113. Principal of SHRC, interview, 5/5/1997.
114. Principal of KSSC, interview, 4/2/1997.
115. Principal of SHRC, interview, 5/5/1997.
116. OPEN Chairman, interview, 24/3/1997.
117. OPEN lobbyist, interview, 17/3/1997.
118. RSAR Coordinator, interview, 3/6/1997.
119. *Ibid.*
120. Sir Richard Greenbury was the Chairman of Marks & Spencer. Former Home Office Minister 2, interview, 10/6/1997.
121. Iain McLaurin is the former CEO of Tesco. Former Home Office Minister 2, interview, 10/6/1997.
122. Former Home Office Minister 2, interview, 10/6/1997.
123. The motor accessory defence, used in 1987, was premised on the fact that most DIY items (such as paint, tools, tiles, carpets, etc.) could be used in caravans. Motor accessories were exempt under Section 47 of the Shops Act.
124. Article 30 provides 'quantitative restrictions on imports and all measures having equivalent effect shall be prohibited between member states'. The Article has direct effect and gives rights for individuals which national courts must protect and enforce.
125. The Shops Act was within 'the rule of reason', but the question of proportionality was a problem. UK Sunday trading law was potentially a breach of Article 30, although technically the Shops Act 1950 did not breach the Treaty of Rome. *Torfaen BC* v. *B&Q Plc* 145/88 [1990] 1 All E.R 129, 158, para. 17.
126. The eleven other references to the ECJ cases were then withdrawn from the court. SHRC Memorandum on the ECJ ruling on 2 June 1992.
127. *Peterborough City Council* v. *Do It All and Payless DIY* [1990] 2 CMLR 577 QBD. The High Court concluded the Shops Act 1950 did conflict with Article 30 and was a trade rule capable of hindering trade and having the potential to act as a quantitative restriction: 'Sunday trading and Europe', *New Law Journal*, 22 November 1991.
128. The ECJ ruled that while Sunday trading rules were 'measures of equivalent effect to quantitative restrictions' that were relevant to Article 30, they did not make the sale of imported goods more difficult than the sale of domestic goods. The judgment was unexpectedly clear. Cases C-306/88 *Rochdale Borough Council* v. *Anders*, C-304/90; *Reading Borough Council* v. *Payless DIY and others*. 'Sunday trade ruling fails to end open-and-shut case', *Financial Times*, 17 December 1992.
129. 'Sunday trading law decision goes to the High Court', *Financial Times*, 10 July 1990.
130. Under the Shops Act, Section 71 and subsequent edicts: House of Commons Library (1993).
131. Report of the Committee of Inquiry into proposals to amend the Shops Acts (The Auld Committee), Cmd 9376, November 1984, para. 52.
132. Institute of Public Finance report October 1993. 'Councils support Sunday shopping', *Financial Times*, 15 October 1993.
133. PPU lobbyist, interview, 7/3/1997; Sort Out Sunday Coordinator, interview, 1/7/1997.
134. KSSC director, interview, 17/3/1997.
135. 'Battlelines drawn on Sunday Shopping', *The European*, 21 December 1990.

136. KSSC director, interview, 17/3/1997.
137. 'Shepard returns with EC delay on work hours ruling', *Financial Times*, 6 May 1992.
138. 'The Sunday trading trap that means shop till you drop', *The Guardian*, 7 December 1993.
139. GJW lobbyist, interview, 9/5/1997.
140. 'Democratic ideal crashed headlong into old buffer', *The Times*, 9 December 1993.
141. Former senior civil servant 8, interview, 22/4/1998.

5 The Failure of CrossRail

1. House of Commons (1986–87a); and House of Commons (1986–87b), p. 259.
2. Parkinson (1992), p. 283.
3. Dr Tony Ridley, Chairman of LUL, in 'Ticket to a 21st Century Tube', *Daily Telegraph*, 15 August 1988.
4. LT (1993).
5. Senior Treasury civil servant, interview, 23/1/1998.
6. *Ibid*.
7. CLRS proposed six single line schemes in total: two tubes, upgrading of an existing BR line and the CrossRail options. The most promising new lines with the highest benefit/cost ratios were: East–West CrossRail (EWC) and Chelsea–Hackney Line (CHL). 'The Central London Rail Study: Transport Options Ruled Out by Cost', *Financial Times*, 27 January 1989.
8. CrossRail lobbyist 1, interview, 15/1/1998.
9. IGA lobbyist 3, interview, 27/5/1998.
10. Former Minister of State for Transport 1, interview, 5/1/1998.
11. *Ibid*.
12. *Ibid*.
13. The designation of the project as one of national significance is relevant to the Transport and Works Act process. Were the Secretary of State to designate the project one of national significance, legislation would have related to the detail, not the principle, of the Bill.
14. IGA Proposal (nd).
15. Former BR director 2, interview, 1/12/1997.
16. Former Minister of State for Transport 1, interview, 5/1/1998.
17. *Ibid*.
18. *Ibid*.
19. Senior Treasury civil servant, interview, 23/1/1998.
20. Senior civil servant 2, interview, 28/1/1998.
21. Former senior civil servant 4, interview, 25/3/1998.
22. Former senior civil servant 3, interview, 19/2/1998.
23. Corporation of the City of London representative 2, interview, 9/3/1998.
24. CrossRail manager 1, interview, 30/3/1998.
25. CrossRail lobbyist 1, interview, 15/1/1998.
26. *Ibid*.
27. Former BR director 1, interview, 31/3/1998.
28. *Ibid*.
29. IGA lobbyist 3, interview, 27/5/1998.
30. *Ibid*.

31. *Ibid.*
32. Employment figures are from 1988 to 1992: O&Y briefing note to Westminster Council (1992).
33. 'The settlement also provides for the cost of the proposed east–west CrossRail as announced by the Secretary of State for Transport on 5 October. This will connect Paddington and Liverpool Street with stations in between at a cost (in March 1990 prices) of £1.4bn over a number of years': Autumn Statement (1990), pp. 16–17.
34. '"Back to work" plan by Lamont: Squeeze on public sector pay, interest cut and aid for industry cheer Tories', *Daily Telegraph*, 13 November 1992. In the 1992 Autumn Statement the Chancellor of the Exchequer authorised the JLE.
35. 'Autumn Statement: Road plans accelerate but BR feels the pinch', *Daily Telegraph*, 13 November 1992; 'Clarke cuts "will cause rage"', *Daily Telegraph*, 4 October 1993.
36. Senior Treasury civil servant, interview, 23/1/1998.
37. 'Budget '93: Tighter rein to be put on public spending – Red Book details', *Financial Times*, 1 December 1993.
38. Scott Wilson Kirkpatrick (1992). The Bechtel report was undertaken in 1993 (May 1993), p. 1.
39. SG Warburg (May 1993), Part 2, p. 3 and pp. 51–3.
40. LT (1993).
41. Railway Operators (1993), p. 53.
42. Bovis *et al.* (1993).
43. Bovis *et al.* (1993), p. 4.
44. Senior civil servant 1, interview, 4/2/1998.
45. *Ibid.*
46. Senior Treasury civil servant, interview, 23/1/1998.
47. Minors and Grenham (1990); Travers (1994).
48. CrossRail lobbyist 2, interview, 6/4/1998.
49. Former senior civil servant 4, interview, 25/3/1998.
50. Senior Treasury civil servant, interview, 23/1/1998. Confirmed by two subsequent interviews: former Minister of State for Transport 2, interview, 5/2/1998; former senior civil servant 4, interview, 25/3/1998.
51. London Transport executive 3, interview, 25/3/1998.
52. Former senior civil servant 4, interview, 25/3/1998.
53. Former Cabinet Minister 1, interview, 29/1/1998.
54. Senior Treasury civil servant, interview, 23/1/1998.
55. Senior civil servant 6, interview, 15/4/1998.
56. Former Cabinet Minister 1, interview, 29/1/1998.
57. Senior Treasury civil servant, interview, 23/1/1998.
58. Senior Treasury civil servant, interview, 23/1/1998.
59. Senior civil servant 2, interview, 28/1/1998.
60. Senior Treasury civil servant, interview, 23/1/1998.
61. Former Minister of State for Transport 1, interview, 05/1/1998.
62. HC Debs, vol. 213, 12/11/1992, col. 993.
63. Treasury (1992).
64. The Ryrie rules required projects to be evaluated against a theoretical public-sector alternative; joint ventures led by the private sector were encouraged

subject to competition by private-sector bodies; and public bodies were encouraged to enter into operating leases. The Treasury insisted that commercial sponsors should not be allowed to make a return without risk. It was believed that government's 'commercially-unpalatable rules and labyrinthine approvals procedures' had hamstrung private-sector participation: Heald and Geaughan (1997); Newchurch & Co. (1994).

65. IGA lobbyist 3, interview, 27/5/1998.
66. Former senior civil servant 3, interview, 19/2/1998.
67. Former Cabinet Minister 1, interview, 29/1/1998.
68. Former senior civil servant 3, interview, 19/2/1998.
69. Senior Treasury civil servant, interview, 23/1/1998.
70. Parkinson (1992), p. 283.
71. Former senior civil servant 3, interview, 19/2/1998.
72. Former senior civil servant 5, interview, 21/1/1998.
73. The year 1992 was spent carrying out design work and detailed planning: 'Ministers delay London rail plan', *Financial Times*, 5 March 1993.
74. Cabinet approved the decision in May 1993. HC Debates, WA, vol. 225, 24/5/1993, col. 405. The Bill proceeded to a Second Reading, which it obtained with no division in June 1993.
75. *Ibid.*
76. Former Cabinet Minister 2, interview, 24/2/1998.
77. Former Minister of State for Transport 1, interview, 5/1/1998.
78. Senior Treasury civil servant, interview, 23/1/1998.
79. Former Cabinet Minister 2, interview, 24/2/1998.
80. Former Minister of State for Transport 1, interview, 5/1/1998; confirmed by former Cabinet Minister 2, interview, 24/2/1998.
81. Former managing director of London Underground, interview, 9/2/1998.
82. London Transport executive 3, interview, 25/3/1998.
83. HC Debates, vol. 226, 8/6/1993, col. 201.
84. IGA proposal (nd).
85. HC Debates, vol. 224, 6/5/1993, col. 296; Debates, vol. 224, 13/5/1993, col. 955; Debates, vol. 224, 13/5/1993, col. 957; Debates, vol. 224, 13/5/1993, col. 960. There was a coordinated series of questions in May 1993.
86. London Transport executive 2, interview, 14/1/1998.
87. CrossRail lobbyist 2, interview, 6/4/1998.
88. IGA proposal (nd).
89. IGA proposal (nd).
90. IGA proposal (nd).
91. IGA proposal (nd).
92. On 10 May 1994 the Committee decided by three votes to one that CrossRail should not proceed to full parliamentary scrutiny.
93. The Montagu Report raised the thorny issue of 'affordability': DTp (1996). Sir George Young, Transport Secretary, ordered the promoters not to go ahead with plans 'for the time being': 'CrossRail project to be shelved', *Financial Times*, 30 March 1996.
94. IGA lobbyist 3, interview, 27/5/1998.
95. IGA proposal (nd).
96. Internal CrossRail Guidance notes, *Party Conferences*, (nd).

97. IGA proposal (nd).
98. D. Wilson and Andrews (1993).
99. 'CBI chief attacks London strategy', *Financial Times*, 19 June 1993.
100. Senior Treasury civil servant, interview, 23/1/1998.
101. Former political adviser 2, interview, 11/2/1998.
102. Former managing director of London Underground, interview, 9/2/1998.
103. Senior LT manager, interview, 13/5/1998.
104. Former Minister of State for Transport 1, interview, 5/1/1998.
105. Senior Treasury civil servant, interview, 23/1/1998 (Grade E is formerly a Principal or Grade 7).
106. Confidence in the Prime Minister amongst some Conservative backbenchers was undermined by a compromise over EU voting arrangements: HC Debates, vol. 240, 29/3/1994, col. 802. Mr Marlow said: 'my Right Hon. friend has no authority, credibility or identifiable policy in this vital area of policy, why does he not stand aside and make way for somebody else who can provide the party and the country with direction and leadership?'.
107. Former Minister of State for Transport 1, interview, 5/1/1998.
108. Tower Hamlets adviser, interview, 25/3/1998.
109. Former senior civil servant 4, interview, 25/3/1998.
110. *Ibid.*
111. IGA proposal (nd).
112. *Ibid.*
113. Internal CrossRail Guidance notes, *Briefings*, (nd).
114. Former senior civil servant 4, interview, 25/3/1998.
115. IGA proposal (nd).
116. CrossRail lobbyist 2, interview, 6/4/1998.
117. CrossRail manager 1, interview, 30/3/1998.
118. *Ibid.*
119. Former senior civil servant 4, interview, 25/3/1998.
120. CrossRail lobbyist 2, interview, 6/4/1998.
121. *Ibid.*
122. CrossRail manager 1, interview, 30/3/1998.
123. *Ibid.*
124. Former managing director of London Underground, interview, 9/2/1998.
125. Corporation of the City of London representative 4, interview, 19/2/1998.
126. IGA lobbyist 3, interview, 27/5/1998.
127. Bond Street, Tottenham Court Road, Farringdon and Liverpool Street/ Moorgate. Confirmed in a telephone conversation with the Surveyors' Office, Corporation of the City of London.
128. Former Cabinet Minister 1, interview, 29/1/1998.
129. Former senior civil servant 7, interview, 29/4/1998.
130. D. Wilson and Andrews (1993).
131. Former BR director 2, interview, 1/12/1997.
132. Senior civil servant 6, interview, 15/4/1998.
133. Senior Treasury civil servant, interview, 23/1/1998.
134. 'They would say that, wouldn't they?' Mandy Rice Davies was an acquaintance of Christine Keeler and, through the osteopath Stephen Ward, was introduced to influential London society. She was a witness at Ward's trial for living off the immoral earnings of Keeler and Rice-Davies. In reply to a

suggestion that Lord Astor denied knowing her, she gave the celebrated retort: 'He would, wouldn't he?'.

135. O&Y adviser, interview, 13/2/1998.
136. Steinbruner (1974).
137. Former Cabinet Minister 1, interview, 29/1/1998.
138. *Ibid.*
139. Former political adviser 2, interview, 11/2/1998.
140. HC Debates, vol. 226, 8/6/1993, col. 208.
141. Former Cabinet Minister 2, interview, 24/2/1998. Shenfield was where CrossRail terminated in the east.
142. Transport consultant 2, interview, 2/4/1998.
143. Former Cabinet Minister 2, interview, 24/2/1998.
144. Tower Hamlets adviser, interview, 25/3/1998.
145. *Ibid.*
146. Senior Treasury civil servant, interview, 23/1/1998.
147. Former Minister of State for Transport 1, interview, 5/1/1998.
148. Former Minister of State for Transport 1, interview, 5/1/1998.
149. 'The Chairman now arriving ... Peter Oborne on the intrigue and in-fighting in the hunt for a new head of London Transport', *London Evening Standard*, 8 February 1994.
150. For LT, CrossRail ranked below JLE, preservation of LT as the regulator of London's buses and the provision of resources for the existing network. For BR, CrossRail scarcely registered as a priority; in the London region a higher priority was the replacement of the old slam-door rolling stock.
151. CrossRail manager 1, interview, 30/3/1998.
152. IGA lobbyist 3, interview, 27/5/1998.
153. CrossRail briefing paper, *Hurdles* (nd).
154. Former senior civil servant 7, interview, 29/4/1998.
155. IGA lobbyist 3, interview, 27/5/1998.
156. CrossRail manager 1, interview, 30/3/1998.
157. Former senior civil servant 3, interview, 19/2/1998.
158. IGA proposal (nd). The consultancy also offered 'a monthly review with each client at which the progress of any public affairs activity is measured against the objectives set at the previous month's meeting'.
159. CrossRail lobbyist 2, interview, 6/4/1998.

6 The Success of the Jubilee Line Extension

1. Fanstein (1994), pp. 209–10.
2. Public investment in Docklands transport was massive. Around £4.615bn of public money was used to improve transport links to Docklands (compared with £780m private sector). Investment Programme (in millions): Total Road Schemes – £1411; Total Rail Schemes – £3939. Other schemes, £45. Total of Docklands-related transport spending, £5395m. See LDDC (1997).
3. The Enterprise Zone, created on 26 April 1986 with a 10-year life, allowed looser planning regulations, no business rates and 100 per cent deduction of capital expenditure on industrial and commercial construction from income tax and freedom from rates and a simplified planning process.
4. Former Cabinet Minister 2, interview, 24/2/1998.

5. O&Y executive, interview, 7/3/1997.
6. *Ibid.*
7. Senior London Transport Manager, interview, 13/5/1998. The stated objective of the study was to identify 'the best options for further improving rail access from central London to Docklands and east Thameside in order to accommodate the rapid pace of development in Docklands'. DTp (1989b).
8. O&Y executive, interview, 7/3/1997.
9. O&Y adviser, interview, 13/2/1998.
10. Former political adviser 2, interview, 11/2/1998.
11. *Ibid.*
12. Senior businessman, interview, 30/1/1998.
13. Former political adviser 2, interview, 11/2/1998.
14. HC Debates, vol. 155, 19/6/1989, col. 46.
15. 'East London rail link unveiled', *The Times*, 27 July 1989.
16. Former Cabinet Minister 3, interview, 19/5/1998.
17. Parkinson (1992), p. 290.
18. Sir Keith Joseph was a non-executive director of Bovis, which was working with O&Y: former Cabinet Minister 3, interview, 19/5/1998.
19. Former Cabinet Minister 3, interview, 19/5/1998.
20. Former Cabinet Minister 3, interview, 19/5/1998.
21. Senior civil servant 1, interview, 4/2/1998.
22. HC Debates, vol. 160, 16/11/1989, col. 398.
23. 'Gone to the dogs', *The Times*, 12 May 1992.
24. LDDC (1997).
25. Corporation of the City of London representative 4, interview, 19/2/1998.
26. Former senior civil servant 1, interview, 13/3/1998.
27. Former senior civil servant 4, interview, 25/3/1998.
28. Former Minister of State for Transport 1, interview, 5/1/1998.
29. Former adviser to the Prime Minister 1, interview, 30/4/1998.
30. Former senior civil servant 5, interview, 21/1/1998.
31. Former Cabinet Minister 1, interview, 29/1/1998.
32. Former Cabinet Minister 3, interview, 19/5/1998.
33. O&Y adviser, interview, 13/2/1998.
34. O&Y executive, interview, 7/3/1997.
35. *Ibid.*
36. Senior businessman, interview, 30/1/1998.
37. *Ibid.*
38. Senior civil servant 2, interview, 28/1/1998. The JLE was one of the biggest spending items in 1993–94.
39. 'O&Y warned on Jubilee line cash', *The Independent*, 19 May 1992.
40. HC Debates, vol. 208, 2/6/1992, col. 707.
41. Senior Treasury civil servant, interview, 23/1/1998.
42. Senior civil servant 2, interview, 28/1/1998.
43. Former Minister of State for Transport 1, interview, 5/1/1998.
44. Former Cabinet Minister 1, interview, 29/1/1998.
45. HC Debates, WA, vol. 230, 20/10/1993, col. 810.
46. Letter from Roger Freeman, Minister of State, to Norman Lamont, Chief Secretary to the Treasury, 27 September 1990, private archive.
47. Glaister and Travers (1993), p. 53; HC Debates, vol. 208, 18/5/1992, col. 126.
48. Former political adviser 2, interview, 11/2/1998.

49. Mrs Thatcher's speech in response to Paul Reichmann at the Banqueting House, 11 May 1988.
50. 'Docklands boost: City Viewpoint', *The Sunday Times*, 11 June 1989.
51. *Ibid.*
52. Former Cabinet Minister 1, interview, 29/1/1998.
53. The London Weekend Television lecture, 'Heseltine sees Euro-boost to eastern city dream', *The Guardian*, 13 December 1991.
54. Former senior civil servant 5, interview, 21/1/1998.
55. Senior Treasury civil servant, interview, 23/1/1998.
56. It was anticipated O&Y would pay £40m in March 1992 followed by £60m in March 1993. The remaining £300m would be paid over 20 years after completion. The penalty charges included in the renegotiated private-sector contribution meant that the private sector would pay £2m less for each month the JLE opening was delayed: London Transport executive 4, interview, 11/3/1998.
57. Glaister and Travers (1993), p. 53.
58. Former senior civil servant 4, interview, 25/3/1998.
59. Senior civil servant 1, interview, 4/2/1998.
60. Harold Macmillan in Fairlie (1968).
61. Mrs Thatcher's speech in response to Paul Reichmann at the Banqueting House, 11 May 1988.
62. Former Cabinet Minister 1, interview, 29/1/1998.
63. Mrs Thatcher's speech in response to Paul Reichmann at the Banqueting House, 11 May 1988.
64. Former political adviser 1, interview, 14/11/1997.
65. Former No. 10 Policy Unit member, interview, 2/3/1998.
66. *Business Week*, 28 January 1990, p. 99.
67. Representatives from Transport, Environment, Home Office, DTI, Social Security, Health, Employment, National Heritage, Office of Public Service and Treasury attended a Cabinet sub-committee for London, chaired by the Secretary of State for the Environment.
68. The Minister for Transport in London established the Transport Working Group that brought together representatives from LUL, LDDC, London Buses, Network South East, the Traffic Commissioner, the Traffic Director, the London Regional Passenger Committee, London Chamber of Commerce and Industry, London Passengers' Advisory Committee, and the London Tourist Board.
69. Former Cabinet Minister 1, interview, 29/1/1998.
70. Former senior civil servant 4, interview, 25/3/1998.
71. Former adviser to the Prime Minister 1, interview, 30/4/1998.
72. Former senior civil servant 4, interview, 25/3/1998.
73. Former political adviser 1, interview, 14/11/1997.
74. Senior civil servant 2, interview, 28/1/1998.
75. Former adviser to the Prime Minister 1, interview, 30/4/1998.
76. Senior businessman, interview, 30/1/1998.
77. Senior Treasury civil servant, interview, 23/1/1998.
78. Former senior civil servant 1, interview, 13/3/1998. See O&Y internal memo, subject *Funding Agreement*, 31 January 1990, private archive.
79. Senior businessman, interview, 30/1/1998.
80. O&Y executive, interview, 7/3/1997.
81. Former senior civil servant 4, interview, 25/3/1998.

82. Former political adviser 2, interview, 11/2/1998.
83. Former Cabinet Minister 2, interview, 24/2/1998.
84. 'Funds for only one rail link', *The Times*, 6 October 1989.
85. 'No Canary rescue', *The Times*, 18 May 1992.
86. GJW memo to O&Y, 28 September 1988, private archive.
87. O&Y memo, *Consultation with Local Authorities*, 25 November 1988, private archive.
88. Former No. 10 Policy Unit member, interview, 2/3/1998.
89. Former senior civil servant 1, interview, 13/3/1998.
90. O&Y executive, interview, 7/3/1997.
91. *Ibid.*
92. *Ibid.*
93. *Ibid.*
94. Former senior civil servant 4, interview, 25/3/1998.
95. *Ibid.*
96. *Ibid.*
97. O&Y adviser, interview, 13/2/1998.
98. Former senior civil servant 4, interview, 25/3/1998.
99. Former senior civil servant 4, interview, 25/3/1998.
100. *Ibid.*
101. Former No. 10 Policy Unit member, interview, 2/3/1998.
102. Lobbyist 1, interview, 11/2/1998.
103. Former Cabinet Minister 1, interview, 29/1/1998.
104. *Ibid.*
105. Senior businessman, interview, 30/1/1998.
106. Former political adviser 2, interview, 11/2/1998.
107. Lobbyist 1, interview, 11/2/1998.
108. Former political adviser 2, interview, 11/2/1998.
109. Lobbyist 1, interview, 11/2/1998.
110. Former senior civil servant 4, interview, 25/3/1998.
111. London Transport executive 3, interview, 25/3/1998.
112. Transport consultant 2, interview, 2/4/1998.
113. Former senior civil servant 1, interview, 13/3/1998.
114. Former senior civil servant 1, interview, 13/3/1998.
115. Senior London Transport manager, interview, 13/5/1998.
116. Former Cabinet Minister 1, interview, 29/1/1998.
117. Senior businessman, interview, 30/1/1998.
118. 'Canary comes home to roost: Olympia & York's brave adventure developing Docklands has ended in tears', *Independent on Sunday*, 29 March 1992.
119. Senior businessman, interview, 30/1/1998.
120. *Ibid.*
121. O&Y adviser, interview, 13/2/1998.
122. Fanstein (1994).
123. 'Administrators move in at Canary Wharf', *The Times*, 29 May 1992.
124. Senior businessman, interview, 30/1/1998.
125. London Transport executive 1, interview, 11/12/1997.
126. *Ibid.*
127. Former Cabinet Minister 1, interview, 29/1/1998.
128. Former political adviser 2, interview, 11/2/1998.

129. Former Cabinet Minister 1, interview, 29/1/1998.
130. Tower Hamlets' adviser, interview, 25/3/1998.
131. Former senior civil servant 7, interview, 29/4/1998. The Overseas Development Administration concluded the Pergau hydroelectric dam project was a 'very bad buy'. A high-level understanding, amounting to an oral commitment from Margaret Thatcher to the Malaysian Prime Minister, led ministers to overrule the advice of their officials. The Accounting Officer advised the project should not proceed and required a direction from ministers to incur expenditure. The Foreign Secretary overruled the advice of the Accounting Officer, leading him to submit a 'note of dissent'. Foreign Affairs Select Committee (1993/94); National Audit Office, (1993/94); and Evidence of Sir Tim Lankester, Permanent Secretary, Overseas Development Administration, Public Accounts Select Committee (1993/94).
132. Former Minister for Transport 1, interview, 5/1/1998.

7   Limiting Professional Liability

1. DoE (1995).
2. DTI Consultation Paper (1996).
3. The essence of proportional liability is that defendants should not be forced to pay for harm they are able to prove has been caused by another party.
4. GJW briefing note, *Joint & Several Liability Defined* (nd).
5. ICAEW (1996).
6. The logic of this argument is that 'a potential exposure in millions of pounds up to the statutory cap is as good a deterrent as one of hundreds of millions of pounds which it is known cannot be met': DTI Consultation Paper (1996).
7. Section 310 makes void any arrangements by a company to exempt or indemnify its auditors from liability: ICAEW (1994).
8. UCTA prevents a contracting party from excluding or restricting its liability: DTI Consultation Paper (1996) p. 41; ACCA (1996). Lawyers can contract to limit their professional liability, provided the cap is not below the compulsory minimum level of professional indemnity insurance.
9. DTI Consultation Paper (1996).
10. Sikka (1998). See Law Commission (1993).
11. Freedman and Finch (1997).
12. Limited liability legislation exists but is framed only to protect the assets of sleeping partners.
13. House of Commons, Standards and Privileges Committee First Report. Appendix 114, statement by Andrew Smith to supplement statement dated 28 June 1995.
14. Leigh and Vulliamy (1997), p. 142.
15. IGA lobbyist 1, interview, 10/3/1998.
16. HC, Standards and Privileges Committee First Report. Appendix 114, statement by Andrew Smith to supplement statement dated 28 June 1995.
17. Former minister in correspondence with the author, 12/12/1997.
18. Senior partner 1, Big Five Firm B, interview, 5/8/1998.
19. Senior civil servant 8, interview, 21/10/1998.
20. Senior partner 1, Big Five Firm B, interview, 5/8/1998.
21. Senior civil servant 10, interview, 18/9/1998.

22. City Law firm representative 3, interview, 16/9/1998.
23. 'Limited horizons: Accountants are disappointed by moves to reform the law on liability', *The Independent*, 13 November 1996.
24. Senior civil servant 8, interview, 21/10/1998.
25. Senior civil servant 8, interview, 21/10/1998; confirmed by senior civil servant 10, interview, 18/9/1998.
26. Senior partner 1, Big Five Firm B, interview, 5/8/1998.
27. David Hencke was the investigative journalist on *The Guardian* who broke the story about the linkages between the MP, Neil Hamilton, and the lobbyist, Ian Greer.
28. IGA lobbyist 1, interview, 10/3/1998.
29. Senior partner 1, Big Five Firm B, interview, 5/8/1998.
30. Senior partner 1, Big Five Firm D, interview, 17/8/1998.
31. ICAEW representative 1, interview, 13/8/1998.
32. *Ibid.*
33. Senior partner 1, Big Five Firm A, interview, 4/8/1998.
34. Senior civil servant 10, interview, 18/9/1998.
35. Senior civil servant 9, interview, 19/10/1998.
36. Senior civil servant 7, interview, 1/10/1998.
37. Senior partner 2, Big Five Firm A, interview, 15/9/1998.
38. Senior partner 2, Big Five Firm D, interview, 26/8/1998.
39. Soden (1994), p. 79. Also see Pressler and Schieffer (1988) for 'deep-pocket' issues.
40. Morris and Stevenson (1997).
41. Coopers & Lybrand dropped the computer games software company Eidos in 1997 because it failed to improve its corporate governance arrangements. Arthur Andersen no longer audits companies on the Alternative Investment Market. London Economics (1998).
42. ICAEW (1996).
43. 'The Doomsday Risk', *Financial Times*, 4 February 1997.
44. Freedman and Finch (1997).
45. Senior civil servant 10, interview, 18/9/1998.
46. Senior partner 1, Big Five Firm D, interview, 17/8/1998.
47. Senior partner 2, Big Five Firm D, interview, 26/8/1998.
48. Professor Likierman was Head of Audit and Director of Financial Management Reporting and Audit at the Treasury: DTI (1989).
49. ICAEW representative 1, interview, 13/8/1998.
50. DTI Consultation Paper (1996). First, under proportionate liability the risk of a defendant being insolvent would shift from fellow defendants to the plaintiff. Second, J&S liability already sets formidable hurdles for plaintiffs to prove causation: each defendant must be causally responsible for the whole of that loss (the damage caused is indivisible). Third, proportionate liability would mean a plaintiff would be less likely to recover full damages by being the victim of two wrongs than if he had been the victim of a single wrong. Finally, under proportionate liability, if another wrongdoer becomes insolvent a blameless plaintiff would bear the risk rather than the principal wrongdoer.
51. The form excludes consumers and reallocates some of the uncollected share (up to 50 per cent) of each defendant's proportionate share. But at the time the Law Commission believed 'the policy objections to joint and several liability

to be, at best, insufficiently convincing to merit a departure from principle'. In DTI Consultation Paper (1996), part VII, summary of conclusions.
52. Senior civil servant 8, interview, 21/10/1998.
53. Senior civil servant 9, interview, 19/10/1998.
54. Senior civil servant 8, interview, 21/10/1998.
55. Lobbyist, interview, 30/4/1998.
56. The report concluded that although incentives would be weakened by a softer liability regime, the large firms' reputations would act as a substitute. It found Institutional shareholders had little incentive to get involved in the company's corporate governance because they were implicitly 'insured' by the auditors' deep pockets. High-risk sectors were being screened and were finding it difficult to get access to the capital market. Unlimited liability is a blunt instrument and does not act as an incentive to act well. Unlimited liability encourages defensive auditing. The report concluded J&S liability should be replaced with proportionate liability and a statutory cap. 'Cap will bring benefits', *Accounting*, May 1998, p. 13.
57. Senior civil servant 9, interview, 19/10/1998.
58. Senior civil servant 7, interview, 1/10/1998.
59. Senior civil servant 9, interview, 19/10/1998.
60. The Cadbury Report on Corporate Governance, established in response to companies with clean audit reports failing, suggested corporate governance reforms to allow auditors to comment on internal processes and suspicion of fraud: *Committee on the Financial Aspects of Corporate Governance*, 1992. It wanted auditors to report on the effectiveness of internal controls and explain their responsibilities for preparing accounts and recommended, but not in the code, that accountants draw up guidelines to rotate partners responsible for a particular company.
61. Institute of Chartered Accountants Scotland (1996).
62. Senior partner 1, Big Five Firm B, interview, 5/8/1998.
63. Senior civil servant 9, interview, 19/10/1998.
64. Senior civil servant 7, interview, 1/10/1998.
65. 'Self-Regulation's Defeat and Legislation's Victory', *Accountancy Age*, 18 March 1993, p. 31; and 'Labour Goes for Regulation – Audit Profession', *Accountancy Age*, 19 March 1993, p. 27; 'Morrison Hits Back at Independence Taunts', *Accountancy Age*, 22 April 1993, p. 21; 'Labour in Plan for Institutes' Regulation', *Accountancy Age*, 26 May 1994, p. 23.
66. S. Bell 'View from the House – Government Paralysed by Threat of Jersey Move', *Accountancy Age*, 8 August 1996, p. 52.
67. Lobbyist, interview 14/5/1997; 'Labour backs liability reform', *Accountancy*, April 1997, p. 11.
68. S. Bell 'The Zeal of Born-Again New Labour', *Accountancy*, April 1997, p. 75; S. Bell 'Letters – Profession Backs Labour on LLP Review', *Accountancy Age*, 24 April 1997, p. 31. In the former article, Bell wrote:

New Labour has consistently advocated reform of joint and several liability law and has even offered to assist the passage of this non-political legislation onto the statute book. The legislation would mean that accountants and other professionals could go about their business in a way that enables them to give the best advice to their clients.

69. Lobbyist, interview, 26/11/1997.
70. Labour Party, *Manifesto for Business*, April 1997.
71. Labour backbench MP, interview, 29/7/1998.
72. 'Letter to the Editor: *Labour line on accountancy prudence* from Stuart Bell MP, Shadow Minister for Trade and Corporate Affairs', *Financial Times*, 18 April 1997.
73. Former minister in correspondence with the author, 9/1/1998.
74. Senior civil servant 7, interview, 1/10/1998.
75. *Ibid.*
76. *Ibid.*
77. Senior civil servant 10, interview, 18/9/1998.
78. Lobbyist, interview, 26/11/1997.
79. 'Bell Denied Place in Blair Government', *Accountancy Age*, 8 May 1997, p. 23; 'Labour Promises Liability Review', *Accountancy*, 13 May 1997, p. 33.
80. Lobbyist, interview, 14/5/1997.
81. DTI Press Release (1998).
82. *Ibid.*
83. HC Debates, Adjournment, 17/6/1997, col. 221, Minister of State DTI.
84. GJW, *Professionals in the World of Lobbying*, company brochure (nd).
85. Senior partner 2, Big Five Firm D, interview, 26/8/1998.
86. Whilst audit standards are controlled by the audit industry, licensing, monitoring, complaints, investigations and appeals are controlled by accountancy bodies which are dominated by the big firms. HC Debates, Adjournment, 17/6/1997, col. 218.
87. Senior partner 1, Big Five Firm D, interview, 17/8/1998.
88. House of Commons Select Committee on the Modernisation of the House of Commons, *Appendix 1, Memorandum submitted by Rt Hon. Ann Taylor MP President of the Council and Leader of the House*, HC 190, 1997–98.
89. Lobbyist, interview 26/11/1997.
90. Senior civil servant 7, interview, 1/10/1998.
91. Senior partner 1, Big Five Firm B, interview, 5/8/1998.
92. GJW, *Professionals in the World of Lobbying*, company brochure (nd).
93. *Ibid.*
94. Lobbyist, interview 11/2/1997.
95. Senior civil servant 7, interview, 1/10/1998.
96. Senior civil servant 7, interview, 1/10/1998.
97. Senior partner 1, Big Five Firm B, interview, 5/8/1998.
98. *Ibid.*
99. Senior civil servant 7, interview, 1/10/1998.
100. Senior partner 1, Big Five Firm B, interview, 5/8/1998.
101. Former minister in correspondence with the author, 9/1/1998.
102. *Ibid.*
103. Senior partner 1, Big Five Firm D, interview, 17/8/1998.
104. Senior civil servant 7, interview, 1/10/1998.
105. Senior civil servant 8, interview, 21/10/1998.
106. Lobbyist, interview 26/11/1997. One senior partner admitted GJW 'have made contact on our behalf with special advisers in the No. 10 Policy Unit and the Treasury': senior partner 2, Big Five Firm D, interview, 26/8/1998.
107. Lobbyist, interview, 30/4/1998.

108. Lobbyist, interview 14/5/1997.
109. Senior partner 1, Big Five Firm D, interview, 17/8/1998.
110. Senior partner 2, Big Five Firm D, interview, 26/8/1998.
111. GJW, *Professionals in the World of Lobbying*, company brochure (nd).
112. Lobbyist, interview, 30/4/1998.
113. *Ibid.*
114. Lobbyist, interview, 11/2/1997.
115. IGA lobbyist 1, interview, 10/3/1998.
116. Senior partner 1, Big Five Firm B, interview, 5/8/1998.
117. Senior partner 1, Big Five Firm D, interview, 17/8/1998.
118. Lobbyist, interview, 30/4/1998.
119. Senior partner 1, Big Five Firm B, interview, 5/8/1998.
120. ICAEW representative 1, interview, 13/8/1998.
121. Senior partner 1, Big Five Firm B, interview, 5/8/1998.
122. Lobbyist, interview, 30/4/1998.
123. Senior civil servant 9, interview, 19/10/1998.
124. Senior civil servant 8, interview, 21/10/1998.
125. Senior civil servant 9, interview, 19/10/1998.
126. Senior civil servant 7, interview, 1/10/1998.
127. Lickiss, M., (1990) 'Auditing Critics short on fact, long on rhetoric', *The Guardian*, 19 December 1990. Under the Companies Act 1989 accountancy bodies act to regulate the industry and defend and advance the public interest.
128. Mitchell and Sikka (1999), p. 7.
129. Senior civil servant 9, interview, 19/10/1998.
130. Senior civil servant 10, interview, 18/9/1998.
131. Including the Institute and Faculty of Actuaries, National Association of Pension Funds, London Investment Banking Association, Institute of Directors, Construction Industry Council and the Building Employers' Confederation.
132. Senior partner 1, Big Five Firm D, interview, 17/8/1998.
133. City law firm representative 2, interview, 28/8/1998.
134. Senior partner 2, Big Five Firm D, interview, 26/8/1998.
135. City law firm representative 2, interview, 28/8/1998.
136. Senior civil servant 9, interview, 19/10/1998.
137. Lobbyist, interview, 30/4/1998.
138. Senior civil servant 9, interview, 19/10/1998.
139. Lobbyist, interview, 11/2/1997.
140. Law Society (1997).
141. Senior partner 1, Big Five Firm A, interview, 4/8/1998.
142. Senior civil servant 10, interview, 18/9/1998.
143. Draft Limited Liability Partnership (Jersey) Law 1995.
144. Sikka (1998).
145. The American Institute of Certified Public Accountants gave US$3.3m between 1991 and 1995, in addition to US$350000 to members of the House Commerce Committee responsible for pushing the legislation through: 'Accountants' Liability Limited', *Accountant*, April 1995, p. 16.
146. 'Thinking the Unthinkable on Joint and Several', *Accountancy Age*, 30 May 1996, p. 56.

147. IGA lobbyist 1, interview, 10/3/1998.
148. *Accountancy*, September 1997, p. 26.
149. Senior partner 1, Big Five Firm B, interview, 5/8/1998.
150. Lobbyist, interview, 26/11/1997.
151. *Accountancy Age*, 4 September 1997.
152. *Financial Times*, 19 September 1997, see Cousins *et al.* (1998).
153. Cousins *et al.* (1998).
154. Senior civil servant 10, interview, 18/9/1998.
155. *Ibid.*
156. Senior partner 1, Big Five Firm D, interview, 17/8/1998.
157. City law firm representative 2, interview, 28/8/1998.
158. Senior partner 2, Big Five Firm D, interview, 26/8/1998.
159. 'More firms look to off-shore registration', *Accountancy Age*, 23 May 1996, p. 1; 'LLP registration tempts Guernsey firms', *Accountancy Age*, 31 October 1996, p. 2; 'Isle of Man to offer cut price LLPs', *Accountancy Age*, 29 August 1996, p. 9.
160. Morris and Stevenson (1997). 'Offshore Trusts – Jersey's Bold Move to LLPs: Limited Liability Partnerships are the latest Jersey initiative', *The Lawyer*, 26 March 1996, p. 26.
161. Jeune had a financial interest in Mourant de Feu & Jeune, the firms' lawyers. See 'Fresh blow to Jersey's Image', *Accountancy Age*, 29 August 1996, p. 1; 'Jersey financial scandal is poised to ensnare Coopers', *Accountancy Age*, 5 September 1996, p. 2.
162. 'Partnership law inquiry', *Financial Times*, 10 November 1996. The legislation's preface paid tribute to PriceWaterhouse, Ernst & Young for their contribution to the legislation.
163. 'Jersey enacts LLP law at last', *Accountancy*, June 1998, p. 20.
164. Senior partner 1, Big Five Firm D, interview, 17/8/1998.
165. *Ibid.*
166. Senior partner 1, Big Five Firm B, interview, 5/8/1998.
167. Mitchell, A., (1996) 'Limited Liability Through the Looking Glass', *Accountancy*, August 1996, p. 62.
168. Senior civil servant 8, interview, 21/10/1998.
169. Senior civil servant 9, interview, 19/10/1998.
170. Senior civil servant 8, interview, 21/10/1998.
171. Sikka (1998). See *Financial Times*, 28 June 1996, p. 22; 24 July 1996, p. 9; HC Debates, WA, 7/11/1996, col. 700.
172. Bell argued 'there must be reform of joint and several liability law to stop professions seeking out off-shore havens': 'View from the House – Government Paralysed by Threat of Jersey Move', *Accountancy Age*, 8 August 1996, p. 52.
173. 'Jersey law's reception makes Brindle bridle', *Accountancy*, September 1996, p. 29.
174. Senior civil servant 9, interview, 19/10/1998.
175. At the time Heseltine was Cabinet Office Minister. The Cabinet Office housed the Competitiveness Division. The Labour government returned the Competitiveness Division to the DTI. The plan was dropped because it would come too late to stop the rush offshore. 'Tories plan Jersey quick-fix', *Accountancy Age*, 18 July 1996, p. 1; 'Isle of Man to offer cut price LLPs', *Accountancy Age*, 29 August 1996, p. 9.

176. Senior civil servant 9, interview, 19/10/1998.
177. 'Government pledges to resolve LLP problem', *Accountancy Age*, 26 September 1996, p. 2; 'Heseltine in bid to stop Big Six move to Jersey: Accountants threaten offshore registration', *Financial Times*, 15 June 1996.
178. 'Jersey stirs debate on professional liability – It seems that Jersey's proposed LLP law has spurred the government on the mainland into action', *The Lawyer*, 3 September 1996, p. 3.
179. Senior civil servant 8, interview, 21/10/1998.
180. As argued by Morris and Stevenson (1997).
181. Senior civil servant 7, interview, 1/10/1998.
182. Senior civil servant 10, interview, 18/9/1998.
183. The seventh largest USA firm, Laventhol and Horwath, collapsed in 1990 amid US$2bn in liabilities and growing fears about bankruptcy. The USA savings and loans crisis of the early 1990s saw state governments act to limit liability: Anderson *et al.* (1992). Arthur Andersen estimated USA firms faced claims of US$30bn: Fearnley (1993) 'Practical Answers Needed, Not Political Claptrap', *Accountancy*, December, p. 76.
184. 'Auditing firms – USA Big Six in move to limit liability', *Accountancy*, 15 July 1994, p. 11.
185. 'USA firms go for LLPs', *Accountancy*, September 1994, p. 11.
186. 'USA firms protect partners', *Financial Times*, 4 August 1994. Under the USA law partners' assets are protected if a lawsuit is brought against one of the partners. The assets of the firm and negligent partners are at risk.
187. McLean (1995) 'Auditors' Liability: all they want is a level playing field', *Accountancy*, May p. 83.
188. Pressler and Schieffer (1988).
189. The President opposed aspects of the law reform but he did not attack joint and several reform. The vote to override the President's veto was 319–100 in the House of Representatives and 68–30 in the Senate.
190. The Act relates to lawsuits over the purchase and sale of securities. Joint and several applies if defendants engaged in actual fraud. Proportionate liability applies otherwise, decided by the judge. The Act distinguished between consumer actions and larger business claims. 'Accountancy: Congress comes to the aid of the Auditors. Richard Waters explains why USA firms feel a change in the law has given them some respite against liability injustices', *Financial Times*, 11 January 1996.
191. 'Senate passes limited liability legislation', *Accountancy*, August, p. 12.
192. Senior civil servant 9, interview, 19/10/1998.
193. *Ibid.*
194. Senior civil servant 8, interview, 21/10/1998.
195. Senior partner 1, Big Five Firm D, interview, 17/8/1998.
196. Senior civil servant 7, interview, 1/10/1998.
197. Senior civil servant 10, interview, 18/9/1998.
198. Senior partner 2, Big Five Firm A, interview, 15/9/1998.
199. Senior civil servant 8, interview, 21/10/1998.

Bibliography

ACCA (1996) *Joint and Several Liability: A Response from the Chartered Association of Certified Accountants, Appendix: Consideration of Contractual Limitation of Liability*, London, ACCA.

Access Opinions (1991) *Survey for SHRC through the Political Opinion Panel*, London, Market Access.

Acemoglu, D. and Gietzmann, M. (1997) 'Auditor Independence, Incomplete Contracts and the Role of Legal Liability', *European Accounting Review*, vol. 6, no. 3, pp. 355–75.

Adams, A. (1981) *The Iron Triangle*, New York, Council on Economic Priorities.

Adonis, A. (1993) *Parliament Today*, 2nd edn, Manchester, Manchester University Press.

Aidt, T. (1997) 'Cooperative lobbying and endogenous trade policy', *Public Choice*, vol. 93, nos. 3–4, pp. 455–76.

Ainsworth, S. (1993) 'Regulating lobbyists and interest group influence', *Journal of Politics*, vol. 55, no. 1, pp. 41–56.

Ainsworth, S. (1997a) 'Representation and institutional stability', *Journal of Theoretical Politics*, vol. 9, no. 2, pp. 147–65.

Ainsworth, S. (1997b) 'The role of legislators in the determination of interest group influence', *Legislative Studies Quarterly*, vol. XXII, no. 4, pp. 517–33.

ALA, Docklands Consultative Committee (1990) *10 Years of Docklands: How the Cake was Cut*, London, Association of London Authorities.

Alderman, G. (1984) *Pressure Groups and Government in Great Britain*, Harlow, Longman.

Alderman, G. (1988) 'Pressure groups: a mixed blessing', *Contemporary Record*, vol. 2, no. 1, pp. 2–4.

Allison, G. (1969) 'Conceptual models and the Cuban Missile Crisis', *American Political Science Review*, vol. 63, no. 3, pp. 689–718.

Allison, G. (1971) *Essence of Decision: Explaining the Cuban Missile Crisis*, Boston, MA, Little, Brown.

Allison, G. and Halperin, M. (1972) 'Bureaucratic Politics: A Paradigm and some Implications', in Tanter, R. and Ullman, R. (eds), *Theory and Policy in International Relations*, Princeton, NJ, Princeton University Press.

Allison, G. and Szanton, P. (1976) *Remaking Foreign Policy*, New York, Basic Books.

Almond, G. (1988) 'The Return to the State', *American Political Science Review*, vol. 82, no. 3, pp. 853–74.

Almond, G. and Powell, B. (1966) *Comparative Politics: A Developmental Approach*, Boston, MA, Little, Brown.

Almond, G. and Verba, S. (1963) *The Civic Culture: Political Attitudes and Democracy in Five Nations*, Princeton, NJ, Princeton University Press.

Amata, E. and Zylan, Y. (1991) 'It Happened Here: political opportunity, the New Institutionalism and the Townsend movement', *American Sociological Review*, vol. 56, pp. 250–65.

Andersen, S. and Eliassen, K. (1991) 'European Community Lobbying', *European Journal of Political Research*, vol. 20, pp. 173–87.

Andersen, S. and Eliassen, K. (1995) 'EU Lobbying: The New Research Agenda', *European Journal of Political Research*, vol. 27, no. 4, pp. 427–41.

Anderson, D., Bromberg, A., Egan, B., Griffin, C., Schoenbrun, L. and Szalkowski, C. (1992) 'Registered LLPs', *Texas Bar Journal*, July 1992, pp. 728–37.

Ascher, K. (1987) *The Politics of Privatisation: Contracting Out Public Services*, London, Macmillan – now Palgrave.

Askham, T., Burke, T. and Ramsden, D. (1990) *EC Sunday Trading Rules: Current EC Legal Developments*, London, Butterworths.

Association of Chartered Certified Accountants (1996) *Joint and Several Liability*, London, ACCA.

Association of Professional Political Consultants, (nd) *Introductory Paper*, London, APPC.

Atkinson, M. and Coleman, W. (1989a) *The State, Business and Industrial Change in Canada*, Toronto, University of Toronto Press.

Atkinson, M. and Coleman, W. (1989b) 'Strong States and Weak States: Sectoral Policy Networks in Advanced Capitalist Economies', *British Journal of Political Science*, vol. 19, no. 1, pp. 47–67.

Audit Commission (1986) *Performance Review in Local Government*, London, Audit Commission.

Auditing Practices Board (1994) *The Auditors' Right and Duty to Report to Regulators in the Financial Sector*, London, Auditing Practices Board.

Auditing Practices Board (1995) *The Audit Agenda*, London, Auditing Practices Board.

Austen-Smith, D. (1993) 'Information and Influence: Lobbying for Agendas and Votes', *American Journal of Political Science*, vol. 37, no. 3, pp. 799–833.

Austen-Smith, D. (1998) 'Allocating access for information and contributions', *Journal of Law, Economics, and Organization*, vol. 14, no. 2, pp. 277–303.

Austen-Smith, D. and Wright, J. (1994) 'Counteractive Lobbying', *American Journal of Political Science*, vol. 38, no. 1, pp. 25–44.

Austen-Smith, D. and Wright, J. (1996) 'Theory and Evidence for Counteractive Lobbying', *American Journal of Political Science*, vol. 40, no. 2, pp. 543–64.

Autumn Statement (1990) HMSO, Cm 1311, Public Expenditure Plans.

Bacheller, J. (1977) 'Lobbyists and the Legislative Process: The Impact of Environmental Constraints', *American Political Science Review*, vol. 72, pp. 252–63.

Baggott, R. (1988) 'Pressure Group Politics in Britain: Change and Decline?', *Talking Politics*, vol. 1, no. 1, pp. 25–30.

Baggott, R. (1992) 'The Measurement of Change in Pressure Group Politics', *Talking Politics*, vol. 5, no. 1, pp. 18–22.

Baggott, R. (1995) 'From Confrontation to Consultation? Pressure Group Relations from Thatcher to Major', *Parliamentary Affairs*, vol. 48, no. 3, pp. 484–502.

Bailey, A. (1996) 'Public Expenditure Control from the point of view of a Spending Department', in Corry, D., *Public Expenditure: Effective Management and Control*, London, Dryden Press.

Barberis, P. (ed.) (1995) *The Whitehall Reader: The UK's administrative machine in Action*, Buckingham, Open University Press.

Barberis, P. (1996) *The Elite of the Elite: Permanent Secretaries in the British Higher Civil Service*, Aldershot, Dartmouth.

Barnes, N. (1984) 'New Shopper Profiles: Implications of Sunday Sales', *Journal of Small Business Management*, July 1984, London.

Barnes, N. (nd), *The Seventh Day: A Profile of the Sunday Shopper*, Southeastern Massachusetts University.

Barnett, J. (1982) *Inside the Treasury*, London, Deutsch.

Bauer, R., Pool, I. and Dexter, L. (1963) *American Business and Public Policy: The Politics of Foreign Trade*, New York, Atherton Press.

Baumgartner, F. (1989) 'Independent and Politicized Policy Communities: Education and Nuclear Energy in France and the United States', *Governance*, vol. 2, no. 1, pp. 42–66.

Baumgartner, F. (1996) 'Public Interest Groups in France and the United States', *Governance*, vol. 9, no. 1, pp. 1–22.

Baumgartner, F. and Jones, B. (1993) *Agendas, Alternatives and Public Policies*, New York, HarperCollins.

Baumgartner, F. and Leech, B. (1996a) 'Good Theories Deserve Good Data', *American Journal of Political Science*, vol. 40, no. 2, pp. 565–9.

Baumgartner, F. and Leech, B. (1996b) 'The Multiple Ambiguities of Counteractive Lobbying', *American Journal of Political Science*, vol. 40, no. 2, pp. 521–42.

Baumgartner, F. and Leech, B. (1996c) 'Problems in the Study of Lobbying', Paper presented to the American Political Science Association, San Francisco, 29 August–1 September 1996.

Baumgartner, F. and Leech, B. (1998) *Basic Interests: The Importance of Groups in Politics and in Political Science*, Princeton, NJ, Princeton University Press.

Baxt, R. (1990) 'The Liability of Auditors – The Pendulum Swings Back', *Company and Securities Law Journal*, vol. 8.

Bechtel (May 1993) 'CrossRail: A Joint Venture. Report on Re-examination', Part 1, not published.

Beckwith, R. and Stott, W. (1978) *This Day*, Basingstoke, Marshall Morgan & Scott.

Beer, S. (1982) *Modern British Politics: Parties and Pressure Groups*, Faber & Faber.

Bell, S. (1996) 'Government Paralysed by Threat of Jersey Move', *Accountancy Age*, 8 August 1996.

Bell, S. (1997) 'Accountancy Regulation in the National Interest', *Accountancy Age*, 3 April 1997, p. 10.

Bell, S. (1997) 'Letter-Profession Books Labour on LLP Review', *Accounting Age*, 24 April.

Bell, S. (1997) 'The zeal of born-again New Labour', *Accountancy*, April 1997.

Benjamin, R. and Duvall, R. (1985) 'The Capitalist State in Context', in Elkin, S., (ed.), *The Democratic State*, Lawrence, KS, University Press of Kansas.

Bennett, R. (1997) 'The Impact of European Economic Integration on Business Associations: The UK Case', *West European Politics*, vol. 20, no. 3, pp. 61–90.

Berry, J. (1977) Lobbying for the People: The Political Behavior of Public Interest Groups, Princeton, NJ, Princeton University Press.

Berry, J. (1989a) *The Interest Group Society*, 2nd edn, Boston, Little, Brown.

Berry, J. (1989b) 'Subgovernments, Issue Networks and Political Conflict', in Harris, R. and Milkis, S. (eds), *Representing Interests and Interest Group Representation*, Boulder CO, Westview Press.

Berry, J. (1997) *The Interest Group Society*, 3rd edn, New York, Longman.

Berry, S. (1991) 'The Growth and Development of the Commercial Lobbying Industry in Britain During the 1980s', PhD Thesis, Birkbeck College, University of London.

Berry, S. (1992) 'Lobbyists: Techniques of the Political "Insiders"', *Parliamentary Affairs*, vol. 45, no. 2, pp. 220–32.

Berry, S. (1993) 'The Rise of the Professional Lobbyists: A Cause for Concern?', *Political Quarterly*, vol. 64, no. 3, pp. 344–51.

Biffen, J. (1989) *Inside the House of Commons*, London, Grafton.

Big Eight (1994) *Reform of Auditor Liability*, London, Coopers & Lybrand.

Big Six (1992) *The Liability Crisis in the United States – the Impact on the Accounting Profession*, Washington, DC.

Biggs, S. (1992) *An Analysis of the Select Committee on Members' Interests' Proposal for a Register of Professional Lobbyists*, Brunel University, Working Papers no. 24.

Birnbaum, J. (1992) *The Lobbyists: How the Influence Peddlers Get Their Way in Washington*, New York, Times Books.

Birnbaum, J. and Murray, A. (1987) *Showdown at Gucci Gulch: Lawmakers, Lobbyists and the Unlikely Triumph of Tax Reform*, New York, Random House.

Blomley, K. (1985) 'The Shops Act 1950: The Politics and the Policing', *Area*, vol. 17, no. 1.

Boléat, M. (1996) *Trade Association Strategy and Management*, London, Association of British Insurers (ABI).

Bovis *et al.* (1993) *CrossRail Cost Effectiveness*, December 1993, Commissioned by the Department of Transport. (Other authors include Sir Alexander Gibb, P&O, Geoconsult, MVA Consultancy, Schroders, Michael Schabas.)

Bow Group/Public Policy Unit (1991) *The Whitehall Wall; Barriers Between Industry and Government – and how to eliminate them*, London, Bow.

Boylan, R. (1995) 'An Optimal Auction Perspective on Lobbying', *Political Economy Working Paper*, Washington University in St Louis, December.

Braggins, J., McDonagh, M. and Barnard, A. (1992) *The American Presidential Election 1992 – What Labour Can Learn*, London, The Labour Party.

Brazier, M. (1993) *Street on Torts*, 9th edn, London, Butterworths.

British Council of Churches and Free Church Federal Council (1985) *A Critique of the Auld Report*, London.

British Interest Group Project (1992) 'What is Studied When Pressure Groups are Studied?', Aberdeen, Aberdeen University Press.

Brown, F. (1990) 'The Defeat of the Shops Bill, 1986', in Rush, M. (1990b) (ed.), *Parliament and Pressure Politics*, Oxford, Oxford University Press.

Brown, F. (1994) 'Influencing the House of Lords: The Role of the Lords Spiritual 1979–1987', *Political Studies*, vol. 42, no. 1, pp. 105–19.

Brown, P. (1996) 'Going Offshore – Jersey's LLP plans take shape', *Accountancy*, July.

Browne, W. (1988) *Private Interests, Public Policy and American Agriculture*, Lawrence, KS, University of Kansas Press.

Browne, W. (1990) 'Organized Interests and Their Issue Niches: A Search for Pluralism in a Policy Domain', *Journal of Politics*, vol. 52, no. 2, pp. 477–509.

Browne, W. (1995) *Cultivating Congress: Constituents, Issues and Interests in Agricultural Policymaking*, Lawrence, KS, University Press of Kansas.

Brownhill, S. (1990) *Developing London's Docklands – Another Great Planning Disaster*, London, Paul Chapman.

Bruce-Gardyne, J. (1986) *Ministers and Mandarins*, London, Sidgwick & Jackson.

Bruce-Gardyne, J. and Lawson, N. (1976) *The Power Game*, London, Macmillan – now Palgrave.

Burch, M. and Wood, B. (1989) *Public Policy in Britain*, 2nd edn, Oxford, Basil Blackwell.

Burnham, J. (1995) *The Politics of the Civil Service: The Thatcher Legacy*, PAVIC. London, Politics Association Resource Centre.

Burns, J. (1963) *The Deadlock of Democracy*, Englewood Cliffs, NJ, Prentice-Hall.

Burrell, M. (1991) 'Lobbying the Regions', *Public Relations*, 5 January, Institute of Public Relations (IPR).

Burrows, A. (1996) 'Reform of Joint and Several Liability – Is there a Case for Proportional Liability?, paper presented at the Accountants' Liability Conference, organised by Euroforum, London, 28 June 1996.

Burton-Jones, S. (1989) *New Facts for Auld*, Jubilee Centre Publications, Cambridge.

Butler, A. and Smith, D. (1986) 'Lobbying the British Parliament', *Public Relations Consultants' Association*, London.

Butler, R. (1993) 'The Evolution of the Civil Service – A Progress Report', *Public Administration*, vol. 71, pp. 395–406.

Butt-Philip, A. (1987) 'Pressure Groups in the European Community and Informal Institutional Arrangements', in Butler, R. and Taskaloyannis, P. (eds), *Experiences in Regional Cooperation*, Maastricht, European Institute for Public Administration.

Cabinet Office (1998) *Guidance for Civil Servants: Contacts with Lobbyists*, London, Cabinet Office.

Callaghy, T. (1984) *The State Society Struggle: Zaire in Comparative Perspective*, New York, Columbia University Press.

Cammins, A. and Haider, D. (1996) 'Governments as interest groups: intergovernmental lobbying and the federal system' [review], *Publius*, vol. 26, no. 2, pp. 143–5.

Campbell, C. and Wilson, G. (1995) *The End of Whitehall: Death of a Paradigm?*, Oxford, Basil, Blackwell.

Campbell, J. (1989) 'A Note from the Guest Editor', *Governance*, vol. 2, no. 1, pp. iii–iv.

Campbell, J., Baskin, M., Baumgartner, F. and Halpern, N. (1989) 'Afterwards on Policy Communities: A framework for comparative research', *Governance*, vol. 2, no. 1, pp. 86–94.

Campbell, S. (1998) 'Grass-roots Lobbying vs Coalition Lobbying: Transnational Strategies and the 1994 MFN Decision', *International Politics*, vol. 35, no. 2, pp. 187–206.

Carpenter, D., Esterling, K. and Lazer, D. (1998) 'The Strength of Weak Ties in Lobbying Networks: Evidence from Health-Care Politics in the United States', *Journal of Theoretical Politics*, vol. 10, no. 4, pp. 417–44.

Casey, M. (1991) *The Power of the Lobbyist: Regulation and Vested Interest*, Occasional Paper no. 32, Edinburgh, The David Hume Institute.

Cater, D. (1964) *Power in Washington*, New York, Random House.

Cates, P. (1988) 'Realities of Lobbying and Governmental Affairs', in Heath, R. (ed.), *Strategic Issues Management: How Organisations Influence and Respond to Public Interests and Policies*, London, Jossey Bass.

Cawson, A. (1985) *Organised Interests and the State: studies in Meso-Corporatism*, Sage series in Neo-Corporatism, London, Sage.

Chapman, R. (1997) *The Treasury in Public Policy-Making*, London, Routledge.

Chappell, H. (1981) 'Campaign Contributions and voting on the cargo preference bill: A comparison of simultaneous models', *Public Choice*, vol. 36, no. 2, pp. 301–12.

Chappell, H. (1982) 'Campaign Contributions and Congressional Voting: A Simultaneous Probit-Tobit Model', *The Review of Economics and Statistics*, vol. LXIV, pp. 77–83.

Chartered Institute of Public Finance and Accountancies (CIPFA) (1996), *Submission to the DTI Investigation of Joint and Several Liability by the Common Law Team of the Law Commission*, London, CIPFA.

CIPFA (nd), *Shopping Hours Reform – Sunday Trading*, London, CIPFA.

Choate, P. (1990) *Agents of Influence: How Japan Manipulates America's Political and Economic System*, New York, Alfred Knopf.

Christiansen, L. and Dowding, K. (1994) 'Pluralism or State Autonomy? The Case of Amnesty International (British Section): the Insider/Outsider Group', *Political Studies*, vol. XLII, no. 1, pp. 5–15.

Chua, S. (1995) 'The Auditor's Liability in Negligence in Respect of the Audit Report', *Journal of Business Law*, January, pp. 1–20.

Chub, J. and Peterson, P. (eds), (1989) *Can the Government Govern?*, Washington, DC, Brookings Institute.

Cigler, A. and Loomis, B. (1995) *Interest Group Politics*, 4th edn, Washington, DC, Congressional Quarterly Press.

Cladeira, G. and Wright, J. (1988) 'Organized Interests and Agenda Setting in the US Supreme Court', *American Political Science Review*, vol. 82, no. 4, pp. 1109–27.

Cockerell, M. (1997) *A Word in the Right Ear*, BBC2 television documentary, January 1997.

Cockerell, M., Hennessy, P. and Walker, D. (1985) *Sources Close to the Prime Minister: Inside the Hidden World of the News Manipulators*, London, Macmillan – now Palgrave.

Coen, D. (1997) 'The evolution of the large firm as a political actor in the European Union', *Journal of European Public Policy*, vol. 4, no. 1, pp. 91–108.

Coen, D. (1998) 'The European business interest and the nation state: large-firm lobbying in the European Union and member states', *Journal of Public Policy*, vol. 18, no. 1, pp. 75–100.

Coffin, C. (1987) *Working with Whitehall*, London, CBI.

Cohen, M., March, J. and Olsen, J. (1972) 'A garbage can model of organisational choice', *Administrative Science Quarterly*, vol. 17, pp. 1–25.

Cole, M., 'British Pressure Groups in the European Community: The Challenge of Brussels', *Parliamentary Affairs*, vol. 45, no. 1, pp. 92–107.

Committee on Standards in Public Life (1995) *First Report: Standards in Public Life*, CM2850-I, May 1995, HMSO.

Committee on Standards in Public Life (1998) *Fifth Report: The Funding of Political Parties in the United Kingdom*, Cm 4057-1, Volume 1, and Cm 4057-2, Volume 2, The Stationery Office.

Communication Group (1994) *Your Guide to Westminster and Whitehall*, London, Communication Group.

Compass Partnership (1996) *Trade Association Performance: Report on a Benchmarking Exercise of Large Trade Associations*, London, Association of British Insurers (ABI).

Compass Partnership (1997) *Trade Association Performance: Report of a Benchmarking Exercise of Trade Associations*, London, Association of British Insurers (ABI).

Confederation of British Industry (1987) *Working with Politicians*, London, CBI.

Connor, L. (1984) 'Stopping Sunday Trading', *Justice of the Peace*, vol. 148, no. 39, p. 614–615.

Connor, W. (1989) 'Shops Act Enforcement: A Strategy to Win', a paper delivered to the conference on Successful Enforcement Strategies on Sunday Trading, 8 December.

Conservative Party (1987) *General Election Campaign Guide 1987*, Conservative Party, London.

Consumers' Association (1993) *Sunday Shopping – A Call for Deregulation*, London, Consumers' Association.

Consumers for Sunday Shopping, *Newsletter*, various editions.

Conway, M. (1991) 'PACs in the Political Process', in Cigler, A. and Loomis, B., *Interest Group Politics*, 3rd edn, Washington, DC, Congressional Quarterly Press.

Cook, J. (1995) *The Sleaze File*, London, Bloomsbury.

Corporation of London (1990) *Report by Segal Quince Wicksteed on the Economic Harm of Poor Transport Links*, London, Corporation of London.

Cortel, A. (1997) 'Centralization, Access, and Influence: The Reagan Administration and the Semiconductor Industry's Trade Complaints', *Governance*, vol. 10, no. 3, pp. 261–85.

Cousins, J. and Sikka, P. (1993) 'Accounting for Change: Facilitating Power and Accountability', *Critical Perspectives on Accounting*, March, pp. 53–72.

Cousins, J., Mitchell, A. and Sikka, P. (1993) 'Secret Government and Privileged Interests', *Political Quarterly*, vol. 64, no. 3, pp. 306–14.

Cousins, J., Mitchell, A., Sikka, P. and Willmott, H. (1998) *Auditors: Holding the Public to Ransom*, Colchester, Essex University, Association for Accountancy and Business Affairs.

Crawford, K. (1939) *The Pressure Boys: The Inside Story of Lobbying in America*, New York, J. Messner.

Currie, D. (1985) 'Lobbying in Europe', in *House Magazine*, 29 November 1985.

Cyert, R. and March, J. (1963) *A behavoural theory of the firm*, Englewood Cliffs, NJ, Prentice-Hall.

Dahl, R. (1956) *Preface to Democratic Theory*, Chicago, IL, University of Chicago Press.

Dahl, R. (1961) *Who Governs?*, New Haven, CT, Yale University Press.

Dahl, R. (1971) *Polyarchy, Participation and Opposition*, New Haven, CT, Yale University Press.

Dahl, R. (1982) *Dilemmas of Pluralist Democracy: Autonomy vs Control*, New Haven, CT, and London, Yale University Press.

Dahl, R. (1991) *Modern Political Analysis*, Englewood Cliffs, NJ, Prentice-Hall.

Dargie, C. and Locke, R. (1999), *From the Active to the Enabling State: The Changing Role of the Senior Civil Service in Comparative Perspective*, Oxford, Nuffield College, 15–16 January.

Darke, M. (1997) 'Lobbying by law firms: a study of lobbying by national law firms in Canberra', *Australian Journal of Public Administration*, vol. 56, no. 4, pp. 32–46.

Davies, M. (1985) *Politics of Pressure: The Art of Lobbying*, London, BBC.

Davies, M. (1989) 'The End of the Affair: Duty of Care and Liability Insurance', *Legal Studies*, vol. 9, pp. 67–83.

Dawson, H. (1967) 'Relations Between Farm Organisations and the Civil Service in Canada and Great Britain', *Canadian Public Administration*, vol. 4, 450–71.

De Smith, S. and Brazier, R. (1994) *Constitutional and Administrative Law*, Harmondsworth, Penguin.

De Vires, W. (1960) 'The Michigan Lobbyist', unpublished PhD thesis, Michigan State University.

Deakin, D. (1989) 'Rational economic behaviour and lobbying on accounting issues: evidence from the oil and gas industry', *The Accounting Review*, vol. LXIV, no. 1, pp. 137–51.

Dearlove, J. (1973) *The Politics of Policy in Local Government: The Making and Maintenance of Public Policy in the Royal Borough of Kensington and Chelsea*, Cambridge, Cambridge University Press.

Dearlove, J. and Saunders, P. (1991) *Introduction to British Politics: Analysing a Capitalist Democracy*, Cambridge, Polity Press.

Deutsch, K. (1963) *The Nerves of Government: Models of Political Communication and Control*, London, Macmillan – now Palgrave.

Dexter, L. (1969a) *How Organisations are Represented in Washington*, Indianapolis, IN, Bobbs-Merrill.

Dexter, L. (1969b) *The Sociology and Politics of Congress*, Chicago, IL, Rand McNally.

Diamond, P. (1989) 'Local Government and Sunday Trading', *The Law Society's Gazette*, no. 28, 19 July 1989.

Diamond, P. (1991a) 'Dishonourable Defences: The Use of Injunctions and the EEC Treaty – case study of the Shops Act 1950, *The Modern Law Review*, vol. 54, no. 1, pp. 72–87.

Diamond, P. (1991b) 'Sunday service: trading restrictions', *Solicitors' Journal*, May.

Diamond, P. (1993) 'Sunday Trading Revisited', *Solicitors' Journal*, 25 June.

Docklands Access Steering Group (1982), *Public Transport Provisions for Docklands*, London, Docklands Access Steering Group.

Docklands Public Transport and Access Steering Group (1982), *Public Transport Provision for Docklands – a summary and assessment of schemes*, London.

DoE (1995) *Latent Defects Liability and 'Build' Insurance: Consultation Paper* London, HMSO.

DoE, Department of Transport, GLC, LT, Docklands Development Organisation (1980), *A Study of Lower Cost Alternatives to the Jubilee Line in Docklands*, London.

DoE, GLC, BR, LT (1974) *London Rail Study*, London.

Doig, A. (1984): *Corruption and Misconduct in Contemporary British Politics*, Harmondsworth, Penguin.

Doig, A. (1986a) 'Access to Parliament and the rise of the Professional Lobbyist', *Public Money*, vol. 5, no. 4, pp. 39–43.

Doig, A. (1986b) 'A Question of Balance: Business Appointments of Former Senior Civil Servants', *Parliamentary Affairs*, vol. 39, no. 1, pp. 63–78.

Doig, A. (1986c) 'Influencing Westminster: Registering the Lobbyists', *Parliamentary Affairs*, vol. 39, no. 4, pp. 517–35.

Doig, A. (1988) 'The Dynamics of Scandal in British Politics', *Corruption and Reform* vol. 3, pp. 323–30.

Doig, A. (1990a) 'An Apparent Abuse in the use of Dining Rooms: The British Parliament and Lobbying', *Corruption and Reform*, vol. 5, no. 3, pp. 189–203.

Doig, A. (1990b) *Westminster Babylon*, London, Allison & Busby.

Doig, A. (1991) 'The Ethics of Lobbying: Why James VI [I] was Right', in Jordan, G. (ed.), *The Commercial Lobbyists*, Aberdeen, Aberdeen University Press.

Doig, A. (1993) 'The Double Whammy; The Resignation of David Mellor', *Parliamentary Affairs*, vol. 46, no. 2, pp. 167–78.

Doig, A. (1994) 'Full Circle or Dead End? What next for the Select Committee on Members' Interests', *Parliamentary Affairs*, vol. 47, no. 3, pp. 355–73.

Doig, A. (1995a) 'Good Government and Sustainable Anti-Corruption Strategies: A role for independent anti-corruption agencies?', *Public Administration and Development*, vol. 15, no. 2, pp. 151–66.

Doig, A. (1995b) 'Untangling the Threads of Sleaze: The Slide into Nolan' *Parliamentary Affairs*, vol. 48, no. 4, pp. 562–78.

Doig, A. (1996a) 'From Lynskey to Nolan: The Corruption of British Politics and Public Service?', *Journal of Law and Society*, vol. 23, no. 1, pp. 36–56.

Doig, A. (1996b) 'Next Steps to the Supremacy of Parliament?', *Parliamentary Affairs*, vol. 49, no. 3, pp. 509–11.

Doig, A. (1997) 'Truth-telling and Power', *Parliamentary Affairs*, vol. 50, no. 1, pp. 143–65.

Doig, A. (1998) '"Cash for Questions": Parliament's response to the offence that dare not speak its name', *Parliamentary Affairs*, vol. 51, no. 1, pp. 36–50.

Donoughue, B. (1995) contribution to a seminar on 'Ethical and Effective Lobbying' organised by Bruce Naughton Wade, 21 March.

Dowding, K. (1991) *Political Power and Rational Choice*, Aldershot, Edward Elgar.

Dowding, K. (1994) 'Policy Networks: Don't Stretch a Good Idea too Far', in Dunleavy, P. and Stanyer, J. (eds), *Contemporary Political Studies*, Belfast, Political Studies Association.

Dowding, K. (1995a) 'Model or Metaphor? A Critical Review of the Policy Network Approach', *Political Studies*, vol. 43, pp. 136–58.

Dowding, K. (1995b) *The Civil Service*, London, Routledge.

Dowding, K. (1996) *Power*, Buckingham, Open University Press.

Drew, E. (1983) 'Charlie, Portrait of a Lobbyist', in Cigler, A. and Loomis, B., *Interest Group Politics*, Washington, DC, Congressional Quarterly Press.

Drewry, G. (1975) 'Declaring MPs; Interests', *New Law Journal*, 4 September, pp. 863–4.

DTI Consultation Paper (1996) *Feasibility Investigation of Joint and Several Liability*, A Report by the Common Law Team of the Law Commission, London, HMSO.

DTI Press Release (1998) P/98/699, *Accountancy Reform: Regulation and Liability*, 17 September 1998.

DTI (1989) *Professional Liability – Report of The Study Terms* (Chairman Professor Andrew Likierman), London, HMSO.

DTI (1996) *A Best Practice Guide For The Model Trade Association*, London, DTI.

DTI (1997) *Limited Liability Partnership – A New Forum of Business Association for Professions* (URN 97/597), London, DTI.

DTI (1998) *Modern Company Law for a Competitive Economy*, London, DTI.

DTI (1999) *Limited Liability Partnerships: Draft Regulations – A Consultation Document* (URN 99/1025), London, DTI.

DTp (1989a) *Central London Rail Study*, with BR/Network South East/LT/LUL.

DTp (1989b) *East London Rail Study*, London, DTp.

DTp (1990) *Central London Rail Study – A Report on Further Work*, London, DTp.

DTp (1992) *New Opportunities for the Railways – the Privatisation of BR*, London HMSO, Cm 2012.

DTp (1996) *CrossRail Study: Final Report*, March (more commonly referred to as the 'Montagu Report').

Dubs, A. (1988) *Lobbying: An Insider's Guide to the Parliamentary Process*, London, Pluto.

Dudley, G. and Richardson, J. (1996a) 'Promiscuous and Celibate Ministerial Styles: Policy Change, Policy Networks and British Roads Policy', *Parliamentary Affairs*, vol. 49, no. 4, 566–584.

Dudley, G. and Richardson, J. (1996b) 'Why Does Policy Change Over Time? Adversarial policy communities, alternative policy arenas, and British trunk roads policy 1945–95', *Journal of European Public Policy*, vol. 3, no. 1, pp. 63–83.

Dudley, G. and Richardson, J. (1998) 'Arenas without Rules and the Policy Change Process: Outsider Groups and British Roads Policy', *Political Studies*, vol. XLVI, pp. 727–47.

Dunleavy, P. (1988) 'Group Identities and Individual Influence: Reconstructing the Theory of Interest Groups', *British Journal of Political Science*, vol. 18, Part 1, pp. 21–49.

Dunleavy, P. (1991) *Democracy, Bureaucracy and Public Choice*, Hemel Hempstead, Harvester Wheatsheaf.

Dunleavy, P. (1995a) 'Policy Disasters: Explaining the UK's Record', *Public Policy and Administration*, vol. 10, no. 2, pp. 52–70.

Dunleavy, P. (1995b) 'Reinterpreting the Westland Affair: Theories of the State and Core Executive Decision-Making', in Rhodes, R. and Dunleavy, P., *Prime Minister, Cabinet and Core Executive*, London, Macmillan – now Palgrave.

Dunleavy, P., Weir, S. and Subrahmanyam, G. (1995) 'Sleaze in Britain: Media Influences, Public Response and Constitutional Significance', *Parliamentary Affairs*, vol. 48, no. 4, pp. 602–16.

Dunsire, A. (1990) 'Holistic Governance', *Public Policy and Administration*, vol. 5, no. 1, pp. 4–19.

Easton, D. (1960) *The Political System*, New York, Alfred A. Knopf.

Eckstein, H. (1960) *Pressure Group Politics: The Case of the BMA*, Stanford, CA, Stanford University Press.

Eckstein, H. (1975) 'Case Study and Theory in Political Science', in Greenstein, F. and Polsby, N. (eds), *Handbook of Political Science, Volume 7: Strategies of Inquiry*, Reading, MA, Addison-Wesley.

Eckstein, H. (1988) 'A Culturalist Theory of Political Change', *American Political Science Review*, vol. 82, no. 3, pp. 789–804.

Edsall, T. (1988) *Power and Money*, New York, W.W. Norton.

Elkin, S. (1989) 'The Political Theory of American Business', *Business in the Contemporary World*, Spring.

Ellis, N. (1988) *Parliamentary Lobbying: Putting the Business Case to Government*, London, Heinemann.

Erola, J. (1991) 'Ethics and Lobbying: A Business Perspective', *Canadian Public Administration*, vol. 34, no. 1, pp. 90–4.

European Commission (1996) *The Role, The Position and the Liability of the Statutory Auditor within the European Union*, Green Paper, para. 4.18.

Evans, D. (1991) 'Lobbying the Committee: Interest Groups and the House Public Works and Transportation Committee', in Cigler, A. and Loomis, B., *Interest Group Politics*, 3rd edn, Washington, DC, Congressional Quarterly Press.

Evans, D. (1996) 'Before the Roll Call: Interest Group Lobbying and Public Policy Outcomes', *Political Research Quarterly*, vol. 49, no. 2, pp. 287–304.

Evans, P., Rueschemeyer, D. and Skocpol, T. (eds) (1985) *Bringing the State Back In*, Cambridge, Cambridge University Press.

Fabrini, S. (1988) 'The Return to the State: A Critique', *American Political Science Review*, vol. 82, no. 3, pp. 891–901.

Fairchild, M. (1997) *The Power of the Media and How to Measure it: A Client Guide to Media Evaluation*, London, Association of Media Evaluation Companies.

Fairchild, M., (forthcoming), *Research and Evaluation Toolkit*, London, International Committee of Public Relations Consultants Associations.

Fairlie, H. (1968) *The Life of Politics*, London, Methuen.

Familybase (1987) *The Family Charter: A New Initiative to Relieve Economic Pressure on the Family*, Cambridge, Jubilee Centre Publications.

Fanstein, S. (1994) *The City Builders: Property, Politics and Planning in London and New York*, Cambridge, MA, Blackwell.

Farrell, D. (1998) 'Political Consultancy Overseas: The Internationalization of Campaign Consultancy', *Political Studies and Politics*, vol. XXXI, no. 2, pp. 171–6.

Fearnley, S. (1993) 'Practical Answers Needed, Not Political Claptrap', *Accountancy*, December, p. 76.

Financial Times, 23 December 1985 (survey of business – extent of commercial political lobbyist hiring).

Finch, V. (1992) 'Board Performance and Cadbury on Corporate Governance', *Journal of Business Law*, pp. 581–95.

Finch, V. (1994a) 'Corporate Governance and Cadbury: self-regulation and alternatives', *Journal of Business Law*, pp. 51–62.

Finch, V. (1994b) 'Personal Accountability and Corporate Council: The Role of Directors' and Officers' Liability Insurance', *Modern Law Review*, vol. 57, no. 6, pp. 880–915.

Finer, S. (1958) *Anonymous Empire*, London, The Pall Mall Press.

Finer, S. (1966) 2nd edn, *Anonymous Empire*, London, The Pall Mall Press.

Fisher, J. (1994) 'Political Donations to the Conservative Party', *Parliamentary Affairs*, vol. 47, no. 1, pp. 61–72.

Fleisher, C. (1995) *Public Affairs Benchmarking: A Comprehensive Guide*, Washington, DC, Public Affairs Council.

Fleisher, C. (ed.) (1997) *Assessing, Managing and Maximizing Public Affairs Performance*, Washington, DC, Public Affairs Council.

Flynn, A., Gray, A., Jenkins, W. and Rutherford, B. (1988) 'Making indicators perform', *Public Money and Management*, vol. 8, no. 4, pp. 35–41.

Foreign Affairs Select Committee (1993/94) *Public Expenditure – Pergau hydro-electric project, Malaysia – the aid and trade provision and related matters*, third report with proceedings and evidence (HC 271i to vii), HC 271.

Foundation for Public Affairs (1992) *The State of Corporate Public Affairs*, Rochester, NY, Center for Organizational Development.

Fowler, L. and Shaiko, R. (1987) 'The Grass Roots Connection: Environmental Activists and Senate Roll Calls', *American Journal of Political Science*, vol. 31, no. 3, pp. 484–510.

Francis, J. (1987) 'Lobbying against proposed accounting standards: the case of employers' pension accounting', *Journal of Accounting and Public Policy*, vol. 6, pp. 35–57.

Franklin, R. (1996) 'Keeping it Bright, Light and Trite: Changing Newspaper Reporting of Parliament', *Parliamentary Affairs*, vol. 49, no. 2, pp. 298–315.

Freathy, P. and Sparks, L. (nd), *Sunday Working in the Retail Trade: Scotland and England and Wales Compared – a summary of research findings*, Stirling, Institute for Retail Studies, University of Stirling.

Freedman, J. (1993) 'Accountants and Corporate Governance: Filling a Legal Vacuum', *Political Quarterly*, vol. 64, no. 3, pp. 285–97.

Freedman, J. and Finch, V. (1997) 'Limited Liability Partnerships: Have Accountants Sewn up the "Deep Pockets" Debate?', *Journal of British Law*, September, pp. 387–423.

Freedman, J. and Power, M. (1991) 'Law and Accounting: Transition and Transformation', *Modern Law Review*, vol. 54, no. 6, pp. 769–91.

Frendreis, J. and Waterman, R. (1985) 'PAC Contributions and Legislative Behavior: Senate Voting on Trucking Deregulation', *Social Science Quarterly*, vol. 66, no. 2, pp. 401–12.

Fritschler, A. (1975) *Smoking and Politics*, 2nd edn, Englewood Cliffs, NJ, Prentice-Hall.

Furlong, S. (1992) 'Interest Group Influence on Regulatory Policy', PhD dissertation, American University, Washington, DC.

Furlong, S. (1997) 'Interest Group Influence on Rule Making', *Administration and Society*, vol. 29, no. 3, pp. 325–47.

Gais, T. and Walker, J. (1983) *Pathways to Influence in American Politics: Factors affecting the Choice of Tactics by Interest Groups*, presented at the annual meeting of the Midwest Political Science Association.

Gais, T. and Walker, J. (1991) 'Pathways to Influence in American Politics', in Walker, J., *Mobilizing Interest Groups in America*, Ann Arbor, MI, University of Michigan Press.

Galbraith, J. (1963) *American Capitalism*, Harmondsworth, Penguin.

Gamson, W. (1968) *Power and Discontent*, Homewood, IL, The Dorsey Press.

General Accounting Office (1984) *Designing Evaluations*, Methodology Transfer Paper no. 4, Program and Methodology Division, Washington, DC, General Accounting Office.

Giddens, A. (1986) *The Constitution of Society*, Oxford, Polity Press.

Giddings, P. (1995) *Parliamentary Accountability: A Study of Parliament and Executive Agencies*, London, Macmillan – now Palgrave.

Gietzmann, M., Ncube, M. and Selby, M. (1997) 'Auditor Performance, Implicit Guarantees, and the Valuation of Legal Liability', *International Journal of Auditing*, vol. 1, no. 1, pp. 13–30.

Gietzmann, M. and Quick, R. (1998) 'Capping Auditor Liability: The German Experience', *Accounting, Organization and Society*, vol. 23, no. 1, pp. 81–103.

Gilligan, M. (1995) 'Comments on Verdier's Public Aid to Private Industry: The Role of Policy Networks', *Comparative Political Studies*, vol. 28, no. 1, pp. 43–61.

Gilligan, M. (1997) 'Lobbying as a Private Good with Intra-Industry Trade', *International Studies Quarterly*, vol. 41, no. 3, pp. 455–74.

Glaister, S. *et al.* (1991) *Transport Options for London*, London, Greater London Group, LSE.

Glaister, S. and Travers, T. (1993) *The City Research Project: Meeting the Transport Needs of the City*, London, Corporation of London.

Glanville, S. (1997) 'Partnership Liability – All Aboard the LLP Train? (Whether Ireland Should adopt UK Proposals for Limited Liability Partnerships)', *Commercial Law Practitioner*, vol. 4, no. 9, pp. 226–9.

GLC (1983) *Working for Better Transport: A Record of Achievement*, London, GLC.

GLC (1985) *Public Transport in London: The next 10 years*, London, GLC.

Glynn, J., Gray, A. and Jenkins, B. (1992) 'Auditing the Three Es: The Challenge of Effectiveness', *Public Policy and Administration*, vol. 7, no. 3, pp. 56–70.

Goldwasser, D. (1997) 'The Private Securities Litigation Reform Act of 1995 – Impact on Accountants', *The CPA Journal*, pp. 72–5.

Gopoian, D. (1984) 'What Makes PACs Tick? An Analysis of the Allocation Patters of Economic Interest Groups', *American Journal of Political Science*, vol. 28, no. 2, pp. 259–81.

Gordon, C. (ed.) (1983) *Erskine May's Treatise on the Law, Privileges, Proceedings and Usage of Parliament*, London, Butterworths.

Grant, W. (1978) 'Insider Groups, Outsider Groups and Interest Group Strategies in Britain', University of Warwick, Department of Politics Working Paper 19.

Grant, W. (1989) *Government and Industry: A comparative analysis of the US, Canada and the UK*, Aldershot, Edward Elgar.

Grant, W. (1993a) *Business and Politics in Britain*, 2nd edn, London, Macmillan – now Palgrave.

Grant, W. (1993b) 'Pressure Groups and the European Community: An Overview,' in Mazey, S. and Richardson J. (eds), *Lobbying in the European Community*, Oxford, Oxford University Press, pp. 27–46.

Grant, W. (1995) *Pressure Groups, Politics and Democracy in Britain*, 2nd edn, London, Harvester Wheatsheaf.

Grant, W. and Marsh, D. (1977) *The CBI*, London, Hodder & Stoughton.

Grant, W., Paterson, W. and Whitson, C. (1988) *Government and the Chemical Industry*, Oxford, Clarendon Press.

Grantham, C. (1989) 'Interest Representation: Parliament and Political Consultants', *Parliamentary Affairs*, vol. 42, no. 4, pp. 503–18.

Grantham, C. (1990) 'Interest Representation', Wroxton papers in Politics, Paper A8 1990, Wroxton College.

Grantham, C. and Seymour-Ure, C. (1990) 'Political Consultants', in Rush, M. (ed.), *Parliament and Pressure Politics*, Oxford, Clarendon Press.

Gray, P. (1996) 'Disastrous Explanations – or Explanations of Disaster? A Reply to Patrick Dunleavy', *Public Policy and Administration*, vol. 11, no. 1, pp. 74–83.

Gray, V. and Lowery, D. (1993a) 'The Diversity of State Interest Group Systems', *Political Research Quarterly*, vol. 46, no. 1, pp. 81–97.

Gray, V. and Lowery, D. (1993b) 'Stability and Change in State Interest Group Systems: 1975–1990', *State and Local Government Review*, vol. 25, pp. 87–96.

Gray, V. and Lowery, D. (1994) 'Interest Group System Density and Diversity: A Research Update', *International Political Science Review*, vol. 15, no. 1, pp. 5–14.

Gray, V. and Lowery, D. (1995) 'The Demography of Interest Organization Communities: Institutions, Associations and Membership Groups', *American Politics Quarterly*, vol. 23, no. 1, pp. 3–32.

Gray, V. and Lowery, D. (1996a) 'A Niche Theory of Interest Representation', *The Journal of Politics*, vol. 58, no. 1, pp. 91–111.

Gray, V. and Lowery, D. (1996b) *The Population Ecology of Interest Representation*, Ann Arbor, MI, University of Michigan Press.

Gray, V., Lowery, D. and Hansen, S. (1997) 'The population ecology of interest representation: lobbying communities in the American states' [review], *Journal of Politics*, vol. 59, no. 3, pp. 936–8.

Greenwood, J. (1996) 'The Management of Interest Representation in the European Union', Paper for the American Political Science Association, San Francisco, 29 August–1 September.

Greenwood, J. (1998a) 'Regulating lobbying in the European Union', *Parliamentary Affairs*, vol. 51, no. 4, pp. 587–99.

Greenwood, J. (ed.) (1998b) 'The Regulation of Lobbying', A Special Edition of *Parliamentary Affairs*, vol. 51, no. 4, pp. 487–626.

Greenwood, J. and Thomas, C. (1998) 'Regulating Lobbying in the Western World', *Parliamentary Affairs*, vol. 51, no. 4, pp. 487–99.

Greer, I. (1985) *Right to be Heard; A Guide to Political Representation and Parliamentary Procedure*, London, Ian Greer Associates.

Greer, I. (1991) 'Making Use of Westminster', in Jordan, G. (ed.), *The Commercial Lobbyists*, Aberdeen, Aberdeen University Press.

Greer, I. (1997) *One Man's Word: The untold story of the cash-for-Questions Affair*, London, André Deutsch.

Greer, P. (1994) *Transforming Central Government: The Next Steps Initiative*, Buckingham, Open University Press.

Grefe, E. and Linsky, M. (1998) *The New Corporate Activism: Harnessing The Power of Grassroots Tactics for your Organization*, New York, McGraw-Hill, Primus Custom.

Grenzke, J. (1990) 'Money and Congressional Behavior', in Nugent, M. and Johannes, J. (eds), *Money, Elections and Democracy*, Boulder, CO, Westview Press.

Grobstein, M. and Liggio, C. (1993) 'A Global Look at Accountants' Litigation', *Journal of Economics and Management Strategy*, vol. 2, no. 3, pp. 395–400.

Gronbech, E. (1998) 'The Emergence of Professional Lobbyists in Britain 1970–1997', M.Litt Thesis, University of Oxford.

Gwilliam, D. (1987) 'The Auditor's Responsibility for the Detection of Fraud', *Professional Negligence*, vol. 5 (Jan./Feb.), pp. 5–10.

Gwilliam, D. (1992) 'The Auditor and the Law: Some Economic and Moral Issues', in Bromwich, M. and Hopwood, A. (eds), *Accounting and the Law*, London, Prentice-Hall, pp. 191–204.

Gwilliam, D. (1997) 'Changes in the Legal Environment', in Turley, S. and Sherer, M. (eds), *Current Issues in Auditing*, 3rd edn, London, Paul Chapman.

Haas, E. (1957) *The Uniting of Europe*, Stanford, CA, Stanford University Press.

Haass, P. (1992) 'Introduction: Epistemic Communities and International Policy Co-ordination', *International Organization*, vol. 46, no. 1, pp. 1–35.

Hall, P. (1986) *Governing the Economy: The Politics of State Intervention in Britain and France*, Cambridge, Polity Press.

Hall, R. (1996) *Participation in Congress*, New Haven, CT, Yale University Press.

Hall, R. and Wayman, F. (1990) 'Buying Time: Moneyed Interest and the Mobilization of Bias in Congressional Committees', *American Political Science Review*, vol. 84, no. 3, pp. 797–820.

Hansen, J. (1991) *Gaining Access: Congress and the Farm Lobby 1919–1981*, Chicago, IL, University of Chicago Press.

Hanson, D. (1985) *Litigation Against Auditors – what is the cost and where does it fall?*, London, Arthur Andersen.

Hardcastle, A. (1988) 'Going to the Government, cap in hand', *Accountancy*, January, pp. 15–16.

Harden, I. (1993) 'Money and the Constitution: Financial Control, Reporting and Audit', *Legal Studies*, vol. 13, no. 1, pp. 16–37.

Harman, R. (1993) 'Railway Privatisation: Does it Bring New Opportunities?', *Public Money and Management*, January–March, pp. 19–25.

Harris Research Centre (1996) *Parliamentary Perceptions of the Lobbying Industry*, London, Harris.

Harris, P. and Lock, A. (1996) 'Machiavellian Marketing: The Development of Corporate lobbying in the UK', *Journal of Marketing Management*, vol. 12, pp. 313–28.

Harrison, R. (1980) *Pluralism and Corporatism: The Political Evolution of Modern Democracies*, London, George Allen & Unwin.

Hawkinson, B. (1997) 'What We've Learned from the 1996 "State of Corporate Public Affairs" Survey', in Fleisher, C. (ed.), *Assessing, Managing and Maximizing Public Affairs Performance*, Washington, DC, Public Affairs Council.

Hayes, M. (1978) 'The Semi-Sovereign Pressure Groups: A Critique of Current Theory and an Alternative Typology', *The Journal of Politics*, vol. 40, no. 1 pp. 134–61.

Hays, R. (1991) 'Intergovernental Lobbying: Towards and understanding of issue priorities', *Western Political Quarterly*, vol. 44, no. 4, pp. 1081–98.

Heald, D. and Geaughan, N. (1997) 'Accounting for the Private Finance Initiative', *Public Money and Management*, July–September, pp. 11–16.

Heinz, J., Laumann, E., Nelson, R. and Salisbury, R. (1993) *The Hollow Core: Private Interests in National Policymaking*, Cambridge, MA, Harvard University Press.

Heinz, J., Laumann, E., Salisbury, R. and Nelson, R. (1990) 'Inner Circles or Hollow Cores? Elite Networks in National Policy Systems', *Journal of Politics*, vol. 52, no. 2, pp. 356–90.

Helco, H. (1974) *Modern Social Politics in Britain and Sweden*, New Haven, CT, Yale University Press.

Helco, H. (1978) 'Issue Networks and the Executive Establishment', in King, A., (ed.), *The New American Political System*, Washington, DC, American Enterprise Institute, pp. 87–124.

Helco, H. and Wildavsky, A. (1974) *The Private Government of Public Money*, London, Macmillan – now Palgrave.

Hennessy, P. (1986) *Cabinet*, Oxford, Basil Blackwell.

Hennessy, P. (1989) *Whitehall*, London, Secker & Warburg.

Hennessy, P. (1995) *The Hidden Wiring: Unearthing the British Constitution*, London, Gollancz.

Hepherd, Winstanley and Pugh (1988) *The REST proposals: A critical analysis*, commissioned for the Shopping Hours Reform Council.

Herring, P. (1929) *Group Representation Before Congress*, New York, Russell & Russell.

Herring, P. (1936) *Public Administration and the Public Interest*, New York, McGraw Hill.

Hewitt, P. (1989) *A Cleaner, Faster London: Road Pricing, Transport Policy and the Environment*, London, Institute of Public Policy Research IPPR.

HMSO (1994) *Pressure groups*, London, HMSO.

HMSO, *Shops (Early Closing Days) Act 1965*, London.

HMSO, *The Shops Act 1950*, London.

Hocking, B. (1990) 'Bringing the Outside in: The Role and Nature of Foreign Interest Lobbying', *Corruption and Reform*, vol. 5, pp. 219–33.

Hodder-Williams, R. (1996) 'British Politicians: To rehabilitate or not', *Parliamentary Affairs*, vol. 49, no. 2, 285–97.

Hogg, S. and Hill, J. (1995) *Too Close to Call: Power and Politics – John Major in no. 10*, London, Warner Books.

Hogwood, B. and Gunn, L. (1984) *Policy Analysis for the Real World*, Oxford, Oxford University Press.

Hojnacki, M. and Kimball, D. (1998) 'Organized interests and the decision of whom to lobby in Congress', *American Political Science Review*, vol. 92, no. 4, pp. 775–90.

Holbech, B. (1991) 'Policy and Influence', in Jordan, G. (ed.), *The Commercial Lobbyists*, Aberdeen, Aberdeen University Press.

Holgate, G. (1983) 'Never on a Sunday: Seven Day Trading', *Justice of the Peace*, vol. 147, no. 43, pp. 679–82.

Holgate, G. (1984a) 'The Extent of an Authority's Duty on Sunday Trading', *Justice of the Peace*, vol. 148, no. 48, pp. 763–65.

Holgate, G. (1984b) 'Video Hire Shops and the Shops Act 1950: A Postscript', *Justice of the Peace*, vol. 148, no. 18, pp. 282.

Holliday, I. (1992) 'The Politics of the Channel Tunnel', *Parliamentary Affairs*, vol. 45, no. 2, pp. 188–204.

Hollingsworth, M. (1991) *MPs for Hire: The Secret World of Political Lobbying*, London, Bloomsbury.

Hollingsworth, M. (1994) *A Bit on the Side*, London, Bloomsbury.

Hollingsworth, M. (1997) *Tim Bell: The Ultimate Spin Doctor*, London, Hodder & Stoughton.

Home Office (1984) *The Shops Acts Late Night and Sunday Opening*. Report of the Committee of inquiry into proposals to amend the Shops Acts, HMSO, London.

House Magazine (1996) Special issue: *Parliamentary Lobbying*, no. 703, vol. 21, 29 January.

House of Commons (1986–87a) Third Report from the Transport Committee, session 1986–87 'Financing of Rail Services', vol. 1, Report and Minutes of Proceedings, HC 383 I.

House of Commons (1986–87b) Third Report from the Transport Committee, session 1986–87 'Financing of Rail Services', vol. 2, Evidence, HC 383 II, p. 259.

House of Commons (1987–8) First Special Report from the Transport Committee, session 1987–88, *Government Observations on the First, Second and Third Reports of the Committee Session 1986–87*, Cm 420.

House of Commons Library (1986) 'Shops Bill (Bill 94 of 1985/86)', Research Paper 86/7, 4 March.

House of Commons Library (1988) 'Employment Bill 1988/89 (Bill 8)', Research Paper 988/8, 14 December.

House of Commons Library (1992) 'Sunday Trading', Research Paper 281, 11 February.

House of Commons Library (1993) 'Sunday Trading: the Shops Bill 1992–93', Research Paper 93/2.

House of Commons Library (1995a) 'Aspects of Nolan – MPs and Lobbying', Research Paper 95/60.

House of Commons Library (1995b) 'The Nolan Resolutions', Research Paper 95/61.

House of Commons Library (1995c) 'Aspects of Nolan – Parliamentary self-regulation', 23 May 1995 Research Paper 95/65.

House of Commons Library (1995d) 'Parliamentary Pay and Allowances', 4 July 1995 Research Paper 95/74.

House of Commons Library (1995e) 'Members' Financial Interests', 11 July 1995 Research Paper 95/86.

Humphries, C. (1991) 'Corruption, PACS and the Strategic Links between Contributions and Lobbying Activities', *Western Political Quarterly*, vol. 44, no. 2, pp. 353–72.

Hunter, F. (1953) *Community Power Structure*, Chapel Hill, NC, University of North Carolina Press.

Hurlston, M. and Whittaker, N. (nd), *Out of the Blue Laws – The Impact of Sunday Trading in Massachusetts*, A Report for Woolworth Holdings.

ICAEW (1987) *Heads of Profession call for Enquiry into Liability Reforms*, London, ICAEW.

ICAEW (1992) *Understanding an Audit*, London, ICAEW.

ICAEW (1994) *Auditors' Professional Liability* (memorandum submitted to the DTI), FRAG 8/94, London, ICAEW.

ICAEW (1995) *Auditors' Liability: The Public Interest Perspective*, London, ICAEW.

ICAEW (1996) *Joint and Several Liability – Finding a Fair Solution: A Discussion Paper on Professional Liability*, London, ICAEW.

ICAEW (1997) *Limited Liability Partnership: A memorandum submitted in May 1997 to DTI in response to consultation paper, 'Limited Liability Partnership: A new form of business association for professions'*, February, Tech 7/97.

IGA Proposal (nd), *A Public Affairs Programme for CrossRail*, London, IGA.

Institute of Chartered Accountants Scotland (ICAS) (1994) *Auditors' Liability*, Edinburgh, ICAS.

Institute of Chartered Accountants Scotland (ICAS) (1996) *Response to the Law Commission Paper: 'Feasibility Investigation of Joint and Several Liability*, Edinburgh, ICAS.

Institute of Chartered Accountants of Ireland (1996), *Response to the Consultation Document of the DTI on the Law Commission's Feasibility Investigation of Joint and Several Liability*, Dublin, Institute of Chartered Accountants of Ireland.

Jack, A. (1994) 'Crying Wolf Too Often over the 'Liability Crisis'', *Financial Times*, 16 June.

Jackson, P. and Lavender, M. (eds) (1996) *Public Services Yearbook 1996–97*, London, Harrap.

Jackson, P. and Palmer, B. (1989) *First Steps in Measuring Performance in the Public Sector: A Management Guide*, London, Public Finance Foundation.

Jaffer, S. and Morris, C. (1985) *Sunday Trading and Employment*, London, Institute for Fiscal Studies.

Jenkins, B. (1997) 'Accounting for auditors', *Parliamentary Review*, January.

Jessop, B. (1983) 'The Democratic State and the National Interest', in Coates, D. and Johnston, B. (eds), *Socialist Arguments*, Oxford, Martin Robertson.

Jessop, B. (1990a) *Putting the Capitalist State in its Place*, Cambridge, Polity Press.

Jessop, B. (1990b) *State Theory: Studies in and Beyond the Capitalist State*, Cambridge, Polity Press.

John, P. (1998) *Analysing Public Policy*, Critical Political Studies Series, London, Pinter.

Johnson, J. (1995) 'Limited Liability for Lawyers: General Partners Need Not Apply', *The Business Lawyer*, vol. 15, p. 85.

Johnson, L. (1985) 'The Effectiveness of Saving and Loans Political Action Committees', *Public Choice*, vol. 46, no. 3, pp. 289–304.

Jones, B. (1994) *Reconceiving Decision Making in Democratic Politics*, Chicago, IL, Chicago University Press.

Jones, B. (1995) 'Pressure Groups', in Jones, B., Gamble, A., Kavanagh, D., Moran, M., Norton, P. and Seldon, A. (eds), *Politics UK*, London, Prentice-Hall.

Jones, G., Wincott and Travers, T., *Transport Infrastructure Planning and Implementation: A Comparative Study*, London, LSE, December 1990.

Jones, N. (1995) *Spin Doctors and Soundbites: How Politicians Manipulate the Press and vice versa*, London, Cassell.

Jones, N. (1999) *Sultans of Spin: The Media and the new Labour Government*, London, Gollancz.

Jones, W. and Keiser, R. (1987) 'Issue Visibility and the Effects of PAC Money', *Social Science Quarterly*, vol. 68, no. 1, pp. 170–6.

Jordan, G. (1981) 'Iron Triangles, Woolly Corporatism and Elastic Nets: Images of the Policy Process', *Journal of Public Policy*, vol. 1, no. 1, pp. 95–123.

Jordan, G. (1985) 'Parliament under Pressure', *Political Quarterly*, vol. 56, no. 2, pp. 174–82.

Jordan, G. (1989) 'Insider Lobbying: The British Version', *Political Studies*, vol. XXXVII, no. 1, pp. 107–13.

Jordan, G. (1990a) 'The Pluralism of Pluralism: An anti theory?', *Political Studies*, vol. 38, no. 2, pp. 286–301.

Jordan, G. (1990b) 'Policy Community Realism versus 'New' Institutionalist Ambiguity', *Political Studies*, vol. 38, no. 3, pp. 470–82.

Jordan, G. (1990c) 'Sub-Governments, Policy Communities and Networks: Refilling the old bottles', *Journal of Theoretical Politics*, vol. 2, no. 3, pp. 319–38.

Jordan, G. (ed.) (1991a) *The Commercial Lobbyists*, Aberdeen, Aberdeen University Press.

Jordan, G. (1991b) 'The Professional Persuaders', in Jordan, G. (ed.), *The Commercial Lobbyists*, Aberdeen, Aberdeen University Press.

Jordan, G. *et al.* (1992) 'Assumptions About the Role of Groups in the Policy Process: The British Policy Community Approach', *British Interest Group Project*, December.

Jordan, G. (1998) 'Towards regulation in the UK: from 'general good sense' to 'formalised rules'', *Parliamentary Affairs*, vol. 51, no. 4, pp. 524–37.

Jordan, G. and Moloney, K. (1993) 'Why are Lobbyists Successful: God, Background or Training', LSE Symposium, March 1993 (unpublished).

Jordan, G. and Maloney, W. (1997) 'Accounting for Subgovernments: Explaining the Persistence of Policy Communities', *Administration and Society*, vol. 29, no. 5, pp. 557–83.

Jordan, G., Maloney, W. and McLaughlin, A. (1992a) 'Assumptions about the role of groups in the policy process: The British policy community approach', *British Interest Group Project*, working paper series 4, Aberdeen, University of Aberdeen.

Jordan, G., Maloney, W. and McLaughlin, A. (1992b) 'Insiders, Outsiders and Political Access?', *British Interest Group Project*, Working Paper Series 3, Aberdeen, University of Aberdeen.

Jordan, G. and Richardson, J. (1979) *Governing Under Pressure: The Policy Process in a Post-Parliamentary Democracy*, Oxford, Basil Blackwell.

Jordan, G. and Richardson, J. (1982) 'The British Policy Style or the Logic of Negotiation?' in Richardson, J. (ed.), *Policy Styles in Western Europe*, London, George Allen & Unwin.

Jordan, G. and Richardson, J. (1987a) *British Politics and the Policy Process: An Arena Approach*, London, Unwin Hyman.

Jordan, G. and Richardson, J. (1987b) *Government and Pressure Groups in Britain*, Oxford, Oxford University Press.

Judge, D. (1990) *Parliament and Industry*, Aldershot, Dartmouth.

Judge, D. (1992a) 'The "effectiveness" of the post-1979 select committee system – the verdict of the 1990 procedure committee', *Political Quarterly*, vol. 63, no. 1, pp. 91–100.

Judge, D. (1992b) 'Parliament and Industry: Bridging the Gap', *Parliamentary Affairs*, vol. 45, no. 1, pp. 52–65.

Judge, D. (1993) *The Parliamentary State*, London, Sage.

Judgment of the European Court (16 December 1992) Cases C-306/88 Rochdale *Borough Council* v. *Anders*; C-304/90 *Reading Borough Council* v. *Payless DIY and others*; C-169/91 *Stoke-on-Trent and Norwich City Councils* v. *B&Q*. *Times European Law Report*, 17 December 1992.

Kassim, H. (1995) 'Policy Networks, Networks and European Policy Making: A Sceptical View', *West European Politics*, vol. 17, no. 4, pp. 15–27.

Kavanagh, D. (1992) 'Changes in the political class and its culture', *Parliamentary Affairs*, vol. 45, no. 1, pp. 18–33.

Kavanagh, D. (1995) *Election Campaigning – the New Marketing of Politics*, Oxford, Basil Blackwell.

Kay, J. and Morris, C. (1984) *Effects of Sunday Trading: The Regulation of Retail Trading Hours*, London, Institute for Fiscal Studies, Report 13.

Kay, W. (1995) 'A Word in Your Ear Minister', *Marketing Business*, May.

Keatinge, R. (1995) 'Limited Liability Partnerships: The Next Step in the Evolution of the Unincorporated Business Organisation', *The Business Lawyer*, vol. 15, p. 147.

Keefe, W. (1988) *Congress and the American People*, 3rd edn, Englewood Cliffs, NJ, Prentice-Hall.

Key, V. (1964) *Politics, Parties and Pressure Groups*, New York, Crowell.

Kingdon, J. (1995) *Agendas, Alternatives and Public Policies*, New York, HarperCollins.

Knoke, D. (1990) *Organizing for Collective Action: The Political Economies of Associations*, Hawthorne, Aldine de Gruyter.

Kohler-Koch, B. (1997) 'Organised Interests in the EC and European Parliament', Paper presented for the colloquium *Pluralisme, Lobbyisme et Construction Européenne*, 20–2 March, Brussels.

Kollman, K. (1997) 'Inviting friends to lobby: interest groups, ideological bias, and Congressional committees', *American Journal of Political Science*, vol. 41, no. 2, pp. 519–44.

Kollman, K. (1998) *Outside Lobbying: Public Opinion and Interest Group Strategies*, Princeton, NJ, Princeton University Press.

Kooiman, J. (1993) 'Social-political governance: introduction', in Kooiman, J. (ed.), *Modern Governance*, London, Sage.

Krasner, S. (1978) *Defending the National Interest*, Princeton, NJ, Princeton University Press.

Krasner, S. (1984) 'Approaches to the State: Alternative Conceptions and Historical Dynamics', *Comparative Politics*, vol. 16, no. 2, pp. 223–46.

KSSC (1987a) *The Fight for Scotland's Sunday*, Cambridge, Jubilee Centre Publications.

KSSC (1987b) *Why Keep Sunday Special – Summary of Case*, Cambridge, Jubilee Centre Publications (a paper stating the arguments against total deregulation).

KSSC (1987c) *Consensus on New Sunday Principle*, Cambridge, Jubilee Centre Publications.

KSSC (1987, 1990, 1991, 1993) *Campaign Update*, November.

KSSC (1988) *The REST Proposals: How to Bring Sense and Consistency to the Law on Sunday Trading*, Cambridge, Jubilee Centre Publications.

KSSC (1989) *Keep Sunday Special Appeal to Attorney General for Action*, Cambridge, Jubilee Centre Publications, 8 December.

KSSC (nd), Flyers on Sunday Trading, Cambridge, Jubilee Centre Publications.

KSSC (nd), *The Case for Maintaining Certain Restrictions on Sunday Trading*, Cambridge, Jubilee Centre Publications.

KSSC (nd), *The REST Proposals*, Cambridge, Jubilee Centre Publications.

KSSC and Keep Sunday Coalition (1987) *Sunday Trading: How to Tidy up the Law*, Cambridge, Jubilee Centre Publications.

Labour Party (1990) *Moving Britain into the 1990s: Labour's New Programme for Transport*, London, Labour Party.

Lang, R. (1989) *Scotland's Sunday Under Pressure: A Survey of the Extent and Growth of Sunday Trading in Scotland 1977–1988*, Cambridge, Jubilee Centre Publications.

Langbein, L. (1993) 'PACs, Lobbies, and Political Conflict: The Case of Gun Control', *Public Choice*, vol. 75, no. 3, pp. 254–71.

Langbein, L. and Lotwis, M. (1990) 'The Political Efficacy of Lobbying and Money: Gun Control in the US House, 1986', *Legislative Studies Quarterly*, vol. 15, no. 3, pp. 413–40.

Larkson, R. (1997) 'Corporate lobbying of the International Accounting Standards Committee', *Journal of International Financial Management and Accounting*, vol. 8, no. 3, pp. 175–203.

Latham, E. (1952) 'The Group Basis of Politics: Notes for a Theory', *American Political Science Review*, vol. 46, no. 2, pp. 376–97.

Latham, M. (1994) *Constructing the Team*, London, Department of the Environment, July.

Laumann, E. and Knoke, D. (1987) *The Organisational State*, Wisconsin, University of Wisconsin Press.

Law Commission (1993) *Contributory Negligence as a Defence in Contract*, London, HMSO.

Law Society (1996) *Joint and Several Liability: A Report by the Law Society's Special Committee*, London, Law Society.

Law Society (1997) *Limited Liability Partnership: Response by the Law Society to the Department of Trade and Industry's Consultation Paper*, London, Law Society.

Law Society Special Committee, *Joint and Several Liability*, London, Law Society.

LDDC (1986) *Canary Wharf Regional Impact Study*, London, LDDC.

LDDC (1997) *Starting from Scratch: The Development of Transport in London Docklands*, London, LDDC.

LDDC, *Annual Reports*, London, LDDC.

Leech, B. and Baumgartner, F. (1998) *Lobbying Friends and Foes in Washington*, paper funded by the National Science Foundation Doctoral Enhancement Grant.

Leigh, D. and Vulliamy, E. (1997) *Sleaze: The Corruption of Parliament*, London, Fourth Estate.

Lindblom, C. (1959) 'The Science of Muddling Through', *Public Administration Review*, vol. 19, no. 2, pp. 79–89.

Lindblom, C. (1977) *Politics and Markets*, New York, Basic Books.

Lindblom, C. (1982) 'Another State of Mind', *American Political Science Review*, vol. 76, no. 1, pp. 9–21.

Lindblom, C. (1984) 'Comment on Vogel', in Bock, B. (ed.), *The Impact of the Modern Corporation*, New York, Columbia University Press.

Linsell, R. (1997) 'Wither the LLP Movement? Advantages of using Jersey Limited Liability Partnership until Government Enacts UK proposals, despite Inland Revenue's view that Jersey LLP in corporation', *Accountancy*, vol. 120, pp. 76–7.

Local Government Review (1988) 'Open House for Sunday Shopping', 10 December. London, Association of County Councils.

Lombardi, M. and Swan, M. (1997) 'Pioneers of Partnership Law: Jersey's LLP Law and DTI Consultative Proposals for Similar Provisions', *The Lawyer*, vol. 112, p. 18.

London Economics (1993) *The Economic Impact of Alternative Sunday Trading Regulations*, London, London Economics.

London Economics (1998) *The Economics of Audit Liability: A Report for the International Federation of Accountants*, London, London Economics.

Loughlin, M. (1992) *Public Law and Political Theory*, Oxford, Clarendon Press.

Loughlin, M. (1996) 'Understanding Central–Local Government Relations', *Public Policy and Administration*, vol. 11, no. 2, pp. 48–65.

Lowery, D. and Gray, V. (1997) 'How some rules just don't matter: the regulation of lobbyists', *Public Choice*, vol. 91, no. 2, pp. 139–47.

Lowery, D. and Gray, V. (1998) 'The dominance of institutions in interest representation: a test of seven explanations', *American Journal of Political Science*, vol. 42, no. 1, pp. 231–55.

Lowi, T. (1964) 'American business, public policy, case studies and political theory', *World Politics*, vol. 16, pp. 677–715.

Lowi, T. (1969) *The End of Liberalism*, New York, Norton.

Lowi, T. (1971) *The Politics of Disorder*, New York, Basic Books.

Lowi, T. (1972) 'Four systems of policy, politics and choice', *Public Administration Review*, vol. 32, no. 4, pp. 298–310.

Lowi, T. (1988) 'The Return to the State: A Critique', *American Political Science Review*, vol. 82, no. 3, pp. 875–901.

LRT, LDDC, BR, Network South East (1988) *Docklands Public Transport Strategic Plan: Discussion Document*, London, LT.

LT (1987) *London Docklands Public Transport Access Study*, London, LT.

LT (1993) 'Cost Effectiveness Review: Responses to Government's 23 Points', August.

LT Planning (1993) *Comments on the Proposal for an Integrated Rail Link for London*, London, LT.

Maass, A. (1951) *Muddy Waters: Army Engineers and the Nation's Rivers*, Cambridge, MA, Harvard University Press.

Mackenzie, W. (1955) 'Pressure groups in British Government', *The British Journal of Sociology*, vol. 6, no. 2, pp. 133–48.

Magleby, D. and Nelson, C. (1990) *The Money Chase: Congressional Finance Reform*, Washington, DC, Brookings Institute.

Magleby, D. and Patterson, K. (1998) 'Consultants and Direct Democracy', *Political Studies and Politics*, vol. XXXI, no. 2, pp. 160–9.

Majone, G. (1989) *Evidence, Argument, and Persuasion in the Policy Process*, New Haven, CT, Yale University Press.

Malbin, M. (1984) 'Looking Back at the Future of Campaign Finance Reform: Interest Groups and American Election', in Malbin, M. (ed.), *Money and Politics in the United States*, Chatham, NJ, Chatham House.

Mancuso, M. (1993) 'The Ethical Attitudes of British MPs: A Typology', *Parliamentary Affairs*, vol. 46, no. 2, pp. 179–91.

Mancuso, M. (1995) *The Ethical World of British MPs*, London, McGill-Queen's University Press.

Manley, J. (1983) 'Neo-Pluralism: A Class Analysis of Pluralism I and Pluralism II', *American Political Science Review*, vol. 77, no. 2, pp. 368–89.

March, J. and Olsen, J. (1984) 'The New Institutionalism: Organizational Forces in Political Life', *American Political Science Review*, vol. 78, no. 3, pp. 734–49.

March, J. and Olsen, J. (1989) *Rediscovering Institutions: The Organisational Basis of Politics*, New York, Free Press.

March, J. and Olsen, J. (1996) 'Institutional Perspectives on Political Institutions', *Governance*, vol. 9, no. 3, pp. 247–64.

Marsh, D. (1983) *Pressure Politics*, London, Junction Books.

Marsh, D. (1995a) 'The Convergence between Theories of the State', in Marsh, D. and Stoker, G. (eds), *Theory and Methods in Political Science*, London, Macmillan – now Palgrave, pp. 268–87.

Marsh, D. (1995b) 'State Theory and the Policy Network Model', *Strathclyde Papers on Politics*, no. 102, Strathclyde, Strathclyde University.

Marsh, D. (1998) *Comparing Policy Networks*, Philadelphia, PA, Open University Press.

Marsh, D. and Grant, W. (1977) 'Tripartism: Reality or Myth', *Government and Opposition*, vol. 12, no. 2, pp. 194–211.

Marsh, D. and Rhodes, R. (1992) *Policy Networks in British Government*, Oxford, Clarendon Press.

Marsh, I. (1986) *Policy Making in a Three Party System: Committees, Coalitions and Parliament*, London, Methuen.

Mazey, S. and Richardson, J. (1992) 'British Pressure Groups in the European Community: The Challenge of Brussels', *Parliamentary Affairs*, vol. 45, no. 1, pp. 92–108.

McCarty, N. and Rothenberg, L. (1996) 'Commitment and the campaign contribution contract', *American Journal of Political Science*, vol. 40, no. 3, pp. 872–904.

McConnell, G. (1966) *Private Power and American Democracy*, New York, Alfred A. Knopf.

McFarland, A. (1987) 'Interest Groups and Theories of Power in America', *British Journal of Political Science*, vol. 17, pp. 129–47.

McFarland, A. (1991) 'Interest Groups and Political Time: Cycles in America', *British Journal of Political Science*, vol. 21, pp. 257–84.

McFarland, A. (1993) *Co-operative Pluralism*, Lawrence, KS, University Press of Kansas.

McLean, D. (1995) 'Auditors' Liability: all they want is a level playing field', *Accountancy*, May, p. 83.

McLeod, R. (1998) 'Calf exports at Brightlingsea', *Parliamentary Affairs*, vol. 51, no. 3, pp. 345–57.

Medvic, S. (1998) 'The Effectiveness of the Political Consultant as a Campaign Resource', *Political Studies and Politics*, vol. XXXI, no. 2, pp. 150–5.

Medvic, S. and Lenart, S. (1997) 'The Influence of Political Consultants in the 1992 Congressional Elections', *Legislative Studies Quarterly*, vol. 22, pp. 61–77.

Merin, M. and Schon, D. (1991) 'Frame-Reflective Policy Discourse', in Wagner, P., Weiss, C., Wittrock, B. and Wollman, H. (eds), *Social Sciences, Modern States, National Experiences and Theoretical CrossRoads*, Cambridge, Cambridge University Press.

Merino, B. and Kenny, S. (1994) 'Auditor Liability and Culpability in the Savings and Loan Industry', *Critical Perspectives on Accounting*, vol. 5, pp. 179–93.

Middlemas, K. (1986) *Power, Competition and the State. vol. 1. Britain in Search of a Balance*, London, Macmillan – now Palgrave.

Middlemas, K. (1990) *Power, Competition and the State. vol. 2. Threats to the Post-War Settlement: Britain 1961–1974*, London, Macmillan – now Palgrave.

Middlemas, K. (1991) *Power, Competition and the State. vol. 3. The End of the Post-War Era: Britain since 1974*, London, Macmillan – now Palgrave.

Milbrath, L. (1963) *The Washington Lobbyists*, Chicago, IL, Rand McNally.

Miller, C. (1985) 'The Phenomenon of Lobbying', *Catalyst*, vol. 1, no. 4, pp. 87–96.

Miller, C. (1987) *Lobbying Government: Understanding and Influencing the Corridors of Power*, Oxford, Basil Blackwell.

Miller, C. (1988) 'Lobbying: New Trends in the UK', *Contemporary Record*, London, Institute of Contemporary British History.

Miller, C. (1991) 'Lobbying: The Development of the Consultation Culture', in Jordan, G. (ed.), *The Commercial Lobbyists*, Aberdeen, Aberdeen University Press.

Miller, C. (1997) 'Lobbying – The Key Principles', Hawksmere Conference, 8 December.

Mills, C. (1993) 'CN Special Report: Lobbying', *Association of County Councils* 14 May.

Minors, M. and Grenham, D. (1990) *London Borough Elections May 1990*, London, London Research Centre.

Mitchell, A. (1986a) 'A House Buyer's Bill – How Not to Pass a Private Member's Bill', *Parliamentary Affairs*, vol. 39, no. 1, pp. 1–18.

Mitchell, A. (1996a) 'Consumers Need Protection From 'Selfish' Audit Profession', *Accountancy Age*, 6 June 1996.

Mitchell, A. (1996b) 'Exposing the Real Motives of the ICA Liability Campaign', *Accountancy Age*, 22 August 1996.

Mitchell, A. (1997) 'Consuming interest', *Parliamentary Review*, January, p. 64.

Mitchell, A., Puxty, T., Sikka, P. and Willmott, H. (1991) *Accounting for Change: Proposals for Reform of Audit and Accounting*, Discussion Paper 7, London, Fabian Society.

Mitchell, A., Puxty, A., Sikka, P. and Willmott, H. (1994a) *The Auditor Liability Charade*, Colchester, Essex University, Association for Accountancy and Business Affairs.

Mitchell, A., Puxty, T., Sikka, P. and Willmott, H. (1994b) 'Ethical Statements as Smokescreens for Sectional Interests: the case of the UK accountancy profession', *Journal of Business Ethics*, vol. 13, no. 1, pp. 39–51.

Mitchell, A. and Sikka, P. (1996) *Corporate Governance Matters*, Discussion Paper 24, London, Fabian Society.

Mitchell, A. and Sikka, P. (1999) 'Jersey: Auditors' Liabilities versus People's Rights', *Political Quarterly*, 1999, vol. 70, no. 1, pp. 3–15.

Mitchie, D. (1998) *The Invisible Persuaders*, London, Bantam Press.

Moloney, K. (1996) *Lobbyists for Hire*, Aldershot, Dartmouth.

Monopoly and Mergers Commission (1991) *London Underground Limited*, London.

Moore, Peter (1991) *A Market in Influence? A Study of Personnel, Clientele, Methodology and Effectiveness in a Leading UK Government Relations Consultancy*, Middlesex, Brunel University.

MORI (April 1993) *Sunday Shopping Behaviour: Research Study Conducted for Shopping Hours Reform Council*, London, MORI.

Morris, P. and Stevenson, J. (1996) 'Auditors, Negligence and Incorporation', *Business Law Review*, vol. 17, p. 54.

Morris, P. and Stevenson, J. (1997) 'The Jersey Limited Liability Partnership: A New Vehicle for Professional Practice', *Modern Law Review*, vol. 60, no. 4 pp. 538–51.

Mortimer, R. (1995) 'Public Perceptions of Sleaze in Britain', *Parliamentary Affairs*, vol. 48, no. 4, October.

Mucciaroni, G. (1995) *Reversals of Fortune: Public Policy and Private Interests*, Washington, DC, Brookings Institute.

Nash, M. (1984) 'The Law of Sunday Markets', *New Law Journal*, vol. 134, no. 6178, pp. 1019–22.

National Audit Office (1992) *Case Studies as a Method of Evidence Collection and Analysis*, London, National Audit Office.

National Audit Office (1993/94) *Pergau hydro-electric project*, report by the Comptroller & Auditor General 1992/93, HC 908; Public Accounts Committee, *Overseas Development Administration – Pergau hydro-electric project*, 17th Report, HC 155.

National Audit Office (nd), *A Framework for Value for Money Audits*, London, National Audit Office.

National Audit Office (nd), *Designing and Carrying Out a Survey*, London, National Audit Office.

Neustadt, R. (1963) 'Testimony, United States Senate, Committee on Government Operations, Subcommittee on National Security', *Administration of National Security*, 26 March, pp. 82–3 in Allison (1969).

Neustadt, R. (1964) *Presidential Power*, New York, John Wiley & Sons Inc.

Neustadt, R. (1970) *Alliance Politics*, New York, Columbia University.

Neustadtl, A. (1990) 'Interest-Group PACmanship: An Analysis of Campaign Contributions, Issue Visibility and Legislative Impact', *Social Forces*, vol. 69, no. 1, pp. 549–64.

Newchurch & Co (1994) *The Newchurch Guide to Private Finance*, London, Newchurch & Co.

Nordlinger, E. (1981) *On the Autonomy of the Democratic State*, Cambridge, MA, Harvard University Press.

Nordlinger, E. (1987) 'Taking the State Seriously', in Weinder, M. and Huntingdon, S. (eds), *Understanding Political Developments*, Boston, MA, Little, Brown.

Nordlinger, E. (1988) 'The Return to the State: Critiques', *American Political Science Review*, vol. 82, no. 3, pp. 875–85.

Norris, S. (1996) *An Autobiography: Changing Trains*, London, Random House.

Norton, P. (ed.) (1985) *Parliament in the 1980s*, Oxford, Basil Blackwell.

Norton, P. (1991) *New Directions in British Politics*, Aldershot, Edward Elgar.

Notes on the London Economy and Employment Seminar, held on 11 June 1996, organised by London Transport Planning in association with the Government Office for London.

O&Y (1988) *Proposal for Second Rail Line to Docklands*, London, O&Y.

O&Y briefing note to Westminster Council (1992) *Reasons for Proceeding Immediately with the Construction of the Jubilee Extension*, London, O&Y.

O'Leary, B. (1987) 'Why was the GLC abolished?', *International Journal of Urban and Regional Research*, vol. 11, no. 2, pp. 193–217.

O'Shaughnessy, N. (1988) 'High Priesthood, Low Priestcraft: The Role of Political Consultants', *European Journal of Marketing*, vol. 24, no. 2, pp. 7–23.

Oliver, D. (1995) 'The Committee on Standards in Public Life: Regulating the Conduct of Members of Parliament', *Parliamentary Affairs*, vol. 48, no. 4, pp. 590–601.

Olson, M. (1971) *The Logic of Collective Action: Public Goods and the Theory of Groups*, Cambridge, MA, Harvard University Press.

Page, E. (1998) *Insiders and Outsiders: An Empirical Examination*, Hull, University of Hull.

Parkinson, C. (1992) *Cecil Parkinson – Right at the Centre: An Autobiography*, London, Weidenfeld & Nicolson.

Parris, M. (1995) *Great Parliamentary Scandals – Four Centuries of Calumny, Smear and Innuendo*, London, Robson Books.

Parsons, W. (1982) 'Politics without promises: the crisis of 'overload' and governability', *Parliamentary Affairs*, vol. 35, no. 4, pp. 421–35.

Parsons, W. (1989) *The Power of the Financial Press: Journalism and Economic Opinion in Britain and America*, Aldershot, Edward Elgar.

Parsons, W. (1996) *Public policy: An Introduction to the Theory and Practice of Policy Analysis*, Aldershot, Edward Elgar.

Peters, B. Guy (1984) *The Politics of Bureaucracy*, 2nd edn, New York, Longman.

Plowden, W. (1994) *Ministers and Mandarins*, London, Institute of Public Policy Research.

Pollitt, C. (1993) *Managerialism and the Public Services*, Oxford, Basil Blackwell.

Pollock, J. (1927) 'Regulation of Lobbying', *American Political Science Review*, vol. 21, pp. 335–41.

Polsby, N. (1963) *Community Power and Political Theory*, London, Yale University Press.

Popper, K. (1959) *The Logic of Scientific Discovery*, London, Hutchinson.

Post, G. (1991) 'Ethics and Lobbying: A Government Perspective', *Canadian Public Administration*, vol. 34, no. 1, pp. 84–9.

Post, J. (1993) 'The Status of US Corporate Public Affairs', *Research in Corporate Social Performance and Policy*, vol. 13, Greenwich, CT, JAI Press.

Powell, C. (1992) 'Jersey as a Business Centre', in Ross, E. (ed.), *The Financial and Business Handbook of the Channel Islands*, 5th edn, Jersey, Ashton & Denton.

Power, M. (1994) *The Audit Explosion*, London, Demos.

Power, M. (1997) 'The Perils of the Audit Society', *LSE Public Service Seminar Series no. 4*, London, LSE.

Power, M. (1998) 'Auditor Liability in Context', *Accounting, Organization and Society*, vol. 23, no. 1, pp. 77–9.

Power, M. (forthcoming), 'Making Things Auditable', *Accounting, Organizations and Society*.

PPU (1987) *The Government Report*, London, September.

PPU (1991a) 'Bid Lobbying: The Complete Guide', London, October.

PPU (1991b) *The Campaign Guide*, London, October.

PRCA and ICO (1997) *How to get real VA£UE from Public Relations*, London, International Committee of Public Relations Consultants Associations.

Pressler, L. and Schieffer, K. (1988) 'Joint and Several Liability: A Case for Reform', *Denver University Law Review*, vol. 64.

Presthus, R. (1974) *Elites in the Policy Process*, Cambridge, Cambridge University Press.

PriceWaterhouse (1990) *Value for Money Auditing*, London, Gee & Co.

Priest, G. (1987) 'The Current Insurance Crisis and Modern Tort Law', *Yale Law Journal*, vol. 96, no. 2, pp. 1521–90.

Pross, P. (1975) *Pressure Group Behaviour in Canadian Politics*, Toronto, McGraw Hill.

Pross, P. (1986) *Group Politics and Public Policy*, Oxford, Oxford University Press.

Pross, P. (1991) 'The Rise of the Lobbying Issue in Canada: "The Business Card Bill"', in Jordan, G. (ed.), *The Commercial Lobbyists*, Aberdeen, Aberdeen University Press.

Pryor, A. (1997) 'Dealing with Whitehall and Westminster', Hawksmere Conference, 8 December.

Public Accounts Select Committee (1993/94) *Pergau Hydro-Electric Project*, Seventeenth Report, Minutes of Evidence on 17 January 1994, HC 155.

Purnell, N. and Armstrong, R. (1998) *Report to the Association of Professional Political Consultants on GJW and GPC*, APPC, London, 29 July.

Puro, M. (1984) 'Audit firm lobbying before the Financial Accounting Standards Board: an empirical study', *Journal of Accounting Research*, vol. 22, no. 2, pp. 624–66.

Pyper, R. (1995) The British Civil Service, London Prentice-Hall/Harvester Wheatsheaf.

Quinlan, M. (1994) 'Changing Patterns in Government Business', *Public Policy and Administration*, vol. 9, no. 1, pp. 27–35.

Quinn, D. and Shapiro, R. (1991) 'Business Political Power: The Case of Taxation', *American Political Science Review*, vol. 85, no. 3, pp. 851–74.

Radice, G. and Pollard, S. (1992) *Southern Discomfort*, London, Fabian Society.

Radice, G. and Pollard, S. (1993) *More Southern Discomfort a year on – Taxing and Spending*, London, Fabian Society.

Radice, G. and Pollard, S. (1994) *Any Southern Comfort*, London, Fabian Society.

Railway Operators (1993) 'CrossRail Financing Review: Cost Effectiveness Study', October, not published.

Ranleagh, J. (1991) *Thatcher's People – An Insider's Account of the Politics, the Power and the Personalities*, London, HarperCollins.

Rauch, J. (1994) *Demosclerosis: The Silent Killer of American Government*, New York, Random House.

Read, M. (1988) 'The Shops Bill 1985', *Essex Papers in Politics and Government*, no. 61 (December).

Rechtman, R. and LarsenLedet, J. (1998) 'Regulation of lobbyists in Scandinavia – a Danish perspective', *Parliamentary Affairs*, vol. 51, no. 4, pp. 579–86.

Regan, P. (1988) 'The 1986 Shops Bill', *Parliamentary Affairs*, vol. 41, no. 2, pp. 218–35.

Regerster, M. (1989) *Crisis Management: How to Turn a Crisis into an Opportunity*, London, Business Books.

Report of the Committee on the Financial Aspects of Corporate Governance (1992), Cadbury Committee, December.

Rhodes, E. (1994) 'Do Bureaucratic Politics matter? Some Discomforting Findings for the US Navy', *World Politics*, vol. 47, pp. 1–41.

Rhodes, R. (1980) 'Analysing Intergovernmental Relations', *European Journal of Political Research*, vol. 8, pp. 289–322.

Rhodes, R. (1985) 'Power Dependence, Policy Communities and Inter-Governmental Networks', *Public Administration Bulletin*, no. 49.

Rhodes, R. (1990) 'Policy Networks: A British Perspective', *Journal of Theoretical Politics*, vol. 2, no. 3, pp. 293–317.

Rhodes, R. (1991) 'Theory and Methods in British Public Administration: the view from political science', *Political Studies*, vol. 39, no. 3, pp. 533–54.

Rhodes, R. (1992a) *Beyond Westminster and Whitehall: The Sub-Central Governments of Britain*, London, Routledge.

Rhodes, R. (1992b) 'New Directions in the Study of Policy Networks', *European Journal of Political Research*, vol. 21, no. 1–2, pp. 181–205.

Rhodes, R. (1994a) 'The hollowing out of the state', *Political Quarterly*, vol. 65, no. 2, pp. 138–51.

Rhodes, R. (1994b) 'State-Building without a Bureaucracy: the case of the United Kingdom', in Budge, I. and McKay, D., *Developing Democracy*, London, Sage.

Rhodes, R. (1995a) 'The Institutional Approach', in Marsh, D. and Stoker, G. (eds), *Theory and Methods in Political Science*, London, Macmillan – now Palgrave.

Rhodes, R. (1995b) 'The Study of Political Institutions', in Stoker, G. and Marsh, D. (eds), *Theories and Methods in Political Science*, London, Macmillan – now Palgrave.

Rhodes, R. (1996a) 'From institutions to dogma: tradition, eclecticism and ideology in the study of British public administration', *Public Administration Review*, vol. 55, pp. 1–11.

Rhodes, R. (1996b) 'The new governance: governing without government', *Political Studies*, vol. 44, no. 4, pp. 652–67.

Rhodes, R. (1997) *Understanding Governance: Policy Networks, Governance, Reflexivity and Accountability*, Buckingham, Open University Press.

Rhodes, R. and Dunleavy, P. (eds) (1995) *Prime Minister, Cabinet and Core Executive*, London, Macmillan – now Palgrave.

Rhodes, R. and Marsh, D. (1992a) 'New directions in the study of policy networks', *European Journal of Political Research*, vol. 21, no. 1, pp. 181–205.

Rhodes, R. and Marsh, D. (1992b) 'Policy Networks in British Politics: A critique of existing approaches', in Marsh, D. and Rhodes, R. (eds), *Policy Networks in British Government*, Oxford, Clarendon Press.

Richardson, J. and Jordan, G. (1979) *Governing Under Pressure*, Oxford, Martin Robertson.

Richardson, J. and Kimber, R., 'Lobbying and Administrative Reform and Policy Styles. The Case of Land Drainage', *Political Studies*, vol. XXVI, no. 1, pp. 47–64.

Ridley, F. and Doig, A. (1995) *Sleaze: Politicians' Private Interests and Public Reactions*, Oxford, Oxford University Press.

Roger Tym & Partners and Drivers Jonas (1981) *Docklands Rail Study: Assessment of Development Impact*, London, Drivers Jonas.

Rogers, B. (1994) *An Apolitical Policy Process? Divergence Between the Theory and Practice of Policy-Making in British Politics – A Case Study*, Middlesex, Brunel University.

Ronit, K. and Schneider, V. (1998) 'The strange case of regulating lobbying in Germany', *Parliamentary Affairs*, vol. 51, no. 4, pp. 559–67.

Rose, R. (1974) *Politics in England Today*, London, Faber & Faber.

Rose, R. (1993) *Lesson-Drawing in Public Policy*, Chatham NJ, Chatham House.

Roth, A. (1988) *Parliamentary profiles [A–D], [E–K] (1990) [L–R] and [S–Z]*, 2nd edn, London, Parliamentary Profiles.

Rothenberg, L. (1992) *Linking Citizens to Government: Interest Group Politics at Common Cause*, New York, Cambridge University Press.

Rush, M. (1990a) 'Lobbying Parliament', *Parliamentary Affairs*, vol. 43, no. 2, pp. 141–8.

Rush, M. (1990b) *Parliament and Pressure Groups*, Oxford, Clarendon Press.

Rush, M. (1994a) 'Career patterns in British politics: first choose your party…', *Parliamentary Affairs*, vol. 47, no. 4, pp. 566–82.

Rush, M. (1994b) 'Registering the Lobbyists: Lessons from Canada', *Political Studies*, vol. XLII, no. 4, pp. 630–45.

Rush, M. (1998a) 'The Canadian experience: the lobbyists registration act', *Parliamentary Affairs*, vol. 51, no. 4, pp. 516–23.

Rush, M. (1998b) 'One man's word: the untold story of the cash-for-Questions affair' [review], *Parliamentary Affairs*, vol. 51, no. 2, pp. 284–6.

Rydz, D. (1979) *The Parliamentary Agents: A History*, London, London Royal Historical Society.

Ryle, M. (1991) 'Recent Procedural Change in the Commons', *Parliamentary Affairs*, vol. 44, no. 4, pp. 470–80.

Sabatier, P. (1988) 'An Advocacy Coalition Model of Policy Change and the Role of Policy Orientation Therein', *Policy Sciences*, vol. 21, no. 2, pp. 129–68.

Sabatier, P. (1991) 'Towards Better Theories of the Policy Process', *Political Science and Politics*, vol. 24, no. 1, pp. 144–56.

Sabatier, P. and Jenkins-Smith, H. (eds) (1993) *Policy Change and Learning: An Advocacy-Coalition Approach*, Boulder, CO, Westview.

Sabato, L. (1985) *PAC Power: Inside the World of Political Action Committees*, New York, W.W. Norton.

Sabato, L. (1989a) 'PACs and Parties', in Nugent, M. and Johannes, J. (eds), *Money, Elections and Democracy*, Boulder, CO, Westview Press.

Sabato, L. (1989b) *Paying for Elections: The Campaign Finance Thicket*, New York, Priority Press.

Sabato, L. (1990) *PAC Power: Inside the World of Political Action Committees*, 3rd edn, New York, W.W. Norton.

Saint-Martin, D. (1998) 'The New Managerialism and the Policy Influence of Consultants in Government: An Historical-Institutionalist analysis of Britain, Canada and France', *Governance*, vol. 11, no. 3, pp. 319–56.

Salamon, L. and Siegfried, J. (1977) 'Economic Power and Political Influence: The Impact of Industry Structure on Public Policy', *American Political Science Review*, vol. 71, no. 3, pp. 1026–43.

Salisbury, R. (1975) 'Interest Groups', in Greenstein, F. and Polsby, N. (eds), *Handbook of Political Science in Non-Governmental Politics*, vol. 4, Reading, MA, Addison-Wesley, pp. 171–228.

Salisbury, R. (1983) 'Interest Groups: Towards a New Understanding', in Ciglar, A. and Loomis, B., *Interest Groups*, Washington, DC, Congressional Quarterly Press.

Salisbury, R. (1984) 'Interest Representation: The Dominance of Institutions', *American Political Science Review*, vol. 78, no. 1, pp. 64–76.

Salisbury, R. (1990) 'The Paradox of Interests in Washington DC: More Groups Less Clout', in King, A. (ed.), *The New American Political System*, Washington, DC, American Enterprise Institute.

Salisbury, R. (1994) 'Interest Structures and Policy Domains: A Focus for Research', in Crotty, W., Schwartz, M. and Green, J. (eds), *Interests and Interest Group Representation*, Washington, DC, University Press of America.

Salisbury, R. and Heinz, J. (1970) 'A Theory of Policy Analysis and Some Preliminary Applications', in Sharkansky, I. (ed.), *Policy Analysis in Political Science*, Chicago, IL, Markham.

Salisbury, R., Heinz, J., Laumann, E. and Nelson, R. (1987) 'Who works with whom? Interest group alliances and opposition', *American Political Science Review*, vol. 81, no. 4, pp. 1217–34.

Schattschneider, E. (1935a) *Politics, Pressures, and the Tariff*, New York, Atherton.

Schattschneider, E. (1935b) *The Semi-Sovereign People*, New York, Holt, Rinehart & Winston.

Schattschneider, E. (1942) *Party Government*, New York, Rinehart.

Schlozman, K. (1984) 'What Accent the Heavenly Chorus? Political Equality and the American Pressure System?', *The Journal of Politics*, vol. 46, no. 4, pp. 1006–32.

Schlozman, K. and Tierney, J. (1983) 'More of the Same: Washington Pressure Group Activity in a Decade of Change', *Journal of Politics*, vol. 45, no. 2, pp. 351–77.

Schlozman, K. and Tierney, J. (1984) 'What Accent the Heavenly Chorus? Political Equality and the American Pressure System', *Journal of Politics*, vol. 46, no. 4, pp. 1006–32.

Schlozman, K. and Tierney, J. (1986) *Organised Interests and American Democracy*, New York, Harper & Row.

Schluter, M. (1986) *Family Roots or Mobility*, Cambridge, Jubilee Centre Publications.

Schluter, M. and Lee, D. (1988) *Keeping Sunday Special – The Fight Against the Shops Bill*, London, Marshall Pickering.

Schroedel, J. (1986) 'Campaign Contributions and Legislative Outcomes', *The Western Political Quarterly*, vol. 39, no. 3, pp. 371–90.

Scott, A. and Hunt, M. (1965) *Congress and Lobbies: Image and Reality*, Chapel Hill, NC, University of Carolina Press.

Scott Wilson Kirkpatrick (1992) 'CrossRail: Audit of Estimated Cost', Final Report, Volume 1, October.

Scottish Law Commission, 'Report on Civil Liability – Contribution', SLC no. 115.

Scottish Law Commission, 'Report on Prescription and Limitation of Actions (Latent Damage and other Related Issues)', SLC no. 122.

Searing, D. (1991) 'Roles, Rules and Rationality in the New Institutionalism', *American Political Science Review*, vol. 85, pp. 1239–60.

Searing, D. (1993) 'Backbench and Leadership roles in the House of Commons', *Parliamentary Affairs*, vol. 48, no. 3, pp. 419–39.

Select Committee on Members' Interests: *Parliamentary Lobbying, Minutes of Evidence and Appendices* (1984–85 Session, HC408); (1987–88 Session, HC518); (1988–89 Session, HC44); (1989–90 Session, HC135); (1990–91 Session, HC586).

Select Committee on Standards in Public Life, *First Report* (together with Minutes of Proceedings and Memoranda) Session 1994–95 (637 and 816).

SG Warburg (May 1993) *CrossRail: A Joint Venture. Report on Re-examination.*

Shafer, P. (1994) *Adding Value to the Public Affairs Function – Using Quality to Improve Performance*, Washington, DC, Public Affairs Council.

Shaiko, R. (1998) 'Reverse Lobbying', in Cigler, A. and Loomis, B., *Interest Group Politics*, 5th edn, Washington, DC, Congressional Quarterly Press.

Shechter, Y. (1998) 'Interests, Strategies and Institutions: Lobbying in the Pharmaceutical Industry of the European Union', PhD Dissertation, December, London, LSE.

Shell, D. (1991) 'The British Constitution in 1990', *Parliamentary Affairs*, pp. 265–81.

SHRC Briefing Notes. *Sunday Trading the Story so Far; Sunday Trading the Options; Consumer Attitudes and Consumer Behaviour; The SHRC Options and Statutory Protection for Shop Workers; Shops and Shoppers; Sunday Trading the Bull Points; Some of the Effects of the Powell Bill; The Powell Bill 'Puzzling and Theme-less' A Legal Opinion.*

SHRC (1988) *Making Sense of Sunday*, London, SHRC.

SHRC (1991) *Shopping Hours – Putting the Record Straight*, London, SHRC.

SHRC (1994) *Sunday Trading Bill – Options Debate Briefings*, London, SHRC.

SHRC (nd), *The Case for Change*, London, SHRC.

SHRC (nd), *Scotland's Sunday Safe*, London, SHRC.

SHRC (nd), *Sunday Trading in Scotland: The TESCO Experience*, London, SHRC.

SHRC/SOS, *Time For Change: The Sunday Shopping Action Pack*, London, SHRC.

Sikka, P. (1992) 'Audit Policy-Making in the UK: the case of the auditors' considerations in respect of going concerns', *European Accounting Review*, December, vol. 1, pp. 349–92.

Sikka, P. (1996) 'Secrecy is the Aim of Those who want Limited Liability in Jersey', *Accountancy Age*, 5 September 1996.

Sikka, P. (1997) 'Regulating the UK Auditing Profession', in Sherer, A. and Turley, S. (eds), *Current Issues In Auditing*, London, Paul Chapman.

Sikka, P. (1998) *A Comment on Limited Liability Partnerships (Insolvent Partnerships) (Jersey) Regulations*, working paper.

Sikka, P. and Willmott, H., 'Illuminating the State-Profession Relationship: Accountants acting as Department of Trade and Industry Investigators', *Critical Perspectives of Accounting*, vol. 6, no. 4, pp. 341–69.

Singleton-Green, B. (1990) 'Limiting Auditors' Liability', *Accountancy*, July, pp. 97–8.

Skocpol, T. (1979) *States and Social Revolutions*, Cambridge, Cambridge University Press.

Skocpol, T. (1980) 'Political Response to Capitalist Crisis: Neo-Marxist Theories of the State and the Case of the New Deal', *Politics & Society*, vol. 10, no. 2, pp. 155–201.

Skocpol, T. (1982) 'Bringing the State Back In', *Items*, vol. 36, New York, Social Science Research Council in Almond (1988).

Skocpol, T. (1985) 'Bringing the State Back In: Strategies of Analysis in Current Research', in Evans, P., Rueschemeyer, D. and Skocpol, T., *Bringing the State Back In*, New York, Cambridge University Press.

Skocpol, T., Abend-Wein, M., Howard, C. and Goodrich-Lehmann, S. (1993) 'Women's Associations and the Enactment of Mothers' Pensions in the United States', *American Political Science Review*, vol. 87, no. 3, pp. 686–701.

Smith, H. (1988) *The Power Game: How Washington Works*, New York, Random House.

Smith, M. (1986) 'The Lobbyist's Business', *Government and Industry*, Harlow, Longman.

Smith, M. (1990) 'Pluralism, Reformed Pluralism and Neo-Pluralism: the Role of Pressure Groups in Policy-Making', *Political Studies*, vol. 38, no. 2, pp. 302–22.

Smith, M. (1991a) 'The Agricultural Policy Community: The rise and fall of a closed relationship', in Marsh, D. and Rhodes, R. (eds), *Policy Networks in British Government*, Oxford, Clarendon Press.

Smith, M. (1991b) 'From Policy Community to Issue Network: Salmonella in eggs and the new politics of food', *Public Administration*, vol. 69, no. 2, pp. 235–55.

Smith, M. (1992) 'The Agricultural Policy Community: Maintaining a Closed Relationship', in Marsh, D. and Rhodes, R. (1992) *Policy Networks in British Government*, Oxford, Clarendon Press.

Smith, M. (1993) *Pressure, Power and Policy: State Autonomy and Policy Networks in Britain and the United States*, Hemel Hempstead, Harvester Wheatsheaf.

Smith, M. (1995a) 'Interpreting the Rise and Fall of Margaret Thatcher: Power Dependence and the Core Executive', in Rhodes, R. and Dunleavy, P. (1995) *Prime Minister, Cabinet and Core Executive*, London, Macmillan – now Palgrave.

Smith, M. (1995b) 'Pluralism', in Marsh, D. and Stoker, G. (eds), *Theories and Methods in Politics*, London, Macmillan – now Palgrave.

Smith, M. (1999) *The Core Executive in Britain*, London, Macmillan – now Palgrave.

Smith, Martin, (1991) 'Issue Advocacy in Parliament: the Case of the National Consumer Council', in Jordan, G. (ed.), *The Commercial Lobbyists*, Aberdeen, Aberdeen University Press.

Smith, R. (1984) 'Advocacy, Interpretation, and Influence in the US Congress', *American Political Science Review*, vol. 78, no. 1, pp. 44–63.

Smith, R. (1988) 'Political Jurisprudence, the 'New Institutionalism,' and the Future of Public Law', *American Political Science Review*, vol. 82, no. 1, pp. 89–108.

Smith, R. (1993) 'Agreement, Defection, and Interest-Group Influence in the US Congress', in Riker, W. (ed.), *Agenda Formation*, Ann Arbor, MI, University of Michigan.

Smith, R. (1995) 'Interest Group Influence in the US Congress', *Legislative Studies Quarterly*, vol. 20, no. 1, pp. 89–139.

Smith, T. (1995) 'Political Sleaze in Britain: Causes, Concerns and Cures', *Parliamentary Affairs*, vol. 48, no. 4, pp. 551–61.

Soden, J. (1994) 'The Frightening Spiral of Litigation', *Accountancy*, November.

Sorauf, F. (1992) *Inside Campaign Finance: Myths and Realities*, New Haven, CT, Yale University Press.

Souza, C. (1998) *So You Want To Be A Lobbyist?*, London, Politicos.

SRU Ltd (nd), *Qualitative Research into the Effects of Sunday Trading in Scotland*, London, SHRC archives.

Stapleton, J. (1991) 'Duty of Care and Economic Loss: A wider agenda', *Law Review Quarterly*, vol. 107 (April), pp. 249–97.

Stapleton, J. (1995a), 'Duty of Care: Peripheral Parties and Alternative Opportunities for Deterrence', *Law Review Quarterly*, vol. 111 (April), pp. 301–45.

Stapleton, J. (1995b) 'Tort, Insurance and Ideology', *Modern Law Review*, vol. 58, no. 6, pp. 820–45.

States of Jersey Policy and Resources Committee (1995) *2000 and Beyond – Strategic Policy Review 1995*, Part 1, States of Jersey.

Steele, A. (1997) *The Economics of Audit Liability*, Coventry, Warwick Business School.

Steer Davies & Gleave (1988) 'Proposals to Extend the Bakerloo Line to Docklands', unpublished, prepared for O&Y.

Steer Davies Gleave (1992) *Tower Hamlets Rail Strategy (An Integrated Rail Link for London)*, August, London, O&Y.

Steer Davies Gleave (nd), 'Isle of Dogs and Leamouth Employment Forecast 1991–2000', in *Transport Supplement*, Canary Wharf, O&Y.

Steinbruner, J. (1974) *The Cybernetic Theory of Decision: New Dimensions of Political Analysis*, Princeton, NJ, Princeton University Press.

Stewart, J. (1958) *British Pressure Groups: Their Role in Relation to the House of Commons*, London, Clarendon Press.

Sunday Shopping Campaign (1993) *Freedom Without a Free-For-All: Queen's Speech Special*, London, SHRC.

Sunday Shopping Campaign (nd), *Campaign Pack*, London, SHRC.

Sunday Shopping Campaign (nd), *Store Manager's Campaign Action Pack*, London, SHRC.

Sunday Shopping Campaign (nd), *Sunday Shopper Newsletter*, London, SHRC.

Sutton, T. (1984) 'Lobbying of Accounting Standard-Setting Bodies in UK and the USA: A Downsian Analysis', *Accounting, Organisations and Society*, vol. 9, no. 1, pp. 81–95.

Swatasky, J. (1987) 'The Insiders: Government, Business and the Lobbyists', Toronto, McClelland & Stewart.

Syvret, R. (1996) 'Jersey – The International Finance Centre', in *The Jersey Financial Services Handbook*, Jersey, Ashton & Denton.

Tandy, P. and Wilburn, N. (1992) 'Constituent Participation in Standard-Setting: the FASB's First 100 Statements', *Accounting Horizons*, vol. 6, pp. 47–58.

Tebbit, N., 'Lobbying – Influencing the Parliamentary Process', *The House Magazine*, 29 November 1985.

Terry, F. (1994) 'Transport Policy – A Review of 1993', in Jackson, P. and Lavender, M., *The Public Services Yearbook 1994*, London, CIPFA, Public Finance Foundation.

Terry, F. (1996) 'The Private Finance Initiative – Overdue Reform or Policy Breakthrough?', *Public Money and Management*, January–March.

Thain, C. and Wright, M. (1995) *The Treasury and Whitehall: The Planning and Control of Public Expenditure, 1976–1993*, Oxford, Clarendon Press.

The Government's Response to the First Report from the Committee on Standards in Public Life, Cm 2931, July 1995, London, HMSO.

The National Association of Sunday Shopworkers Newsletter.

Thomas, C. (1998) 'Interest group regulation across the United States: rationale, development and consequences', *Parliamentary Affairs*, vol. 51, no. 4, pp. 500–15.

Thomson, S., Stancich, L. and Dickson, L. (1998) 'Gun control and Snowdrop', *Parliamentary Affairs*, vol. 51, no. 3, pp. 329–44.

Thurber, J. (1998) 'A Slate of Candidates, a Recession of Economists, an Advice of Consultants', *Political Studies and Politics*, vol. XXXI, no. 2, pp. 145–9.

Tomkins, C. (1987) *Achieving Economy, Efficiency and Effectiveness in the Public Sector*, Edinburgh, Institute of Chartered Accountants in Scotland.

Townsend, C. and Schluter, M. (1985) *Why Keep Sunday Special*, Cambridge, Jubilee Centre Publications.

Townsend, C. and Schluter, M. (1986) *Fight for Scotland's Sunday*, Cambridge, Jubilee Centre Publications.

Transport Select Committee (1988) *LRT fares policy*, HC416.

Transport Select Committee (1997) *London Transport Minutes of Evidence*, 19 February, 327i–ii.

Travers Morgan (1973) *Docklands Redevelopment Proposals for East London*, London, Travers Morgan.

Travers, T. (1994) *London Borough Council Elections May 1994*, London, London Research Centre.

Travers, T. and Glaister, S. (1991) *Transport Options for London*, London, The Greater London Group, LSE.

Travers, T. and Glaister, S. (1993) *Meeting the Transport needs of the City*, London, The City Research Project, Corporation of London.

Treasury (1988a) *A New Planning Total*, Cm 441, London, HMSO.

Treasury (1988b) *Policy Evaluation: A Guide for Managers*, London, HMSO.

Treasury (1988c) *Private Finance in Public Expenditure*, London.

Treasury (1991) *Economic Appraisal in Central Government: A Technical Guide for Government Departments*, London, HMSO.

Treasury (1992) *Private Finance – Guidance for Departments*, press notice, 139/92.

Truman, D. (1951) *The Governmental Process*, New York, Alfred A. Knopf.

Turnor, R. (1996) 'Jersey Stirs Debate on Professional Liability', *The Lawyer*, 3 September.

Turpin, C. (1996) 'Responsibility in Government', *Public Policy and Administration*, vol. 11, no. 2, pp. 35–47.

USDAW, 'The Choice Must be Hours', Report on Shops Legislation.

Vandermark, A. (1994) 'Lobbying and Registration: Biting the Bullet or Shifting the Focus?', *Talking Politics*, vol. 7, no. 1, pp. 34–40.

Vaughan, D., Samuels, J., Barling, G., Davidson, N. and Anderson, D. (nd), *Reforming the Law on Sunday Trading: A Legal Review of the Options for Reform in the Sunday Trading Bill – Second Joint Opinion*, Hepherd, Winstanley and Pugh.

Verdier, D. (1995) 'The Politics of Public Aid to Industry', *Comparative Political Studies*, vol. 28, no. 1, pp. 3–42.

Vogel, D. (1983) 'The Power of Business in America – A Reappraisal', *British Journal of Political Science*, vol. 13, pp. 19–43.

Waldegrave, W., Secrett, C., Bazalgette, P., Gaines, A., Parminter, K. and Riddell, P. (1996) 'Pressure Group Politics in Modern Britain', *The Social Market Foundation*.

Walker, J. (1983) 'The Origins and Maintenance of Interest Groups in America', *American Political Science Review*, vol. 77, no. 2, pp. 390–406.

Walker, J. (1989) 'Policy Communities as Global Phenomena', *Governance*, vol. 2, no. 1, pp. 1–5.

Walker, J. (1991) *Mobilizing Interest Groups in America*, Ann Arbor, MI, University of Michigan Press.

Wallis, J. and Dollery, B. (1997) 'Autonomous Policy Leadership: Steering a Policy Process in the Direction of a Policy Quest', *Governance*, vol. 10, no. 1, pp. 1–22.

Ward, G. (1994) 'Towards a Fairer System for Auditors' Liability', *Accountancy*, April, pp. 80–1.

Ward, G. (1996) 'Time to be Fair to Auditors', *Accountancy*, June, p. 84.

Ward, G. (1997) 'The blame drain', *Parliamentary Review*, January, p. 62.

Warhurst, J. (1987) 'Lobbyists and Policy Making in Canberra', *Current Affairs Bulletin*, vol. 64, no. 3 (August), pp. 13–19.

Warhurst, J. (1990) 'Political Lobbying in Australia', *Corruption and Reform*, vol. 4, pp. 173–87.

Warhurst, J. (1998) 'Locating the target: regulating lobbying in Australia', *Parliamentary Affairs*, vol. 51, no. 4, pp. 538–50.

Washington Representatives 1998, New York, Columbia Books.

Weetman, P., Davie, E. and Collins, W. (1996) 'Lobbying on accounting issues: Preparer/user imbalance in the case of the Operating and Financial Review', *Accounting, Auditing and Accountability Journal*, vol. 9, no. 1, pp. 59–76.

Welch, W. (1982) 'Campaign Contributions and Legislative Voting: Milk Money and Dairy Price Supports', *Western Political Quarterly*, vol. 35, pp. 478–95.

Whelan, C. and McBarnet, D. (1989) 'The "Crisis" in Professional Liability Insurance', *The Geneva Papers on Risk and Insurance*, vol. 14, no. 53, pp. 296–307.

Whiteley, P. and Winyard, S. (1987) *Pressure for the Poor: The Poverty Lobby and Policy Making*, London, Methuen.

Whiteley, P. and Winyard, S. (1988) 'The Poverty Lobby in British Politics', *Parliamentary Affairs*, vol. 41, no. 2, pp. 195–208.

Whittaker, N. (1984) *Sunday Trading – Lessons from Sweden*, London, Woolworth Holdings plc.

Wiggins, C., Hamm, K. and Bell, C. (1992) 'Interest-Group and Party Influence Agents in the Legislative Process: A Comparative State Analysis', *The Journal of Politics*, vol. 54, no. 1, pp. 82–100.

Wildavsky, A. (1964) *The Politics of the Budgetary Process*, Boston, MA, Little, Brown.

Wilks, S. and Wright, M. (1987) *Comparative Government Industry Relations*, Oxford, Clarendon Press.

Williams, S. (1985) *Conflicts of Interest: The Ethical Dilemma in Politics*, Vermont, Gower.

Willis, J. (1987) 'Docklands – Planning the Initial Railway', *Highways and Transportation*, August/September.

Willis, J. (1997) *Extending the Jubilee Line: The Planning Story*, London, LT.

Wilson, D. (1998) 'The need for lobbying', *Public Money and Management*, vol. 18, no. 4, pp. 4–5.

Wilson, D. and Andrews, L. (1993) *Campaigning – the A–Z of Public Advocacy*, London, Hawksmere.

Wilson, G. (1977) *Special Interests and Policy-Making*, London, John Wiley.

Wilson, G. (1981) *Interest Groups in the United States*, Oxford, Clarendon Press.

Wilson, G. (1990) *Interest Groups*, Oxford, Basil Blackwell.

Wilson, G. (1991) 'Contract Lobbying in the USA', in Jordan, G. (ed.), *The Commercial Lobbyists*, Aberdeen, Aberdeen University Press.

Wilson, J. (1973) *Political Organizations*, New York, Basic Books.

Wilson, J. (1980) *The Politics of Regulation*, New York, Basic Books.

Wirl, F. (1994) 'The Dynamics of Lobbying – A Differential Game', *Public Choice*, vol. 80, nos 3–4, pp. 307–24.

Wittingberg, E. and Wittingberg, E. (1989) *How to Win in Washington*, Oxford, Basil Blackwell.

Woodhouse, D. (1998) 'The Parliamentary Commissioner for standards: lessons from the 'cash for questions' inquiry', *Parliamentary Affairs*, vol. 51, no. 1, pp. 51–61.

Wooton, G. (1970) *Interest Groups*, Englewood Cliffs, NJ, Prentice-Hall.

Wright, J. (1985) 'PACs, Contributions and Roll Calls: An Organizational Perspective', *American Political Science Review*, vol. 79, no. 2, pp. 400–14.

Wright, J. (1989) 'PAC Contributions, Lobbying and Representation', *Journal of Politics*, vol. 15, no. 3, pp. 713–29.

Wright, J. (1990) 'Contributions, Lobbying, and Committee Voting in the US House of Representatives', *American Political Science Review*, vol. 84, no. 2, pp. 417–38.

Yin, R. (1984) *Case Study Research: Design and Methods*, London, Sage.

Yishai, Y. (1998) 'Regulation of interest groups in Israel', *Parliamentary Affairs*, vol. 51, no. 4, pp. 568–78.

York, K. (1987) *Lobbying Information and Welfare*, PhD thesis, University of Virginia.

York, S. and Larson, R. (1993) 'Lobbying behaviour and the development of international accounting standards', *European Accounting Review*, vol. 3, pp. 531–54.

Zeigler, H. (1964) *Interest Groups in American Society*, Englewood Cliffs, NJ, Prentice-Hall.

Index